D0498479

THE CROWN JEWELS

THE CROWN JEWELS

THE BRITISH SECRETS
AT THE HEART OF THE
KGB ARCHIVES

NIGEL WEST

AND

OLEG TSAREV

YALE UNIVERSITY PRESS
NEW HAVEN AND LONDON

First published in the United Kingdom in 1998
by HarperCollins*Publishers*. Published in
the United States in 1999 by Yale
University Press.

Set in Sabon by Rowland Phototypesetting Ltd,
Bury St Edmunds, Suffolk, United Kingdom.
Printed in the United States of America.

Library of Congress
Cataloging-in-Publication
Number 98-88428.
ISBN 0-300-07806-4
(pbk.: alk. paper)

A catalogue record for this book is
available from the British Library.

The paper in this book meets the guidelines
for permanence and durability of the Committee
on Production Guidelines for Book Longevity
of the Council on Library Resources.

10 9 8 7 6 5 4 3 2 1

CONTENTS

ACKNOWLEDGEMENTS

Clearly, much of the material in this book has not been declassified in the United Kingdom and therefore technically remains secret. Very few of the original documents have been sent to the Public Record Office at Kew, and none of the original MI5 or Secret Intelligence Service material is ever likely to be. In embarking on this project it was not the intention of either author to jeopardize British security, so every document has been submitted prior to publication to the Ministry of Defence. We should like to express our thanks to the Secretary of the D Notice Committee for his help in enabling this book to be published in its full form.

We are also indebted to the late John Costello for persuading the Russian Federation Intelligence Service to open its archives, and to Yuri Kobalaze for supervising our access. Also our gratitude is due to the Chief of the SVR archives, Aleksandr P. Byelozyorov, and his staff for their patient support, and to the members of the SVR Declassification Board.

All photographs are from the KGB archives, with the exception of those of Kim Philby, which is reproduced by permisssion of Mrs Rufina Philby, and Edith Tudor Hart (courtesy of Wolf Suschitzky).

Abbreviations

ACP	Austrian Communist Party
AERE	Atomic Energy Research Establishment
ARCOS	All-Russian Co-operative Society
CHEKA	All-Russian Commission on Counter-Revolution
FBI	US Federal Bureau of Investigation
FCD	Soviet First Chief Directorate
FUSAG	First United States Army Group
GC & CS	Government Code & Cypher School
GPU	Soviet Intelligence Service
GRU	Soviet Military Intelligence
GUGB	Chief Directorate of Soviet State Security
G2	US Military Intelligence
G-2	Irish Military Intelligence Service
INO	Foreign Department of Soviet State Security
IPI	Indian Political Intelligence
KGB	Soviet Intelligence Service
KI	Soviet Committee of Information
MEW	Ministry of Economic Warfare
MGB	Soviet Ministry of State Security
MI5	British Security Service
MI6	British Secret Intelligence Service
MI14	British Military Intelligence on Germany
MoI	Ministry of Information
MOPR	Monarchist Association of Central Russia
NID	Naval Intelligence Division
NKGB	People's Commissariat for State Security
NKID	People's Commissariat of Foreign Affairs
NKVD	People's Commissariat of Internal Affairs
OGPU	Soviet Intelligence Service
ONI	US Office of Naval Intelligence
OSS	US Office of Strategic Services
RCMP	Royal Canadian Mounted Police
RIS	Radio Intelligence Section of SIS
RSFSR	Russian Soviet Federal Socialist Republic
RSIC	Radio Security Intelligence Conference
RSS	Radio Security Service
SHAEF	Supreme Headquarters Allied Expeditionary Force
SIM	Italian Military Intelligence Service

SMERSH	Soviet Military Counter-Intelligence
SO2	Special Operations / 2
SOE	Special Operations Executive
SVR	Russian Federation Foreign Intelligence Service

Soviet Intelligence

The Foreign Department's Official Titles

Foreign Department, CHEKA	December 1920–February 1922
Foreign Department, GPU	February 1922–November 1923
Foreign Department, OGPU	November 1932–July 1934
7th Department, GUGB	July 1934–July 1939
5th Department, GUGB	July 1939–February 1941
First Directorate, NKGB	February 1941–July 1941
First Directorate, NKVD	July 1941–April 1943
First Directorate, NKGB	April 1943–March 1946
First Directorate, MGB	March 1946–March 1947
KI, Council of Ministers	March 1947–February 1949
KI, Ministry of Foreign Affairs	February 1949–January 1952
First Chief Directorate, MGB	January 1952–March 1953
Second Chief Directorate, MVD	March 1953–March 1954
First Chief Directorate, KGB	March 1954–July 1991

Chiefs of the Foreign Department at Moscow Centre

Yakov C. Davydov	1920–21
Soloman G. Mogilevski	1921–22
Mikhail A. Trilisser	1922–30
Artur C. Artusov	1930–36
Abram A. Slutsky	1936–38
Zelman I. Passov	1938
Sergei M. Spiegelglass	1938–9
Vladimir G. Dekanozov	1939
Pavel M. Fitin	1939–46
Pyotr N. Kubatkin	1946
Pyotr V. Fedotov	1946–49
Sergei R. Savchenko	1949–52
Vasili S. Ryasnoy	1952
Yevgeny P. Pitovranov	1953
Aleksandr M. Korotkov	1953–54
Aleksandr S. Panyushkin	1954–56
Aleksandr M. Sakharovski	1956–72
Fyodor K. Mortin	1972–74

Rezidents *in London*

LEGALS BASED AT THE EMBASSY

N. N. Alekseyev	1924–25
N. V. Rakov	1925–27
P. A. Zolotussky	Feb–May 1927
Yevgeny P. Mitskevich	1932–33
Max M. Zinde	1933–35
Adolf S. Chapsky	1936–37
Grigory B. Grafpen	1937–38
Anatoli V. Gorsky (Acting)	1938–Feb 1940
Anatoli V. Gorsky	Dec 1940–1943
Ivan A. Chichayev	1941–45
Konstantin M. Kukin	1945–47
Nikolai B. Rodin	1947–52
Georgi M. Zhivotovsky	1952–53
Sergei L. Tikhvinsky	1953–55
Yuri I. Modin	1955–56
Nikolai B. Rodin ('Korovin')	1956–61
Nikolai B. Litvinov	1961–62

ILLEGALS

Vasili Spiru	1930–31
Yevgeny P. Mitskevich	1931–32
Ignaty Reif (Acting)	1933–34
Aleksandr N. Orlov	1934–35
Arnold Deutsch (Acting)	1935–36
Theodor Mally	1936–37
Arnold Deutsch (Acting)	1937
Konon Molody ('Gordon Lonsdale')	1955–61

Introduction

For the greater part of this century Britain and the Soviet Union were locked in a clandestine war fought, largely unseen, by professional intelligence officers and their co-opted collaborators. Even during the four years when the two nations were officially allied, during the Second World War, the conflict continued on both sides.

Occasionally details of the murky world of espionage would be revealed, through official denunciations of the adversary's misconduct, usually manifested by the arrest of spies or expulsion of diplomats, or by more unorthodox disclosures: the publication of personal memoirs, the defection of a key player or propaganda given to some covert coup. Both sides conformed roughly to the same rules, frequently adopted the same tradecraft, and often appeared even to conspire to avoid needlessly embarrassing the opponent. In one particular area, this paradox has been manifest: the precise details of how successful each had been.

Since the end of the Cold War, greater openness has been prevalent in both East and West, and for the first time the custodians of what were the KGB's most treasured secrets have been made available to researchers. Among the most closely-guarded documents of all are those which belonged to the Third Department of the First Chief Directorate, a series of cardboard-bound files containing original papers and photographic prints of Whitehall's most classified material, acquired by the KGB's British branch. This collection became known to the very few trusted officers allowed to view them as 'the crown jewels', the tangible results of espionage conducted on a grand scale in England over many years, by Soviet intelligence personnel attached to the 'legal' *rezidentura* at the embassy, the 'illegals' who operated without any diplomatic immunity, and the individual agents, some motivated by money, others by ideology, who risked long prison terms to betray their country's secrets. This material is at the heart of the archive and consists of a mass of authentic official files extracted in their original form and photographed for immediate transmission to Moscow. Many were considered so sensitive, their sources so vulnerable, that they have been read by fewer than four people since they were consigned to the heavy steel vaults of the First Chief Directorate's operations building at Yasenevo, now the headquarters of the Russian Federation's Foreign Intelligence Service, the SVR.

Not all the Soviet spies mentioned in this book will be familiar even to the *cognoscenti*. Several entire networks escaped the attention of the British Security Service, MI5, and in the case of the spy ring run by the Foreign Editor of the now defunct *Daily Herald*, to prosecute his sources, who were moles in the Metropolitan Police Special Branch, was considered too embarrassing. As for the more notorious names of those recruited at Cambridge University, much has been written about them, although only Kim Philby and John Cairncross have written accounts of their duplicity for publication. What remains unknown until now is exactly the nature and the scale of the damage they inflicted on Britain. Few will be unaffected by the depth of treason indulged in by these spies who evidently spent hundreds of hours, in the dead of night, answering detailed questionnaires from their contacts and writing long and comprehensive accounts of the secret work with which they had been entrusted by British governments. To read Anthony Blunt's description of MI5's latest eavesdropping device, jotted down on the Security Service's headed stationery so that the KGB could warn the Communist Party that it was the subject of a surveillance operation, or to see Guy Burgess's offer to murder the Welsh academic Goronwy Rees so as to ensure his silence, is quite breathtaking, even after the passage of so many years.

The story of the London *rezidentura* is all the more remarkable because, although there has been much speculation over precisely what it accomplished and exactly who it succeeded in recruiting, no one hitherto has been given access to its files to establish what really happened. What emerges is a bizarre tale of plotting and intrigue, with dedicated master spies being summoned home to Moscow to be liquidated, leaving willing sources abandoned; of almost paranoid counter-intelligence analysts detecting deception and manipulation where there was none; and dedicated professional case officers suffering muddle and incompetence from their over-zealous recruits.

CHAPTER I

The Reds are Coming

From the middle of the nineteenth century rebellion against the autocratic Tsarist regime was brewing in Russia, stirred up by various factions of anarchists, Communists and Bolsheviks. In response to a failed uprising in 1905, Tsar Nicholas II granted some concessions including a parliament of sorts, but when he took Russia into the First World War on the side of the Allies public discontent boiled over. The October Revolution of 1917 created the world's first Communist state, with the seasoned revolutionary Lenin at its head.

The new Soviet administration in Moscow did not immediately contemplate the creation of an intelligence service, but this does not mean that no intelligence operations were conducted. Russia rapidly collapsed into civil war and the foreign powers intervened in the conflict, providing the White Guards, anti-Communist forces fighting for the restoration of the Romanov royal family, with arms and bases. Inevitably, intelligence activity became necessary.

The first Soviet intelligence officer to be sent abroad on a secret assignment was Aleksei F. Filippov, an undercover agent of the Extraordinary Commission known by its initials as the CHEKA. Between January and March 1918 he travelled to Finland several times to clarify the political situation there and to assess the morale of the Russián Fleet, then stationed in Finnish ports with its headquarters, the Centrobalt, located in Helsingfors. A former editor of the Russian business newspaper *Dyengi* (Money), and the director of his own bank, Filippov reported important information about the intention of the Finnish government to remain neutral, about unrest in the Russian fleet fomented by anarchist agitators, and about a raid being prepared by the Finnish Schutzkorps on the military arsenal in Vyborg. In his diary, still retained in Moscow, Filippov recalled how the head of the CHEKA, Felix Dzerzhinsky,

asked me to help him. It was about the time the VCHEKA was being organized, at 2 Gorokhovaya Street in St Petersburg, when there were only three workers. I agreed, without pay, to supply him with information from industrial, banking and conservative circles.

As the situation in Finland deteriorated he was despatched there, and one of his reports survives:

> The state of the Russian troops in Finland is most desperate. Germany is intending to apply military pressure on Petrograd [formerly St Petersburg later Leningrad] from the north and to move Russia away from the sea with the purpose of capturing huge stocks of food in Helsingfors and Vyborg. German troops plan to occupy the Aland Islands. Emergency measures are of immediate necessity.

From the autumn of 1918 onwards, very limited Soviet intelligence operations were conducted by the CHEKA along the frontier and into the neighbouring territories. On 19 December 1918 the Central Committee of the Russian Communist Party issued a decree setting up a Special Department of the CHEKA to deal with counter-revolutionary activities and espionage within the army and navy, the principal fighting forces in the Civil War, and a resolution on the special departments of the CHEKA dated 6 January 1919 entrusted the Special Department with the task of organizing and running agent networks abroad and in Russian territory occupied by foreign powers and the White Guards, such as Archangel and around the Caspian Sea. However, it was nearly a year before the realization dawned that it was necessary to extend intelligence operations beyond the occupied territories to certain cities in Western Europe. As was stated in the resolution of the All-Russian conference of the heads of special departments, held in December 1919, 'the internal counter-revolution is led from abroad, where the White Guards centres, operating without danger, carry out their activities continuously and systematically.' It was not until the spring of 1920 that a special intelligence section, known as the Foreign Department, was created within the CHEKA's Special Department, and the question of setting up overseas bases, or *rezidenturas*, was addressed for the first time. The directive that created the Foreign Department stressed the need to establish *rezidenturas* in the Soviet missions abroad and recommended that only the Head of Mission should know the identity of the *rezident*, who should be assisted by one or two subordinates. Illegal *rezidents* of the Foreign Department were to be despatched to those countries where there were no official Soviet missions, but they might also be sent, as the need arose, to countries with legal *rezidenturas* where they could operate independently. At this point the Chief of the CHEKA's Special Department, Vyacheslav R. Menzhinsky, was preoccupied with the war in Poland

and he clarified the Department's counter-intelligence role in an order dated 27 February 1920:

> Counter-intelligence officers should be sent abroad with the task of studying all the ways by which the Poles sent their agents in our rear; the most experienced officers, crossing the front line, should try to penetrate the enemy intelligence service.

Thus the CHEKA, reacting step by step to the practical need to protect Soviet power, detached pure intelligence work from counter-intelligence, recognizing the functions which are inherent in any modern intelligence service: legal, illegal and counter-intelligence. However, the planning of intelligence work on paper was unable to keep up with developments, for the rout of the White Army was followed by the Soviets' defeat in Poland where the Red Army almost reached Warsaw before both sides were forced to accept Lord Curzon's settlement terms in 1920. The British ultimatum forced the Soviet government to halt offensive operations, enabling Britain, France and the USA to use the ensuing pause to supply Poland with weapons and ammunition. The Polish troops counter-attacked and occupied the Western Ukraine and Western Byelorussia. 'The weakest link in our military machine is undoubtedly intelligence gathering, a fact which became especially evident during the Polish campaign. We advanced blindly on Warsaw and suffered disaster,' observed a paper adopted in September 1920 by the Central Committee's Politburo. 'Bearing in mind the international situation in which we find ourselves, the question of our intelligence should be adequately addressed. Only a well-organized, well-directed intelligence service can save us from blindly floundering.' Accordingly, the Politburo set up a special commission, headed by the veteran Bolshevik Felix Dzerzhinsky, to reorganize intelligence work; among its members were Stalin and Dmitri I. Kursky. Following the commission's recommendations, the CHEKA issued an order, No. 169 signed by Dzerzhinsky on 20 December 1920, setting up the Foreign Department:

1. The Foreign Department of the Special Department of the CHEKA to be disbanded and the Foreign Department of the CHEKA to be set up.
2. The entire staff, property and affairs of the Foreign Department of the Special Department of the CHEKA to be put at the disposal of the newly organized Foreign Department of the CHEKA.
3. The Foreign Department of the CHEKA to be subordinate to the Head of the Special Department, Comrade Menzhinsky.
4. Comrade Davydov is appointed Head of the Foreign Department.

He should submit within a week the establishment of the Foreign Department to the Presidium for approval.

5. With the publication of this order all relations with foreign countries by the People's Commissariat for Foreign Affairs, the People's Commissariat for Foreign Trade, the Central Bank and the Comintern Bureau should be conducted only through the Foreign Department.

This order marks the beginning of the history of the Intelligence Department of the State Security Services of the USSR and its direct successor, the present Foreign Intelligence Service of the Russian Federation. In its early days the Foreign Department, or INO, was a small and simply organized agency consisting of its Chief and two assistants, a secretariat, an agent and a foreign section, with a visa office to handle the Department's responsibility for issuing passports and visas.

Its first Chief, Davydov, whose real name was Yakov C. Davtyan, was a professional revolutionary. He had been arrested by the police in St Petersburg in 1908, but skipped bail and escaped to Belgium where he studied at the Brussels polytechnic. Interned by the Germans during the First World War, he had returned to Russia only after the revolution. He fought in the Civil War and later carried out a number of important assignments for the People's Commissariat for Foreign Affairs. In particular, he went to France on a mission for the Red Cross to arrange the return of Russian soldiers. He was personally known to Lenin and Dzerzhinsky and in 1920 he was appointed Head of the Baltic Department of the People's Commissariat for Foreign Affairs. Dzerzhinsky considered him the most suitable candidate for the post of Head of Intelligence and, while occupying that post under the name Davydov, he continued to work for the Commissariat. In 1922 he was appointed political representative in Estonia, Lithuania and China, where he continued to carry out assignments for Dzerzhinsky, as had been agreed when he officially left the INO. This was an unusual arrangement, indicative of what was happening at the time, for as well as working as a diplomat he acted as chief *rezident*, supervising all the regional *rezidents* in China. He was so enthusiastic about his unofficial role that after a year in China he reported to the Centre:

A few words about our special work. It goes well. If you follow my reports to you, you see that I have managed to cover almost all of China. Nothing of importance escapes me. Our contacts are expanding. In general I dare say that not a single move of the Whites remains unknown to me. I find out everything quickly and in good time.

Davtyan's self-praise was quite justified. In Mukden the local *rezi-dentura* had penetrated the Japanese security service and acquired the White Russian counter-intelligence archive for the whole of the Far East, which was promptly sent to Moscow by courier. However, his preoccupation with undercover activities led to him falling from favour on the diplomatic front and he thought Peking would be his last appointment. In fact he continued to hold other senior posts, first in France and then as ambassador in Iran, Greece and Poland. Eventually he was recalled to Moscow and perished in the purges in 1938.

Davtyan-Davydov was briefly succeeded as Head of the Foreign Department by Solomon G. Mogilevsky, who was killed in an air accident, and then in 1922 by Mikhail A. Trilisser, who had headed the Western and Eastern Europe Section since August 1921 and remained in office until 1930. Trilisser was also an old underground party worker who had spent eight years in prison and exile. During the Civil War he had been military commissar and head of the Cheka in Siberia and the Far East. In 1918 he was captured by bandits and was about to be hanged when a group of partisans attacked and he was cut down from the tree from which he was dangling. To the astonishment of the partisans and the doctors, he survived the experience. During Trilisser's leadership of the Foreign Department Soviet intelligence really developed, a period marked by the recruitment of agents under a foreign flag, the wide use of émigrés for intelligence tasks and, to make up for the small number of permanent staff, the organization of independent agent networks and the use of talent spotters. Unusually for such a senior official, Trilisser often travelled abroad to meet agents, for example to Berlin, insisting that he wanted to keep up his knowledge of work in the field. In 1926, on Dzerzhinsky's recommendation, Trilisser was promoted to the post of Deputy Chairman of OGPU, the Soviet security service, where he continued to retain responsibility for intelligence operations.

Trilisser was responsible for developing the 'overseas' or 'foreign unit', actually the *rezidenturas* of the Foreign Department of the CHEKA, in which the main tasks were described thus:

> All intelligence activities in foreign countries are conducted with the following aims in mind: the identification, on the territory of each state, of counter-revolutionary groups operating against the RSFSR; the thorough study of all organizations engaged in espionage against our country; the elucidation of the political course of each state and its economic situation; the acquisition of documentary material on all the above requirements.

The struggle against the counter-revolution abroad, known as the 'White Line', was considered the main assignment by the leadership of Soviet Intelligence up to the end of the 1930s when the activities of the Russian All-Services Union (ROVS) were brought to a halt.

From 1922 onwards the OGPU's Foreign Department succeeded in placing its agents in virtually all the most active groups – Boris Savinkov's People's Union for the Defence of the Motherland and Freedom; the Russian All-Services Union; the Brotherhood of the Russian Truth; the National Labour Union – and gaining control of the communication channels with their agents in the Soviet Union. The joint operations of the OGPU's Counter-intelligence Department and Foreign Department, known as Syndicate-2, which lured Savinkov back to Russia, and The Trust, which trapped the British spy Sydney Reilly, are well known. However, other important operations along the 'White Line' have remained secret. These included the infiltration by N.N. Alekseyev's agents, under the guise of refugees from Moscow and Kharkov, of the organizations run by S.V. Petlyura, Hetman Skoropadsky and Savinkov in Prague and Paris, thus providing information on the journeys of their emissaries to Russia. An OGPU agent, Nikolai Kroshko, infiltrated the immediate circle of the head of the White emigrant agent network, Vladimir Orlov, and managed to lay hands on part of Orlov's archives. As a result of a clandestine intervention with the Berlin authorities, Orlov was prosecuted by the German police and deported. A former Russian naval lieutenant, pretending to be the British agent Kerr (codenamed VIKTOR), arrived in Berlin to investigate the anti-Bolshevik White émigré organizations and recruited, allegedly on behalf of British intelligence, the leader of the Brotherhood of Russian Truth, Aleksandr N. Kolberg.

The Whites were regarded as dangerous adversaries because of a series of assassinations of Soviet officials. In 1923 two Whites named Konradi and Polunin killed Vaclav Vorovosky, then the General Secretary of the Soviet delegation to the Lausanne Conference, and four years later a monarchist, B. Koverda, killed the Soviet ambassador to Poland, P.L. Voykov, an act that coincided with the discovery of a huge bomb in the embassy's chimney. In the same year five White officers were caught after a bomb injured thirty people attending a Party club in Leningrad.

Notwithstanding the importance of its work on the White Line, the Foreign Department paid considerable attention to foreign or, as it was then called, diplomatic, economic and, from 1925 onwards, scientific-technological intelligence. These intelligence operations were conducted both by the legal *rezidenturas*, which were set up in foreign countries as and when diplomatic relations were established with them, and by illegal *rezidenturas*. The first legal *rezidentura* was opened in Berlin in 1922, when, for the first time, a Western European country gave formal recognition to the Soviet Union. Germany was a convenient country from which to carry out intelligence operations against Poland, Romania, Czechoslovakia, Bulgaria and the countries immediately bordering on the Soviet Union, and for many years Berlin was maintained as the West European centre of the OGPU's Foreign Department, controlling the agent networks in Paris, Vienna, London and Rome. The Berlin *rezidentura* obtained a great deal of valuable information concerning the negotiating positions of the West European countries at the Genoa conference held in 1922 to discuss the recognition of the Soviet Union; on Petlyura's intentions 'to counteract the intention of the ruling circles in Europe' to agree recognition; on the preparations by a group of White officers from Avalov's army to assassinate the Bolshevik delegates; the interception of messages from Petlyura's people to the Supreme Monarchistic Council; on Savinkov's plan to assassinate Lenin after having gained control of the security arrangements for the Soviet delegation. The activities of the German police against the Soviet Embassy in Berlin and on those of French intelligence in Kronstadt were also uncovered.

Diplomatic recognition of the Soviet Union by successive West European countries in the mid-1920s created conditions for the economic development of the country, and the task of reconstruction became a priority with the adoption of the first five-year plan. The improvement in the Soviet Union's international status opened up opportunities for setting up legal *rezidenturas* in West European countries, and the Foreign Department, which at that time formed part of the OGPU's Secret Operations Directorate, adopted a more complex structure to control the *rezidenturas* abroad: the Northern sector, which supervised the *rezidentura* in Stockholm with its substations in Copenhagen, Helsingfors, Revel, Riga and Lübeck; the Polish sector, which directed the Warsaw *rezidentura* and its substation in Danzig, operating in East Prussia, Galicia and the Carpathian Ukraine; the Central European sector, which controlled the *rezidentura* in Berlin with its substations in Paris, Rome and Brussels as well as the London *rezidentura*, which was, in part, responsible for intelligence gathering in the USA; the South European and Balkan sector which handled the *rezidentura* in Vienna with substations in Prague, Budapest, Belgrade, Sofia and Bucharest as well as the *rezidentura* in Constantinople responsible for Egypt and Algeria; the Eastern sector working through the missions in the Caucasus, against Turkey and Persia and, from the Far Eastern republic, against Japan, China and, partly, the USA; the American sector controlling the *rezidenturas* in New York and Montreal.

Although the first legal *rezidentura* in London opened in 1924, a few surviving documents mention that an attempt was made to start intelligence activities in Great Britain two years earlier. A copy of a letter from the GPU to the Secretary of the Central Committee of the Russian Communist Party Valerian Kuibyshev, dated 9 September 1922, requested confirmation of

> the appointment of the plenipotentiary of the GPU in London, Comrade Krasny, who will be on the staff of the Diplomatic Mission of the RSFSR in London. Comrade Krasny will have four assistants for technical tasks. The question of Comrade Krasny's posting to London was agreed verbally with Comrade Krasin [head of the Soviet trade delegation to Britain, and effectively first Soviet ambassador to London].

At a meeting of the Organizing Bureau of the Central Committee of the RCP(b) held on 18 September 1922, Krasin's assistant asked about Krasny's background and was informed that

> Comrade Krasny, who has been a member of the Social Democratic Workers Party since 1904, did party work in Poland and was twice sentenced to hard labour, each time to six years. He served seven years in a hard labour camp and two and a half years in a concentration camp. He was tried together with Comrade Dzerzhinsky. He passed a party purge in Vienna. He served in Soviet Budapest and Upper Silesia. His work consisted of editing newspapers and other publications. Comrade Krasny is an experienced and seasoned worker.

Joseph J. Krasny, alias Rothstadt, had indeed acquired, in the course of his forty-five years, considerable experience in underground party work and his contact with Dzerzhinsky had not been limited to sharing the same dock. According to a book by Dzerzhinsky's wife, *The Years of the Great Battles*, Krasny (meaning 'red' in Russian) was among her husband's closest comrades; she recalled that he had been arrested 'in Krasny's flat, which I knew well'. Having arrested Krasny first, the police lay in wait there for three days. The biography in his personal file makes no mention of his intelligence experience. Indeed, at the time of his posting to London, he was head of the joint *rezidentura* of the Foreign Department of the GPU and the Registration Directorate of the General Staff of the Red Army in Vienna. Linked organizationally to Berlin, the Vienna *rezidentura*, among other things, acted as a base for operations in the Balkans. In a letter to Mikhail Trilisser, dated 27

March 1922, Krasny described his penetration of General Wrangel's White Army headquarters:

> My organization for the Balkans is fairly large and has the potential for expansion, as the need may arise. Certain contacts are extremely valuable. I have, for instance, somebody who frequents Wrangel's house and another individual is a good acquaintance of General Klimovich, the Chief of Wrangel's intelligence department.

In June 1922, Krasny was recalled to Moscow to discuss his possible posting to London, and on 12 October he wrote from Vienna that he had wound up his affairs and applied for a British visa. Few details survive in the files, but operational accounts, which show that his wife supervised British affairs in the Foreign Department of the OGPU between 1925 and 1928, tend to confirm his transfer to London. However, he left intelligence work soon afterwards and devoted himself to organizing the archives of the Polish Communist Party and setting up the Central Publishing House in Moscow.

If the Krasny mission remains subject to some doubt, all his successors are listed in the archive, even if a few rate only minimal mention. The first OGPU *rezidentura* in London was set up in the Soviet diplomatic mission in the summer of 1924, after the establishment of diplomatic relations, by Nicolai Alekseyev, code-named OSKAR, with the help of one permanent assistant, his typist L. Orlova. In 1925, Alekseyev was replaced by N.V. Rakov, code-named VALDEMAR, who was assisted by Belopolsky, codenamed MATVEI, acting as his deputy. This remained the *rezidentura*'s full establishment until February 1927 when P.A. Zolotussky filled the post, but only until May when he was recalled to Moscow following the severing of diplomatic relations by Stanley Baldwin's Conservative government. Thus, during the first three years of the *rezidentura* there were three *rezidents* in London, and it would be unrealistic to expect any intelligence agency to build a new apparatus so quickly, and with such such a frequent change of *rezidents*. The lack of much information in the files, apart from the names of the first London *rezidents*, is explained by the fact that they were all repressed in the purges of 1937. As for individual files on agents, none were used until 1930, and even then the practice was haphazard at the outset.

From the start the *rezidentura*'s principal source was B-1, otherwise known as HERMAN, a *Daily Herald* correspondent who was well known in British left-wing circles and the British Communist Party as William Euer. B-1 had a number of subsources with whom he maintained regular contact in his capacity as a journalist: a typist in the Foreign Office, identified in the documents only by the letter 'F'; source 'O' in the India Office, sources 'Y', 'Z' and 1, 2, 3, 4 in the Home Office and Scotland Yard. There is no indication in the documents that any of them knew the final destination of the information they supplied. In addition there were a number of sources, from B-2 to B-16, among Russian émigrés and employees of various Soviet agencies in London who were frequently also émigrés. One significant document gives a general picture and, at the same time, an analysis of the work done in London. *The Report on the state of the London rezidentura as of 1 January 1927* was written by Yelena Krasnaya, who was working at that time as the special plenipotentiary of the external section of the Foreign Department of the OGPU.

Aged twenty-seven, Yelena A. Krasnaya had led an eventful life as an underground party worker. Born in Krakow in 1900 to the family of a lawyer, she had been educated at home and had specialized in French language and literature. She spent some time in London giving lessons and learning English and, gifted in the extreme, she sat her gymnasium finals in 1918. She was admitted to the juridical faculty of Krakow University and joined the Polish Communist Party in 1919, becoming actively engaged in propaganda work until she came to the attention of the police and spent three months in a Czech prison. After she was expelled from Switzerland she lived illegally in Austria, Germany and Belgium. Since such a young, well-educated and already experienced underground worker could be very useful to the intelligence service, she was sent in May 1921 by the Russian Communist Party to work in the OGPU's Foreign Department. Her first posting abroad was to the Vienna *rezidentura*, together with her husband Joseph Krasny, and she continued to work in intelligence much longer than her husband, until 1929. There are indications that Trilisser valued her highly. At the end of January 1929, following the call of the Moscow Party Committee for senior party workers to do manual labour, she asked the OGPU's party cell to release her and started work as a typesetter in a printing works. In 1930 she was mobilized by the Central Committee to help in the collectivization of agriculture in the frontier districts of Kitaigorod and Proskurov. Later she did construction work in Kuznetzk and from 1934 she attended courses in the Institute for Red Professors. Like many other revolutionary idealists, she was liquidated during Stalin's purges.

In her detailed report on the London *rezidentura*, Krasnaya added some further information on B-1 and noted that officially he was a member of the Independent Labour Party, but considered himself a Communist and collaborated with the British Communist Party, supplying it with information about Scotland Yard. The British Central Committee trusted him completely and valued him highly as an energetic and intelligent worker. 'The motives for his working for us,' recorded Yelena Krasnaya, 'are material assistance [i.e. payment] and access to information, thanks to which he builds up his career as a journalist and passes for a clever fellow. He is a man of "substance" and is received in respectable circles, politically educated and conversant with diplomatic practices.' Contact had been established with him for the first time in 1921, and in the spring of 1922 B-1 went to Vienna where he met the local *rezident*, Joseph Krasny. In 1923 or 1924 B-1 visited Moscow and 'gave M.A. a signed statement'. That is, B-1 gave the Chief of the Foreign Department, Mikhail Trilisser, a written agreement to collaborate with the OGPU.

Krasnaya noted that 'the material supplied by B-1 and his group is, to a large extent, of value'. She conceded, however, that 'in many cases, where it is impossible to check the veracity of his reports, the suspicion arises a) that his reports constitute clever speculation, based on logical conclusions drawn from newspaper reports; this suspicion is supported by the fact that, up to the recent threat of loss of contact (in the summer of 1926), the source provided mainly information on the East, which it is difficult to verify, and very little on his own country; b) that he is an unconscious or conscious tool for planting provocative disinformation by the Foreign and Home Office; c) that he is unnaturally interested in our good relations with Urquart [unidentified].' As a gifted analyst, Krasnaya also tried to look at the other side of the coin:

However, apart from this, one should also take into account the positive aspects. Thus, for instance, when the oil magnate Boris Zaid (of Standard Oil) proposed that he should publish in the *Daily Herald* the negotiations between Deterding and Serebryakov, he consulted comrades Rosengoltz and Maisky on the matter, after which he turned down the proposal.

Krasnaya concluded that, 'In the given situation this source may be considered, in spite of everything, one of the best informants of the London *rezidentura*.' Apart from B-1's subsources 'F' in the Foreign Office and 'O' in the Home Office, Krasnaya mentions two highly-placed Old Etonians in the Foreign Office, Sir Arthur Willert and John D. Gregory, as his contacts. At that time Willert was, as Head of the News Department, effectively the Foreign Office press officer while Gregory, a former chargé d'affaires in Bucharest, was an Assistant Secretary. It is also notable that B-1 used his sub-sources 1, 2 and 4 for watching White émigrés and other individuals of interest to Soviet intelligence.

All the London *rezidentura*'s sources worked for money which varied from £25 to £60 per month. Yelena Krasnaya's thorough analysis included two tables in the report which evaluated the quality and quantity of the reports from the main sources (except economic information).[1]

While complaining that the greatest shortcoming of diplomatic (i.e. political) information from London was the absence of any documentary material, so that she had to be constantly vigilant for signs of deception, Krasnaya pointed out that it was always up to date. 'An example of this is the fact that the London *rezidentura* reported the "new course" in British policies in China and the expected mission of a special envoy of the Foreign Office to Canton a month earlier than other *rezidenturas*. London also reported the deal which Ramsay MacDonald did with the government over his party's opposition to the Prime Minister's Chinese policy, in the beginning of December of last year, a month before he made a statement to this effect.'

Evaluating the counter-intelligence information, Krasnaya noted that it was 'very extensive. Every month we receive an average of fifty reports of a counter-intelligence nature. This material is obtained through a Party source who has informers in the Home Office and Scotland Yard. A number of these reports sound very true. There have been cases when the informers of our sources have rendered extremely useful service by removing from the police archives material compromising the party. For instance, after the search of the premises of the Central Committee of the Communist Party in the autumn of 1925, they removed the most compromising documents, thanks to which the Blue Book, published by the Home Office in 1926, made a very feeble impression and did not contain any really secret material.' She concluded:

> Generally speaking, one can say that the diplomatic information received from London is disseminated by us in processed form (or in the form of monthly or weekly intelligence bulletins) to the People's Commissar for Foreign Affairs and, partly, to Comrades Rykov and Stalin, sometimes (rarely) to the Intelligence Directorate of the Red Army. These bulletins are generally appreciated.

Apart from the absence of documentary material, Yelena Krasnaya noted some of the London *rezidentura*'s operational disadvantages.

There was a lack of experienced sources, despite the willingness of some senior Whites to co-operate with the Soviets – even adherents of Kerensky, leader of the Russian Provisional Government overthrown by the revolution.

> It is a shortcoming of the person in question who, because he speaks Russian badly as well as for other reasons, is not suitable for direct contact with Whites (even if one allows for this being possible from the point of view of security). All the same, possibilities exist in this respect. A clear example is General Bagratuni, the former Chief of Staff under Kerensky and Assistant Chief of Intelligence with the Tsarist Army Staff, who has retained a number of his old contacts and has sold his wife to Deterding; he would be quite ready to sell himself to us, but there is nobody who can negotiate with him, though he could be of great service. From Lady Deterding's correspondence, it is clear that it would not be difficult to make her acquaintance and this might be worth trying. There is also the possibility of compromising and recruiting the former White consul, Onu, who has kept his old contacts and who is at present helping Sablin in his work on ARCOS and other Soviet economic agencies in London on behalf of Scotland Yard.

Krasnaya believed there were plenty of opportunities to develop sources of political information. 'It follows from information produced by other *rezidenturas* and also from documentary material, that if the London *rezidentura* and, even better, the illegal *rezidentura*, had people on their staff with the necessary qualifications, it would be possible to recruit contacts in the Italian, French, Lithuanian, Polish and Afghan embassies as well as in the Association of British Interests in China which is, in fact, a consulting body of the Foreign Office and determines British policy in the Far East.'

In the list of the London *rezidentura*'s sources, Yelena Krasnaya omitted B-13, although his information always originated in London, as the information files of that time indicate. This was Major-General Pavel P. Dyakonov, formerly on the General Staff and the Tsar's Representative in Northern France. A graduate of the General Staff Academy, he had fought in the Russo-Japanese War of 1904–5 and had acquired a good knowledge of English, German and French, which assisted his transfer to London in July 1914 as an assistant military attaché. In January 1916 he was appointed commander of the Russian Expeditionary Corps' Special Regiment, fighting the Germans in France. Having won the Légion d'Honneur and been promoted to the rank of general, he was posted back to London as military attaché in 1917 and remained there until the Russian Military Mission was closed in 1920, when he moved to Paris. By the end of 1923, Dyakonov had become disenchanted with the constant quarrelling in the higher circles of the White émigrés and their attempts to ingratiate themselves with foreign governments. For patriotic reasons he decided to serve the Soviet Union and in March of that year he sent a letter to the interim chargé d'affaires in London in which he requested to be granted Soviet citizenship and to be employed in his main speciality, military representation. Receiving no answer, he sent a second letter a month later as a reminder. This time Soviet Intelligence established contact with him and succeeded in persuading him that he could be of greater use if he kept his position in the immediate circle of the Grand Duke Cyril, a cousin of the murdered Tsar whom his supporters always called His Imperial Majesty and who was recognized by them as the sovereign of Russia. According to his personal file, his recruitment was completed in London on 26 May 1924.

In the 1920s the Soviet Government saw military intervention by the White Guards, a considerable number of whom were well-trained officers who had fought in the First World War and in the Civil War, assisted by foreign governments, as the main external threat. By chance Dyakonov found himself in the very centre where plans of this kind were being hatched because he was one of those who carried out Grand Duke Cyril's most secret and sensitive instructions. Accordingly, the information he supplied fully met the intelligence service's expectations, revealing the intentions of the White émigrés.

In a message dated 19 June 1925, Dyakonov reported that a meeting presided over by Cyril had been held two days earlier to discuss organizing the officers and soldiers of the Corps of the Imperial Army and Navy in France and other European countries. Apart from Dyakonov himself, the meeting was attended by Lieutenant-General Lokhvitsky and Lieutenant-General Shilling, Major-General Alyanchikov, Rear-Admiral Prince Gregory Trubetskoy, Colonel Count Osten-Saken and Colonel Kozlyannikov. The Grand Duke had opened the meeting with a speech in which he pointed out that the number of officers and soldiers who had joined the Corps was so large that it had become necessary to turn it into a well-structured military organization. At the same time, according to Cyril, events were taking shape in Russia which could require the active intervention of the Imperial Army against the Soviet government. The main obstacle to such intervention was lack of the necessary funds. The money donated in America had, so far, not been received and it was quite impossible to predict when it would arrive. Another obstacle, continued Cyril, was the absence of territory where the forces could be assembled, but in this respect negotiations were in progress with a certain power, and there was every reason to hope that they would very shortly be concluded successfully. In the discussion which followed the meeting decided that as soon as the territory became available, the officers and men would be transferred there and training for possible military action would begin. When the money arrived, arms would be purchased and stored on the territory.

After the meeting, Count Osten-Saken took Dyakonov aside and told him that 'the Sovereign' had summoned him the following day to discuss a very important matter. On 18 June Dyakonov was received by Cyril in the presence of Count Osten-Saken. The Grand Duke told them that

a situation has, at present, arisen in China which seriously threatens British interests in that country. It is a fact that there is considerable alarm in British financial circles, for hundreds of millions of pounds are at stake, invested by the British in Chinese enterprises. This development should be used to further our aims by:

1. Pointing out to influential British political and financial circles that the source of the present unrest in China is the Soviet government.
2. Offering the assistance of the forces of the Emperor Cyril which could seize a stretch of territory along the Trans-Siberian railway line, somewhere near Lake Baikal, and in this way cut off communications between China and Moscow.
3. In this way, without the support of Moscow, the revolutionary movement in China will peter out from the very start.
4. In return for this assistance the British will undertake to provide the necessary funds, recognize Cyril as Emperor, as soon as his forces consolidate their position on Russian territory, and render him every assistance in his further struggle against the Soviets.

Cyril explained that he had chosen Dyakonov to carry out this vital mission and was sending him to London to conduct negotiations with important political and financial figures, and instructed him to make use of all his former contacts and acquaintances. Thus the OGPU's Foreign Department became acquainted with the Grand Duke's secret plans and was able to monitor developments at first hand, for Dyakonov did not waste time in carrying out the Grand Duke's instructions. On 29 July 1925 he gave Soviet Intelligence details of the report he had submitted to Cyril on the results of his trip to London. Dyakonov reported that on arrival in London on 9 July 1925 he had contacted the War Office through Captain

Chaplin RN and on the following Monday he had been received
by the head of the Far Eastern Department of the War Office,
Colonel (Sir) Robert Finlayson.

> I described to the Colonel the situation which at present exists in
> China and pointed out to him that it was such that British interests
> and the national interests of Russia coincided and were closely inter-
> twined. Both for us, White Russians, and for the British, the principal
> enemy are the Bolsheviks. Saying that I was speaking on behalf
> of a military organization in the Far East, which was headed by
> Lieutenant-General Lokhvitsky (in accordance with the latest instruc-
> tions received before I left Paris, I did not mention that, apart from
> the above organization, I had also been sent to London on orders
> of His Imperial Majesty), in whose name I offered our assistance to
> isolate China from the Bolsheviks by cutting off its communications
> with Soviet Russia. Without entering into details and mentioning
> any exact figures to Colonel Finlayson, I told him which forces were
> at our disposal and what our plan of action was. I then explained
> that in order to carry out this plan we needed money, and we asked
> the British, if they wanted to act together with us, to give us this
> money. Colonel Finlayson listened very attentively to what I had to
> say, put some additional questions to me, gave every sign that he
> was very interested in my proposal and said that he would report
> everything to his chief who would appoint a day for further dis-
> cussions.

A day or two later Finlayson telephoned Captain Chaplin and
told him that he had been instructed to invite Dyakonov to the
Foreign Office for further discussions, upon which a final decision
would depend. Dyakonov should get in touch with a Mr Stanley
who, he explained, was already in the picture. Stanley received
Dyakonov on 16 July, listened to everything he had already told
Finlayson, and promised to report the matter to the Assistant Secretary of State who would see Dyakonov personally. On 21 July
Stanley again received Dyakonov and told him that the Assistant
Secretary of State was very busy and was sorry he could not meet
him personally, but he had been instructed to say that

> The situation is such, at present, that we cannot openly come to
> your assistance. This does not mean that we refuse to hold any
> further discussions on this matter, but only that the present time
> is not suitable for many reasons. On the contrary, we find the pro-
> posal you have put to us extremely interesting and as soon as the
> situation changes we shall, in all probability, resume the discussions
> ourselves.

To Dyakonov's objection that any delay might be complicated by the Siberian climate and political circumstances, making it impossible to do anything, Stanley replied: 'Perhaps you could start this action of yours independently, without our help. Once it has started and we are faced with an accomplished fact, it may be easier for us to come to your aid.' He asked Dyakonov to leave him his Paris address and Chaplin to keep in touch. 'As I left,' wrote Dyakonov, 'Mr Stanley said, "Don't lose hope, General. Maybe in a month or so the situation will change and we shall meet again here and make arrangements for the implementation of your plan."'

It looks from Dyakonov's report to his 'sovereign' that Cyril had assessed the mood of the British quite accurately, though the talks did not amount to anything more than a polite brush-off. Undeterred, Colonel Korotkevich used other channels to approach influential circles and he spoke with a committed anti-Communist, Godfrey Locker-Lampson MP, Under-Secretary of State at the Foreign Office, who said that an early decision could hardly be expected since the government was completely preoccupied by the coal strike which had created considerable difficulties for the country. 'The principal question is,' added Locker-Lampson, 'does the Grand Duke Nikolai Nikolayevich know about the supposed uprising, and is it undertaken with his blessing?' Locker-Lampson promised to talk about the operation in the Far East to the Chancellor of the Exchequer, Winston Churchill, but Korotkevich and Lokhvitsky himself considered that the opportunity for an operation in 1925 had been missed and nothing could be done until the following spring. Cyril therefore sent instructions to Korotkevich and Chaplin in London to act more energetically and to get in touch with Lord Birkenhead, Secretary of State for India. However, the general opinion was that the British, if they would talk at all, would only do so with Dyakonov, whom they knew best.

Information was also received in August 1925 about similar approaches made by the White émigrés to the French government. According to Lieutenant-General Lokhvitsky, who was friendly with Sainte-Emile Lechère, Aristide Briand's Chef de Cabinet, Dyakonov reported that the French Foreign Minister was to be accompanied by the Director of the Political Department of the Ministry, Phillipe Bartello, on a visit to London on 10 August to discuss an intervention plan with the British. The French, who wanted the operation to be led by Nikolai Nikolayevich, were believed to have far-reaching intervention plans embracing the Baltic states, and in this connection the Estonian Minister, Pust, was also expected to participate.

The information about the Whites' discussions with the British and the French so alarmed the Soviet government that it decided to fire a warning shot or, to use the contemporary terminology, to take active measures, through the Soviet press. Accordingly *Izvestia* disclosed that the French government was holding discussions with White émigré representatives in France, naming Lokhvitsky as being involved. When Lechère met Lokhvitsky, after the former's return from London, he told him about the *Izvestia* article and added that as a result 'he could now be accused of dealings with Russian anti-Bolsheviks ... In general, we [officials of the French Foreign Ministry] are being watched,' he told Lokhvitsky, and refused to discuss the results of his trip to London.

On 27 August Chaplin arrived in Paris from London and said that he had met Mr Stanley from the Foreign Office, who had told him that the Assistant Secretary of State was interested in Dyakonov's proposal, but for the time being the British were adopting a waiting posture and the question would be considered again after 10 September when senior Foreign Office and War Office officials returned from leave. According to Chaplin, the British were worried about developments in China and felt that something had to be done about the aggressive Chinese. 'Locker-Lampson continues to lobby for support of the operation and wants to know Nikolai Nikolayevich's attitude to this idea.' Locker-Lampson was told that Nikolai Nikolayevich would not object.

In addition to the political considerations which acted as a restraint, there were other issues, such as the strengthening of left-wing British trade unions. In 1926 the British Embassy in Moscow closely monitored the visit of the miners' leader, Arthur Cook,[2] and there was also considerable anxiety in Whitehall about the difficulty of determining the point at which force should be applied in China.[3] The existing split in the leadership of the White émigré movement only served to support British hesitation in supporting the White intervention. The Foreign Office, for which Locker-Lampson acted as an antenna, received through him information from 'the Cyrilians' that Nikolai Nikolayevich would not object to their action in the Far East, but this did not correspond with the news that the 'Nikolaians' were preparing an independent operation themselves. The British knew this better than anybody else, since they were themselves holding discussions with them on this very topic.

On 5 September 1925, Dyakonov reported information received by him from General Bem, a friend of the Chief of Staff of Wrangel's army, General Evgeni K. Miller, that 'for the past two months the representatives of Nikolai Nikolayevich in London, Prince Byeloselsky-Byelozersky and General Galfter, had been holding talks with

the British on the deployment of the rest of the army against the
USSR. Is there not a connection between the fact that the British
are holding talks with the representatives of Nikolai Nikolayevich
and the delay in continuing discussions with General Dyakonov, the
representative of the Cyrilians, and Lokhvitsky?' asked the author of
the report rhetorically, writing about himself in the third person.

France, the second real force in Europe which could give support,
was also inclined to be cautious about the White initiative. According to Dyakonov's report, Paul Castagne, a press officer at the
French Ministry for Foreign Affairs, said over a lunch with Lokhvitsky held at the end of September 1925 that the French were very
interested in Lokhvitsky's plan, but that France's current economic
situation made it impossible to give financial backing. 'On the other
hand,' continued Castagne, 'relations between France and Britain
are such at present that any attempt by the French to help you would
only result in the British refusing to do the same.' Nevertheless, the
French Ministry for Foreign Affairs appointed the former French
Minister to Portugal as liaison officer with Lokhvitsky, and Castagne asked to be kept informed of all discussions with the British.

Seeing the hesitation of officials in London and Paris, Lokhvitsky
activated his own private channels of influence and established contact with the ninth Duke of Manchester, who was to come to Paris
to conclude an agreement on aid. The Duke undertook, in return for
a commission, to lobby the British government and private capital.
'Lokhvitsky is ready to pay,' wrote Dyakonov, 'since the money
will anyway not be his, but British ... The immediate aim of the
Duke and Lokhvitsky is to convince the British government of the
close link between the internal situation in Britain, events in China
and the foreign activities of the Soviet government and to prove to
the British that a blow at the Bolsheviks in China meant, at the
same time, a blow against communism in Britain.'

In their relations with the White émigrés, the British and the
French took into account the extremely low morale of the White
combat units. General Bem, in a conversation with Dyakonov, mentioned that the mood among the troops of Wrangel's army was
defeatist, discontent was growing and there was a shortage of
money. Because of all that, and not because of a lack of confidence
in their strength – they had 17–18,000 men stationed in Serbia and
Bulgaria – pressure for an early intervention against the Soviets was
gaining support: it would revitalize the army, raise its morale and
make it possible to get money from the foreigners.

The preparations for an attempt on the life of the People's Commissar for Foreign Affairs, Georgi V. Chicherin, which was reported

by Dyakonov on 5 October 1925, served the same purpose. He had received this information from General Nechvolodov, and Dyakonov reported that instructions setting out the desirability of Chicherin's assassination had been received by the local (Paris) branch of the Union of Gallipolians from the Association of Officers Organizations in Serbia. The plan was regarded as tremendously secret and Nechvolodov had only been approached because his unwillingness to be reconciled to the Soviet regime was well known, as was his enthusiasm for action. The Whites had hoped that he might donate some of the money given to him by his wealthy nephew, who was married to Madeleine Bionnet, the owner of a leading Paris fashion house. Nechvolodov contacted Dyakonov to help plan the assassination and find the people to carry it out. On 4 October he informed Dyakonov of the details of the scheme:

1. The attempt will only be carried out if Chicherin comes to Wiesbaden for medical treatment.
2. The choice of Wiesbaden was determined by the fact that it was situated in the French zone of occupation and it was not necessary to get a visa to go there, a procedure always difficult for Russian emigrants.
3. Wiesbaden was subject to German law which did not allow the death sentence.
4. It was proposed to despatch three separate killers, who would together plan the assassination. One of them was Captain Tscheglovitov, a nephew of the former minister, who had already taken part in Polish military operations against the Soviet power. The two others had not yet been recruited.
5. Only people without dependants would be selected so that, in case of arrest, it would not be necessary to provide for their families. The leading figure in this operation among the Gallipolians is General Repyev.

Naturally, having been alerted to the White plot, Soviet Intelligence took steps to prevent it, and operations to infiltrate White émigré circles, and to undermine their military and political organizations both in Europe and the Far East, were intensified.

Apart from information on the Whites' strategic plans, Soviet Intelligence also received during the second half of the 1920s a large number of documents on British foreign policy and the Foreign Office's assessment of the situation in Europe, Persia and China. Hitherto, no word has ever leaked out regarding the source of these documents. It is clear that from about 1924 onwards the OGPU had someone in one of the British embassies but, from the range of problems and territories the papers deal with, it is obvious that there was more than one agent at work. Telegram No. 24 of 21 August 1926 from the British Ambassador to the Baltic states to the Foreign Secretary, Sir Austen Chamberlain, discussed the claim of Lithuania to the town of Memel, ceded by Germany after the First World War and still occupied by Allied troops, and ways of using the dispute to bring about a rapprochement of that country with Poland. No. 315 of 6 September 1926 from Chamberlain to Bogan was on the same question.[4] There was a memorandum to Chamberlain from the British representative to the League of Nations, Robert Cecil, dated 24 September 1926, about his talk with the American Minister in Switzerland, Gibson, on naval disarmament problems;[5] a dispatch from Robert Cecil to the Foreign Office, dated 27 September 1926, on the work of the sub-commission on disarmament at the League of Nations session;[6] Memorandum No.71, dated 3 March 1927, from Cecil to Chamberlain on a conversation with Briand and Paul Boncour on disarmament;[7] an undated memorandum containing instructions from Chamberlain to the Ambassador in Berlin, Sir Ronald Lindsay, on German tactics at the Locarno Conference, which was submitted to the Soviet leadership on 23 February 1927;[8] a selection of letters exchanged by the British Ambassador and High Commissioner in Teheran and the Foreign Office for 1926;[9] and a memorandum from the British Ambassador in Moscow, Sir Robert Hodgson, No. 925 of 7 December 1928, to Chamberlain on the visit of the miners' leader Arthur Cook to Moscow.[10]

The interest of Soviet Intelligence in British policy in China, demonstrated by Krasnaya's report, was very much to the point. The conflict between the various military groups which had degenerated into a civil war in this largest of Asiatic countries had, by the beginning of 1927, put the Chinese question at the heart of Anglo-Soviet relations. The fate of China was regarded as significant in the Soviet Union, which strove for a secure frontier with that country (the longest in Asia), and backed the anti-Western revolutionary movement. Nor was it a matter of indifference to Great Britain, France and other countries, whose considerable financial and industrial interests in China were threatened by those very forces that received the support of the USSR. Notwithstanding a somewhat more stable situation in Europe and moderate development of Anglo-Soviet trade, China became the bone of contention which, after the scandal of the Zinoviev letter in 1924 (see Chapter Two) and accusations of anti-Soviet propaganda by the Kremlin, threatened to create a new crisis in Anglo-Soviet relations.

A retrospective survey of the situation in China is contained in a Foreign Office memorandum, *The foreign policy of HM Government*, dated 5 April 1928 and submitted to the Cabinet. This 44-page document was received by the OGPU's Foreign Department and submitted to the Soviet leadership on 7 August 1928.

Giving a general assessment of the 'Soviet threat', the Foreign Office noted: 'It is very probable that Russia, for a number of years to come, will not be in a position to wage war on any large scale beyond the frontiers of the Soviet Union. What we have to fear from the Soviet Union (independent of its persistent anti-British propaganda) is the gradual strengthening of its influence in spheres which could affect British interests.'[11]

Regarding 'the spheres affecting British interests', the memorandum gave an assessment of the situation in China: 'From 1911 on, a period of civil war commenced in China, a struggle between North and South, between liberal (Kuomintang) and conservative groups, between competing war lords and civilian dignitaries, a period of intrigues which were clearly not based on any principles or patriotism.' The change in relations between China and foreign powers, the Foreign Office submitted, happened as a result of the intervention of Russia which, from 1925 onwards, actively supported the Chinese People's Army in the North and the Kuomintang in the South. General Chiang Kai-shek's Kuomintang was described by the Foreign Office as 'left wing', close to the Communists and Russia. At the same time there were forces designated as 'right wing', anti-Communist and anti-Russian in their sentiments, which did not oppose the establishment of friendly relations with Great Britain. A flagrant expression of anti-British feeling was the attack on the concession in Hankow and the British Consulate-General in Nanking. In order to protect the concession, a British armed contingent was sent to Shanghai. Britain was not ready, however, to use force on a large scale, and the memorandum explains:

> This (Russian) intervention and assistance changed the balance of forces between the warring sides. It introduced an element of bitterness and extremism, which had been absent until then. At the same time, it contributed in some way to a strengthening of hostility towards Britain to an extent that, in ordinary circumstances and in respect of another country, would inevitably have led to war. The state of affairs which arose as a result of the boycott of Hongkong by Canton may be described as a kind of one-sided war in which Britain refused to take up the gauntlet. Such a form of action was chosen because Great Britain considered that in the current amorphous state of China it would be impossible to select a point at which

a decisive blow could be delivered. Allowing itself to be drawn into a war which could not be compared with any previous one, Britain would only play into the Russians' hands, both in the Far East and at home.[12]

Clearly, 'the hand of Moscow' in Chinese affairs caused the British government great concern. It was, however, not ready to take any overt, decisive action, just as it had refrained from giving support to the plan of the Cyrilians in the autumn of 1925, preferring to hold secret discussions with them as well as with the 'Nikolaians', more likely than not so as to keep control of the plans of the White émigrés and the situation within that movement. Instead, the British inspired various kinds of anti-Soviet actions in China, the most notorious of which, from a propaganda point of view, were the raids on the Soviet Consulate in Shanghai and the Soviet Embassy in Peking. British involvement is clear from telegram No. 731, dated 30 July 1928, from the British Ambassador to China, Sir Miles Lampson, to London on the death of General Chang Tse Min and obtained by the Foreign Department of the OGPU. (Chang Tse Min headed the pro-Western forces in China and was close to the British as well as to the Japanese.) 'The raid on the Soviet Embassy, for the assistance in which he remained, I think, always grateful to me, gave him the opportunity to master the situation.'[13] On 6 April 1927 the Foreign Department of the OGPU had received a report from a London source on this question: 'Investigations in official circles in Whitehall prove up to the hilt that ostensibly this is a move on the part of Marshal Chang Tse Min. The masterminds behind the scenes are undoubtedly represented by British, French, German, American, Italian and Japanese interests.'[14]

During 1926, passions mounted in London because of Communist intrigues and China was but one smouldering brand in that fire. Red propaganda and Soviet espionage featured constantly in the British media, raising the temperature, and Whitehall, aware of the Marxist commitment to the overthrow of the rule of the bourgeoisie which was being adopted by the trade unions, became increasingly preoccupied with the strengthening of the left wing in domestic politics. The British Ambassador in Moscow, Sir Robert Hodgson, had taken much interest in the visit of the British miners' leader A.J. Cook at the end of 1926 and had submitted several reports to London. In dispatch No. 925 of 7 December 1926, addressed to Austen Chamberlain, he described Cook's appearance at the 7th Congress of the Soviet Trade Unions and the reception he was given.

Hodgson drew attention to Cook's aggressive statements following the failure of the recent British miners' strike:

> The newspaper *Trud* received a special message from him in which he stated: 'We shall follow your example and will set up a Soviet state . . . No capitalist government will succeed in separating us. We shall work for the destruction of capitalism . . . The British workers, or at any rate a considerable part of them, have applied the lesson of the bitter struggle and begun to understand that there is only one way to the victory of the proletariat – the way of the revolutionary class struggle . . . We have already hundreds of people out of whom new leaders will be forged, capable of taking the place of the traitors . . . capitalist Britain is in decline . . . We need your help, your experience and the teaching of Marx and Lenin in order to be able to get out of the difficulties in which England finds itself today . . . We come to Moscow to acquire new strength, new inspiration, new hope for the forthcoming struggle.[15]

Although Cook's words could be dismissed as revolutionary rhetoric, they were reproduced not only in the secret dispatches of the Foreign Office but in the British popular press and they might have had some effect on the population, particularly those with the most to lose as well as those seeking to inspire hope for a Communist paradise for the workers. Certainly the claim that 61 per cent of the financial support for the striking miners came from the Soviets sounded particularly impressive.[16]

British anger, especially that part of it orchestrated by F.H. Cloe on behalf of the Association of British Creditors of Russia, which demanded the return of its members' money confiscated during the Revolution, manifested itself through the activities of Godfrey Locker-Lampson. A collection of his pamphlets is still to be found in his OGPU dossier, including new words to the tune of the popular song 'Over There':

> Clear the air, clear the air!
> Join our band, save our land
> Everywhere!
> The Reds are cunning, so keep them running;
> Help Locker-Lampson, do your share;
> Let them swear, don't despair!
> Sing our song, wear our badge
> Everywhere!
> Use no mittens, it's Hands off Britain!
> To every alien Red from over, over there.[17]

By the end of 1926, Anglo-Soviet relations had deteriorated to the point where the Foreign Department commissioned an analytical paper from Yelena Krasnaya entitled *On Anglo-Soviet Relations*. Dated 21 December 1926, it gives an idea of the amount of information obtained by Soviet Intelligence and an insight into the problems affecting the strained relations between the two countries. In the section headed 'The activities of anti-Soviet elements', Krasnaya pointed out that 'the most important role in heightening the tension in mutual relations is played by the Bankers Association of which the British financiers Rothschild, Schroeder, Kleinwort, Ambrose & Co, are members.' In the author's opinion, this Association was not interested in direct participation of British capital in the economic life of the Soviet Union, arguing that during the economic depression British capital had found its way to the financial markets through the intermediary of international banks because it did not have its own mechanisms for placing investments overseas.

In this way agreement between Britain and the USSR would doubly affect the interests of this group of international bankers. First, by contributing to the rehabilitation of British industry, such an agreement would divert a considerable part of free banking capital to both the financing of British enterprises and to the provision of loans to the USSR which, in turn, would lead to British capital becoming dearer on the international financial markets. Second, the participation of British finance in the Soviet economy would take away a large share of the profits of international bankers which they now derive almost without limits from the shortage of credit for Russian external trade, now financed through their middlemen at usurious rates.

The report highlighted the close links between the Schroeder group and the Secretary of State for India, Lord Birkenhead, who 'financially fully depends on it'. In the summer of 1926 he had mounted 'an anti-Red campaign on an imperial scale', for which India was to serve as a base, and brought pressure to bear on other departments and the Prime Ministers of the Dominions, in particular Stanley Bruce of Australia. As an indication of Birkenhead's influence, Krasnaya cited the fact that he deputized for Home Secretary while Joynson-Hicks was on leave. 'His nephew, Oliver Locker-Lampson, the initiator of the "chase the Reds out" campaign is completely under Birkenhead's influence and is also dependent on the group of international bankers,' wrote Krasnaya. 'Both Locker-Lampson and [the Home Secretary Sir William] Joynson-Hicks work closely together in their anti-Soviet activities with Russian

White emigrants. Locker-Lampson is also responsible for obtaining information which could compromise Soviet agencies in Great Britain and provoke a rupture of diplomatic relations with the USSR. . . The clearest example of this is the proposal, made by [ex-Ambassador] Sablin to write a number of articles under the guise of intercepted letters of the Moscow opposition. Lampson maintains personal contact with businessmen dealing with Arcos who have experience in working with Soviet agencies in London.'

Krasnaya listed other anti-Soviet factors, such as the activities of the Catholics who influenced the British Cabinet through John Gregory, a senior official in the Foreign Office, Sir Eric Drummond, the Secretary-General of the League of Nations, and two leading members of the Association of British Interests in China, Lord Sidinhead and the director of a tobacco company, Archibald Rowes, 'who, together with Deterding of the Anglo-Persian, are financing Lokhvitsky'.

She noted that 'in the course of the last few weeks the prerequisites for anti-Soviet currents, both in foreign and home policies, considerably increased in decisive British political circles'. This was attributed to disappointment in business circles with the progress of trade negotiations, exacerbated by Krasin's death, and the successful implementation of the foreign policy announced at the Imperial Conference of 1926, which concentrated the formulation of policy in London. In addition, the crushing of the miners' strike was seen to have strengthened the position of Conservative hardliners who had opposed Baldwin's more moderate approach.

Among the foreign policy issues, Krasnaya listed the failure to isolate the Soviet Union, by creating a hostile bloc under British leadership, and the lack of success in negotiating a Soviet guarantee for the security of British colonies and a free hand in South China. In her opinion only a third possibility remained, active anti-Soviet policies, which increased pressure on the Foreign Office, making it 'more and more difficult to maintain its position'. Her paper noted:

> The Foreign Office defended its position against the severance of diplomatic relations with the Soviet Union over a period of several months for considerations which are apparent from a conversation which one of the Under-Secretaries in the present Cabinet had with one of the leaders of the Russian emigrants in London, in which he said: 'The government closely follows the Locker-Lampson campaign, but considers it not a serious manifestation and an attempt to provoke public indignation not consonant with the actual realities. Our intelligence activities in Russia are quite satisfactory at present, but this is only possible because we have an official mission there with

which the Soviet authorities are increasingly compelled to reckon. We receive abundant information from there and all this material shows that the Communist Party is rapidly losing ground and that changes are close at hand. It is still not possible to guess what these changes will lead to and we cannot foresee whether they will be for the better or the worse ... In these circumstances it would be shortsighted to give in to feelings of anger because of the provocative activities of the Soviet government and its agents and break off diplomatic relations, which were established with great difficulty and which enable us to keep our finger on the pulse of the patient. I should add that the rupture of diplomatic relations would not bring us any advantages while doing very little to weaken the position of the Soviet government ... Let Krasin and his Embassy live peacefully in Chatham House, we shall continue to ignore them ... The question of a large loan is completely unrealistic as long as the Soviet government does not carry out all our demands.

It is noteworthy that, in recent months, the Foreign Office, in explaining its old position of 'masterly inactivity' and its policy of 'ignoring' the USSR, is forced more and more on to the defensive. The clearest evidence of this is a memorandum from the Far Eastern Department of the Foreign Office, dated 28 August and written by Unsley [unidentified]. In this memorandum he repeatedly stresses the compelling nature of the restrained policy of the Foreign Office, which takes into account the real possibilities for offensive policies. At the same time, all the démarches and instructions of the Foreign Office show that its leading officials began to realize more and more the need to change this policy and to adopt more active anti-Soviet measures.[18]

Krasnaya affirmed that 'the Foreign Office finds itself at the present time under ever greater pressure on the part of Russophobe groups personified by the War Office, the India Office, the Admiralty, the Locker-Lampson group and Lancashire industrialists ... By the way, the Locker-Lampson group succeeded in collecting 200,000 signatures under a demand to break off relations with the Soviet Union. The India Office, in its turn, is bringing pressure to bear on the Foreign Office by circulating reports of unrest on the Chinese border ... In the opinion of leading officials of the Foreign Office, in spite of all attempts to seek a peaceful solution, the rupture of relations with Canton is extremely likely and in Gregory's opinion a rupture with Canton "means a rupture with the USSR".'

The conclusions of the paper were short: 'Quite independent of further developments in China, the following should be noted:

1. The considerable increase in the activities of anti-Soviet groups and their importance in British public life.

2. The unlikelihood that the Foreign Office will be able to maintain its position of "moderation" in respect of the Soviet Union.'[19]

However, the Foreign Office continued to hold out and an agent report from London, dated 11 February 1927, asserted that, 'The Foreign Office obtained the adjournment of a severance of Anglo-Soviet relations. Chamberlain is of the opinion that the anti-British agitation in China cannot serve as an official reason since this would imply that China formed part of the British Empire. That is why another reason will have to be found.'[20] Eleven days later, on 22 February, another report was received by the OGPU's Foreign Department from an agent in London, to the effect that the British Government was preparing a Note to the Soviet Government expressing dissatisfaction at the anti-British propaganda campaign and citing a list of 'Soviet crimes'.[21] Often the agent reports on British intentions towards the Soviets were supported by documents, as in an undated telegram from the French Ambassador in London to his Ministry, which reached the Foreign Department on 2 April 1927:

I have already reported to you in my previous despatch that there is a move perceptible in the Cabinet here towards breaking off relations with the USSR. John Gregory, the Under-Secretary of State, told me today that anti-Bolshevik feelings began to spread in public opinion with the start of events in China. He was, nevertheless, of the opinion that a rupture of official relations with Moscow would not come about very soon as he could not see what the British government would gain from this. He added, however, that since the attitude of the Soviet government towards Great Britain could become extremely offensive, things might get to a point where the British could no longer tolerate it. I suppose that Mr Baldwin will take this extreme measure only in case public opinion demands it and we are still far from this.[22]

In another undated document, which reached the Foreign Department on 1 April 1927, the Foreign Secretary, Austen Chamberlain, reported his conversation with the Italian Ambassador:

Taking leave, the Ambassador mentioned China, in passing, and the collaboration between the British and Italian authorities in this field. He then remarked that, evidently, HM Government had no intention of replying to the Soviet answer to our Note. I used this occasion to explain to him, as I had already done this morning to the Polish Ambassador, that the extreme moderation and patience of HM Government in the face of the continual provocations on the part of the Soviet government should in no way be attributed to fear for the consequences, whatever they might be, for the mutual relations between the USSR and Great Britain and of a recall of our mission [from Moscow], but are only the result of our view of the state of Europe and our reluctance to introduce new factors of instability and lack of equilibrium in a situation which is already sufficiently tense. Moreover, such a step would, probably, put other powers in an embarrassing position, especially if it were done suddenly and without prior warning. In sending my Note to Mr Rosengoltz [the Soviet Minister in London] I had two objectives in mind: first, to draw the attention of the Soviet government, once more, in a most formal way to the impossible situation which has been created as a result of its policies; second, and this no less important, to draw the attention of other powers to the unstable nature of these [Anglo-Soviet] relations and to warn them of the possibility of circumstances arising which will not allow us to continue any longer to maintain these relations.[23]

On 6 April an agent report arrived of a more categorical nature: 'Diplomatic relations will be severed with Moscow and we have been told further that the British legation in the Soviet capital has already made arrangements to clear out.'[24] The imminent severance of diplomatic relations therefore came as no surprise to the Soviet Union, but the way the breach occurred was unusual, for the British government chose to accuse the Soviets of espionage in Britain and sanctioned a police raid on 49 Moorgate, the premises in the City of London occupied by Arcos and the Soviet Trade Delegation. The raid, executed on 12 May 1927, produced little hard evidence of Soviet espionage, so when the Opposition challenged the Government during a Parliamentary debate on 24 May 1927, the Conservatives took the unprecedented step the next day of publishing a collection of decrypted Soviet diplomatic telegrams which linked the Soviet Embassy to anti-British subversive propaganda. On the same day the Soviet Minister in London, Arkadi P. Rosengoltz, was informed that diplomatic relations were to be severed.

To Soviet Intelligence it was clear why diplomatic relations had been broken off, and how a pretext had been found, but the details only emerged in 1942 when Anthony Blunt came across a fascinating MI5 paper entitled Soviet Espionage in the United Kingdom, (see Appendix I). It described how MI5 had received information from a former employee of Arcos to the effect that a few months earlier he had been working at 49 Moorgate, and had copied at the request of a manager named Dudkin a document entitled Signal Training. Dudkin had supervised the copying but at a vital moment he had been distracted, allowing MI5's informant to make an extra

copy of the cover, which he kept at home. Two months later the
informant was sacked and a Russian was appointed in his place.
Soon afterwards he had mentioned the incident to a friend who
informed MI5, and he had handed over the photocopy which
showed that it was an official publication, *Signal Training*, volume
3, manual No. 11, containing a description and instructions for a
wireless transmitter issued in August 1926 for official use only. It
also bore the following standard warning: 'The information contained in this document should not be transmitted, indirectly or
directly, to the press or any person, not holding an official position
in the service of His Majesty.' MI5's account of this episode noted
that, 'In consequence of this information the Home Office decided
that it was necessary to carry out a raid on the premises at 49
Moorgate. In the room which was occupied by Anton Miller, the
head codist of the Trade Delegation and Arcos, was found, apart
from other documents, a list of secret addresses for contacting party
organizations in different parts of the British Empire and North
and South America. Although neither the original nor a copy of the
army manual were discovered on the premises, there is no doubt
that it had been there earlier. On 24 November 1927 the Prime
Minister announced in the Commons that the documents seized in
the raid and earlier information at the disposal of the authorities,
proved beyond doubt that military espionage and subversive activities in the British Empire and North and South America were conducted from 49 Moorgate.'

As well as giving an account of the Arcos raid, *Soviet Espionage
in the United Kingdom* revealed that by the time of the breach in
diplomatic relations, MI5 was well advanced in its investigation of
Soviet espionage, but had relied on the rather slender evidence of
the missing *Signal Training* manual as a pretext. Enquiries had
begun in April 1927 into what was to become the Wilfred Macartney case which, although it did not lead directly to the Soviet
Embassy in London, could have served as proof of Red espionage
because Macartney was a CPGB member and was convicted of
breaching the Official Secrets Act. Indeed, Blunt's document
revealed that MI5 had been preoccupied since 1924 with another
spy-ring, headed by B-1, the foreign editor of the *Daily Herald*,
'William Norman Euer, a British subject'. Apparently Euer had
been responsible for many of the Russian Intelligence operations
conducted in Britain between 1919 and 1929, but on 24 November
1924 he had made a mistake which had led to an investigation, and
the exposure of his organization. On that day the *Daily Herald* had
published a very compromising advertisement:

Secret Service. A Labour group, carrying out investigations would be very glad to receive information and details from anyone who was connected with the intelligence department or its operations. Write to the following address: Post Box 573, Daily Herald.

By following up this entry in the classified columns MI5 found a man who called himself 'VX' and who was later identified as Euer. An agent was planted near him, but Euer soon became suspicious and broke off contact. However, by the time the meetings stopped, the Security Service had noticed that Euer and the MI5 agent had been kept under observation by other watchers, and in turn had started a counter-surveillance operation which revealed a man and a woman, who were seen to visit the Soviet Embassy in London. The woman was identified as Rosa Edwards, a secretary of the Federated Press of America, a press agency located at 50 Outer Temple and managed by Euer. By intercepting his mail MI5 established that Euer received letters from Paris in the name of Kenneth Milton, containing secret French diplomatic correspondence and reports on the economic and political situation in France, as well as messages from Indian Communists for onward transmission to the Communist Party of Great Britain. In the middle of September the author of the mail from France was identified as George Solcombe, the *Daily Herald*'s Paris correspondent and also the manager of the Paris branch of the Federated Press of America. Euer sent money to Solcombe to pay for the services of officials in the French Ministry for Foreign Affairs and at the end of 1925 MI5 discovered a proposal from Solcombe to send his material directly to Moscow, thereby by-passing London, a suggestion prompted by the arrival in Paris of a very capable man who had previously received this material. This, noted MI5, coincided with the transfer to Paris of the Soviet chargé d'affaires, Christian G. Rakovsky. Further investigations in London led to the identification of several other people connected with Euer, including the Communists Walter M. Holmes, Albert Aller and Walter Dail, all former Scotland Yard detectives who had been sacked following the police strike in 1919, as well as Rosa Edwards, the daughter of a former policeman and private detective, Joe Paul. Dail was the man who followed the MI5 agent planted on Euer, and it was established that he, with the help of private detectives, had also kept watch on foreign embassies in London.

After the raid on Arcos, the activities of Federated Press gradually diminished and in March 1928 it closed down. Nevertheless MI5 maintained its interest and in August 1928 established contact with

Albert Aller, who was short of money; he confirmed that Rakovsky had received material from Euer and had financed his organization. He claimed that Euer had remained in contact with him after he had gone to Paris, and he also disclosed that Euer had two sources in Scotland Yard who had supplied him with weekly reports of a kind useful to the Soviets and the CPGB, and with lists of people on whom MI5 kept a watch. MI5 turned its attention to Euer and he was observed meeting Holmes and Dail at the Fitherston Typewriting Bureau, where Rosa Edwards worked. Intensive surveillance of all three revealed separate meetings between Dail and two people who were seen to visit Scotland Yard; they turned out to be Detective Inspector Hubert Ginhoven and Detective Sergeant Jane of the Special Branch. On 11 April 1929, Dail, Ginhoven and Jane were arrested during a meeting, but in order to avoid a scandal they were simply sacked from the police without any pension. A search of Dail's flat turned up his diary, which showed that he routinely kept watch on the various buildings of the Secret Intelligence and Security Services and on certain Russians living in London, and had conducted counter-surveillance operations for Euer's group. In addition, Dail had received lists of political and public figures about whom Soviet Intelligence wanted information, and other data traced to Scotland Yard. From this evidence MI5 drew the conclusion that during the preceding ten years Euer's organization had received every scrap of information about the Yard's counter-subversion operations.

Soon after the arrest of Dail and the two police officers the typewriting bureau was closed down and Euer went to Poland. After his return, in September 1929, MI5 could not keep a permanent watch on his movements, but decided that his organization had not been active since 1929. Much later Euer became a fervent anti-Communist, but he never revealed the scale of his involvement in Soviet espionage and as his contacts in Scotland Yard escaped prosecution, no details of his network ever became known outside MI5's registry.

CHAPTER II

The Zinoviev Letter

According to the files of the OGPU's Foreign Department, no special investigation was conducted into the origin of that most mysterious of documents, the Zinoviev letter, which played such a decisive role in the downfall of Britain's first Labour government and led to the Conservative victory in the general election of October 1924. Timely publication in the press of what purported to be an undisguised incitement to revolution and mutiny, supposedly despatched to British Communists by the Comintern leader Grigori Zinoviev on the eve of the polls, helped to destroy Ramsay MacDonald's chances.

The absence of an OGPU mole-hunt implies that there was no leak of a genuine document, and it is clear from the archive that the key to the story lies in the flow of agent reports on the activities of a group of forgers among White Guards officers, based mainly in Berlin. Among them, the principal personality who interested the OGPU was Vladimir Grigorievich Orlov, the former chief of intelligence of General Wrangel's army who, after the end of the Civil War, was engaged in fabricating and selling Soviet and Comintern documents as well as preparing his own intelligence bulletins. The OGPU was particularly well-informed about his activities, as is evident from a note in Orlov's dossier, dated 19 March 1929, which states that 'constant taps were kept on Orlov's activities by our sources A/3 and A/25'.[1] However, these activities represented only the tip of the iceberg; the main part of Orlov's work, running a White Guard network of agents abroad, remained concealed until 1945, when new information made it possible for the Soviets to build an accurate retrospective assessment of what Orlov had been up to twenty years earlier. Just as Berlin was being liberated, the Head of the 9th Department of the NKVD's First Directorate, Gukasov, reported in a note dated 23 April 1945 and addressed to the Chief of Intelligence, Pavel Fitin, that the Paris *rezidentura* had seized in Belgium the archives of the former chief of 'the intelligence unit of the Russian General Staff' and was sending them to Moscow.[2]

These documents showed that Orlov had been sent to Western Europe in the spring of 1920 to set up an intelligence network, at a time when it was already clear that the White Guards had lost the Civil War and their last troops were being pushed into the Crimea. Orlov's task was set out in a formal letter of authority given to him by the Chief of the Military Directorate of the Armed Forces in the South of Russia, Major-General Nikolsky, who was then stationed in Sevastopol. Dated 19 May 1920, No. 0476, and addressed to the military attaché in Italy, Nikolsky advised that he had

> sent the Chief of the Intelligence Unit of the General Staff, Councillor of State Orlov, to Western Europe to investigate the situation in respect of agent running by the military agencies and to organize secret anti-Soviet agent networks and communications with the General Staff. I request that you render him every assistance.[3]

Orlov had taken the entire headquarters of the White Guards intelligence organization abroad with him and in a handwritten note headed *The Volunteer Army and Intelligence*, he observed that in the period between 1920 and 1923 the 'central base' was located in Strenski Karlowtzy, near Belgrade, where operations were directed by Generals Kusonsky, Shatilov, Miller and Stanislavsky. The actual agent running was carried out, as in the war years, by Vladimir Orlov. When the central base was moved to Paris, the responsibilities of the leaders of the White movement abroad were redistributed, and in 1923–4 the set-up was described in the following terms:

> The anti-Bolshevik activities inside Russia were directed by General Kutepov (mutinies and uprisings). Prince Sergei Nikolayevich Trubetskoi was in charge of information and intelligence. Cossack affairs were looked after by General Krasnov. All three were subordinate to the Grand Duke Nikolai Nikolayevich.

That Orlov was not alone in supervising the forgeries is clear from the file comment that 'the entire anti-Bolshevik organization of Councillor of State Orlov in Berlin is subordinate to General Kutyepov and Prince Trubetzkoi'.[4] Certainly Orlov retained his previous responsibility for the agent networks, as is borne out by the White Guard intelligence organization's inventory of agents and accounts preserved in his archives, which includes a list of ten 'agents' in Great Britain. However, the White Russian definition of 'agent' would certainly not conform with what is understood by the word today. At the top was an unnamed 'head of the intelligence department of the British War Office', who may have been the Chief of SIS, Sir Mansfield Smith-Cumming, who was sympathetic to the White Russian cause, and in second place was the 'head of the intelligence service of the British Admiralty', presumably the Director of Naval Intelligence. After them was Sir Basil Thomson, described as the 'Director of the higher police', and then 'Major Morten', supposedly the 'head of the Intelligence Department of the Foreign Office', who may have been Major (Sir) Desmond Morton of SIS. In a column marked 'nature of information supplied', was another, headed 'material obtained by all the intelligence agencies on bolshevik activities' and in the column 'on what conditions' was the entry 'in exchange for material obtained by the Central base', which supports the proposition that all involved were engaged in an unofficial exchange of information. The same kind of relationship existed with the foreign editor of *The Times*, Dr Harold Williams, the author of *Russia of the Russians*, who was married to Ariadna Tyrkova, the first woman member of the Duma (the short-lived elected government of pre-revolutionary Russia), and Robert Wilton, the long-serving Russian correspondent for *The Times*, who had served in the Russian Army during the war and afterwards had written *The Last of the Romanoffs*. Also listed was a *Daily Express* correspondent called Hill, who apparently supplied the White intelligence organization with material in return for information from Orlov. Among the paid agents were Mechislav Kuntsevich, allegedly a member of the staff of the 'secret service of the Foreign Office', who received 2,000 francs a month, Lieutenant Sonakhovsky, 'an employee of the British Police department' who received 1,000 francs a month, and Nina Sokhatskaya, described as 'head of the London network', who took office expenses and a monthly salary of 2,000 francs.

Similar agent lists exist for other Western European countries and the accounts for 1921 show that the White intelligence sources were paid a total of 34,100 francs in 1921, while maintenance of the headquarters cost 16,500 francs. Undoubtedly Orlov's position as controller of the agent networks, in contrast to Prince Trubetskoi, the actual organizer of the intelligence work, helped him in his forgery activities, as became clear during his trial in Berlin in 1929. The prosecution produced evidence of his hitherto secret liaison with other intelligence services and of his efforts to fabricate and plant disinformation about the Bolsheviks. As far as the British were concerned, there is a report from 'A-3', an OGPU agent named Nikolai Kroshko who successfully penetrated the forger's immediate circle.

The most interesting thing is what Orlov is doing at the moment. Together with Nelidov he is preparing forged documents for sale to British intelligence. At present are for sale: French intelligence codes, a manual of naval signals, blueprints of factories etc. All this is printed at the Schwale printing works in the Triersche Strasse. Big money is involved. Through Nelidov the design of a Soviet AA gun is being offered for sale (in fact this is the design of a French gun).[5]

Kroshko turned out to be one of the Centre's most remarkable agents. Although born into a poor family he had been educated at a gymnasium and in 1918 had escaped from the Germans to join General Anton Denikin's army. Later he turned up in Poland, where he worked with Boris Savinkov, but by 1920 he had become disillusioned and was recruited to spy on the Whites for Moscow. He proved to be a versatile, well-connected source, with contacts among the Nazis and the *Stahlhelm* auxiliary police; one of his greatest coups was the overnight removal of two suitcases full of documents from the Denikin–Wrangel military mission in Berlin so they could be photographed by the *rezidentura*. However, he only received Orlov's approval after he had made two secret visits to Moscow, in 1925 and 1927. Thereafter he was indoctrinated into the OGPU's forgery techniques and made impressions of Orlov's keys to his apartment and laboratory. When Orlov departed for Mecklenburg, Kroshko removed the evidence of his forgeries, among them the two notorious documents which purported to implicate Moscow in a plot to bribe US Senators Blore and Norris to gain diplomatic recognition for the Soviets. These forgeries were later handed to the US Government and resulted in Orlov's trial in Berlin in February 1929. Following a breach in his own security, Kroshko was forced to flee, and was subsequently given a post at OGPU headquarters. Somehow he survived the purges and died in the late 1960s.

Orlov and his team did not restrict themselves to supplying forgeries to the British, for A-3 also reported to the Centre that 'the Estonians are selling to the Germans and the British, through Orlov (paying him 10 per cent commission), material on Soviet armaments and fortifications (Krasnaya Gorka and Kronstadt), obtained by Estonian Intelligence'.[6]

Naturally British Intelligence actively trawled through the most willing Russian emigrants for agents, and during the course of this exercise stumbled on a Soviet spy who had infiltrated White émigré circles. In 1930 a 'former Russian naval lieutenant' named Kerr, who had worked 'with the English', turned up in Berlin and was identified by the OGPU as Arkady Petrovich Kerr, born in Odessa, who had served with the British mission to Archangel under General Miller. Kerr had been evacuated to Britain and then travelled on special assignments to Reval and Riga. When he arrived in Berlin to 'study the work of emigrant organizations against the Bolsheviks', an official at the Centre noted on the margin of a report submitted by the Berlin *rezidentura*: 'This is comrade Viktor.'[7] Kerr's real mission was to penetrate the Brotherhood of Russian Truth, a White Guards organization which provoked this response when its objectives were published:

> The Brotherhood of Russian Truth disseminates anti-communist propaganda, creates trouble whenever possible for the Soviet administration, organizes acts of terror against commissars and unrepentant communists, organizes and unites all men ready to fight in secret fighting units, provokes mutiny in the ranks of the Red Army and its final object is a general armed rising.[8]

One of the leaders of the Brotherhood in Berlin was Aleksandr N. Kolberg, a former Tsarist public prosecutor who had long worked in Orlov's intelligence organization under the pseudonym Lomonosov, and specialized in the forgery of Soviet and Comintern signatures. Kolberg was recruited by Kerr 'for the British' and was remunerated, never suspecting that he was in fact supplying information to the OGPU's Foreign Department.[9] When this duplicity was eventually discovered, the White Guards were covered in confusion, not least because it had been the head of British Intelligence in the Baltic countries and Poland, a man named Bogomolets, who had approached members of the Brotherhood in an attempt to tap into the organization's networks. Bogomolets had used an agent for this purpose, a Baron Wrede, who was the head of the Brotherhood's Baltic section in Berlin, and, in conversation with Kolberg, Wrede had asked him if he would be willing to work for the British, and learned that he was already doing so. This information was immediately checked by the British and the Foreign Department's agents reported that the former Tsarist military attaché in Paris had been approached by a Captain Smith of the British Army who had asked to be put in touch with Kerr. Soon thereafter another British officer, Lieutenant Eridge, arrived in Berlin from Copenhagen and began an investigation which established that Kerr was in fact working for the Soviets.[10] Source A-250 passed information about Kerr's denunciation to the Foreign Department and reported that Bogomolets was now recruiting a man named Flemmer for the British to

work against the Soviets. The Berlin *rezidentura* commented: 'Bogomolets said there is no Kerr, that is the work of the OGPU.'[11]

If there was a semi-official agreement between the British and the
White Guards to exchange intelligence and act for each other, as
seems likely from the Orlov archive, the British were also covertly
recruiting agents in the White movement while Orlov and his friends
were selling them both genuine and forged material.

Several British historians, including Christopher Andrew and
Richard Deacon, have observed that the Foreign Secretary, Sir
Austen Chamberlain, and both MI5 and SIS had acquired considerable experience in spotting anti-Soviet forgeries and their authors.
Certainly many of the forgeries, such as the Comintern documents
manufactured in Berlin by Sergei M. Druzhelovsky, were crudely
executed in both form and content and it must have been easy
for the British, who were reading the Soviet Trade Delegation's
cipher traffic with the Comintern, to compare the genuine material
with the bogus documents. Whitehall must have been in a position
to distinguish between the two, and in any event the sudden abundance of supposedly authentic classified Soviet documents should
also have given rise to suspicion. What, for instance, could have
motivated the Tsarist Colonel Arnoldi, based in Romania, to offer
for sale 'all the secret publications of the Revolutionary Military
Council'?[12]

Admittedly some of the material supplied by Orlov and his friends
was of quite high quality and, according to A-3, Orlov possessed the
signatures of Bustrem, Trilisser, Yevdokimov, Ausem, Rakovsky,
Proskurov and Smirnov. 'The forgeries look very real,' wrote A-3.
'The signatures are extremely well imitated by Orlov's assistant, the
former public prosecutor, Kolberg. Their authenticity was enhanced
by the fact that Orlov, an experienced specialist, managed to convey
the very essence of the style of Soviet correspondence.'[13] Doubtless
Orlov and his friends were also responsible for the notorious Tris-
siler letters, which sought to compromise the then Chief of the
Foreign Department of the OGPU.[14]

An excellent example of Orlov's art is the documentary evidence
fabricated by him for the libel action brought by Henry Ford, the
car manufacturer, against Herman Bernstein, the journalist who
published a series of articles in the American press accusing Ford
of 'ideological anti-semitism and direct participation in anti-semitic
pogrom organizations', citing his links with anti-semitic White emigrant groups. In particular, documents were produced which purported to throw light on the activities of Russian anarchists in
Constantinople. Ford started legal proceedings and 'is collecting

material against Bernstein in every country,' reported A-3, 'and it is on this that Orlov bases his schemes. He has already been in touch with the representatives of Ford and Brasol (who acted for the supporters of the Grand Duke Cyril in America) and has promised to supply "genuine material", compromising Bernstein.'[15] However, the libel case collapsed in 1927, with Henry Ford making a full retraction.

Quite unintentionally but very opportunely another forger, Sergei Druzhelovsky, came to Orlov's assistance in May 1925 while under interrogation at the Berlin Polizeipraesidium. In order to exonerate himself, he incriminated a number of others, including Bernstein, whom he accused of working for the OGPU. 'This accusation served as the basis for Orlov's work,' wrote A-3. 'The aim of the forgeries was dual: first, to compromise Bernstein by showing that he was a Soviet agent, and second, to depict the Soviet government as a "Jewish gang".' The forgery scheme described by A-3 was based on events which had allegedly taken place in 1922, and linked Bernstein to the CHEKA through an intelligence network in Constantinople headed by Colonels Baliyev and Akatsatov, who routinely kept an eye on the monarchists. Bernstein's role was to plant deception material in the press, but the Constantinople *rezidentura* broke off contact with him because of his excessive demands for money. Around this quite simple but plausible scenario Orlov created an entire correspondence between the CHEKA and the Constantinople *rezidentura*, matched with a series of fabricated instructions from the Centre 'on the struggle against anti-semitism by the most drastic means', together with a number of orders 'on the protection of Jews' and relations with the Jewish sections of the Communist parties. 'This second lot of forgeries,' A-3 reported, 'is very subtly and skilfully constructed and is connected with the Protocols of Zion, but executed with great care and ingenuity.'[16]

Orlov's trump card was the genuine register of the Kharkov CHEKA for 1922, supplied to him by a former CHEKA official named Sumarokov, codenamed JASHIN, who later became one of Orlov's assistants. When Orlov wanted to register newly-created correspondence, he simply inserted an additional page between the real ones. 'A lot of money was spent on this work,' wrote A-3, 'and technically it was of the highest quality. Russian paper was used and the stamps and register pages with headed columns were fabricated on the basis of photostat copies of the originals. All the stamps were those in use in 1922.'[17]

Orlov intended to sell all the forgeries, together with the registers, to Henry Ford and to make a lot of money. 'In a communicative

mood,' A-3 reported, 'he boasted that in the past year he had earned
DM12,000.'[18] However, he was not always successful, as can be
seen from a report from a reliable source dated May 1929 which
was submitted to Trilisser and Artusov:

> Curie (from the Deuxième Bureau of the French General Staff), in
> a conversation with a prominent member of the White emigrant
> movement, recalled the unsuccessful collaboration of the French with
> Orlov, who simply deceived them by fabricating false information
> on the USSR.[19]

Though the Foreign Department knew about some of the forgeries
even before they were offered for sale by Orlov and his friends, it
learned of the Zinoviev letter only after the event. Very soon after
the scandal broke in England, the Centre received two reports which
gave, as subsequent analysis demonstrated, an accurate picture of
the document's origin: perhaps that is why the Foreign Department
did not conduct a special investigation. The first report, from the
Berlin *rezidentura* and received on 11 November 1924, was distributed to Vyacheslav Menzhinsky, Genrikh Yagoda, Artur Artusov
and Nahum Eitingon, and asserted that:

> According to certain information, which requires checking, the Zino-
> viev letter was allegedly fabricated in Riga by Lieutenant Pokrovsky
> (who worked with Biskupsky, connected to Guchkov), who has in
> his possession Comintern stationery and made it up from extracts
> of Zinoviev's speeches with something extra added, and as this was
> a circular, not a letter, it bore no signature. Pokrovsky, who is in
> contact with the British counter-intelligence service, told them that
> he had information that an important letter would be sent that day
> by post from Riga to an agreed address belonging to the British
> Communist Party, which was allegedly given to him. He then posted
> the letter which was duly intercepted by the British. Its further fate
> is known.[20]

The second report, dated 20 November 1924, was sent to Mikhail
Trilisser, the Chief of the OGPU's Foreign Department, by the Intelligence Directorate of the RKKA (Red Army) Staff:

> Attached please find a copy of a report from one of our sources on
> the 'Zinoviev letter':
> 12 November 1924. According to information received by us, Zino-
> viev's letter to London was written in Riga by the White Guards
> intelligence organization. The author of the letter is Pokrovsky. The
> letter was sent, through Polish intermediaries, from Riga to London
> by post and addressed to a well-known English communist, Mac-
> Manus. The British police who keeps taps on the latter's correspon-

dence, photographed the letter and handed it over to the British Foreign Office as genuine.[21]

Ivan D. Pokrovsky is referred to in later Foreign Department documents as a contact of Orlov in Brazil.[22] It is also known that by 1925 they had worked together on the fabrication of documents and, judging by the nature of their relationship and the contents of a letter sent by Pokrovsky to Orlov in May 1925, even earlier. A report from the Berlin *rezidentura* dated 18 May 1925 records that, 'On 10 May, Orlov received a semi-encoded letter from Pokrovsky, who informs him that he had thought up "a new kind of dirty trick to play on the Bolsheviks" by forging something and he asks Orlov if the ordered stationery and stamps are ready. Orlov expresses surprise about the stamps as he is not sure which exactly are needed.'[23] The expression 'a new kind of dirty trick', used by Pokrovsky, raises the question of what 'an old kind of dirty trick' was? Perhaps this was a reference to the Zinoviev letter since, between October 1924 and May 1925, nothing else is known to have been produced that accomplished that kind of furore.

The OGPU's information on Ivan Pokrovsky's participation, received in November 1924, came from two independent sources and was later confirmed by Aleksandr F. Gumansky, another colourful figure among the Berlin White émigrés. His story emerges from a document recovered from the Bureau Liser-Rau, a private intelligence group which featured during Orlov's 1929 trial in Berlin. According to Gumansky, in 1924 Pokrovsky headed an intelligence organization which forged large quantities of Soviet documents that were distributed to Orlov in Berlin, to Shevich in Paris, and to other purchasers. The forgeries, based on genuine Communist Party decrees but with extra names added, were so good that an Englishman had been sent to Riga specifically to work with the organization. As for General Korneyev, he was a Russian officer of English origin who had been granted British citizenship during the World War. In the autumn of 1924 he had requested material that could be used against the British Labour Party in the forthcoming General Election. Pokrovsky responded by sending Korneyev samples, among them the Zinoviev letter, which received approval and formed the basis of a scheme in which a copy of the letter was sent by registered post to the Soviet Embassy in London. At the same time, the Metropolitan Police were tipped off so the letter was intercepted, photographed and replaced with a blank sheet of paper which was delivered to the Soviet Embassy with two policemen watching as the postman obtained a signature to confirm receipt.

When the letter was published in the British press, the Foreign Office requested the Soviet Embassy to inform it of the contents of a letter delivered to it against the official signature. The Embassy's only answer was that the envelope had contained nothing more than a blank sheet of paper.

At the beginning of 1925 Pokrovsky reported by letter to Orlov, and then he and his English partner left Riga and settled in South America. Although unconfirmed, Gumansky's account sounds very plausible,[24] even though the Bureau Liser-Rau did not set out the circumstances of Gumansky's confession. Although a committed opponent of the Soviet system, his attitude towards the Bolsheviks changed after Hitler came to power. A man of unusual ability and great talent for intelligence work, possessing a considerable number of sources in Germany, Poland, Czechoslovakia and neighbouring countries, Gumansky decided a European war was inevitable, and became convinced of Germany's likely aggression against the Soviet Union. In 1934 he began to supply the Soviet Embassy in Prague anonymously, and on his own initiative, with military and political intelligence, and the following year he established personal contact and started to carry out assignments for the Soviets. His information was highly prized by the Centre and eighteen months later he arrived in Moscow where he was put up in a hotel to undergo a friendly debriefing by the NKVD.[25] Naturally the question of the Zinoviev letter came up and Gumansky insisted that,

> It was fabricated in Riga by a certain Pokrovsky, a really talented person, who worked for the British since 1920. British Intelligence in Riga did not establish contact with other British stations in connection with this assignment. I got to know Pokrovsky in 1925 when he was in Berlin on his way to Hamburg from where he was leaving for Brazil. I was invited to meet him by Orlov and in the presence of Orlov himself, the husband of his sister (whose name I have forgotten) and, if I remember rightly, Kolberg, he told us the following: 'My chief, Captain Black, suggested that I should compose a letter addressed to the British communists. I drafted it but not on proper paper and without a signature, not knowing how it would be used. This was before the general elections. Immediately after the elections Black told me that if I left Europe he would make me a downpayment of £500 and arrange for a monthly pension of £15 to be paid to me over a period of two years. He advised me to go to Brazil. I agreed to this proposal as I had long wanted to leave Europe. The British vice-consul in Riga offered to buy my archives for £500. I sold all the old rubbish and am now on my way. He told Orlov the next day that Black was also leaving for Brazil.'[26]

In another part of his testimony Gumansky returned to the Zinoviev letter: 'The Uruguayan documents were fabricated by Pokrovsky, the author of the Zinoviev letter, and Aleksandr Zelinsky. Pokrovsky got £500 for the Zinoviev letter and a recommendation in Buenos Aires, with the help of which he got a job with the Argentinian political police. In 1933, Pokrovsky moved to Montevideo where, with the support of the British Intelligence Service, he was again employed by the local political police as an expert on communist affairs.'[27] Gumansky's sincerity cannot be doubted: he had no reason to lie, he was not under any constraints, and his loyalty to the Soviet authorities remained undiminished when he was arrested and realized that he would be executed. In prison, under sentence of death, he wrote detailed advice on how best to organize Soviet Intelligence in Germany and neighbouring countries, and a bundle of his papers, taken from his cell before his execution in 1939, is preserved in his file.

Leaving aside the vague and contradictory statements made by other forgers, such as Zhemchuzhnikov, Belgardt and Druzhelovsky, the OGPU and its successors decided that everything pointed to Ivan Pokrovsky as the author of the Zinoviev letter, the principal evidence being the two agent reports received by the OGPU's Foreign Department in November 1924, together with Gumansky's account. Alas, very little is known about Pokrovsky himself, who figures just three times in the OGPU files as one of Orlov's agents, first in Riga and later in Brazil. In an undated letter to the editor of the magazine *Anticomintern*, Pyotr V. Glazenap, Orlov wrote: 'Just in case, I am sending you the address of Ivan Dmitrievich Pokrovsky in Brazil. He is a very active man. If you remember him and write to him he can do a lot, especially now, after the coup.'[28] The reference to Pokrovsky's anti-Comintern expertise is clear and it certainly led the OGPU to conclude that he had played a key role, together with British Intelligence, in the fabrication and despatch of the Zinoviev Letter.

CHAPTER III

Rezident in London

The British Government's decision to break off diplomatic relations in May 1927 forced the closure of the London *rezidentura* along with the embassy. However, trade with the Soviet Union continued to thrive, even though some of the Soviet employees of foreign trade organizations were asked to leave the country and those who remained were placed under MI5 surveillance. In deciding who should be expelled, the British authorities received considerable assistance from White Russian émigrés who had grouped themselves around the former Tsarist ambassador to the Court of St James, Yuri V. Sablin. His subordinates kept the Soviet representatives in London under observation and developed their own view, invariably coloured by political opinion, on who was who in the Soviet community in London. This is clear from a letter from Sablin to Giers, his counterpart in Paris, dated 2 July 1927, which fell into Soviet hands soon after it was despatched, informing Giers of the expulsion from England of 'Communist agents'. Sablin complained of Scotland Yard's lack of vision in leaving some key personalities alone:

> Most of these agents are women. The role of women in this question is a significant feature. Even the late Krasin and Rakovsky, who served here, were under special observation by the Soviet political police, which, at the time, was represented here by two extremely attractive young women – the Armenian, Babayants, and the Jewess, Goldfarb. Both were very energetic and the careers of all the employees of the Soviet organizations depended, in one way or another, on the good opinion of these girls. Everything possible was done to get rid of them, but some of the girlfriends of these ladies still continue their surveillance work in London today, to the increasing displeasure of the Soviet staff.[1]

Sablin's indignation and MI5's activities were of only academic interest to the Soviets after the breach of diplomatic relations deprived the Foreign Department of an operational base in London, forcing Mikhail Trilisser and his colleagues to look for new ways to penetrate Whitehall. Without focusing on England alone, the OGPU examined the problem of mounting intelligence operations without the benefit of diplomatic cover and the decisions reached marked the start of a period in the history of Soviet Intelligence which, from the results achieved and the ingenuity of the operations, became known as 'the Golden Decade' or 'the time of the Great Illegals'.

On 16 December 1927 an Austrian citizen named Max Weiner boarded a German ship, the SS *Preussen*, in Leningrad. Nobody accompanied him to the gangway, and once aboard he spoke with no one unless absolutely necessary. A few days later, in Hamburg, Max Weiner disappeared and a Dane, David Fuchs, emerged in his place. This switch in identity was completed effortlessly by a man whose real name was Bertold Karlovich Ilk. Using the codenames BEER and HIRT, Ilk was one of the first of that generation of 'the great illegals' who, among other things, all had very similar backgrounds. Just as Soviet Intelligence had its origins in the Bolshevik underground movement, its staff was also largely recruited from among underground Party workers. The direct link between secret intelligence and the experience of illegal Party work is evident from the Central Committee's decree of 11 July 1919, more than eighteen months before the creation of the Foreign Department of the CHEKA, on the establishment of a department for illegal work attached to the Organizational Bureau of the Central Committee. Its task was to 'leave behind', in places under enemy occupation, 'illegal political workers' to gather information on the military situation and on the enemy's plans and activities. With the end of the Civil War and the shifting of the struggle to the international arena, the 'illegal political workers' were replaced by illegal intelligence operators who were no longer left behind, but deliberately infiltrated into the target capitalist countries. Naturally Germany, with its liberal regime after the war, its geographic location in central Europe and its wide international links, became the main Soviet base of operations by the end of the 1920s. At that time a number of illegal *rezidenturas* and independent groups operated simultaneously from Germany, including those run by JACK, alias Fyodor A. Karin, and KIN, alias Boris J. Bazarov. In developing this large network, the Soviets enjoyed a tremendous advantage: the large number of Communists originating from the Austro-Hungarian Empire who had strong German roots and a good knowledge of Germany and the adjoining central European and Baltic countries, which in those days were referred to by Soviet diplomats as 'peripheral'.

A document prepared by the Chief of the Third Department, O.

Steinbruek, dated 5 March 1931 and headed 'The Immediate Tasks of our Intelligence in the West', acknowledges Germany's importance to the heads of the OGPU's Foreign Department. The report contains a summary of what had been accomplished, and listed the department's objectives:

> Post-war Germany, due to its military-geographical, economic and political situation, is the object of a constant and bitter struggle by various anti-Soviet groups and parties, both outside the country and of groups and parties, linked to them, inside, to influence its foreign policy. The cultivation and the elucidation of the activities of these anti-Soviet groups and parties inside Germany will undoubtedly always lead to the international centres (Britain, America, France) who are fighting us. Germany should be looked upon by our Intelligence Service as a litmus paper. Moreover, Germany offers great advantages for all kinds of anti-Soviet activities inside our Union since there are a large number of German specialists on our territory, German colonists and Russo-Germans, who work in our Soviet institutions and participate in the economic activities of the country. The above as well as the existence of a reasonably well functioning agents network in Germany and the favourable conditions prevailing there for recruiting makes it imperative to concentrate our intelligence thrust on Germany.[2]

Ilk's personal history and service record fitted exactly into the operational plans of the OGPU's Foreign Department of those years, as do those of others of his comrades. He was born in Austro-Hungary in 1896 and studied at the gymnasium and then the Export Academy in Vienna. A Jew by origin, Ilk spoke fluent German, Polish, English and Russian. In 1919 he joined the Galician Communist Party and in 1920 the Austrian Party, where he was at once engaged in underground work. At the beginning of 1921 he was briefly detained in Germany as a Bolshevik without a residence permit and he was arrested again in 1925, this time in Hungary, for underground activities but escaped soon afterwards. On arrival in the Soviet Union he was directed to serve in the OGPU's Foreign Department, which he joined on 14 June 1926.[3]

People such as Ilk, who had experience of underground work, hardly needed any special training in espionage and if they had avoided arrest, leaving no trace of their Communist past in police records, they did not have to change their identity. Arnold Deutsch, for instance, worked abroad under his real name. Hiding his Communist past behind a passport in the name of David Fuchs, Ilk turned up in Germany, quickly made his home there and, taking

advantage of his old connections, soon became the co-owner of a
toy factory and was appointed its managing director. In the middle
of 1928, Mauritz J. Wanshtein, alias Gutchkov and codenamed
JULIUS, was sent to him as his deputy *rezident*. Aged twenty-seven,
JULIUS was an officer of the Foreign Department who had worked
for the Party in Latvia and had been expelled. Ilk's *rezidentura*
proved extremely effective and by the end of 1929 had acquired
ten valuable sources, seven of whom provided documentary information, and thirty sub-agents who also played an important role.
The large number of agents was required because the *rezidentura*'s
wide area of operations extended beyond Germany to Poland and
the Baltic republics, which made intermediaries essential. Between
them Ilk and Wanshtein could not cope with such a vast geographi-
cal area and they set up sub-*rezidenturas* in Warsaw, Danzig, Bres-
lau and Riga. Apart from receiving valuable political and technical
information, Ilk organized supplies of passports both for his own
people and for the Centre.

By the end of 1930 the BEER station had become such a large
intelligence network that, in spite of Ilk's great organizational
talents, it became difficult to control and the need arose to divide
it into smaller, more compact, illegal groups which could provide
greater security. One of these, directed at Eastern Europe and the
Baltic region, was headed by MOND, a former NCO in the Tsarist
army named Ivan N. Kaminsky, who had taken the side of the
Bolsheviks during the Civil War and afterwards fought against the
guerrillas in the Ukraine. Another group remained under the direction of Ilk, who continued to control activities in Britain and
France.[4]

In December 1930 a well-known German journalist was assigned
the task of penetrating THE ISLAND, as Britain was referred to in
the Foreign Department's operational documents. Only his codename OS/29 is known, the prefix 'OS' being the two letters of the
Russian word for island. He had a great number of contacts both
in Germany and abroad, and in the middle of 1929 had set up what
was termed a 'Correspondents Bureau' in London – in fact a small
news agency specializing in the collection of confidential data on
European and American politics and economics. He secured the
co-operation of an English journalist, designated OS/42, and put
him at the head of the whole enterprise, entrusting him with the
acquisition of information and its transmission to Germany. OS/
42, in his turn, recruited a number of other journalists, some working for newspapers and some freelance, as well as the head of a
department of the Board of Trade. They were assigned symbols in

numerical order following OS/42, OS/43, etc., and the Correspondents Bureau operated as a legitimate concern, paying for the information supplied; its operation was sufficiently routine not to require OS/29's permanent presence in London. Two of these agents, OS/43 and OS/44, were to prove particularly valuable, the first working directly for the Foreign Secretary, Arthur Henderson, and the other being a member of Ramsay MacDonald's personal staff. Reporting on a year's work of the Bureau, Ilk wrote to the Centre in August 1930:

> We have made progress in adapting the work of the OS/42 group more to the needs of our organization. Indeed, both OS/42 himself and all his people have given evidence of a serious desire and readiness to achieve this. The weakness in their work in recent times is explained by the fact that many of our sources have been away and that, in general, the summer months make themselves felt. OS/42 and other sources are ready to carry out their tasks, though it is of course important that they should be constantly directed on the spot. OS/43, who was appointed a member of the Far Eastern Commission, about which we have sent you a report, remains in place and has been given the task of processing material from the Far East, which he has agreed to pass on personally to OS/29 for his information. This is already somewhat of an achievement in itself in the case of a civil servant like OS/43 and it took OS/29 considerable efforts to bring him to this point.
>
> OS/44 is already two weeks travelling through Europe charged by Snowden [Philip Snowden, the Labour MP] and MacDonald to study the situation on the spot. At present he is in Warsaw. When he returns home, in the middle of September, we hope to receive quite interesting material from him which he has already agreed to supply. OS/46 has been told to concentrate exclusively on questions of the [financial] blockade and the City. Unfortunately he is a rather ambitious man who sees himself playing a role in high politics (he is quite active in the Zionist movement, being a supporter of the revisionists) but we shall cure him of that.[5]

Curiously, credit for the idea of using journalists as a cover for intelligence work belongs to the British. Shortly after the start of Ilk's operations in England, the Danish newspaper *Berlinske Tidende* published the triumphant memoirs of a British intelligence officer, Captain William Harvey, in which he recalled his work in Denmark during the First World War:

> I began my work in Copenhagen by opening a 'Press Bureau', having first secured employment by two London newspapers who appointed

me their correspondent in Denmark ... I despatched long articles by post to the *Daily Mail* which were written naturally in English in my handwriting and described the situation in Denmark and neighbouring countries. This was completely legal journalistic activity and it was my aim to deceive the Danish police into believing that I was just an ordinary journalist and not a British officer sent here with a special mission.[6]

Material from Ilk's Correspondents Bureau reached Moscow regularly in fairly abundant quantities, but the quality from an intelligence standpoint left much to be desired. Of the fifteen to twenty reports delivered by each mail, only about one-fifth were evaluated in Moscow as 'representing interest or considerable interest' and the Centre voiced concern in a letter from Artusov to Ilk, dated 7 August 1930:

> As far as the work of this group is concerned, its main shortcoming is that it is of a 'correspondent' nature rather than 'ours' and shows an excessive enthusiasm for economic questions, which are not so urgent from our point of view. Try to steer its work firmly towards elucidation of the activities of the imperialist countries and, in the first place, of their home country [of the sources] directly or indirectly aimed against us. We are particularly interested in the following questions:
> (a) work on the mounting of an economic and financial blockade (pay particular attention to the activities of the Norman-Anglo Bank, the Moro-Banque de France, Luther–Germany); (b) the origins and background to the campaign in (c) the question of Franco-German rapprochement and the relations with and role of Britain (pay attention to Sauerwein from MATAN and Rechberg in Germany); (d) the British position in respect of Franco-Italian and Italo-German relations and (e) of course, the attitude of Britain towards us; (f) the participation of Britain in Polish-Rumanian affairs.
> This, roughly, is what it would be most desirable to study at the present time. We shall go into greater detail in our next letters.
> ARTUR.[7]

This critical evaluation, although accepted by Ilk as justified, prompted an explanation of the state of affairs on THE ISLAND in his letter dated 25 August 1930:

> I am under the impression that you do not have a sufficiently clear picture of certain important branches of our work and, in the first place, of ways to reorganize and decentralize my organization (the question with which I was confronted a few months ago) as well as of the methods and ways of working on THE ISLAND, in general,

and in connection with the proposed separation of THE ISLAND organization, in particular.

As you know, we have been working on THE ISLAND for about a year. I have repeatedly written to you about this work, but it seems to me that you still do not have a sufficiently clear idea of what our work on THE ISLAND represents and what could and should be the ways to adapt the sources, who occupy more or less important positions in British society, to the needs of our work.

I fully agree with you in regard to the criticism to which you have subjected the material from OS/42's group. Speaking of the methods by which the organization on THE ISLAND has been built up, I should like to stress, in the first place, that when we started on this work a year ago we found ourselves literally in unknown territory. Whatever the quality of the material received by us from THE ISLAND today, we have nevertheless succeeded in strengthening the personal position of OS/29 on THE ISLAND, legalizing him to such an extent that we now have the possibility of sending him there in complete safety. In addition, this position gives him, without exaggeration, enormous opportunities for establishing new contacts.

You perhaps do not appreciate sufficiently how difficult it is on THE ISLAND for a foreigner to get a work permit, which is a precondition for obtaining a residence permit. Apart from legalizing the work and life of OS/29 on THE ISLAND, we have succeeded in the course of a year in recruiting a number of people, of whom we have at present retained four sources from the OS/42 group.

Assuming from the start that the work on THE ISLAND should be carried out with great caution and systematically, I fully realized that we would obtain results only very slowly. I also, from the start, arranged matters in such a way as to completely exclude the possibility of penetration of the organization by double agents or potential double agents. For this reason and for this reason alone I, from the beginning, gave the work of the OS/42 group the aspect of a semi-legal link by specially setting up a correspondent bureau. This way of legalizing the work had, quite understandably, apart from a positive side, a whole series of negative aspects. It is these aspects which are reflected in the material which we received from our sources, a number of whom occupy quite prominent positions in the government apparatus. It is nevertheless noticeable that over the last 2–3 months a small improvement has taken place in the elucidation of the questions which I have put to the group. In the course of the work, after all these people had become accustomed to their work for us and, first and foremost, to the punctual payment of their salaries, we were able slowly but systematically to put them to work along our lines. However, in the course of this process I came to the conclusion that our man should be permanently present on the spot in order to daily follow and direct the work of this group. So far I have temporarily solved this problem by sending OS/29 quite frequently for more or less lengthy periods to THE ISLAND.[8]

The issue of sending 'a special man' to lead the OS/42 group had been decided already by the Centre, and Artusov conveyed the news to Ilk on 7 August 1930:

Your new officer has left and you will see him on 13–15. We shall from now on call him HOFMAN... He creates a good impression and he should develop into a good operator.

HOFMAN was Julius Hutschnecker, alias Vasili L. Spiru, whose entry into the world of intelligence had been swift even by the standards of those days of miraculous metamorphoses. His file takes only a few lines, starting with a short note addressed to the OGPU from the Central Committee dated 3 June 1930:

To the OGPU,
The allocation department of the CC of the APC(b) puts at your disposal comrade Spiru, Party card No: 020136, for your use. Date of arrival 3 June 1930.
  On 9 June Spiru wrote a statement:
'I enclose the order of the CC of the ACP(b) of 3.06.30 and request that you register me for service with the Foreign Department of the OGPU.'
  The statement was minuted:
To the Foreign Department of the OGPU – please register comrade Spiru for service with the Foreign Department in the position of representative. He will be sent on a prolonged mission by the Foreign Department. Agreed with comrade Messing. M. Gorb.[9]

If Gorb's minute is taken as formally enlisting Spiru in the Intelligence Service, his appearance in Berlin only two months later as an illegal *rezident* represents training in record time. Evidently, having studied Spiru's personal history, the Foreign Department decided he could be sent on active service straight away.

Spiru's personal background was very similar to that of Ilk and Wanshtein, to whom he was to be subordinate. He was born into a Viennese doctor's family in 1898 and finished his gymnasium education in 1915. He was called up by the Austro-Hungarian army and fought on the Italian front, ending the war in 1918 as a second lieutenant, and between March and August 1919 he served in the Red Army of the Hungarian Soviet republic. Spiru's further career lay in journalism and up until 1927 he worked for a number of

'Party and bourgeois newspapers', and in the press bureau of the MOPR's Balkan executive committee. Of greater interest, however, was the clandestine dimension of Spiru's life:

> From 1919 to 1927, I was permanently engaged in underground work: 1919–20 – I was a member of the managing committee of the communist organization of the Bukovina;
> 1920–21 – a member of the managing committee of communist organization of the Banat;
> 1922–24 – a member of the bureau of the CC of the Komsomol in the CC of the Communist Party of Romania;
> 1924–27 – MOPR.

He had been arrested for the first time in Vienna in 1915 and subsequently a number of times in Romania, then once more in Vienna, after which he was expelled by the Austrian police. His arrest in Islavl, Romania, was followed by a prison sentence served from 1921 to 1922. In 1927, Spiru went to the Soviet Union, joined the ACP(b) and was directed to work in the Romanian and German section of Moscow's Communist University of the West. His impressive experience of the underground Party was evidently the best recommendation for work in intelligence. The arrests and prison sentence meant that the police of the countries where he had been detained knew about his Communism, which posed a danger to his security as a future intelligence operator, but this difficulty was easily overcome. In most cases a change of name was sufficient to enable a Communist with a background in the underground to slip past the blacklists of the police and immigration authorities. Thus Spiru adopted the identity of an Austrian, Anton Tauber, and calmly crossed the German border, as Artusov informed Ilk in due course.[10]

Naturally the Foreign Department realized the danger of using people with a Communist past, but the service was small and at that time the Centre had neither the facilities nor the time to give special training to illegals. People with experience and knowledge, like Ilk, Spiru, Bystrolyotov, Mally and Deutsch, represented a useful reserve, although Moscow was aware of shortcomings in the selection of illegals, as is clear from Artusov's subsequent letter to Ilk, dated 7 October 1930:

> My dear friend,
> Our mutual friend HOFMAN, sent to you in connection with the oral instructions given to you and in clarification and addition to our letter N 20/3, will, as you know, work under your direction in enterprise O.

HOFMAN, as we have already briefly described, is a capable, politically perfectly trained comrade. He has, however, never worked for us before and is therefore quite inexperienced in our business. You will have to put in a lot of work before he can be turned into the valuable operator which he promises to become. You will have to warn him (when you entrust him with work) against too much enthusiasm for political effects in the work to the detriment of our tasks.

Artusov was confident he could rely fully on the experienced Ilk who, soon after Spiru's arrival in Berlin, demonstrated considerable ingenuity and imagination in setting him up in England.

As far as the preparation of HOFMAN for work on THE ISLAND (I have only met him today) is concerned, since he is on THE ISLAND as an illegal operator, this will take a little more time and should be properly organized. Certain openings have presented themselves to me to legalize his position in the field with which he is best acquainted – publishing. I have asked OS/29 to find him a job as a German specialist or something like that with one of the British publishing houses, and, at the same time, put him in touch with some very large German publishing house with which OS/29 is connected.[11]

Apparently, Ilk's intelligence network was something more than a classic *rezidentura*, and represented a quite independent foreign branch of the Centre in Europe. In practice, it dealt with problems which, by all the rules, should have been resolved in Moscow, before the despatch of the illegal abroad, such as working out a cover story, creating his cover and supplying supporting documents. All this was left to Ilk's *rezidentura*, which evidently enjoyed rather better facilities than the Centre itself. Spiru was simply planted in Germany and his transformation into an illegal had to be completed on the spot. Further evidence of this is Artusov's request that Ilk should provide Spiru with cover and more reliable documents, contained in the letter of 7 August 1930, in which he announced the illegal's departure:

We have not equipped him here very well and you will have to get him ready for work by providing him with a good cover, boots, etc., without however forcing the pace. Try to agree your plans in this respect with us.[12]

'Boots' is Soviet intelligence jargon for cover document, just as 'book' means passport. This unsatisfactory state of affairs characterized the initial period of the organization of the Soviet Foreign Intelligence Service. The *rezidenturas* enjoyed considerable independence, an arrangement which made for a creative approach to operations, but it posed a threat to security because of the Centre's lack of knowledge, and the consequent lack of co-ordination. After 1930 steps were taken to improve the Centre's liaison with the *rezidenturas*, and in a letter dated 30 November 1931, Ilk was informed that all future correspondence with him would be dealt with by 'one point in the Centre', presumably a single section that had been made responsible for his *rezidentura*.[13]

Ilk entrusted the task of creating a cover for Spiru in Britain to OS/29 who, through his contacts, helped him cultivate the publishing world. In his progress report Spiru wrote that he had acquired contacts in the large German publishing firms of Kiepenheuer and Henius und Schub Verlag. He was introduced to the well-known writers Georg Kaiser and Bertolt Brecht, signed a contract with Kaiser for the English-language rights to one of his popular novels, and even conducted negotiations for the English rights to Karl Kraus's *Die letzten Tage der Menschheit*. Thanks to OS/29's help, Spiru noted, 'years of work were done at one stroke'.[14]

While Spiru established himself in the German publishing world, Ilk supplied him with an Austrian passport in the name of Josef Lahodny, and sent him to England in the first half of October for a few weeks, together with OS/29. Spiru's first, rather humble task was to acquaint himself with conditions in London, and to find out whether it was possible, in principle, to legalize his role as a literary agent.[15]

According to the stamp in Josef Lahodny's passport, he arrived at Harwich on 12 October 1930 and stayed in London at the Piccadilly Hotel, ostensibly conducting business on behalf of the German publishing firm Adalbert Schulz Verlag. Over a meal in Scott's restaurant, OS/29 introduced him to Charles Duff, a press officer from the News Department of the Foreign Office and himself a linguist and author of note, who was pleased to make what he believed was a useful contact in the German publishing world. As a result of their connection, Duff wrote letters of recommendation to British publishers in which he presented Josef Lahodny as 'a literary adviser to a number of German publishing houses'. A copy of one, dated 21 October 1930 and written on Foreign Office letterheading to (Sir) Geoffrey Faber, marked 'Private', survives:

Dear Mr Faber, The bearer of this letter is Joseph Lahodny who is literary adviser to a number of German publishing houses.

Mr Lahodny returns to Germany very soon and will come back to England in a month or so to reside here for some time. He wishes to meet English publishers to consider books for publication in Germany and perhaps to exchange ideas, recommend German books for publication, etc.

I do not know how you are fitted as regards Germany but it occurred to me that you may be interested to meet Mr Lahodny. Yours sincerely, Charles Duff.[16]

Thus Spiru established contact with the publishing firms Geoffrey Bles, Jonathan Cape and Faber & Faber. In addition, Duff gave Spiru a letter of recommendation to Hermon Ould, the General Secretary of the International PEN Club, while a leading literary critic on the weekly *Sunday Referee* introduced him to C.H. Brooks, a well-known translator of German books.[17]

After staying in London for nearly two weeks, Spiru returned to Berlin, having concluded that the cover of a literary agent would be entirely suitable. In his report he wrote that this profession had a number of useful advantages: in the first place, a foreigner could exercise it since it came under the category of free professions and did not need a special permit; secondly it made it possible to travel abroad frequently, and thirdly it opened up vast opportunities for making useful contacts, all of which was eminently suitable for illegal intelligence activities.[18]

On his next journey to England, on 27 November 1930, he was accompanied by OS/29 and this time Spiru was ordered to start his intelligence work, so he was introduced to OS/42 as the new head of the Correspondents Bureau. OS/42 was pleased to retain the job of London editor, and to know that henceforth all organizational and financial issues would be settled on the spot by the new chief. OS/29 also met other sources and subsequently reported that 'OS/43 was prepared to transmit secret information if this did not have to be done by post – OS/42 and OS/44 expressed similar readiness as they were afraid of losing their jobs in conditions of an economic crisis and they had become used to their salaries from the bureau.'[19]

When Spiru visited London again, on 15 January 1931, he obtained an alien's permit which gave 58c Lexham Gardens, Kensington W8, as his permanent address. Ilk reported with satisfaction to the Centre: 'A few days ago I received a communication from HOFMAN in which he reported that he had already received a residence permit, a development he is very pleased about. In addition, he has been accepted as a member of a very well-known English writers club thanks to the warm recommendations of Duff whom you know about. From this development I hope to receive very interesting peripheral information.'[20]

By now well established in London, Spiru began to take an active part in the Correspondents Bureau. In those days few files were kept on individual sources, so the notes written in Spiru's hand in German are probably the only description of the hitherto unknown members of this Soviet intelligence network in London. OS/42, the London editor of the Correspondents Bureau was, in Spiru's words, a professional journalist who was an unlikely candidate for further promotion. The diplomatic correspondent of a London newspaper, he frequently visited Berlin, Rome, Belgrade, Vienna and Budapest. OS/29 met him in Berlin through an American journalist and although this American recommended OS/29 as 'absolutely reliable and beyond all suspicion', OS/42 agreed to the creation of the Correspondents Bureau only after consultation with the Foreign Office. In a conversation with Spiru, OS/42 admitted: 'First I sounded them out whether the setting up of such a bureau would be in Britain's interest and I received a positive reply. Our bureau never spread any information harmful to Britain.' In his own words, 'he hoped that the bureau would grow into a large news agency supplying news to continental newspapers. These ideals,' wrote Spiru, 'covered of course purely material interests. OS/42 is by nature a typical English bohemian who is always short of money and has no firm basis in life.' Through the bureau he hoped to achieve not only honour and fame but also a reasonable income and at first he looked upon the bureau as a kind of press agency, an experiment, as he put it. 'Only gradually,' wrote Spiru, 'was he persuaded that what was required were:

1) ordinary press reports and 2) confidential reports for the information of chief editors of German publications and, finally, secret reports for certain big American businessmen and dealers on the stock exchange. OS/42 is convinced to this day that the bureau has a German-American background. There is considerable evidence to this effect in his whole work and behaviour, but only his closest friend OS/46 knows about this 'American line'. He urged me not to say anything about the 'American line' to any other employees of the bureau. For various reasons, mostly of a material nature, OS/42 has become a fanatic as far as the bureau is concerned which recently has become virtually his only source of income. That is why he is so concerned about it.

All the same, two emotions live in his breast. On the one hand, he wants to remain a good patriot and be in all respects looked upon with favour by the Foreign Office while, on the other, he conceals from it the 'American line' and the fact that OS/43 and OS/44 are collaborating with the bureau, since they, as highly-placed civil servants, are virtually breaking the law.

OS/46, according to Spiru, was a typical international adventurer who served as a source to OS/42. He was born in Russia, in the Kuban region near the Black Sea, and at the time the bureau was set up had twenty-five years' experience of journalism behind him. During the revolution he was sent by the interim government to buy arms in Western Europe and had remained there together with the money entrusted to him. He was acquainted with Kerensky, closely linked to the White émigré newspapers *Rul* and *Posledniye Novosti*, and wrote anti-Soviet articles. Having lived for a long time in Berlin, Brussels and London, he had a great number of contacts throughout Europe. In addition, OS/46 was vice-president of, as Spiru called it, the 'fascist-revisionist wing of the Zionist organization' and, according to OS/42, informed the Foreign Office of all closed meetings of the 'revisionists, hostile to Britain'.

'OS/46, it would seem, understands much better the true nature of the Correspondents Bureau,' wrote Spiru. 'He thinks that it is a semi-official American news agency which works on the brink of economic espionage. He is not prepared to go any further. He is ready to do anything provided he cannot be accused of directly violating the law, even though what he does is in fact illegal.' In the course of a confidential conversation, the contents of which OS/46 asked should not to be communicated to OS/42, he promised Spiru to make all his opportunities available to the bureau. When Spiru remarked that it would be a good thing if his reports could be supported by documents, OS/46 replied, 'No, that I shall never do. There should be no misunderstanding between us on this point. I cannot supply documents, but you may expect from me the best, inaccessible information, real "inside reports". Everything I give you, you may publish. Whether you do so or not makes no difference to me.'

'OS/46, like OS/42 looks upon the Correspondents Bureau as a American-German enterprise,' wrote Spiru. 'He is convinced of its non-Russian and especially its anti-Soviet nature.'

OS/43 had been a civil servant and a former member of the Communist Party, and was much better informed on economic and political topics than the other employees of the bureau, but his uneven, hysterical character, the absence of any journalistic abilities and the fact that he was not a gentleman led to friction with OS/42. OS/43 considered himself a kind of economic courier of the government, and lived in constant fear of giving away official secrets. 'His hysteria,' noted Spiru, 'brings him to seeing today in the bureau the hand of Moscow and tomorrow that of the Wilhelmstrasse. Both OS/42 and I have convinced him of putting this idea out of his mind. Only OS/42 knows about his work in the group.'

OS/44 was the only member of the network who consciously broke the law and handed over official documents. In the past he had given OS/42 certain information for his newspaper in return for money, and thus had become an employee of the bureau. 'Recently OS/44 has firmly refused to collaborate with us. He has been made a head of department and he is afraid that his "unlawful activities" might be discovered. It has, however, proved possible to influence him to such an extent that, in fact, he is supplying good material. It is noteworthy that he has invited OS/29 to the ministry and shown him secret documents.' At the end of his description of the group, Spiru drew certain conclusions:

1. By the very way we have set up the group, we have ourselves set certain limits to its activities.
2. The group has undoubtedly served the ends of widening the periphery [of contacts]. It has provided us with contacts which were beyond our possibilities. That is why its creation was, in principle, right. Certain dangerous aspects were never lost sight of. In certain cases it was the probable control by the Foreign Office which served as a cover for our work.[21]

From Spiru's account it is clear that the Correspondents Bureau was balancing on the brink of illegality, and this explains the uneven quality of the information it passed to the Centre. If the Foreign Office or even MI5 had expressed interest in his activities, the London editor probably would have revealed only the surface of the organization, because the money he needed so badly, for himself and the group's members, was made clandestinely. He must have realized that without the illicit dimension, the rest of the structure would have collapsed. The whole shaky enterprise depended on the Centre's financial support and on the whims of the bureau's ideologically-motivated sources.

It is difficult to say whether the 20 per cent of the bureau's material evaluated as 'of interest and considerable interest' by the Centre was worth the work of the illegals in Berlin or the expenditure, but, as Ilk pointed out, the London operation had to be regarded as the beginning of a much greater undertaking. However, events did not always unfold according to plan, and occasionally a Communist past unexpectedly caught up with a new illegal.

In March 1931, Ilk informed the Centre that Spiru had arrived in Berlin from London on the second of that month, having been summoned by him. 'The fact of the matter is,' explained Ilk, that

HOFMAN, contrary to my instructions not to work with the OS/42 group, and in particular with OS/46, beyond the framework of present activities and only to intensify them in keeping with our instructions to create the necessary periphery, has, probably in pursuit of excessive personal ambitions, exceeded my directives and decided to speak with OS/46 in fairly open terms and suggest to him that he should provide documentary material. This brought about a sharp rebuke on the part of OS/46. I saw in this certain signs which may lead to HOFMAN's denunciation. His position is much more dangerous than I originally thought. I heard about this only on Monday from HOFMAN himself.

Ilk did not exaggerate the gravity of the situation and the second part of his letter sets out events which occur rather more frequently in films than in real life.

Three days before leaving THE ISLAND, HOFMAN was invited by OS/46 to an evening party. The company present had nothing to do with the work. Suddenly, in the middle of the evening, the door opened and a couple entered who turned out to be old friends of HOFMAN and his wife from their Vienna days.

The husband was a Zionist from Lithuania who had studied at Vienna University and knew HOFMAN well as a communist. His wife had also been a good friend of HOFMAN's wife in Vienna, at that time worked legally in our interest, and knew about her activities . . .

Upon entering the room and seeing him, both husband and wife, pleasantly surprised, called out HOFMAN's real name. In a moment a really dangerous situation had developed. OS/46 at once realized what was going on and, turning to HOFMAN, said rather maliciously: 'So you have two surnames. You are leading a double life. We should look more closely into this.'

HOFMAN tried to pass it off as best he could and, according to him, he partly succeeded in this, since the husband and wife, realizing what had happened, tried to back down, apologizing to HOFMAN for having made a mistake. The next day HOFMAN told OS/42 about this 'mistake'. The latter did not take it very seriously, looking upon it as a passing incident. Before his departure HOFMAN once more spoke to OS/46, who completely evaded the question, started a serious conversation about other matters and even took an advance of £10. HOFMAN left, saying that he had to attend a meeting of a publishing company of which he was a shareholder. His departure from England passed off without any incidents.

I personally think that HOFMAN has failed in the eyes of OS/46 and, by the same token, in the work with the OS/42 group.

Ilk further reported another unpleasant development. When Spiru returned to Berlin his landlady there said to him: 'I know that you are not a National Socialist and that is why I want you to know that two weeks ago two men called here and introduced themselves as officials of the Berlin political police. They said they were looking for you in connection with political matters and wanted to know who called on you, whom you phoned and what you were doing. I told them that you were in the publishing business and that you were at present in London at the following address.' Ilk explained that the landlady was a Jewess of about fifty with whom HOFMAN during his visits to Berlin had established good relations. In view of all this, Ilk took decisive action and sent Spiru to a holiday resort in the Harz mountains, 'where one could live without books', and Spiru told his landlady that he was going to the Leipzig trade fair. At this time material arrived from OS/42 which forced Ilk to look for a pretext why Spiru could not return to London. The latter wrote a letter to OS/42 in which he told him that he had had a sharp attack of gallstones, which OS/42 happened to know that he suffered from. At the end of his detailed report Ilk came to a definite decision in respect of his English operation. 'The HOFMAN case will, in all probability, leave a trace which in time could have serious consequences,' he wrote to the Centre on 26 March 1931. 'In any case everything points to the fact that Berlin can no longer remain a base for work on THE ISLAND. Already three weeks ago I came to the conclusion that the time has come that it will have to be transferred to some other location in the West. I think Paris would be the best choice.'[22]

At the same time it was decided, because of HOFMAN's absence, to suspend the Correspondents Bureau. Accordingly OS/29 met OS/42 on 1 June 1931 and explained that this temporary measure was due to what was euphemistically termed 'the economic crisis in Germany', or lack of money. In a letter sent to OS/29 a few weeks later, OS/42 wrote: 'Like you I share the hope and the belief that by the autumn we shall be functioning again; and personally I feel it will be all the more vigorous for this breathing space during the summer months in which time it should be possible to devise reformed systems of editorial, administrative and financial management which should result in the business becoming financially profitable when it is resumed later.'[23]

In spite of this optimistic tone the Correspondents Bureau was doomed, but HOFMAN did not give up altogether and at the end of September he met OS/46 in Holland and arranged to continue working privately for a salary of $250, to be paid, ostensibly, by a large American trust. However, this last effort soon disintegrated for in December 1931, Ilk informed the Centre that Spiru had been arrested by the Berlin police.

> On 3 December 1931, at 9 o'clock in the morning, an official of the Polizeipresidium called at my flat in the Herbertstrasse 16 (where I lived under the name of Julius Pober, a writer from Vienna), and at once took my passport away. He asked me to get dressed and accompany him. I at once realized what it was all about as the official asked me to take with me all other personal documents. I managed to trick the official into leaving the room for ten minutes which enabled me to give my wife instructions how to warn the comrades and hide various documents.

This was how Spiru started his report on what happened to him between 3 and 9 December 1931. At the Polizeipresidium a document from the Berlin Police Directorate was read out asserting that the real Julius Pober, an assistant fitter, was living in Vienna, and that Spiru was holding the passport illegally. The Vienna police requested his arrest and the confiscation of the passport. Then the official tried to elucidate Spiru's real identity, but without success. He was locked up in a cell for the night and the next day he was moved to the counter-intelligence branch, designated Department la, to a room where the walls were hung with frightening posters about foreign espionage. Two officers in turn affirmed that Spiru was either a Frenchman or a Russian and wanted to know how he earned his living and who sent him an envelope with money from Paris. On one of the desks Spiru saw a file entitled 'Akt Lahodny', and on another a photostat of a document with a stamp 'OGPU. Foreign Department'. Fortunately he was not taken in by such tactics and, no progress having been made, he was sent back to his cell.

Spiru wrote that after thinking it over it became obvious that the police was mainly interested in his fake passport and that his fingerprints, once sent to Vienna, would soon enable them to establish his real identity. He also feared that further detention would make it possible, with the help of the police officials who had called at his boarding house in February 1931, to confirm that he was the same Lahodny, thereby endangering the whole organization. Clearly his immediate release was essential, so the next day he disclosed his real name and said that in 1927 he had gone to the Soviet Union as a political refugee, where he had worked as a translator in Moscow and Kharkov. Then, he claimed, the mistrust he had sensed towards him as a member of the intelligentsia had forced him, with the help of Romanian emigrants, to go to Czechoslovakia where he had purchased a passport in the name of Julius Pober. At first he had lived on his savings and money given to him by emigrants, and then he had set up a youth press agency, which happened to be true.

Early in December, Vienna confirmed that the name of the detainee was indeed Julius Hutschnecker and on 9 December Spiru was sentenced to a fine of fifty marks, given a Nansen passport for stateless persons and released.[24] The OGPU was able to confirm these details from Willy Lehman, codenamed BREITENBACH and A-201, who worked in Department 1a. He was later exposed as a Soviet mole in the Gestapo and executed at the same time as other, better-known members of the Soviet network known as the Rote Kapelle. On 12 December he reported: 'A few days ago the Austrian Communist Pober from Vienna, earlier expelled from Prussia, was again arrested in Berlin. He was at first taken to source. Since the latter had no interest in the case he was handed over to the political police (Kriminal-Komissar Heller) which is investigating the matter.'[25]

In another report A-201 mentioned Spiru's real name, established by the police, as 'Hutschnecker, Julius, born 27 November 1898 Luzan, Austrian subject ... arrived in Moscow from Neubabelsberg'.[26] Thus the Berlin police classified the Pober–Hutschnecker case as a political affair, ensuring that Spiru could not work abroad again as an intelligence officer and forcing the Centre to tell Ilk that, 'In view of the difficulties with HOFMAN, we consider it necessary to recall him to Moscow.' Upon his return he was dismissed by the OGPU and he resumed civilian life working for the *Deutsche Zentral Zeitung*; he was lucky to escape the Stalin purges. From 1939 he continued his career as an employee of the MOPR Central Committee and his file ends in the early 1950s, when some interest was shown in him by the Party's Central Committee.

Following the continuing enquiries of German counter-intelligence about Ilk's people, Moscow recalled him and the work he had started was taken over by the illegal groups organized by Karin, Kaminsky and Bazarov. It was a new member of Bazarov's group, Dimitri Bystrolyotov, who was destined to penetrate the deepest into the British Foreign Office.

CHAPTER IV

The Secrets of Room 22

Early in 1930 a diminutive, modestly dressed visitor called at the Soviet mission in Paris and asked to see the military attaché. Introducing himself simply as 'Charlie' when he met the local OGPU *rezident*, he said he was a typesetter in the British Foreign Office's printing house and explained that his job was to decipher incoming telegrams from overseas and prepare them for distribution to other ministries and members of the Cabinet. He was offering to make an additional copy of each telegram and supply it to the Soviets. If the remuneration was satisfactory, he was also willing to provide copies of the Foreign Office's codes and ciphers, which were also printed by his department.[1]

Always suspicious of an *agent provocateur*, the OGPU was cautious. 'Charlie' would give neither his name nor his address, and insisted that he would break off contact if he detected any attempt to establish his true identity. When challenged about why he had selected the Soviet Union for his offer, he replied that the British had penetrated the embassies of most other countries and that he had judged the Soviets the safest to deal with. Satisfied with this explanation, the OGPU arranged for his material to go to Moscow via Boris Bazarov, the illegal *rezident* in Berlin codenamed KIN. The episode was subsequently described by KIN to Dimitri Bystrolyotov, his assistant in Berlin, codenamed ANDREI:

> At first we were quite satisfied by this as long as we believed his story about being a typesetter. Then, as he seemed to delay the delivery of ciphers and failed to pass over top quality telegrams, providing only politically insignificant material, the issue of his true identity arose and we pressed him about the quality of the data. We were also concerned that the choice of the time and place of meetings was always his, and it was clear that we had to take him in hand. The Centre has assigned you this task, ANDREI, and I shall direct the operation on the spot.[2]

Bystrolyotov operated in Berlin under a Czech alias, Josef Sverma, but also had a Greek passport in the name of Alexander Hallas, and a British document identifying him as an English nobleman, Lord Robert Grenville. According to his official biography, prepared in March 1936, which accompanied his application to join the Communist Party, he had been born in the Crimean village of Akchora on 17 January 1901, the illegitimate son of the village school teacher. 'I don't know my father,' Bystrolyotov wrote, 'but when I was about twelve my school friends dropped a hint about my father and I asked my mother about him. The conversation ended with embarrassment and tears and it made such an impression on me that I never raised the subject again.' Evidently this incident deeply affected the boy, for he later said that he had 'looked for his father all his life' and much later believed that he was an illegitimate scion of Count Tolstoy's family, perhaps an explanation for his undoubted literary and artistic ability, not to mention his skill at adopting the identity of an aristocrat, which was to come in useful during his years as an illegal.

The mother was the daughter of a village priest and, in defiance of his wishes, had been educated in Moscow where she had acquired very liberal views. Bystrolyotov's own opinions were not influenced by bourgeois ideology, property or religion and he encountered the revolution 'without any sentiment or opposition. I wasn't interested in politics but I was keen on the sea. I entered nautical school at Anapa, so in the summer I sailed and in the winter I studied.'

He graduated in 1919 and joined the *Rion*, then undergoing repairs in Novorossisk. The Civil War was raging and the Crimea was under the control of General Denikin. Instead of serving with the White Russians, Bystrolyotov decided to flee abroad, and he stole the *Rion*'s compass to sell for Turkish currency. His first attempt to stow away in a ship bound for Constantinople failed when he was discovered, but he escaped and swam to the *Constantin*, where he hid in the coal hold for the voyage to Turkey. Once safely in Constantinople he served briefly on the *Nikolai* which was pledged to the liberation forces of Kemal Ataturk until November 1920, when the ship was handed over to the Soviets in Evpatoria. For the next six months he worked in the communications branch of the Black Sea Fleet and then, when the war ended, joined the merchant navy. Short of work and suffering from undernourishment and poor health, Bystrolyotov accompanied a friend to Constantinople and found work as a stoker, occasionally lodging in a brothel run by Rosa Keizer from Odessa. Later he entered the American College for Christian Youth and, after witnessing the genocide in

Turkish Armenia, suffered a nervous breakdown. He was cared for in the country mansion of a Turkish general, nursed by the Grand Duchesses Dolgoroukova, Trubetskaya and Chavchavadze.

Bystrolyotov made a recovery towards the end of 1922 and was sent by the Red Cross to Czechoslovakia, where schools for White Guard émigrés had been established. However, his contemporaries learned that he had served with the Red Navy and made his life intolerable to the point that he contemplated suicide. Instead he decided, despite the reports of famine, to return home and, following an appeal to the Soviet Consulate, was sent to Leningrad to serve with the Baltic Fleet. However, he ended up in a prisoner-of-war camp in Velikiye Luki, and although ordered to report at Novorossitsk, found no work there either. It was while travelling from Sevastopol to Batumi that he chanced upon two Communists who described how the Revolution should be rebuilding the country. Inspired to help the cause by destroying its enemies, he undertook a long and hazardous journey via Bulgaria, Serbia and Hungary to Prague where, he had been told, the underground struggle was concentrated. Upon his arrival he reported to the Soviet Consulate and offered his services but the astonished consul declared that if he was not a spy he was crazy, and threatened to call the police. However, the émigré community welcomed Bystrolyotov and suggested that he write a report of the famine he had witnessed and the atrocities of the CHEKA. In an attempt to gain their confidence he agreed. When he finally delivered his emotional address he had a packed audience, but after giving an account of the famine he urged those present to return home and help rebuild their country, a provocative suggestion that led to physical assault.

Based at a hostel for refugees, Bystrolyotov found part-time work in a cemetery as an undertaker and started to study medicine at university. Here, while taking a leading role in the students' union, he attracted the OGPU's attention and participated in several schemes to undermine the local White émigré organizations. In 1924 these illicit activities resulted in two arrests and the Czech police seemed determined to expel him, but instead the OGPU's *rezident*, Dneprov, arranged for him to join the Soviet Trade Delegation and recommended that he be recruited as a regular officer. Thus he was sent to Moscow in April 1925, ostensibly as a delegate to the first Congress of Proletarian Students, and interviewed by Gorb and Trilisser's future successor, Artur C. Artuzov. Evidently Bystrolyotov survived this encounter and upon his return to Prague was assigned to work on economic intelligence targets, such as the Skoda factories, with two members of the *rezidentura*, Vilner and Gursky.

Meanwhile he continued his university studies, switching from medicine to law; in 1928 he presented a thesis on the influence of Marx, Lenin and Engels and received a doctorate in law. Following his graduation he was promoted to head of the Trade Delegation's information section and undertook his first recruitment of an Englishman, apparently the son of a senior diplomat who was employed to teach foreign service officials before they were posted to the Soviet Union. He worked at a language school run by General Inostrantsev from his apartment, which Bystrolyotov placed under surveillance to identify all its visitors, among whom was a Royal Navy lieutenant who had been assigned to Moscow with his wife.[3]

Bystrolyotov was later transferred to the political intelligence branch, under the supervision of the *rezident*, Golst codenamed SEMYON, where he was given the task of acquiring the diplomatic codes of a Western European country. His target was a pretty unmarried woman from a good family, codenamed LAROSH, who had turned down SEMYON and Gursky when they had tried to recruit her. Although married to a beautiful Czech named Maria, Bystrolyotov put his duty first when he was instructed to complete the seduction and extract the required secret documents. Where Golst and Gursky had failed, Bystrolyotov succeeded despite 'tears and entreaties', but was then instructed by the Centre to put LAROSH on ice, supposedly because a traitor in Moscow feared exposure. This at least was the interpretation made by Golst, who was equally mystified by the decision, leaving Bystrolyotov to sever relations with the wretched woman by claiming that he was being abruptly withdrawn from Prague. He later encountered her in Dresden, when instructed by the Centre to revive LAROSH, and she made it clear she never believed his excuses.[4]

Another embarrassing episode occurred at the end of 1929 after he had arranged to meet an agent, an engineer at the Skoda works. The rendezvous had been set up by letter and an inexperienced embassy clerk had simply mailed it. Although ordered to post the letter from a mailbox in another part of the city, he had unfortunately stamped it with an embassy stamp, enraging the agent who arrived at the Steiner Hotel to see Bystrolyotov armed with the envelope franked with a large red star and overprinted with the slogan 'Drink Russian Tea'.[5]

The final straw was the recruitment, on Golst's instructions, of the technical secretary of the Czech Union of Industrialists, a potentially useful source of economic intelligence who was believed by the *rezidentura* to be deeply in debt. The target was invited to visit the Trade Delegation, where Bystrolyotov rather unsubtly offered him a wad of banknotes in exchange for information. Insulted, the man spat in his face and stormed out of the building, thereby ensuring that Bystrolyotov was thoroughly compromised.[6] Golst acknowledged that he had become a liability and suggested he take a course at the Academy of Foreign Trade in Moscow. However, as an alternative Golst offered him a role as an illegal in Germany, following his appointment as *rezident* in Berlin. Soon afterwards Golst received a directive dated 2 April 1930 and returned to Moscow for instructions while Bystrolyotov disappeared, leaving his wife Maria in Prague, and emerged in Germany as the illegal codenamed ANDREI (later HANS).[7]

Bystrolyotov's first task as an illegal was to acquire a new identity and for this purpose he visited Henry Havert, a Jew from Odessa who acted as the Greek Consul in Danzig and, according to Golst, was also a swindler and a drug smuggler. In return for a bribe, Havert issued a passport in the name of Alexander S. Gallas which Bystrolyotov used to establish himself in the guise of a Greek businessman, originally from Salonika but brought up elsewhere. In the middle of 1930, Boris Bazarov (KIN) briefed Bystrolyotov on the ARNO case, that of the Englishman who called himself 'Charlie', suggesting that he himself should play the role of a ruthless Chekist, with Bystrolyotov pretending to be an aristocrat who had fallen into the clutches of the Soviets.[8] Equipped with a Czech passport in the name of Lajos Perelly, supposedly an impecunious Hungarian count, Bystrolyotov travelled to Budapest and, having developed a taste for nightclubs and racehorses, established himself in Paris where KIN introduced him to ARNO. After this initial encounter two of Bystrolyotov's assistants, codenamed PEEP and ERIKA, attempted to follow the Englishman home, but he eluded them with what was judged to be professional skill. Bystrolyotov also tried to get ARNO drunk, but the Englishman continued to resist all Soviet efforts to discover his identity. Eventually KIN's surveillance team traced ARNO to the Hotel Napoleon and discovered he was registered as Eric H. Oldwell. Although Bystrolyotov travelled to London in a vain attempt to find Oldwell, he eventually confronted him in his hotel room and learned that his real name was Captain Ernest Holloway Oldham. Soon afterwards his identity was confirmed when he was seen at the Hotel Beau Rivage in Geneva with the British delegation to the League of Nations conference. Subsequent checks confirmed that Oldham lived in Pembroke Gardens, Kensington, so Bystrolyotov called unexpectedly at his house and introduced himself to Oldham's wife as a bank official from Dresden. He entertained her to lunch at the Ritz and after several drinks Lucy Oldham, codenamed MADAM in the Centre's files, disclosed that her husband was an alcoholic who had fallen out with the Foreign Office. Apparently he had been confined at Rendlesham Castle, near Ipswich, for treatment so the following day Bystrolyotov drove to Suffolk to find Oldham, and spent the rest of the month keeping him company. Thereafter their relationship was cemented, according to Bystrolyotov's account which he wrote for the files in December 1968. This is also confirmed by a message from the illegal *rezidentura* dated 9 October 1931, reporting that,

> The improvement in the relationship with ARNO is beyond doubt. ARNO's wife suggested rather insistently that HANS should stay at their house. ARNO suggested the same. Incidentally, ARNO's wife told HANS that when HANS came to them she would introduce him to many colleagues of ARNO who is known to all the chiefs of the Foreign Office.[9]

This offer was considered very attractive by the *rezidentura*, which remained puzzled by Oldham's precise status within the Foreign Office. Oldham himself claimed that he was merely an intermediary who had decided to make a little extra money by helping a more senior figure to whom he passed on most of the money he was paid by HANS and KIN. It was not until after Oldham committed suicide in 1933 that the Soviets learned that he was a cipher expert and the head of the department responsible for the distribution of diplomatic telegrams.[10] According to Bystrolyotov's 1968 report he was given responsibility for the education of Oldham's son, who had been entrusted to the care of a German family living in a villa on the Rhine near Bonn. This apparently gave Oldham a pretext for travelling abroad and allowed him to deliver packets of documents to HANS at frequent intervals. Not all the meetings took place in Germany: some were held in Madrid, Ostend and a resort in Switzerland. On one occasion, when HANS was copying a cipher book overnight in Paris, he accidentally cut his finger on the glass he used to press down the pages. Some blood stained the pages but Oldham was undeterred; apparently security procedures in the Foreign Office were so lax that no one noticed. Their relationship was later described in a message from Boris Bazarov dated 18 April 1932:

> ARNO sees in him an aristocrat, a Hungarian nobleman which impresses him very much (he seems to have seriously believed his legend) who somehow found himself a Bolshevik, but since he is not Russian he is far more acceptable. How exactly he imagines it in his mind is not clear. Obviously he thinks that either HANS was our

prisoner of war or had got lost in Europe. HANS only asks for something, explains the pressure on my part, as if he himself were placed in such a position in which lack of success in the work means transferring him to another, non-European section.[11]

Eventually Lucy Oldham fell in love with the handsome Hungarian count and HANS was instructed to oblige her in the hope that she would continue to be co-operative. She did, and gradually the organization based on ARNO's material expanded to include Stanislav Glinsky, the legal *rezident* in Paris, codenamed PYOTR, and two technical bases, one in Paris under an agent codenamed CHEMIST to process the documents, the other run by Bystrolyotov's wife Maria from a tuberculosis sanatorium in Davos, where she supervised the network's passports and money. The illegal *rezident* in Paris, Theodor Mally codenamed MANN (see Chapter Six), was also involved, but HANS himself never learned the true identities of PEEP and ERIKA, who sometimes acted as couriers and photographers.[12]

While Bystrolyotov failed to persuade ARNO to introduce him to other sources in the Foreign Office, he did claim in 1968 to have procured a British passport in the name of Robert Grenville, supposedly the son of a Lord Grenville who had emigrated to Canada. Whatever the name or title, Bazarov reported to the Centre on 27 July 1932 that, 'Charlie has brought a book [passport] for HANS. This book has been issued not by the Ministry of Home Affairs, as is usual, but by the Foreign Office. This book is British and not Canadian as originally intended, it is like the one Charlie has.'[13]

This was the document Bystrolyotov claims he used to carry dangerous material across borders, but he did not use it for long for fear of having to register at a local British consulate where his thick accent would be bound to arouse suspicion. Exactly what this hazardous cargo was is unclear, but the quantity of Foreign Office telegrams surviving in the Soviet archives indicate the importance of Oldham's access. In a cable dated 28 June 1932, for example, the British ambassador in Berlin, Sir Horace Rumbold, described confidential discussions he had held with the German Foreign Minister Franz von Papen on the subject of the imminent League of Nations conference in Lausanne and the approach to be taken with the French. Similarly, there are details of Cabinet discussions, secret talks with General Schleichen, and information gleaned from the Belgian military attaché in Berlin.[14]

Bystrolyotov's work was so appreciated by the Centre that in November 1932 he was rewarded with a much-prized gun bearing the inscription. 'For a relentless struggle against the counter-revolution from the OGPU Collegium. OGPU Deputy Chairman Balitsky'.[15]

The first sign that all was not well with ARNO can be traced to Bystrolyotov's meeting with him in July 1932, when he passed over the British passport. At the time Bazarov reported that

> HANS has just come back from his trip; this time his partner made him wait for as much as ten days. He has brought nothing interesting. I think this is explained by his careless attitude to his job. He keeps convincing us that his partner was extremely busy in connection with the Lausanne conference so he had no opportunity to interest himself in different matters which are of significance for us.[16]

Thereafter the news deteriorated. On 11 November, Lucy Oldham met Bystrolyotov in Berlin and he sent a report to the Centre:

1. In the middle of October, that is, a week before his arrival in Berlin, ARNO was dismissed from the service. How greatly the chiefs were prejudiced against him is indicated by the fact that not even a partial pension was granted to him. The reason was that for the past two years he had been drinking, and had been working carelessly. For the past six months he had ceased working entirely and had not appeared at the office. He had taken official papers home and lost them, and had failed to answer urgent enquiries. His colleagues had tried to reason with him, but to no avail, so they had given up, with the exception of his former assistant Kemp who still visits him.

2. ARNO's financial situation is bad. He had some money in the bank, but not much. MADAM intends to leave him, to sell the house and car and take her share. She intends to settle in some French resort where there are plenty of Englishmen and work as a housekeeper or companion. If this fails she will become a prostitute. She asked me not to leave her without support.

3. ARNO's physical condition is poor. He will take a rest after the Berlin trip and will recover some of his cheerfulness and capacity for work, but in the end his strength will not last for long and complete disablement will follow within a few months.

4. ARNO declared that he will continue to maintain contact in the future and we agreed to meet in Germany next week. There was no deterioration in our relations because of his abnormal condition. Complete apathy, heavy vomiting and the inability to speak or move has made him impossible to talk to.[17]

Bystrolyotov prepared a plan for Oldham, accepting his illness and his inability to work and offering him a pension for life in return for direct contact with his main source. At the same time, he expressed concern about Oldham's dismissal from the Foreign Office. As Lucy had noted with indignation, her husband had been sacked after twenty years' service without even a pension, but Bystrolyotov assumed that the loss of pension was connected with Oldham's carelessness and drunkenness. Indeed, recalling ARNO's own account of the dismissal of two other officials suspected of treachery, from Peking and Oslo, even though the investigations had proved inconclusive, it was likely that ARNO himself had fallen under suspicion. However, Bystrolyotov acknowledged, following a conversation with Lucy, that Oldham might have been made of sterner stuff than he had realized. Indeed, it turned out that he had deliberately misled Bystrolyotov and Bazarov, for he admitted under pressure that his main source was a captain, whom he declined to name, a Foreign Office official now in retirement who had been willing to make some money by selling secret documents. However, when Bystrolyotov checked his claim with Mrs Oldham, she denied knowing anyone fitting that description, and she also asserted that her husband never went abroad for the Foreign Office. Indeed, according to her, Oldham had not made any recent trips to Geneva and Paris, as he had alleged, 'so not a word he said could be believed', Bystrolyotov concluded.[18]

Bystrolyotov was particularly anxious that Oldham might let the cat out of the bag when drunk and compromise the entire operation; the circumstances of his dismissal demonstrated that he was already under some suspicion. The sensible course would have been to break off contact entirely, but Bystrolyotov wanted to identify the main source. When he arrived in London at Christmas 1932 he found his agent sinking into alcoholism: on '22, 23 and 24 December ARNO drank more and more; our entreaties and reproaches only irritated him with no result. Finally I decided to take the matter into my own hands and demanded that he go to the country for treatment. On the evening of the 25th I went to his house and found ARNO dishevelled and asleep in an armchair, an alcoholic who had completely gone to pieces. I shook him awake but without opening his eyes he reached out for a bottle and drank, thinking that I was his wife. "Go away, you bitch," he said, before falling asleep again. I persuaded MADAM not to give him any more brandy and urged her to call a doctor when he awoke. When he did so, that night, her refusal to give him a drink prompted him to try and strangle her and she was only saved by the doctor who gave him medication and arranged for him to be taken to the country unconscious. ARNO looked awful and MADAM was shattered and wanted to do away with herself. I spent three days persuading her not to commit suicide while she lay sedated in bed with the marks of ARNO's fingers very evident on her throat.'[19]

After treatment at the sanatorium Oldham recovered somewhat, but continued to drink and beat his wife. In May 1933 he travelled to Paris and delivered another batch of Foreign Office documents to Bystrolyotov, claiming that he had no idea of precisely what the sealed package contained, but insisting that he had paid his source in full for the contents. He explained that he had offered to buy the Foreign Office codebook known as 'Book C' from his source, as well as three cipher charts, for about three times the amount he had paid for similar material a year earlier. Once again Bystrolyotov raised the possibility of identifying the source, and giving Oldham a pension, but the spy declined and on 22 June Oldham returned to Paris, accompanied by his wife, but arrived empty-handed, saying that he had been unable to pay his source. Exasperated by Oldham's drinking, which his doctor said was likely to kill him at any time, Bystrolyotov arranged for Oldham to go back to the sanatorium and sent his wife away to a resort for a month.

He planned to live in their house and attempt to restore contact with Oldham's source once he had recovered, and Bazarov in Berlin supported the proposal, but when Bystrolyotov arrived in London on 23 June he discovered a wild scene of drunkenness at Oldham's house. After a fight he had the wretched man detained in a hospital, but while he was undergoing treatment MADAM decided to divorce him and seized the contents of the house. She also engaged a lawyer and demanded half of the £2,000 which she believed her husband had earned through HANS. The lawyer put Bystrolyotov through an uncomfortable interrogation to establish the nature of their business and this awkward episode prompted Moscow to order his immediate withdrawal to the Continent. Still determined to trace Oldham's source, Bystrolyotov appealed against the decision and was allowed to maintain contact in the hope of acquiring a copy of the new Foreign Office cipher book which Oldham was to extract from a Foreign Office safe, having been taught by Bystrolyotov in Hyde Park how to take a mould of the key. While Bystrolyotov waited for him to gain access to the safe he attempted to cultivate Oldham's erstwhile assistant, Kemp, codenamed ROLAND, who had begun to take an interest in the Oldham family. The Centre instructed Bystrolyotov to see if Kemp could identify ARNO's source, and suggested that perhaps it was Kemp himself, so Mrs Oldham invited both men to dinner. Clearly this was a dangerous move, so Moscow made a contingency plan to exfiltrate Bystrolyotov should the need arise. His wife met him on a park bench, one of his regular rendezvous sites, and handed him a package containing a gun, in case he had to commit suicide, and the passport in the name of Alexander Hallas. 'My wife and I said goodbye to one another as if before a battle,' recalled Bystrolyotov.[20]

The dinner proved memorable, not least because, to Bystrolyotov's dismay, Mrs Oldham confessed to her guests that she was concerned about her husband's behaviour. He was making regular trips abroad, he had stolen a diplomatic courier's briefcase from the Foreign Office, and he had obtained a passport in a false name for someone. While Bystrolyotov concealed his anxiety, Kemp announced that he had been instructed to find out if Oldham was engaged in espionage. Still pretending to be an attorney for a bank, Bystrolyotov suggested that the evidence would lead to Germany, and arranged to meet Kemp for lunch at the Ritz the following day so he could give details of Oldham's overseas assets. However, instead of keeping the appointment, Bystrolyotov left England by the first plane, as reported to Moscow by Bazarov on 24 July 1933.[21] The Centre replied on 4 August, praising HANS for the 'selflessness, discipline, initiative and courage' he had displayed 'under the exceptionally dangerous conditions of the last days of work with ARNO'.[22]

Soon afterwards Oldham turned up for a meeting with Bystrolyotov and Bazarov in Switzerland, and the Berlin *rezident* submitted a report on it dated 9 August. Together the two intelligence officers tried to get Oldham to reveal his source, but instead he returned to London, not to his house but a hotel, and continued to gather information for the Soviets, apparently intending to see Bystrolyotov again in September to deliver a list of British Secret Intelligence Service personnel posted abroad. Meanwhile Mrs Oldham kept in touch by letter and informed Bystrolyotov that Kemp had found a job for her and her son. Later she wrote that according to Kemp her husband had been seen drunk in various pubs, and that he had asked Kemp to endorse his passport to give him the status of a diplomatic courier. Kemp had retained the passport and invited Oldham to visit the Foreign Office, but he had taken fright and disappeared from his hotel.[23]

In fact Oldham subsequently committed suicide, and it is clear from MADAM's letters to Bystrolyotov that the Foreign Office conducted an investigation into his death, concentrating on his income in 1932 and 1933. The family solicitor was interviewed in October 1933 in an attempt to discover what she termed her husband's secret life and his connections with Germany, and there was a hint that he and other officials had been suspected by the police of smuggling drugs. Mrs Oldham had alleged that her husband had invariably visited the Foreign Office before his overseas trips, and that he had been paid for his packages by a man named de Vinchy, which was Bazarov's alias. When pressed by the solicitor for Bystrolyotov's address, she had refused to disclose it, claiming that he was an innocent go-between, and not a party to 'the dirty business' into which the Germans supposedly had drawn Ernest. The solicitor responded that Bystrolyotov had robbed her husband, and later Kemp turned up uninvited and denounced Ernest as 'a spy and a smuggler'. He also threatened to have her arrested for complicity if she did not co-operate with the Foreign Office and betray Bystrolyotov, but she refused to do so. From what she learned from Kemp the Centre was able to reconstruct much of ARNO's background:

ARNO remained above suspicion until the middle of 1932, and he was considered an able but undisciplined official. He was allowed to keep his post in spite of his alcoholism and was given extensive time off for treatment. When a codebook disappeared from a safe in the basement of the Foreign Office, ARNO was investigated, and it was established that despite being on sick leave, he was still visiting the office, gaining entry by the side door known as the Ambassador's Entrance. He was forbidden to do so but resumed the practice within a month, and so was dismissed.

After ARNO's visit to Berlin MADAM told ROLAND [Kemp] of £3,000 spent on drink in three weeks, and this prompted a further investigation. ROLAND and a colleague, referred to only as 'B', were instructed to keep an eye on ARNO whenever he visited the Foreign Office, but evidently ARNO had spotted the surveillance. It was during one of these visits that a bundle of telegrams disappeared from the duty cipher clerk's desk. ROLAND rushed around to ARNO's house but discovered that he had already left for the Continent. This was the last delivery made by ARNO.

After a period of treatment in the country, when the Foreign Office tightened up its physical security procedures, ARNO resumed his visits, making up to three a day, and even appeared after working hours, moving from room to room in an agitated state, obviously anxious to be left alone. ROLAND had arranged for a file to be left unattended and ARNO would have been arrested if he had taken it, but doubtless he sensed a trap. On another occasion ARNO visited ROLAND's room and the keys to his safe went missing. A search established that ARNO had left the building, and soon afterwards the keys were found with traces of wax on them.

When ROLAND learned from MADAM, during their dinner together, about the theft of the courier's briefcase and the forged passport he was instructed to gain as much evidence as possible from HANS so ARNO could be arrested. However, ROLAND soon established that HANS was not at the hotel he had named, and the police reported that no one with HANS's name was registered in London, which meant that he had used another name to gain entry to the country. This gave the Foreign Office good reason for handing the entire matter over to the police, but when ARNO was questioned he said that HANS had left the country that morning by train.

It became evident from what ROLAND said to MADAM that the Foreign Office had no idea that ARNO had conducted a meeting with HANS in Switzerland, and their version of ARNO's stay in Vienna and Berlin, a wild binge with prostitutes, was intended to enrage her. In fact, of course, ARNO had been to Interlaken, which had also escaped their notice. Nevertheless, HANS's letters and telephone calls had been intercepted, as had the money he had sent to ARNO by mail. Anyone connected with ARNO was interrogated and MADAM noted indignantly that TOMMY and SHELLEY had co-operated with enthusiasm, even to the point of suggesting that she should be arrested as an accomplice.[24]

Mrs Oldham's account of the Foreign Office investigation was considered very useful by Moscow, especially as it tended to confirm what was already known to Bazarov and Bystrolyotov and indicated that the affair was regarded in London as one of German espionage; it is a key objective of all illegal operations to mislead the opposing security apparatus. Indeed, the MADAM–HANS–ARNO triangle had been constructed so skilfully that even Lucy Oldham believed in the German interpretation and, determined to protect her 'Hungarian count', cast de Vinchy (Bazarov) in the role of villain.

In retrospect Bystrolyotov took the view that he had helped prolong Oldham's life by a few months, his demise from greed and drunkenness being inevitable. Having read the widow's account, he remarked: 'Only in English novels does everything go smoothly for the intelligence services, all ends meet and the Tower of London mercilessly swallows those who have touched upon the secrets of the British Empire. I accept that I could have ended up in the Tower, but only if Vansittart [the head of the Foreign Office] had been willing to wash his dirty linen in public and the matter had been entrusted to anyone other than ROLAND.'[25]

Indeed, according to Kemp, the Foreign Office had not experienced such a case in the past 300 years, a fact doubtless appreciated by Sir Robert Vansittart.

Surprisingly, the loss of Oldham did nothing to undermine Bystrolyotov's enthusiasm for his work, and his knowledge of the Foreign Office made him the ideal candidate to continue the cultivation of SHELLEY. However, he could not risk returning to London.

One of Oldham's first tasks for the Soviets had been to identify his Foreign Office colleagues to Bystrolyotov. One of those working in the British delegation to the League of Nations in Geneva, code-named BOY, seemed a difficult prospect to recruit but one which Bystrolyotov and Bazarov were convinced was promising. Since Bystrolyotov, masquerading as a Hungarian count, would attract too much attention in Geneva if he approached BOY, and since he was already engaged in a dangerous game with the international adventurer ROSSI, who was supplying him with ciphers, Henri Pieck was summoned to Switzerland to assist. The decision was taken collectively by Bystrolyotov, Bazarov and the famous illegal Theodor Mally. At that time Pieck, codenamed COOPER, was working for Ignace Reiss, codenamed RAIMOND, who had recruited him in 1930. Pieck was Dutch by birth, a painter by profession and a Communist by ideology: in 1935 he had been awarded the coveted engraved pistol by the Chief of the Foreign Department, Abram A. Slutsky. Bystrolyotov noted that COOPER

> had three merits: devotion to the cause, honesty in financial matters and straightforwardness in his work and relations with us. COOPER's character has attributes which help him to work. He is a good actor who plays his role naturally, sometimes masterfully, finds his bearings quickly in conversation, manoeuvres well and is always ready for initiative, for active conducting of the business; intelligence in the sense of the general knowledge of people, culture, political training, all this immediately puts him in a favourable light with the object of recruitment. Love for intelligence work bordering on a passion, a romantic attitude to his role close to that of an actor's enjoyment.

All this was supported by 'a genuine citizenship, legal passport, origin from a "good family", prepossessing appearance, a very suitable profession which opens doors in society to him, fluency in Dutch, German, English, French and several other languages (perhaps Italian and Danish)' and his special ability 'to approach women'.

Bystrolyotov also recognized some of COOPER's weaknesses, his tendency 'to get carried away, which makes him act and then think', and that he was 'absolutely unable to play the role of a reactionary'. He was also 'Bohemian, disorderly, untidy, inaccurate, incoherent and undisciplined'. According to Bystrolyotov, Pieck was 'a person with a weak will, extremely kind, warm hearted, mild and sentimental' and 'an ideal talent-spotter, not at all a bad recruiter, but that's all. He is unable to put pressure on somebody, to grab him, to overcome him, to blackmail, to threaten to kill.'[26]

There seems to be a reflection of Bystrolyotov's own character in his description of COOPER's personality, as is clear from his memoirs, written after sixteen years in a labour camp between 1938 and 1954. He too was kind, sometimes sentimental, but still sufficiently professional to disarm ROSSI physically and psychologically, and push a prominent member of the French intelligence service, codenamed JOSEPH, into a corner. Both Pieck and Bystrolyotov were examples of the phenomenon of the kind person in a cruel world.

COOPER took up residence in the Hotel Beau Rivage in Geneva to establish contact with BOY, but only managed to meet him when he moved into rooms above his apartment and started to visit a bar frequented by Englishmen. He made friends with several, or so Bazarov reported to Moscow on 12 March 1933, and was commissioned to paint the portrait of an influential Englishwoman who could prove useful. Pieck was optimistic about building on his growing popularity among the British community and developing his relationship with the local vice-consul, a Captain John Harvey who had been involved in Admiralty signals during the First World War. Codenamed CHIEF, Harvey had indiscreetly confided in Pieck during Ramsay MacDonald's official visit to Rome in May 1933 and had urged him not to leak to the newspapers information he had disclosed. This was considered evidence of Pieck's acceptance by the British, as was his introduction to Harvey's family and the knowledge that his daughter NORA was to marry SHELLEY, another consular official. He later described how late one evening after dinner he was invited by SHELLEY and TOMMY to visit the Consulate while the officials studied the latest telegrams. He was also urged to call in at Room 22 when he was next in London, and join Harvey and his colleagues for a drink in their local pub. On 25 December 1933, Bystrolyotov reported that COOPER had witnessed the two Britons opening a combination lock safe and examining the contents.[27]

While COOPER waited for the right moment to approach BOY, he realized that young SHELLEY had fallen into debt. He had spent much of his December salary on drink and before his departure for home some of his cheques were in danger of bouncing, an offence that would bring him instant dismissal. COOPER lent him the money he needed, and a further loan soon afterwards, regarded by Bystrolyotov as an investment in the future. His opinion of SHELLEY was confirmed by Oldham who regarded him as a wastrel, uninterested

in politics, who was in the hands of the money-lenders. Apparently
SHELLEY supported an elderly mother and an unemployed sister,
as well as an unsustainable lifestyle based on entertaining his friends
in bars and music-halls. His financial misfortune prevented him
from realizing his ambitions, to marry NORA and buy her a car.
Bystrolyotov had a scheme to exploit these weaknesses.

In early March 1934, SHELLEY spent a week with Pieck and his
wife at their house in Geneva, where elaborate arrangements had
been made to present them as a well-to-do couple, complete with
maid and car. Finally Pieck explained that his wealth was in part
due to information he supplied to a senior financier, and SHELLEY
admitted that he had once been paid fifty francs to answer a journalist's question. He agreed to complete a questionnaire for Pieck the
next time he visited Geneva, in return for £500, and this was
reported by Bystrolyotov. The Centre responded on 4 April 1934,
instructing Mally to ensure that the material was passed over 'on
the Continent, and not on THE ISLAND'. Although SHELLEY seemed
unconcerned about supplying information about other countries,
for example about Germany and Mussolini's policy towards central
and southern Europe, he expressed doubt about his ability to give
'the bank' specialist economic data and suggested that he approach
another Foreign Office colleague for help. This idea was swiftly
vetoed by Pieck, who stressed the dangers of bringing strangers
into their scheme; he was privately anxious about having someone
planted in the network by the security authorities.

Bystrolyotov accepted that there would be delays before SHELLEY
became productive and his opinion was endorsed by Ignace Reiss,
through whom his report was channelled: 'The hesitations that took
place are a positive sign and I am sure that the maiden, partly
infatuated, partly tempted, will finally lose her virginity.' The Centre
also counselled caution, taking the view on 19 April that, 'SHELLEY
is considered here classic and model work' although the counter-
intelligence repercussions from ARNO were still unknown. In fact
SHELLEY had made his first modest delivery by 20 April which
delighted its recipients because it included extracts from official
telegrams which he had copied out by hand. It was relatively trivial,
containing material available in the newspapers and indicating that
SHELLEY was politically naive, but he seemed to understand what
his contacts wanted.[28]

At the end of May SHELLEY gave more material to Pieck and
dictated some notes, but he pointedly refused to supply any manuscript papers and refused to bring original telegrams to the house
to be copied. Nevertheless, he agreed to continue helping Pieck and

mentioned that he was about to complete a comprehensive analysis of Britain's economic position. This was reported by COOPER on 23 July 1934 and the following month SHELLEY produced enough excerpts to prove that he 'has sat down to processing serious secret correspondence'. The following month SHELLEY agreed, for £1,000, to make fortnightly reviews of the most important instructions to ambassadors and their telegrams home. Pieck was delighted, but when they met next, at the end of August, SHELLEY had been overcome by fear and protested that he was unwilling to take any further risks. He declared that he would not work for the bank any more: it was all very well for the banker to sit in a comfortable office in absolute safety, with no idea of the danger. When Pieck enquired what had prompted his change in attitude, SHELLEY answered that 'nothing has happened but I don't want to go to prison just before the wedding'.[29]

When SHELLEY had calmed down Pieck returned to the topic of working for the bank but, as Bystrolyotov reported to the Centre in a letter dated 8 October 1934, 'the clandestine meeting came to nothing. SHELLEY did not promise to do anything by some fixed time.' However, after SHELLEY visited the next session of the League of Nations his future father-in-law had raised the subject of his financial situation and SHELLEY confided that he had started working part-time as an intermediary for a bank. Harvey gave his approval to this arrangement, saying that one could only contemplate marriage when one has saved up sufficient money. Accordingly, SHELLEY asked Pieck for a loan, but Pieck refused and brought the conversation around to 'work for the bank'. SHELLEY said that there were very few telegrams in Geneva and that most of the longer documents went to London by courier. Although he expressed a willingness to resume making copies of telegrams, he arrived empty-handed at his next meeting with Pieck, which was in Paris on his way back to London from Geneva. On 8 October 1934, Bystrolyotov reported deadlock to Moscow. SHELLEY's financial difficulties were matched by the problems posed by his marriage, which would increase the financial pressure while making secret meetings more complicated to arrange. However, he advised against a confrontation with SHELLEY, pointing out that thus far his relationship with Pieck had been good and saying that antagonism should be avoided. He was confident that, despite the so far unproductive investment, SHELLEY was coming around to the idea of being a source.

SHELLEY's potential remains unknown. He works in a room with twenty other officials, at a table at which sit four others. Only a small part of the correspondence passes through his hands, which he cannot copy on the spot. He must look for material in other rooms, in which he has no official business. Whether this is a consequence of measures taken after the ARNO case is not known. SHELLEY carefully conceals all details regarding his work so it is extremely difficult to give him guidance. Maybe the fear he expressed in July was a result of his having been caught somewhere he was not supposed to be.[30]

Mally relayed Bystrolyotov's message to Moscow, adding that SHELLEY had asked Pieck 'to come to THE ISLAND'. Pieck was instructed to go only if SHELLEY had something to offer, and to make it clear that he was not willing to undertake an expensive and futile chase across Europe. Evidently SHELLEY was short of money, and it was agreed that a waiting game was the best method of applying pressure. Sure enough, when Pieck next visited London at the end of October SHELLEY asked him for £50. Pieck said that earning money was better than borrowing, and urged him to pass on the weekly summaries of the diplomatic telegrams he had access to, adding that the bank would pay well for them. But he made the mistake he had been warned of, that handing over money would simply delay matters, and lent him the £50. A month went by and SHELLEY failed to keep his promise. At that point Bystrolyotov was in Moscow, on his first short leave for years, so on 4 December the Centre gave new instructions to Mally. The Deputy Chief of the INO, Boris Berman, codenamed ARTYOM, directed that 'we must stop treating SHELLEY ceremoniously' and ordered him 'to threaten him good and proper'. He suggested it be put to SHELLEY, as 'the bank' had made a substantial investment in him, the bank wanted a return and intended to demand it back, if necessary through the courts. Bystrolyotov left for Paris on 18 December and the following day the Centre informed Mally, declaring that if he had not had an opportunity to confront SHELLEY, the imminent arrival of HANS would make the task easier. In fact, Mally had already despatched Pieck to London to threaten SHELLEY, but it was Bystrolyotov who submitted the report on the meeting.[31]

Having listened to COOPER, SHELLEY declared that this was either an attack of nerves on the part of a bank director or some intelligence work, for only an intelligence officer would generously lend money and then demand information and threaten a scandal. Far from being intimidated, he declared that he was ready to begin repaying the debt and promised to find COOPER some alternative sources who had a knowledge of Germany, but he refused point-blank to supply any material, insisting he would never submit to blackmail. Thus, according to COOPER, SHELLEY appeared to regard himself as untouchable, his only concern being for COOPER.[32]

The only positive element in this fiasco was SHELLEY's suspicion that Pieck, who had played his hand with characteristic skill, might have an intelligence connection, which was interpreted in Moscow as evidence of the briefings MI5 were presumed to have given Foreign Office staff, perhaps in the wake of the ARNO affair. Certainly the first sign of SHELLEY's reluctance to co-operate had emerged at the end of August which, Bystrolyotov speculated, may have coincided with a Security Service effort to tighten procedures following Oldham's lapse. Bystrolyotov contemplated a further blackmail attempt, but the Centre vetoed the idea because the resulting scandal would only serve to scare off SHELLEY's colleagues and 'friends among whom our other recruiters and comrades are working'. Accordingly, Bystrolyotov admitted defeat and asked for the Centre's approval for his new instructions to COOPER, which required him to 'travel to THE ISLAND and get down to MAG'.[33]

MAG, who first appeared in the Centre's files in a letter from Bystrolyotov dated 8 October 1934, was a Foreign Office cipher clerk of Irish extraction named Captain John Herbert King who, according to Pieck, had been introduced to him by SHELLEY:

In Geneva COOPER became acquainted with a cipher clerk named King. He is about fifty years old, an Irishman who lived in Germany for about ten years and speaks German perfectly. A lively and inquisitive person, not stupid but well-educated. He draws a sharp distinction between himself with his cultured ways and the 'pompous fools' of Englishmen. He likes music and is knowledgeable, and is keen on the theatre. He is very eccentric and likes magic.[34]

Bystrolyotov concurred with Pieck's assessment and added that, 'King is in dire need of money because he has to support himself on a small salary, as well as his grown-up son, a student, and his wife. In spite of his length of service he is not given promotion because of his Irish background, and he likes to have a drink at someone else's expense ... He would borrow money and being an Irishman does not like the English and makes friends easily with foreigners.'

Evidently King had come to admire COOPER as a painter and they had drunk beer together, but Mally had been wary of pursuing him beyond assigning him the codename MAG, partly because he did not want to complicate SHELLEY, but mainly because of the danger that King might draw the attention of other cipher clerks. 'Even though COOPER has given the impression that he would be easier to handle than either SHELLEY or TOMMY,' reported Mally, 'we have forbidden him to even think about it.'[35]

By early 1935 the situation had changed, with SHELLEY having categorically rejected further contact with 'the bank' although he remained friendly with Pieck. Bystrolyotov gave COOPER two months to complete MAG's recruitment or give him up. The assignment was accomplished by 17 February, when Moscow informed Bystrolyotov, who was then in Paris, that celebrations should be postponed until he had taken possession of 'the document familiar to you bearing the inscription "the property of H.M. Government".'[36]

On 20 February, in a letter sent to the Centre by courier, Bystrolyotov gave an account of the background to King's recruitment. Apparently Pieck had been introduced by SHELLEY to a prominent architect, Cameron Kirby, through whom he had met a number of bankers and who had recommended him for membership of the prestigious Albany Club in London. By exploiting his new circle of friends, Pieck had met a number of Dutch businessmen and an official of the Netherlands Ministry of Trade. This official had been made responsible for disposing of two million cans of lard which the Dutch government had acquired for the unemployed, but which had become the subject of a political scandal. Pieck was invited to find a buyer for the cans, and receive a commission of 100,000 florins, which he was to share with his English partners, including SHELLEY. This transaction gave Pieck an excuse to make regular visits to London and he eventually set up a company, with the official as a sleeping partner, to import Dutch butter and cheese. The business was boosted by its selection by the Netherlands Ministry of Trade to decorate all the Dutch pavilions at international trade fairs. Simultaneously, Pieck collaborated with his English wholesalers to establish the Joint Stock Company of International Barter, a company described by Bystrolyotov as engaged in 'selling air'.[37]

Encouraged by Bystrolyotov, Pieck widened his range of social contacts in London and became friendly with the Albany Club's secretary, a man named Partridge, who arranged for him to join the Society of Painters. Two of the Society's patrons, Brigadier-General Reginald Kentish and Sir Walter Peacock, proved to be short of money and anxious to start an antiques business, so Pieck latched on to them. Unmarried, and a professional soldier until his retirement in 1922, Kentish had founded the National Playing Fields Association, while Sir Walter Peacock, who had spent much of his life in the service of the Prince of Wales, was a member of the Royal Fine

Art Commission. Suitably impressed by Pieck's new acquaintances, SHELLEY asked to be introduced to Peacock, and a dinner was arranged at which, according to Pieck, 'SHELLEY behaved like a servant'. Captain King was also tremendously impressed by Pieck and his social prowess, and asked Pieck to arrange for his son to meet Sir Walter Peacock in the hope that he might employ the young man. However, at the last moment the dinner had to be cancelled because King's son did not possess a tailcoat, and MAG could not afford to buy him one at short notice. This humiliating experience proved an ideal opportunity to conclude MAG's recruitment. 'To be accepted by high society requires money,' explained Pieck. 'To acquire friends one must dance, drink, drive a car and spend money. When one has those, one can obtain a post as a private secretary. Kessler [Sir Henri Deterding's representative on the Royal Dutch Shell Oil board] took on six young fellows from Oxford. It only takes a word from a wife or daughter for such a magnate to offer a suitable position.'

Evidently MAG conceded that his son's future could only be secured with big money, and he listened enthusiastically when Pieck made his pitch, describing how a large bank known to him routinely speculated on the international stock markets and paid £100 a month for political information. 'If there is to be a war between Italy and Abyssinia, shares in the Italian factories fulfilling Mussolini's military orders will rise, and if the Luftwaffe is legalized [development of a German air force had been barred under the Treaty of Versailles] shares should be bought in the German aircraft industry.' Pieck suggested that he would be willing to hand over 60 per cent of his salary from the bank in return for this kind of information. King acknowledged that it would be easy for him to make notes of the documents that passed through his hands, whereupon Pieck suggested that it would be easier if he simply took the originals. King promised to think the matter over, and when they next met Pieck was well prepared, having gained experience from his collaboration with SHELLEY. He claimed that he had been involved in plenty of highly successful speculation which had been well rewarded by the bank, and King agreed to start work immediately. He also suggested that the weekly Foreign Office summaries, intended for circulation to the Cabinet, did not contain the most important telegrams, which were only copied to the Permanent Secretary. He revealed that he worked in a section of the Foreign Office handling the most sensitive material, telegrams that were despatched overseas in the morning, and the replies which were received in the afternoon. King suggested that they find a method of meeting at eleven p.m. daily, when he could supply copies of the telegrams 'so they could be on the banker's desk the next morning'. He also said that he would not tell his son of what he was doing, and suggested that he and Pieck distance themselves socially so as to avoid suspicion.[38]

Pieck was delighted by the new recruit's initiative, but had two reservations. One was King's reluctance to hand over original documents, preferring to rely on notes and extracts, and the other was his insistence on setting up a regular channel of communication. He wondered whether King was perhaps too good to be true, possibly planted by the British, but he was reassured by Mally and Bystrolyotov who expressed confidence in their ability to examine King's material and judge its authenticity.

King's first delivery included his notes of Foreign Office telegrams and a fascinating verbatim account, given to Pieck on the morning of 29 March 1935, of the Foreign Secretary Sir John Simon's recent audience with Adolf Hitler. Simon had listed the German Chancellor's demands for revision of the Treaty of Versailles: an air force at least the equal of France's, the elimination of the Polish Corridor (the strip of land giving Poland access to the Baltic and dividing East Prussia from Germany proper) and the return of Germany's colonies. King also supplied a sensational analysis of the international situation in anticipation of the forthcoming conference at Stresa. Sir John Simon took the view that if British policy failed, and a unified stand against Germany collapsed, war might be the consequence within a matter of months.[39]

When passing on this information King insisted that Pieck commit it to memory and burn the actual paper because its discovery would immediately alert the Foreign Office to the leak. Pieck agreed and offered King £50, which was declined with a request that it be put into a secret bank account, together with any bonuses earned through the successful exploitation of his tips. 'I expect up to £500 a time,' he said. 'We must trust one another. You know that a couple of words to the right person over the telephone will ensure you will never go home. However, you can talk to me and I believe in you and in the bank.' After a couple of whiskies King confided that at their first meeting he had taken Pieck for a foreign intelligence officer. Then, in London, he had wondered if he had been sent by British counter-intelligence to test him.

Pieck told him that the bank demanded originals because 'it could not risk huge sums of money on oral information' and King accepted the logic of his argument. As for its authenticity, Bystrolyotov noted that much of the material had already been confirmed by the press, for Sir John Simon had made a statement regarding the Luftwaffe and had admitted Hitler's demands over the Polish Corridor. 'MAG does not disinform and does not look for easy earnings,' wrote Bystrolyotov. 'He is very careful and is counting on years of work and thousands of pounds of income. MAG says that in THE ISLAND he is a foreigner and he does not regard his work for us as dishonest. The whole business comes down, in his opinion, to danger and receiving danger-money.'[40]

He first turned his attention to the book in which the most important incoming telegrams were registered after they had been deciphered, and after a summary had been prepared for senior Foreign Office personnel. However, what had seemed practical in theory turned out to be impossible to implement. MAG worked in the cipher room with SHELLEY and TED, but on the afternoon shift they operated in pairs, one writing the decrypted text onto a flimsy in pencil while the other read the telegram. The flimsy was then passed on to the next room where the King's Messengers, who were ranked more senior than the cipher clerks, awaited their assignments. They were responsible for typing the telegrams, destroying the original flimsies, and entering summaries into a log known as the Day Register. The incoming telegrams were then passed for internal distribution to the office messengers, who were usually retired warrant officers, while the outgoing telegrams were circulated to the senior staff for approval before being sent abroad. MAG handled the Day Register every day, entering new telegrams, but on the occasion he attempted to read some of the other pages he was noticed by one of the couriers who challenged him. Alarmed by this experience, MAG decided that he could not use the Day Register and instead concentrated on the Foreign Office daily bulletins, which hitherto had been supplied by ARNO [Oldham]. According to SHELLEY, ARNO and MAG, these files are kept in the couriers' room and MAG had no official access to them, as he discovered when he tried to look at one, and was spotted by a courier who warned him not to take 'his book', indicating that each was the responsibility of an individual courier. They were in constant use by the couriers, who kept them permanently in their sight making access impossible, so MAG opted for old copies of the daily bulletins which were scheduled for destruction. The document shredder, which in ARNO's time had stood in the basement, is now in a ground-floor corridor, not far from MAG's room. However, when he chose his moment to steal the bulletins from the machine, which was guarded, he was asked why he was in that particular corridor, and who he was looking for. MAG had no excuse and therefore had abandoned the attempt.

In these circumstances MAG was left with the telegrams which he handled legitimately.[41]

From King's description of his office Bystrolyotov concluded that neither he, nor the unidentified TED nor SHELLEY could be of much use, a disappointment for which MAG cursed the Foreign Office. His experience duplicated that of SHELLEY, who had tried to steal a document, but was spotted and scared to death. However, having a rather different relationship with Pieck, SHELLEY had not been entirely candid about the security procedures which had prevented him from performing, and instead had used some spurious moral excuses to conceal his failure. Inevitably the Centre concluded that it would have to forget about the cipher clerks and concentrate instead on the couriers and the distribution room where ARNO had been in charge.[42]

Bystrolyotov's pessimism concerning Herbert King soon proved to be premature. He turned out to be rather more ingenious than he had been given credit for, as he demonstrated on 16 April when he met Pieck and presented him with a decrypted cable from the Prime Minister, Stanley Baldwin, to Sir John Simon. King explained that he had personally deciphered the telegram, which was too important to be included in the weekly summary. His purpose in bringing it was to show 'the banker' the kind of material he handled, and the source of the information he usually dictated to Pieck, who undertook to destroy the cable immediately it had been studied by the banker. Indeed, King insisted that he place it inside an envelope marked 'To Be Destroyed Immediately' and, in case of an accident, that this be inserted into another envelope addressed to Pieck's wife.[43]

At a further meeting held on 4 May 1935, King produced a shorthand record of all the incoming telegrams received that day which he dictated to Pieck. However, this arrangement proved unsatisfactory as Pieck made mistakes in taking down the dictation, so King started to write the texts of the telegrams himself. Finally he was reluctantly persuaded to hand over the shorthand note, protesting that the form on which it was written identified his exact room, number 22 in the Foreign Office, and his handwriting might also betray him. 'Remember,' he warned, 'I am an Irishman and I am either one hundred per cent your friend or your enemy. Do not let me down.' He declined Pieck's offer of £100, instructing him to keep it in his secret account and, when Pieck expressed astonishment at his behaviour, explained that as an Irishman he 'did everything to the extreme'. King added that he could not be bought, but had agreed to help the bank because, as a foreigner he was unconnected with the state which employed him, and that anyway the political information he collected was for the use of capitalists, which was precisely what he was doing.[44]

As HANS (Bystrolyotov) noted in his report to the Centre on 9 May, 'the first stage of the recruitment is completed. MAG has agreed to work for us and has proved himself. Further development depends on us, not him, but someone is required to receive his daily deliveries.' To this Mally appended the caution that consideration should be given to MAG's sudden access to documents which he had previously said were denied him. 'Combined with the fact that he trusts COOPER [Pieck] too much, it might suggest that we have stepped right into the jaws of the lion. Perhaps his initial disinclination to pass material was influenced by a lack of confidence in COOPER, and maybe fear as well. As you can see from HANS's report, it really is not easy for him to extract documents, and he can only get a limited number of them, so that is why he wanted to move to the distribution room.'[45]

Early in May 1935, King took three weeks' leave on the Continent and brought with him a large number of the pink outgoing flimsies and white incoming telegrams. He explained to Pieck that he now had access to a very large amount of papers which were not intended to be copied by being retyped. He revealed in a moment of candour that he had feared a trap set by the Secret Intelligence Service, but was satisfied after he had made discreet enquiries about Pieck with SHELLEY and other officials. Only when his suspicions had been dispelled did he decide to proceed. The fact that King had attempted to check up on Pieck was later discovered, as Bystrolyotov reported on 5 June 1935.

> MAG said that after his first lunch with COOPER he had returned to CHIEF [Captain John Harvey] and had reported that a foreigner had entertained him, and that Geneva was full of suspicious characters. He had sought his advice and CHIEF had replied that Pieck was a personal friend and deserved complete trust. This, according to MAG, had enabled him to develop his friendship with COOPER, but when the latter offered him work with the bank he had suspected that he might be CHIEF's agent.[46]

Although King had insisted that the daily summaries were uninteresting, Pieck had demanded sight of them, asserting that the bank was used to receiving them. King responded that he now knew the bank's previous source had been Ernest Oldham, but Pieck had never heard of Oldham and was able plausibly to deny all knowledge of him. Undeterred, King denounced Oldham as 'a fool who took documents openly and ruined himself'. At a subsequent meeting with Mally in August 1936, Oldham's name came up again and King disclosed some additional details of the ARNO case. He claimed that Oldham had been working for the French, and the story of his suicide was untrue; the Intelligence Service had eliminated him and then placed his body next to a gas tap. However, Oldham's fate had not deterred King for he soon had plenty of files on stream. 'MAG works with clockwork precision,' reported Bystrolyotov to the Centre on 26 June. 'At present he is supplying four types of material: weeklies, separate telegrams that later go into the weekly summaries, telegrams that are too sensitive to be included in the summaries, and his personal information based on what he has heard or read. The separate telegrams sometimes reach us very quickly. For example, the telegram already cabled to you was received within two hours of its arrival at the Foreign Office. This is a special category of telegram marked with the letter "K" which is too secret to be included in the summary, but instead is distributed in triplicate.'[47]

By October 1935 the cipher clerk's access had broadened considerably and Bystrolyotov reported on 10 October that King, 'on his own initiative, and after a number of failures, had acquired a key to the safe belonging to the head of the cipher department, and he can now extract files which are not included in the secret bulletins'. However, some of King's material proved useless because of the time it took to reach Moscow, the delay being caused by Pieck's lack of an excuse to stay in London permanently. Although Bystrolyotov expressed an interest in going to England, the Centre forbade him to. Instead, Mally arrived in London in September to set up a local base of operations, a flat in Buckingham Gate, conveniently near the Foreign Office, rented by Pieck's business partner Conrad Parlanti. Ostensibly it was a studio, and King called almost every day, drawing the curtains as a signal that he had left some papers to be photographed by an illegal sent especially for the task. The film was then delivered to the legal *rezidentura* for processing and urgent information was transmitted to Moscow immediately. By early June 1935, Mally had recommended Alexander Orlov for this important assignment, knowing that he was already well established in London under excellent cover, but the Centre turned this suggestion down because Orlov and Arnold Deutsch were already fully committed to the ring that had penetrated the Woolwich Arsenal (see Chapter Six) and to the Cambridge network, and instead nominated Walter Krivitsky, codenamed GROLL. This choice seemed inexplicable at the time because Krivitsky spoke no English and had no knowledge of photography, but despite Mally's reservations, which he expressed to the Centre, he had to brief Krivitsky on the King case and supervised a meeting with Krivitsky and Pieck in December 1935. It was only after this meeting that Krivitsky agreed to abandon the idea of running King in England. Mally had already excluded himself back in June, having observed that he 'could not sit on THE ISLAND. I have neither a book [passport] nor cover, and it is impossible to go there frequently without cover because the frontier control is polite but thorough.'[48]

By the end of 1935 the situation had become desperate. Pieck was being blackmailed by his first wife's husband who had hired a private detective to follow him and had threatened to expose his Communist past and 'his shady business deals'. Although the Centre was confident that the detective would discover nothing about Pieck's true occupation, Mally reported on 25 November that he would not 'let COOPER go to THE ISLAND for contact with MAG any more. One must consider him under surveillance. He will extract himself eventually, given the right circumstances, the conditions for which already exist.' Accordingly, Pieck was obliged to limit his contact with King to meetings on the Continent until his personal affairs could be regularized. This left King without a controller in London, a situation deemed unacceptable. 'To put MAG on ice for two or three months does not seem possible,' reported Mally to the Centre in a letter written in German dated 9 December 1935. 'This would completely demoralize him. The only possible way out of the situation would be if I took over MAG temporarily. I have advanced this suggestion without any enthusiasm and I don't like the idea of a six-month stay on THE ISLAND at all, simply because of a single case, but perhaps we can penetrate much deeper and succeed in getting a collection [of codes and ciphers].' His first meeting with King took place on 6 January 1936 at Pieck's office in London, but what he termed 'a technical misunderstanding' arose. Pieck had given him the wrong key so he could not unlock the office door, and he was unable to wait by the entrance because he saw a police constable on the street corner. Pieck supplied the correct key the following day and Mally arrived the same afternoon to meet King. 'MAG came. I had seen him previously in Paris from a distance but this time I gained a different impression. He is a big fellow, not quite so tall as I am, and grey, but by no means an old man. After an exchange of passwords our conversation began and although he was obviously excited and uneasy, he tried to compose himself.'[49]

Mally introduced himself to King as 'Peterson', saying that his

wife was related to 'the banker', and proffered a letter confirming
that he had responsibility for handling the bank's most secret affairs.
At first cautious, King responded by observing that Mally's accent
did not sound Dutch and asked what was his nationality. Mally
explained that he was Austrian, but Hungarian by birth, and after
being calmed by a glass of whisky, King relaxed. By the end of the
meeting he had written a letter to the banker:

> I have received your letter dated 4th. I am sending you perhaps
> the most important communication I have yet sent. I have absolute
> confidence in you and I feel sure that this communication is safe. I
> appreciate your caution – you are absolutely correct – and I hope
> one day to have the pleasure of meeting you. In the meantime I hope
> our service will be to your satisfaction. I wish you a very happy and
> prosperous New Year, Yours very sincerely, Johnson.[50]

In a short postcript he requested a brief meeting with Pieck, who
was then still in London, and on that occasion he handed over, on
Mally's instructions, the documents to which he had referred. Mally
commented that King had 'painted me in such bright colours that
I didn't recognize myself' and submitted a report to the Centre
confirming the cipher clerk's political opinions, which indicated his
co-operation with the Soviets could not be based on ideological
considerations. 'He spoke to me about Socialism, and about the
fact that he had studied it and how good it would be if one could
rid the world of poverty, hunger, war and prison. But all this is
theory. Socialism in practice is the terrors of Bolshevism, it is chaos,
the power of the mob, Jews and endless bloodshed. I am against
Fascism but if here, in this country, I had to choose between Sir
Oswald Mosley and British Labourites, I would choose the former
for the latter logically led to Bolshevism. Here is a left-wing man for
you.' King also hated Mussolini, considering him 'crazy, a belated
imitator of British imperialism'. He also, though to a lesser extent,
hated Hitler, who was in his opinion 'a maniac but an honest person,
and anyhow he has saved Germany from Communism'. King
thought the English aristocracy 'good for nothing, in the first place
because it is English, and in the second because it mixed with Jews
and other lower classes. The Irish and Scottish nobility is a quite
different matter,' he said. 'It is clear of foreign taint and it has
preserved its race. All the talented and outstanding people of Great
Britain were either Irishmen, Scotsmen or even Jews,' he argued.
Mally simply commented, 'You see the logic'.[51]

When Mally initiated a conversation about ciphers, King
explained how they were used and attempted to prove that they

were impossible to break. Feigning ignorance, Mally encouraged King to be indiscreet and then observed that 'theoretically all ciphers can be broken for they are based on the law of permutational theory of higher mathematics and the proof of this is the well-known historical fact that during the war the British broke the German cipher'. Finally he added that ciphers 'are not necessarily made impregnable by reciphering charts'.

King was clearly 'stunned, even frightened' by Mally's expertise and asked if he had been a cipher clerk too. Mally denied this but remarked that 'one doesn't have to be a cipher clerk. It is enough to be a spy to have an idea about ciphers. In the course of my work I happened to come across people who sell ciphers.' King replied that he would never sell ciphers, not even for £10,000, which prompted Mally to say that he would not offer to buy them, and certainly would not agree to a price of £10,000.[52]

Turning the conversation to ciphers was, of course, entirely deliberate on Mally's part, as the Soviet objective was to extract British ciphers from King, but then 'the bank' would lose its cover and be revealed as a foreign intelligence agency. King would face a choice: to go on selling secrets to a bank concealed under the veil of commerce, or pure espionage. With characteristic subtlety, Mally intended to let King ponder precisely who he was really dealing with. Naturally, Soviet Intelligence always wondered just how far King believed the tale about 'the bank' and Mally's provocative hints had undermined the principal cover story. 'I am afraid to say he doesn't believe it. Most likely he still believes, but harbours doubts.'[53]

The conversation about ciphers obviously intrigued King. At a later meeting he returned to the subject without prompting, disclosing that a friend of his, now dead, had successfully deciphered a German telegram during the war and mentioning that he had been lucky that the German communication was only enciphered and not reciphered. Reporting this to the Centre, Mally announced that 'this was a clear hint about ARNO'.

After these preliminary meetings with King, Mally made a series of recommendations about how he should be handled in the future and suggested that he be encouraged to get more quality material, including ciphers and information about the British Intelligence services, 'both military and naval. Then,' mused Mally, 'we would have to explain who he was working for, and this "who" must not be us.' According to what was known of King's political views, 'it can be the Americans, or it may be someone else. It may strike you that we may even have to switch him over to the Germans, not the

Nazis but the Reichswehr, or to anti-Nazi business circles.'[54]

While Mally prepared his future collaboration with King, other events took place which placed the whole arrangement in jeopardy. On 31 January 1936, Pieck threw a house-warming party at his new flat and among those invited were his lawyer, his partner Conrad Parlanti, and the British commercial attaché in The Hague, John Hooper. When the party was in full swing Hooper asked his host to spare him a few moments in private, and revealed to Pieck that 'we know about your past and keep a constant watch on you. I want to know whether you are still in the same business,' meaning the Comintern. The Dutchman did not deny 'the sins of my youth', but insisted that he had long abandoned political activity and was now entirely preoccupied with commerce and painting. At this point Hooper had identified several of Pieck's business contacts in London, demonstrating that he had been kept under surveillance, and that the commercial attaché was connected with MI5. Hooper had learned from Parlanti the Westminster address of the company's offices, 34 Buckingham Gate, and received Pieck's undertaking that he would not use the premises for, and would no longer engage in, 'nonsense'. Apparently satisfied by Pieck's promise, Hooper offered to issue him with a card that would facilitate his entry into the UK in the future. Pieck declined the offer politely, asserting that he had never encountered a problem entering England, but Hooper remarked that although he may not have experienced any difficulty, the authorities always acted one way and thought something entirely different. When Parlanti visited Hooper on routine business next day the attaché asked him about Pieck's income and produced a schedule listing the Dutchman's profligate expenditure.[55]

Despite John Hooper's obvious interest, Pieck felt sure that MI5 had not discovered his intelligence role, and had no knowledge of his links to SHELLEY and King. However, the fact that Hooper had learned his company's address in Buckingham Gate, which had been used as a safe house in which to meet the Foreign Office clerk, was sufficient reason to sever the connection. Pieck alerted GROLL (Krivitsky) to the danger and told Mally that no more meeting would be held at the flat. A replacement was rented and the meetings were resumed with the previous frequency.

Pretending that he had been offered the local agency of a British company, Pieck approached Hooper and asked him to provide a reference, claiming that he was anxious to clear his name of any suspicions that may have arisen. Having extracted Pieck's file, which included information about his place and date of birth and his parents, Hooper challenged him about his membership of the Communist Party in Holland in 1920 under the name Donat, and the fact that he had been sent by the Party to the Soviet Union in 1929. This last item Pieck denied, protesting that he had gone on behalf of a publishing firm that had paid for the trip. The file also contained details of all Pieck's visits to England, the last being a stay at the Victoria Hotel where all his business contacts had been noted.

Persuaded by Pieck that he was entirely legitimate, Hooper agreed to amend the dossier, asking only how it was possible for the son of a naval officer to get mixed up with revolutionary ideas. Pieck explained that he had been influenced by a trip he had made to Hungary in 1919, accompanied by a *Times* correspondent, and had allowed his paintings to express his radical views. Later, he said, he had abandoned revolutionary activity to support his family, which was more important to him. Suitably impressed, Hooper asked Pieck to put his story in writing, asserting that this was the only way to set the record straight and to persuade the Dutch intelligence service that he had given up his commitment to Communism. Indeed, at one moment Hooper hinted that he might like to participate in one of Pieck's companies, Seekant.[56]

Hooper's attitude to Pieck is best explained as an attempt to recruit him for the British. Doubtless he would have been asked to re-establish contact with his old Communist friends in much the same way that, as we shall see, Olga Gray was recruited to penetrate the Communist Party of Great Britain and, ultimately, the Woolwich Arsenal spy-ring.

What remains in Pieck's personal file in Moscow does not make it clear whether he had permission to disclose the purpose of his trip to Hungary in 1919, and it is unknown whether he had any further contact with Hooper. In fact he was forbidden to undertake any more operations in England and his dossier shows only that there was a discussion about sending him to Austria, leaving a gap in the official biography between August 1936 and June 1941, when the *rezident* in London, Anatoli Gorsky (VADIM), reported that Anthony Blunt (TONY) had come across MI5's file on 'Pieck, alias Donat'.

Blunt revealed that 'Jack' Hooper had worked for the British in Holland until the Nazi occupation, and then had transferred to MI5 headquarters in London. According to Kim Philby, Pieck was spotted again in 1946, this time in the company of Richard Laming, an SIS officer under attaché cover at the British Embassy. Apparently Tómas Harris of MI5 was to be despatched to The Hague to investigate Pieck's contacts, but this would have proved fruitless as Pieck had not been used operationally since he had come to the attention of the British and Dutch authorities.[57]

After the alarming events of February 1936, Mally continued to run John King and the amount of documents the cipher clerk removed from the Foreign Office increased steadily. On 25 March Mally reported to the Centre that MAG had delivered 'seventy separate documents (telegrams) and dailies for the 14th, 18th, 19th and 21st March are being forwarded from him with this mail'. About 70 per cent of the material was received from MAG on the very day of their registered arrival at the Foreign Office. Only 30 per cent of the material was two (maximum four) days old. On 9 May this amount had escalated to 'eighty-nine telegrams, two weeklies and one despatch (Eden's report)', and on 24 May it was 'ninety-five telegrams and one special summary', virtually swamping the Centre's capacity to process such large amounts, which of course was increased by additional material supplied by WAISE (Donald Maclean) and the spy in Rome codenamed DUNCAN (see Chapter Five). A year later, in April 1937, King's delivery comprised '113 telegrams and four summaries' which prompted concern in Moscow about duplication, especially after Maclean joined the Foreign Office and became productive. An analysis dated 19 June 1936, sent to the *rezident* in London, observed that 'about 30 per cent of MAG's material was repeated by DUNCAN, and now we receive it thrice, and if the documents get into the summary, four times. Nevertheless, we should not refuse to accept material from any of the sources simply because it is repeated. To reduce the mail you may tear up on the spot any duplicates or information of little value, until the arrival of the legal' (OGPU officer). Although the quantity of documents flowing in caused an administrative burden on those handling it, it did have the advantage of enabling the Centre to compare items so as to check on their authenticity and to prevent the deliberate insertion of disinformation by a hostile intelligence agency.

Contact with King was finally broken off with Mally's departure from London in the summer of 1937, and since there is no record of any attempt to restore it between 1937 and 1939, the period of Stalin's purges, it must be assumed that none was made. King himself was arrested in October 1939, but it was not until 5 June 1941 that the Centre learned the full background of his betrayal by the defector Walter Krivitsky from Anthony Blunt, who supplied the relevant MI5 report to Anatoli Gorsky (VADIM). According to the Security Service, 'Krivitsky told Isaac Don Levine in 1939, who in turn reported to MI5, that a Foreign Office cipher clerk named King was a Soviet agent working for a man named Pieck in Holland'.[58]

The complete text extracted from MI5's registry, entitled *Soviet Espionage in the United Kingdom* (see Appendix I), provided a review of the five principal cases investigated by the Security Service since the Arcos raid in May 1925, and received a warm welcome in Moscow. The subjects covered were Wilfred Macartney and George Hansen; Percy Glading, George Whomack and Albert Williams; Robinson Walker and Michael Kaptelsky; A. A. Dotchenko; and John King. Blunt's willingness to delve into MI5's registry and retrieve a file that the Soviets were interested in must have been an invaluable asset for Moscow.

CHAPTER V

Codename DUNCAN

By 1936 Soviet Intelligence had successfully developed three really good sources in the British Foreign Office. Donald Maclean and John King are now well-known, but the third, Francesco Costantini, is almost completely unknown.

Strictly speaking, Costantini did not work in the Foreign Office: he held a low-grade post as the Ambassador's servant in the chancery of the British Embassy in Rome where he was locally employed. Variously codenamed D3, DUNCAN and finally LANGLE, Costantini had been recruited to work for the Soviets in 1924 by an officer of the Rome *rezidentura* named Sheftel through D1, another Italian who had been employed at the pre-Revolution Russian Embassy in Rome.[1] Despite Costantini's relatively low status and lack of education, he had long mixed with diplomats and had acquired their style and manners. His espionage was motivated by money and, from the very start of his work up to 1937, was one of the Soviets' most important sources of information. That he was highly valued by the People's Commissariat for Foreign Affairs is demonstrated by a letter dated 15 October 1933 from the Centre to the Rome *rezidentura*:

> Comrade Litvinov has asked us why he has not received for already more than a year material on this [British] Embassy. He added that this material at the time was of great use to him.

The hiatus referred to, caused by DUNCAN's mysterious but temporary disappearance, soon ended, and in January 1934 the *rezidentura* reported that it had dispatched the following Foreign Office documents:

1. On the plans for German rearmament and the three stages of the reform of the German Army (up to 1938) according to data supplied by the Deuxième Bureau of the French General Staff to the British Military Attaché in Paris.
2. Cipher telegrams about Eden's visit to Berlin, Paris and Rome

and the talks about German rearmament (with secret proposals from Hitler).

3. A survey of the Japanese–American strategic positions in the Pacific, composed by the Tokyo Embassy.

4. A report on the implementation of the Japanese Naval programme in 1933 and the budget for 1934–5.

5. On Japanese–German relations and the recognition by Germany of Manchuria [annexed by Japan in 1931].

6. Plans and prospects of German foreign policy, as evaluated by the Berlin Embassy.

7. A memorandum by [Sir John] Simon on the position of China in case of war between the USSR and Japan.[2]

In addition, DUNCAN also provided invaluable details of British codes, ciphers and one-time pads, as listed by the Centre:

the diplomatic code Political-8; the Consular Code M-28; the Naval Intelligence code Reporting Officers Cypher; the diplomatic code K; the Interdepartmental Cipher; the India Office Cipher.

DUNCAN was also able on several occasions to pass the British diplomatic bags to the Rome *rezidentura*; they were restored to the building once the contents had been copied. His access within the Embassy made him an exceptional agent, but the Soviet case officers who ran him began increasingly to suspect that he was also working for the Italian military intelligence agency, known as SIM. The first fears, voiced in 1928, were grounded on the entirely justifiable concern that his position in the British Embassy, which made him so attractive as a source to the Soviets, must also have attracted the interest of their Italian counterparts who simply would not have been earning their keep if they did not try to recruit him. Indeed, as an Italian national, Constantini seemed an obvious target, and as he lacked any moral or ideological motives he would have been unlikely to refuse an offer. The *rezidentura* again raised this issue in a letter dated 29 September 1930, reporting DUNCAN's remark that 'for him only the British represented a danger and he was not afraid of the Italians'.[3] However, in the absence of any real evidence, other than this ambiguous comment, the Centre opted to continue working with him because of the great value placed on his information.

Over the years that followed, however, the question of double dealing remained a preoccupation. In April 1934 the *rezidentura* reported that among the material supplied by DUNCAN was a note in an unknown hand requesting payment owed. This, combined with the undeniable fact that Costantini was not very conversant with the documents he supplied and never seemed able to give very clear explanations of how he had obtained them, led to the conclusion that he was not working alone, but was using someone else who was demanding his share of the financial rewards.

The illegal *rezident* Akselrod, codenamed OST, who had been running DUNCAN since early 1935, decided to get the truth out of him, and in May 1935 he extracted the admission that he was linked to the local security service which was interested in British Embassy staff. But he alleged that he had told the Italian Counter-Intelligence Service that he had no access.[4]

However, in a message to the Centre dated 24 September 1935, OST disclosed that DUNCAN routinely transmitted the same British documents to the Italians as he had passed to Soviet Intelligence. He came to this conclusion because when the Soviet Ambassador told the legal *rezident* Zhuravlyov, codenamed MAKAR, about his conversation with the Italian Deputy Minister for Foreign Affairs, he quoted the Italian as using characteristic expressions which MAKAR had encountered in DUNCAN's material. Secondly, judging by the volume, quality and content of the material, which was often damaging to Italy, the Italian security service did not appear to be controlling its flow to the Soviets, as might be expected. Thirdly, OST asserted that DUNCAN was no longer working at the British Embassy. This last and most sensational conclusion was based on DUNCAN's ignorance of the names of Embassy officials: moreover, when documents were returned to him after they had been copied, he did not go to the Embassy, but to an entirely different district. Finally, it was easy for him to leave Rome for lengthy periods, and invariably he was unable to fix more than one meeting at a time, suggesting that he did not enjoy regular employment. When all this was considered with the note from an unknown person found in his material in April 1934, OST deduced that DUNCAN had been running his own source inside the British Embassy.

The accuracy of this conclusion was confirmed at a meeting in November 1935, when DUNCAN suddenly mentioned the need to have an assistant in the Embassy so as to widen his access. This was interpreted by OST as an attempt to put his source on a legal footing, and during a discussion in France in August 1936, where the pair had gone on holiday, he confronted DUNCAN directly with the charge that he was not working at the Embassy. Taken aback, DUNCAN admitted that he had resigned five years earlier, fearing the consequences of the discovery of his acquaintance D1. He also confessed that he had an assistant who had started working there as an administrative officer before he had left. Further, he admitted that he had sometimes given British documents, which did not need to be returned, to the Italian Counter-Intelligence Service.[5]

OST gave the unknown source in the British Embassy the codename DUDLEY and in February 1937 obtained the admission that it was DUNCAN's own brother, Secondo.

OST's illegal group was disbanded in August 1937 when the legal *rezident* Markov, codenamed OSKAR, was denounced. Contact with DUNCAN was suspended, with the exception of a few rare control meetings with PLATON, one of the *rezidentura*'s officers. Nevertheless, PLATON obtained a full confession in October 1938, in return for an agreed sum of money. DUNCAN recounted how at the very start of his co-operation with the Soviets he had made contact with the Italian Counter-Intelligence Service in order to safeguard himself in case something went wrong. He claimed that he had only given the Italians documents which were due for destruction, for which he received a monthly salary of 4,000 lire. The really valuable documents, he said, he only gave to his Soviet contacts.[6]

At the beginning of 1939, DUNCAN disappeared to reappear only in 1944 when he visited the Soviet mission in Rome. In conversation with the new *rezident*, Nikolai M. Gorshkov, who had arrived in the capital with the Anglo-American forces as an Allied representative, he explained what had happened to him in the intervening years. Apparently his co-operation with SIM had continued till 1937, and he had been run by Alberto Perini, the officer responsible for maintaining surveillance on the British and Soviet Embassies. Perini had introduced him to another officer named Tadamo, alias Taddei, but at the beginning of the war DUNCAN moved to Milan, and later to Albania, where he lost contact with SIM. However, his brother Secondo, who had been left by the British as caretaker of the Embassy property, had continued to co-operate with SIM right up to the arrival of the Allies. When the British returned he was reinstated as a protocol and administrative officer, but they quickly learned from the SIM archives of his duplicity and he had been questioned about his contacts with Perini and Tadamo. Under interrogation Secondo had admitted supplying SIM with British secrets.[7] This, apart from confirming DUNCAN's previous admissions, suggested that the British might be aware of his co-operation with the Italian authorities, too, but it was not clear whether Secondo had given this away, or evidence had been found in the SIM archives, or perhaps DUNCAN himself had been questioned. In any event, in case he really was an *agent provocateur*, it was decided not to renew operational contact with him, although he was given some financial support on the few occasions that he asked for it.

In July 1949, DUNCAN made a further visit to the Soviet Embassy and reported that a British intelligence officer had told his brother that he had learned about his Soviet connections from a certain Russian. In return for his confirmation, he said, Secondo had been promised half a million lire. This assertion was regarded as a provocation and an attempt by DUNCAN to extort money, so contact with him was terminated.[8]

What remains unclear is whether the Italian Counter-Intelligence Service ever knew about DUNCAN's work for the Soviets, from DUNCAN himself or perhaps from having kept him under surveillance. If the Italians had discovered this link, it could reasonably be assumed that the British would have uncovered it in the SIM archives. It is more likely that the Italians never realized that DUNCAN was in touch with the Soviets as he would hardly have volunteered the information himself. His principal anxiety had been to cover himself for the illicit possession of documents removed from the British Embassy, and a candid confession to the Italian authorities almost certainly would have deprived him of a considerable additional income. Most probably the Italians trusted him enough not to keep a watch on him, and thereby failed to discover his Soviet links. If they did find out about them, it is difficult to understand why they took no action against OST's illegal group, which ran other valuable agents as well as DUNCAN, and allowed the leakage of documents damaging to the Italian government. If DUNCAN had been operating for Soviet Intelligence under Italian control, his admission to OST that he was in contact with the Italian service could have been extraordinarily, perhaps terminally, dangerous. The fact that DUNCAN reported that Perini, his Italian handler, was responsible for keeping a watch on both the British and Soviet Embassies remains strange. If one were to assume, in spite of the evidence to the contrary, that the Italians really had known about DUNCAN's link with the Soviets, and had manipulated him, the whole operation would look extremely effective from an Italian standpoint.

As for the British, their discovery that the Costantini brothers were Soviet spies was entirely unexpected and came far too late for them to take any counter-measures. In fact Francesco had not resigned but was sacked for some act of dishonesty by the Ambassador, Sir Eric Drummond, and Secondo had been suspected of having been the cause of a massive leakage of documents from the Embassy which had been the subject of a major investigation. Major Valentine Vivian, then head of the counter-espionage branch of the Secret Intelligence Service, had undertaken a rigorous review of the

Embassy's security in February 1937, following the theft of Lady Drummond's diamond necklace, and at the end of the month had submitted a damning report, *Security of Documents in HM Embassy Rome*, to the Foreign Office. In it Secondo was identified as a likely cause of the breach in security, and Francesco, who had been dismissed earlier, also came under suspicion, but certainly was never considered as a possible Soviet agent. Major Vivian accurately traced the loss of papers back to 1924 and observed that Secondo might

> have been directly or indirectly responsible for any, or all, of the thefts of papers or valuables which have taken place, or are thought to have taken place, from this mission. He was, I understand, not quite free of suspicion of being himself concerned in a dishonest transaction for which his brother, then also a Chancery servant, was dismissed a short while ago. Moreover, although the Diplomatic Staff at the time did not connect him with the matter, I am clear in my own mind that the circumstances of the loss of two copies of the 'R' Code from a locked press in the Chancery in 1925 point towards S. Costantini, or his brother, or both, as the culprits.[9]

Although the British authorities did correctly identify the breach in security, they did not appreciate the seriousness of the lapse until the Soviet defector Walter Krivitsky revealed at the end of the war that the NKVD *rezident* in Rome, Leon Helfand, had been tapping into a British source there since 1924.[10] Although this disclosure remained secret, the former Austrian Chancellor Kurt von Schuschnigg claimed in his memoirs that in 1937 the Italians had employed 'a confidential agent' who 'was a member of the immediate entourage of the British Foreign Minister'.[11] He knew this because he had seen a photostat of a letter from the Permanent Under-Secretary at the Foreign Office, Lord Vansittart, addressed to Sir Anthony Eden. Von Schuschnigg's revelation appeared to be supported by a reference in the diaries of Count Ciano, published in the same year, which suggested that the Italian secret service had enjoyed access to classified British documents.[12] When this issue was raised in the Commons in December 1947 the Minister of State at the Foreign Office, Hector McNeil, explained that an unnamed Italian servant 'had been able to remove documents from the Embassy in Rome over a considerable period'.

> This servant, apprehended after the war, admitted what he had done and stated that he had received considerable sums of money from the Italian authorities. We also believe that Count Ciano was in the habit of boasting that he had a source in the Foreign Office which

provided him with the contents of secret files affecting Italy. It is thought, however, that this was the device by which Ciano sought to cover up the actual source of information, which we now know to have been the Rome Embassy.[13]

With no possibility of prosecuting either Costantini brother for the thefts, McNeil made the British Government's displeasure known to his Italian counterpart and the matter was consigned to the archives, the Soviets satisfied from both the public statements and from Guy Burgess, who was then McNeil's private secretary, that the NKVD's role had gone undetected.

CHAPTER VI

The Great Illegals

Technically Arnold Deutsch could not be categorized as an illegal, as he always used his real name and travelled on his own genuine Austrian passport. Nevertheless, as a member of the section dealing with the Foreign Department's illegal *rezidenturas*, he was always regarded as an illegal, and he certainly practised their tradecraft. He can be classed as one of the generation of 'the Great Illegals', and takes the credit for recruiting no fewer than seventeen agents in Britain, some of whom provided valuable information over decades. Perhaps not surprisingly for such an accomplished professional, very little has been published about either him or his colleague Theodor Mally. Considering that this pair were directly responsible for the extraordinary success achieved in THE ISLAND it is appropriate that their individual files should be extracted from the archives and made public for the first time.

According to the NKVD officer's Special Questionnaire completed by Deutsch in 1935, evidently while he was on leave in Moscow, his full name was Arnold Genrikhovich Deutsch and he had worked in the Comintern's Department for International Relations under the name Stephan Lang, which was also the name on his Party card. Deutsch gave his date of birth as 21 August 1904, his nationality as Austrian Jew, and his citizenship as Austrian. His education had been five years of primary school, eight in a gymnasium, followed by five in Vienna University's chemistry faculty. He had joined the Austrian Communist Youth Organization in 1922 and the Austrian Communist Party in 1924; membership of the Soviet Communist Party dated back to 1931. He had been employed by the Comintern in Vienna from December 1928 to December 1931, and as an NKVD officer since August 1932 had been posted to Paris, Vienna and London. Under the heading 'knowledge of foreign languages', Deutsch had written 'German, French and English fluently, can read and write Italian and Spanish'. Between 1928 and 1932 he operated for the Comintern in Greece, Romania, Palestine, Syria, Germany and Czechoslovakia.

His twenty-eight-year-old wife, Fini Pavlovna, worked from 1931 to 1935 as 'Liza Kramer' on special assignment in the Department for International Relations. She was a candidate member of the Soviet Communist Party, a member of the Austrian Communist Party, and by profession a teacher. While in the Department for International Relations in Moscow, she attended the Communist University for Western Youth (KUNMZ).

Deutsch's father, Genrikh Abramovich Deutsch, was a businessman, then aged sixty-five, and his mother, Katya Emmanuelovna, was sixty-one. His wife's father, Pavel Rubel, was a shopkeeper who had died in 1934, her mother was Frieda Moiseyevna Rubel, aged sixty-one. According to Deutsch, his parents and his wife's belonged to the lower middle class, but he pointed out that they were members of the Austrian Social Democratic party. In conclusion, Deutsch listed the few NKVD officers he knew: A.F. Karin, L. Nikolsky, O.G. Mueller, Dmitri Smirnov, I. Reif and R. Gurt.[1]

Rather less mundane is the curriculum vitae written by Deutsch on 15 December 1938:

I was born in Vienna (Austria) in 1904. My mother and father are Jewish and of Slovakian origin. My father was a country school teacher. After they moved to Vienna, he worked for a merchant. He was called to the colours in 1916 and served in the Austrian Army as an ordinary soldier till 1919. From 1919 to 1920 he was a rag-and-bone man and later sold ready-made clothes and underwear from a stall as he did not have his own shop. In 1927 he hired a bookkeeper. After Hitler incorporated Austria and already under Schuschnigg, as a Jew he had to give up his business and live on the income from his house, which he had bought in 1931–2. On what means he lives at the moment, I cannot say as I have not heard from him for several months. Since about 1910 right up to its prohibition in 1934 he was a member of the Austrian Social Democratic Party.

About my relations with my parents. My mother is the daughter of a courier. I have always had good relations with her. My father was a religious Jew and he tried to force me in every way, including beatings, to become one too. The final conflict with my father arose because of my political activities, which called forth all his wrath and hatred. My mother, on the other hand, defended me and helped me in this regard. In the beginning of 1929 I left my parents and from that time on I have maintained relations with my family only for my mother's sake. He persecuted my two younger brothers even more than me because they were materially dependent on him. He forced them to have nothing to do with the communist movement. They also hated him.

From 1910 to 1915 I attended the primary school and from 1915 on the gymnasium in Vienna. During the first years, inasmuch as my father was serving in the army, I received a scholarship. Later, I did not have to pay any school fees at all because of my high marks. From 1923 to 1928 I studied physics, chemistry and philosophy at Vienna University and got a degree of Doctor of Philosophy.

In 1920 I became a member of the Free Union of Socialist Students, an organization of Communist and socialist students. In 1922 I joined the Austrian Communist Youth Organization, where I worked permanently as a leader of a propaganda group, partly in the district, partly in the Central Propaganda Department. In 1924 I became a member of the Austrian Communist Party. I did propaganda work in the district. Later I worked also in the MOPR [International Workers Relief Organization] and was a member of the Central Committee of the Austrian MOPR. Several comrades know me from the time I worked in the Austrian Communist Youth Organization and the Communist Party: Koplenig, General Secretary of the Austrian Communist Party, Fuernberg, representative of the Austrian Communist Party with the IKKI [Executive Committee of Comintern], Heksman, member of the CC of the ACP, and his wife. All three are at present living in Moscow in the Hotel Luxe.

After my studies at the University in 1928, I was sent by the ACP to Moscow as a member of the Austrian workers' delegation to the Spartakiad [the USSR's version of the Olympic Games]. After my return to Vienna, I worked for about three months as a chemical engineer in a textile factory. In December 1928, comrades Koplenig and KONRAD, at that time Secretary of the Austrian Communist Youth Organization, recommended me for work in the underground organization of the Department for International Relations of the Comintern in Vienna. This was underground liaison and courier work. In October 1931, because of the bad work of some of the members of our apparatus, we were discovered.

In January 1932 I was summoned to Moscow. Up to May I remained without work. Then I was sent on a temporary assignment to Greece, Palestine and Syria. In August of that year I returned to Moscow and I was told that I had been sacked and would work in a factory.

The Head of the Department for International Relations was Abramov. Something about my attitude to Abramov, who later turned out to be an enemy of the people. I once said something to a colleague which implied criticism of Abramov's work. This colleague told Abramov about this and the latter forced me to write a statement to the effect that I would never again criticize his organization. Abramov sent one of his creatures, a certain 'Willy' to Vienna, with whom I and certain other members of the Department did not get on because he tried to introduce an anti-party, bureaucratic spirit into our organization. When 'Willy' later returned to Moscow, I believe he encouraged Abramov in his dislike of me. I heard recently that 'Willy' was arrested a year ago by our security people.

When comrade Georg Mueller heard that I had been sacked from the Department of International Relations, he offered me work in our department. Mueller was at that time already working in the department and I knew him from the time of his work in the Vienna organization. I was also recommended by comrade Urdan, at present Head of Department in the People's Commissariat for Heavy Industry.

In January 1933 (up to October 1932 I had been ill with typhoid fever in Moscow), I was sent by our department to Paris to work for KARIN. I carried out technical tasks for him, photography etc., and set up crossing points across the French frontier to Belgium, Holland and Germany. Apart from this, I tried to establish contact with fishermen in France, Holland and Belgium in order to use fishing boats to install radio equipment, in case of war. I invited comrade Luksy, the adopted daughter of the Hungarian revolutionary writer A. Gabor, and the daughter of the literary translator Olga Galperina to join in our work. Both are now in Moscow.

In October 1933 I was told that I would be sent to Britain on operational work. I then went to Vienna and recruited STRELA (GERTA) and JOHN in our organization [neither has been identified]. In February 1934 I went to London alone where I recruited EDITH [Edith Tudor Hart], whom I already knew in Vienna.

In London I worked with [Ignaty] Reif from April till June 1934 and from June till July 1935 with SCHWED [Alexander Orlov]. In August 1935, I went to Moscow on leave where I remained till November 1935. After that I returned to London and worked there: from November 1935 till April 1936 by myself, from April 1936 till the end of August 1936 with MANN [Mally], then up to January 1937 again by myself and till June 1937 again with MANN and later, till November 1937, again by myself.

During my work in London I personally recruited a number of people. As a cover I studied psychology at London University. I completed these studies with the exception of the last examination. In London I found one of my relatives, a cousin, whom I had not met until then and who is the owner of a large British film company [unidentified]. I started working for him as a cover in the capacity of head of the psychological and advertising department. I worked for ten months for him and the monthly salary of £20 sterling I gave to our organization. He agreed to obtain a work permit for me, necessary for foreigners, but as I had come to Britain on a student visa, the British police refused to issue me with a work permit and I was obliged to leave England in September 1937, together with my family. In November 1937 I returned for ten days to London in order to conserve our network there. On 23 November 1937 I returned to Moscow.

In 1932, I was transferred by a commission of the CC of the All-Union Communist Party from the Austrian Communist Party to the ACP (b) and at the end of March of this year (1938) I passed the renewal of party cards successfully. At the beginning of 1938 I received Soviet citizenship.

About my wife Fini or Sylvia. Born 1907. I have known her since 1922. We married in 1924. In the same year she joined the Austrian Communist Youth Organization. She worked at the time as a teacher in a children's home. In 1927 she became a member of the Austrian Communist Party. In 1931 she was sent to Moscow to attend the radio school of the Comintern and she remained there till 1932. Up to 1934 she worked as a radio operator at one of the Comintern stations. From 1934 till the beginning of 1936 she studied at the KUNMZ. In February 1936, i.e. only after Abramov's removal, who up to then because of his dislike for me had resisted this in every way, she joined me in London where she gave birth to a child. After my return to Moscow my wife and child, on the instructions of the leadership, remained abroad for another nine months. My wife arrived in Moscow on 1 September 1938.

I have two brothers. One is 27 years of age and the other 26. The elder was a tailor and was for some time a member of the Austrian Communist Youth Organization, but later left because of my father's opposition. Later he became a member of the Schutzbund [the Austrian Socialists' armed force] and took part in the February revolt in 1934. My younger brother worked as an engraver but continued his studies at night. He passed the entrance examination to the University and studied at the medical faculty. He only had to pass a few more examinations when Austria was incorporated and he was obliged to abandon his studies. He was also a member of the Schutzbund and took part in the February revolt. During the administration of Dollfuss and Schuschnigg he worked in the underground organization of the MOPR. In August 1938 my brothers succeeded in obtaining visas for Argentina and leaving Austria. Both are now living in Buenos Aires. One works as a tailor and the doctor became an errand boy.

I know English and German fluently, speak French fairly well and can read and understand Italian and Dutch. STEPHAN. 15 December 1938.[2]

In addition to this full autobiography by Deutsch, there are various documents in his personal file which make it possible to clarify certain episodes. Thus in other autobiographical notes Deutsch writes that in 1920 he became a member of the revolutionary group of the intelligentsia named after the journal *Clarté*, founded by the French left-wing novelist Henri Barbusse. In 1927 because of his Communist activities he was suspended from the university for six months. After the discovery of the bureau of the Department of International Relations in Vienna in 1931, Deutsch writes that he had to go into hiding for two months after which he was summoned to Moscow.[3]

An episode hitherto completely unknown shows that Deutsch's first contacts with Soviet intelligence were fairly active and lasted for quite a while before he was invited in the autumn of 1932 to work in the Foreign Department. In a brief, undated note Deutsch wrote that in 1930–1 a girl he knew introduced him to an official of the GPU who entrusted him with a few tasks. Deutsch in his turn introduced the Soviet intelligence officer to EDITH, who later went to Britain. The inventive young chemist made up a few recipes for invisible ink and obtained passports for the Vienna *rezidentura*.[4]

Arnold Deutsch was highly appreciated as an operative. The illegal *rezident* in London, Alexander Orlov, wrote to the Centre on 8 September 1935, while Deutsch was on leave in Moscow:

> I am very pleased that he was of use to you and that you were attentive to him and treated him as a comrade. STEPHAN is a very serious worker and a devoted compatriot [Communist]. Very valuable for our work. He has already accomplished much and if directed rightly he can be of great use. He deserves that our organization show appreciation of his work in such a way that it would increase his zeal tenfold and, most importantly, that he should know that for the Centre he is not some unknown technical assistant. I am therefore of the opinion that if our department awarded him a diploma, a revolver, a watch or something like that, it would be only just and very useful for our work. STEPHAN never lets one down and the trust put in him is fully justified.[5]

The Centre reacted immediately to Orlov's suggestion and in October recommended that Deutsch be rewarded with a revolver. The text of the recommendation addressed to Abram Slutsky, then the Head of the Foreign Department is an interesting sign of the times, clarifying certain details of Deutsch's status in the intelligence service:

Arnold Deutsch, an assistant of SCHWED, is an Austrian citizen, a member of the Austrian Communist Party since 1924, a member of the All-Union Communist Party (B) since December 1931 under the name Stephan Lang, born in Vienna 21 May 1904. In view of the fact that comrade Deutsch, due to the conditions of underground work, is not a Soviet citizen he is not on the permanent staff of the Department and is listed as a secret employee. Comrade Deutsch works illegally abroad for the Foreign Department since 1932. During his work in group 'G' comrade Deutsch proved himself in various aspects of underground work as an extremely combative and loyal operator. Comrades SCHWED and MANN, who work with him, note his exceptionally meritorious work for the group such as, for instance his recruitment of SÖHNCHEN [Philby], his smooth contacts with ATTILA and HEIR [unidentified], his great initiative in organizing the technical work of the group (photography, safekeeping of material, etc.). In view of the above request that comrade Deutsch be awarded a revolver. Head of group 'G'. Slavatinsky 17 October 1935.[6]

There is no indication in the files that Slavatinsky's request, supported by Alexander Orlov, was approved and that Deutsch was awarded the revolver.

Like Mally, Arnold Deutsch experienced difficulty with his attempt to legalize his stay in Britain. The problem became more serious in the summer of 1937 when his studies at London University ended, and he started work in his relative's film company without the required work permit. His application was refused without explanation, probably because there was no special reason why this work should be done by a foreigner.

Deutsch's efforts to start his own business in England met with similar lack of success, and Mally did not exclude the possibility that 'they have there something against him personally and that possibly he has been living here too long without any visible sources of income because the authorities know nothing about the salary he is getting from his relative'. Finally Deutsch suggested a solution, that he should leave England for a short while and return as a graduate student on a scholarship. The plan was approved by the Centre and by his relative who was to give him the scholarship, so in the middle of September 1937 Deutsch prepared to leave for Paris. However, in a letter dated 9 September, he informed the Centre that towards the end of the preceding week a policeman had called at his flat, armed with a document which Deutsch could see bore his name. In order to pre-empt any questions about his income and occupation, Deutsch had volunteered to the policeman that he was 'sorry it is such a mess here but we are leaving on 15 September'. The policeman asked if he was going abroad, and from which port he was intending to leave, explaining that his solicitor had been in correspondence with the Home Office for the past nine months, and that the police had been instructed to establish his intentions. When Deutsch replied that he was to travel from Dover, the policeman answered that the matter was settled.[7]

Perhaps disconcerted by the visit from the polite policeman, Deutsch put his affairs in order and arranged to make contact with some of his sources, namely Donald Maclean, John Cairncross and Guy Burgess, who intended to visit an exhibition in Paris.

Deutsch's principal assignment in Paris was to put the NKVD *rezident* in Spain, Alexander Orlov (SCHWED), in touch with Kim Philby who was going to Spain as a *Times* correspondent. To report to the Centre on the meeting he organized for Orlov and Burgess, who was acting as an intermediary for Philby, Deutsch used his own personal method which consisted of sending postcards to a fictitious address in Moscow. 'Liebe Karl, Ich bin unterdessen in Paris und habe die Sache des Zusammentreffens Mädchens und Schweds erledigt,' he wrote. (Dear Karl, I am in Paris just now and have dealt with the business of bringing together Maiden and Schwed.)[8]

Although Deutsch always intended to return to London, the defections of Ignace Poretsky and Walter Krivitsky in the summer of 1937 made this impossible as he was known to Krivitsky (GROLL), an embarrassing fact he disclosed in a letter to the Centre from Paris dated 23 October 1937:

> Comrade DUCHE [Sergei Spiegelglas, Deputy Head of the NKVD's 7th Department] told me that I should put on record all I know about GROLL. GROLL met my wife before I myself met him. He knew the name of my wife's mother from the Vienna days. When in June 1936 I was in Paris, MANN [Mally] first introduced me to him. He asked me for a cover address in Paris and also to find an Austrian communist girl, who could help him in his work. I introduced him to LUKSY [unidentified] and her husband. When I lost contact with him, he rang me up in my hotel having presumably got my address from MANN. GROLL was a little aware of the nature of our work in London: he knew that we worked with young people and he knew about the man in the F.O.[9]

Deutsch returned only briefly to London to put his agent network on ice, and later he reported to DUCHE on what had happened in February 1938:

> Dear Comrade Spiegelglas,
> When in the beginning of November I went to London, I received

instructions from you to put all our people on ice for a period of three months. I paid them all their salary up to 1 February and arranged with them that by that time somebody would get in touch with them. It is now already the end of February and as far as I know only PFEIL and JOHN have been contacted. For various reasons I consider it of great importance to renew contact with our comrades, if not personally then at least by letter. All our people are young and do not have much experience in our work. For them a promise by us can be relied upon as something absolutely certain. Many of them count on our money, as they depend on it for their livelihood. In the interest of our further work, I told them that I was going to Spain which to us is a more important battlefield than Britain. If they do not hear from us they are bound to be disappointed. They are all working for us out of conviction and with enthusiasm and they may start thinking that they have been let down. I don't want to be alarmist but in the interest of our further work we should avoid anything that could cause them to become disappointed, that could shake the faith in our reliability and punctuality. Particularly in view of the recent events (GOT) [see below, p. 115] it is essential to show them a) that this has nothing whatsoever to do with us and b) that we are in place and continuing the work which for all of them has become their life's mission.

I should like to point once more to the special composition of our group. They all believe in us. They are convinced that we are always in place, always everywhere, that we fear nothing, never leave anybody to their fate, that we are first and foremost accurate, exact, reliable. The success of our work has been based on the fact that we have so far never disappointed them. It is just now very important from a psychological point of view that they hear from us even if we do not start working with them at once. STEPHAN.[10]

Deutsch remained temporarily inactive although there were repeated attempts to send him abroad on a mission, the first being in December 1937, almost as soon as he had arrived in Moscow, when Slutsky suggested to People's Commissar Nikolai Yezhov that he should be sent to the USA as an illegal *rezident*. A second, similar minute was sent on 15 March 1938 by Spiegelglas to the Deputy People's Commissar for Internal Affairs, Mikhail Frinovsky. However, it was quite pointless to arrange a foreign assignment for Deutsch at a time when the intelligence service was being decimated, the senior personnel being replaced as fast as they were arrested. On 11 October 1938 the new Head of Intelligence, Passov, sent a minute to Lavrenti Beria, then the People's Commissar for Internal Affairs, on a different topic:

At the end of 1937, the eminent recruiter of the illegal apparatus, the temporary employee Comrade Lang, Stephan Georgievich, was summoned back to the Soviet Union. His recall was connected with the treachery of RAIMOND [Ignace Reiss], who knew where he worked. For eleven months he has been without work being maintained at our expense. Bearing in mind that the question of his work abroad cannot be decided now, I request your agreement to finding work for comrade Lang outside our organization.

Two days later Beria replied: 'Arrange other temporary work for him outside the NKVD'.[11]

It is quite possible that Beria's uncharacteristic generosity saved Deutsch's life, but the danger had not passed completely. Another minute, dated 19 December 1938, concerned the payment of Russian lessons for Deutsch and was addressed to Passov's replacement Dekanozov (a security Commissar, 3rd Grade) from Senykin, an assistant to the Head of the 5th section. This was remarkable, for usually Deutsch's affairs were only handled by the most senior officers, such as Slutsky, Spiegelglas and Passov. On 29 December Dekanosov replied 'Comrade Senykin! Don't waste my time. STEPHAN should be thoroughly vetted and not be taught languages.'[12]

Dekanosov's minute marked probably the lowest point in Deutsch's career, but in 1939 the intelligence service began to recover from the purges and interest in Deutsch also revived. In March 1939 he was visited by a security officer, Lieutenant Kazhdan, who asked him to write a number of essays on Britain, beginning with one on the country's political structure, and an account of the former illegal *rezidentura* in London; this is where Deutsch's famous psychological portraits of Philby, Maclean, Burgess and their comrades first appeared.

Sensing the improving climate, and the imminent start of a war in Europe, Deutsch sent Pavel Fitin, the new Head of Intelligence, a note seeking a personal interview in which he pointed out that he had spent twenty-one months without work. Prompted by this reminder, Fitin wrote to Beria on 31 December 1940 suggesting that Deutsch be sent to the USA as illegal *rezident*, with Boris Kreshin as his assistant, to renew contact with the sources codenamed 19th, NIGEL [Michael Straight] and MORRIS, and to recruit new agents in the defence industry and ministries, as well as recruiting agents for work in Europe. The proposal also included the suggestion that Deutsch and Kreshin should travel to the US disguised as Jewish refugees from the Baltic.[13]

Accordingly, Deutsch was sent to America in 1941, travelling through the Indian Ocean on the SS *Kayak*, but when war broke out in the Far East he was stuck in Bombay, and was forced to return to Moscow via Teheran, arriving on 1 April 1942. The second attempt to get him to the USA ended in disaster on 7 November 1942 when the SS *Donbass* was sunk by a U-boat in the Atlantic. Mortally injured, Deutsch died while heroically trying to save the lives of others.

Curiously, the decision to use Deutsch again as an operational illegal was taken by the Centre after Anthony Blunt had passed Gorsky the contents of his MI5 dossier in March 1941. Blunt's report indicated MI5's certainty that Deutsch was a Soviet intelligence agent and contained several details, including the dates that he had travelled to Britain. Although the file contained no information on any of Deutsch's contacts, it did note that he had been vouched for by his uncle the film producer, who had been investigated together with his immediate circle on suspicion that they might be linked to Soviet or German intelligence.

Although it is not clear from Blunt's report exactly when MI5 started to investigate Deutsch's uncle, either as soon as Deutsch had arrived in England, or soon after Krivitsky's interrogation, when Deutsch had already left the inhospitable ISLAND, it is certain that any doubts which may have existed in the minds of counter-intelligence about his role as a Soviet agent would have been eliminated by the testimony of the defector Walter Krivitsky.

Like Deutsch, Theodor Mally belongs to the generation of 'the Great Illegals', not just because of his connections with his colleagues Boris Bazarov, Dmitri Bystrolyotov, Alexander Orlov and Sergei Spiegelglas, but for his recruitment of the Foreign Office cipher clerk John King and his role in the expansion of the Cambridge group during his period as the illegal *rezident* in London.

Hitherto Mally has been inaccurately known in the literature as a priest, a former chaplain in the Austro-Hungarian army, who sided with the revolution and served it as an intelligence officer. These incorrect biographical data originate from Krivitsky, although Kim Philby and Donald Maclean also refer to Mally in their notes as a former priest. Indeed, it is not impossible that he used this unusual detail of his earlier life to give himself more colour in the eyes of his contemporaries, and in the indictment which concludes his case, prepared in 1938, he is called a 'former Catholic priest' and later an 'officer in the Austro-Hungarian Army'. Apparently his accusers wanted to emphasize Mally's social origins.[14]

Theodor Stepanovich Mally was a Hungarian, born in 1894 at Temesvar (now Timisoara, Romania) into the family of an official of the Ministry of Finance. Having passed through eight classes of the Gymnasium he entered one of the Catholic monastic orders and studied theology and philosophy at an unnamed seminary. After ordination as deacon he left holy orders and was a layman when he volunteered for the army. His change from a soldier of God to a soldier with a gun therefore took place long before he was confronted with the realities of the Russian revolution, and was connected with something other than a conversion to Marxism. In December 1915 Mally passed out of the Military Academy with the rank of cornet. In 1915–16 he served as second lieutenant in the Austro-Hungarian army and in July 1916, fighting on the Russian front, he was taken prisoner. He moved from one PoW camp to another until May 1918, and was in Poltava, Kharkov, Rostov, Penza, Astrakhan, Orenburg and Chelyabinsk, learning Russia's geography from its railway lines, roads and country lanes.

In 1918, Mally volunteered for the Red Army and continued to serve until 1921, experiencing all the hardships of the Civil War. He fought against the White Czechs near Chelyabinsk and later against the White armies of Kolchak, Wrangel and Makhno. In November 1918 he was captured by Kolchak's counter-intelligence and was imprisoned in Krasnoyarsk and later in a concentration camp until he was liberated by the Red Army in December 1919. In 1921 he was directed to work in the CHEKA and for the next five years operated in the Crimea as a clerk, registrar, counter-intelligence agent, investigator, secretary of the Secret Operations Section, Head of the Secretariat and Head of the Eastern Section.

In 1926 he left the Crimea and for six months worked as executive secretary of the department for political refugees belonging to the International Workers' Relief Organization (MOPR). A transfer to Moscow took him to OGPU headquarters; for four years he operated as Assistant Head of the Counter-Intelligence Department, and between 1930 and 1932 as an officer of the OGPU's Special Department. In 1932 he was transferred to intelligence duties as Assistant Head of the Foreign Department's 3rd section until June 1934 when he was sent abroad on a lengthy assignment which lasted until July 1937.

According to his OGPU file, Mally was decorated in 1924 with the insignia of the Crimean Central Executive Committee, and in 1927 awarded a diploma and silver cigarette case by the Collegium of the OGPU. In 1932 he was granted the insignia of 'Honorary Chekist', but on 20 September 1938

Right: Vladimir Orlov, the master forger and formerly General Wrangel's Chief of Intelligence, now believed to have played a key role in the Zinoviev letter affair.

Below left: Mikhail Trilisser, Chief of the Foreign Department in 1922–30, on holiday in the Crimea with his wife and son.

Below right: Boris Bazarov, one of the first Soviet illegals in Germany, with his wife. Based in Berlin, Bazarov pioneered the infiltration of illegals into England, and in 1930 supervised the penetration of the Foreign Office by recruiting the code clerk Ernest Oldham.

Yelena Krasnaya, author of the 1927 report on the London *rezidentura* which listed dozens of Soviet sources.

Nikolai Alekseyev, the first 'legal' *rezident* in London, who arrived with diplomatic status and a single assistant in the summer of 1924.

Artur Artusov with his daughter; he was the mysterious spymaster in Moscow who supervised the early development of the Soviet networks in London.

Fyodor Karin, code-named JACK, who ran an independent illegal network in Germany in the 1920s that established the future of Soviet espionage in Europe.

Right: Vasili L. Spiru, one of the first Soviet illegals to operate in England, where he arrived posing as a German publisher in October 1930.

Below: Theodore Mally, one of the great pre-war illegals who helped run the Cambridge spies.

Bertold Ilk, the illegal *rezident* in Germany who ran a toy factory as cover and later started a news agency in London, through which he organised a major spy ring that penetrated Scotland Yard and the Foreign Office.

Arnold Deutsch, the brilliant Soviet recruiter, pictured with his daughter. He was the charismatic handler who personally approached Burgess, Blunt, Cairncross and Maclean, while ostensibly studying psychology at London University.

Sergei Spiegelglass, Chief of the
Foreign Department, 1938–9.

Grigori Grafpen, the London
rezident in 1937–8, who was
executed in Stalin's purge.

Passport 1 (top):

2

ΧΑΡΑΚΤΗΡΙΣΤΙΚΑ
SIGNALEMENTS

Συζύγου — Femme

Ἐπάγγελμα / Profession — *Έμπορος / Négociant*

Τόπος καὶ χρόνος γεννήσεως / Lieu et date de naissance — *Θεσ/νίκη 40 / Salonique 40*

Διαμονή / Domicile — *Αρ.../...*

Πρόσωπον / Visage — *régulier*

Χρῶμα ὀφθαλμῶν / Couleur des yeux

Χρῶμα κόμης / Couleur des cheveux

Ἰδιαίτερα σημεῖα / Signes particuliers

ΤΕΚΝΑ — ENFANTS

Ὄνομα / Nom	Ἡλικία / Age	Γένος / Sexe

3

Συζύγου — Femme

Φωτογραφία / Photo

Ὑπογραφὴ κατόχου / Signature du titulaire
καὶ τῆς συζύγου / et de sa femme — *Alexander Gallas*

ΥΠΟΓΡΑΦΗ ΤΟΥ ΧΟΡΗΓΗΣΑΝΤΟΣ ΤΟ ΔΙΑΒΑΤΗΡΙΟΝ ΥΠΑΛΛΗΛΟΥ:
SIGNATURE DE L'AGENT DELIVRANT LE PASSEPORT:

Le gérant de la chancellerie consulaire Demetrios

Passport 2 (bottom):

1.50

— 2 —

OSOBNÝ POPIS
SIGNALEMENT

Manželka — Femme

Zamestnanie / Profession — *obchodník / Commerçant*

Rodisko a dátum narodenia / Lieu et date de naissance — *Komárno 23. XII. 1894*

Bydlisko / Domicile — *Bratislava*

Obličaj / Visage — *oblý - ovale*

Barva očí / Couleur des yeux — *hnedá - brune*

Barva vlasov / Couleur des cheveux — *čierna - noire*

Zvláštné znamenie / Signes particuliers — *—*

DETI — ENFANTS

Meno / Nom	Vek / Age	Pohlavie / Sexe

— 3 —

Manželka — Femme

Fotografia

PODPIS MAJITEĽA
SIGNATURE DU TITULAIRE — *Lajos ...*

A JEHO MANŽELKY
ET DE SA FEMME

Podpis úradníka vydávajúceho cestovný pas:
Signature de l'agent délivrant le ...

Left: The Greek passport in the name of Alexander Gallas used by the ace illegal Dmitri Bystrolyotov to visit London. He was forced to flee when his best source, Ernest Oldham, committed suicide.

Below left: Dmitri Bystrolyotov's false Czech passport in the name of Lajos Perelly.

Right: Bystrolyotov adopted the identities of a Hungarian count and an English aristocrat to find suitable targets for recruitment. Among others he ran Herbert King, Ernest Oldham and several other hitherto undiscovered spies in the Foreign Office.

Below: Bystrolyotov's wife Maria and their son Ensio. She was based in Davos, Switzerland, while her husband recruited spies inside the Foreign Office.

Willy Brandes with his wife, who travelled on Canadian passports and pretended to represent a New York furniture manufacturer. He supervised the Woolwich Arsenal spy ring but disappeared from his London flat in November 1937, just as MI5 was closing in.

Clockwise from far left:

Adolf Chapsky, code-named KLIM, the *rezider* who worked in London under diplomatic cover a Anton Shuster until he w recalled in 1937 and executed in a purge.

Boris Berman, deputy Chief of the Foreign Department, who super-vised the recruitment of SHELLEY and other spies in the Foreign Office.

Ivan Chichayev was the NKVD's official liaison officer with British Intelligence during the Second World War.

Henri Pieck, codenamed COOPER, was a gifted painter as well as an ideologically motivated spy. He often visited London to help the illega *rezidentura* service spies inside the Foreign Office and successfully recruite Captain John Harvey, th British consul in Geneva.

the Military Collegium of the Supreme Court of the USSR sentenced Comrade Mally to death under article 58-6 of the Criminal Code. By Order No. 4/N-04358 of 14 April 1956, the Military Collegium of the Supreme Court of the USSR Comrade Mally was rehabilitated.[15]

Mally was married twice, and in 1923 had a son, Theodor, by his first wife, about whom nothing is known. His second wife, Lidya Grigorievna (Lifa Girshevna) Razba, was born in Riga in 1906. His personal file throws very little light on his intelligence work abroad, this information being dispersed in various operational files, but it is known that, having based himself in Paris, he supervised operations in Holland and those of the Bystrolyotov – COOPER – MAG group in Britain.

Mally arrived in London at the beginning of 1936 to work with John King, codenamed MAG, having visited the country twice in 1935 for the same purpose, using the cover of a trader in old clothes. His trips to London were necessary because he had turned down Krivitsky as unsuitable for working with MAG and the Centre had transferred Krivitsky to Holland. While collaborating with MAG, Mally maintained contact with Paris through a group of go-betweens known only by the codenames SHTURMAN, RANCY, APO-THEKER and MADELEINE. In April 1936, Mally was summoned to Paris by Sergei Spiegelglas, who suggested that he should take over the London illegal *rezidentura* from Alexander Orlov, who had fled to Moscow for fear of being discovered. Part of Mally's assignment had been to collect political intelligence with the emphasis on hand-ling Donald Maclean, codenamed WEISE. Technical intelligence from the Woolwich Arsenal group was to be put on ice temporarily. In Paris, Mally made contact with Orlov's assistant, Arnold Deutsch, and he returned to London in the middle of April 1936.

Once established in London, Mally began to work intensively with Maclean and also met Philby and Guy Burgess, who sometimes drove him in his car into the country. Mally wrote that Percy Glad-ing, codenamed GOT, the initiator of the group of scientific and technical intelligence, suggested that the group should be re-activated and expanded, and in the autumn of 1936, when Mally returned on leave to the Soviet Union, he wrote a minute based on a note from Deutsch, who was running GOT, on the ring's current status and potential. As a result the Centre decided to send another illegal to London to supervise the group; this was the agent who later became known to MI5 as Willy Brandes. Direct control was handed to Brandes by Deutsch himself at the end of January 1937. With the return of Mally to London in January 1937 political intelligence collection was expanded by the recruitment of Anthony Blunt (TONY), Michael Straight (NIGEL) and John Cairncross (MOLIERE), whom Mally never met personally, but he was introduced by Deutsch to the founder of a ring known as the Oxford group, a man codenamed SCOTT (see Postscript).

The *rezidentura* needed a flat in which to hold meetings with GOT and to process his scientific material, and Glading suggested that 'a contact of Harry Pollitt' (leader of the Communist Party of Great Britain) named Olga Gray should rent the flat. Olga Gray was unmarried and although she had never been a Party member, she had been known to GOT for a number of years and had travelled to India as a Party courier. Pollitt trusted her sufficiently to give her the central contact to groups in India and she was also used for other illegal Party tasks. Mally never met her, but he did see her once from a distance in a café on Cheapside and described her as 'aged 35 to 40, pale blonde and not very attractive'.

A flat was found in Holland Road, Kensington, and before it was used operationally Mally took the precaution of leaving a suitcase there. As it showed no signs of having been secretly opened the site was approved, and when Mally visited he introduced himself to Olga Gray as Mr Peters. He did not detect any hostile surveillance, but during the subsequent prosecution at the Old Bailey, and from information from MI5's files extracted by Anthony Blunt, the rest of the story emerged. Olga Gray turned out to have been an MI5 agent who penetrated the CPGB, and although only three members of the Woolwich Arsenal ring were convicted of stealing military secrets, and Brandes himself managed to leave England in time, Soviet Intelligence suffered irreparable damage in that field.[16]

Messages exchanged between Mally and the Centre show that Mally was constantly at risk of exposure while he was abroad, as were most of his colleagues. The danger came not so much from the activities of the counter-intelligence service, but rather from their very weak cover and the problem of 'legalization'. Mally's withdrawal to Moscow in the middle of 1937 was more to do with the impossibility of remaining in Britain with his inadequate cover than any summons to face liquidation. He had been confronted by 'legalization' from the moment he first arrived in Paris in June 1934; on 9 October he wrote to the Centre that he was travelling on a Yugoslav passport, but after the murder of the King of Yugoslavia, 'I do not envy myself for having it.' He also possessed an American passport, 'according to which I am eight years younger than I really am. What is more, I am supposed to be a Jew. All this makes things rather difficult.'

The assassination of King Alexander in Marseilles led to police checks on all Yugoslavs in Paris and those who could not give satisfactory answers were arrested. 'They have not found me yet because I left the hotel for a private flat two days before the murder, but undoubtedly in a day or two they will come and I cannot answer the simplest questions ... In short, I am leaving for Holland on an Austrian passport (also not very satisfactory) and shall stay there until things die down ... I shall send mail from Holland with HANS [Bystrolyotov]. All the work for the time being is conducted there. I think I shall move from there to Switzerland.'[17]

The Centre responded to Mally's complaint with the offer of several passports, and the one he selected became known to MI5 after his discovery in London. In answer to Moscow's suggestion, Mally wrote on 27 December 1934 that he would 'take the name HARDT. I can be a trader, chemist, doctor, engineer. Birthplace, Oldenburg in Burgenland. 21 January 1894. Lida – the same, 18 January 1906.'[18]

Certainly Mally's American passport was far from perfect. As he complained in a letter to the Centre, dated 24 April 1935 and despatched soon after his return from a business trip to Moscow between January and March 1935, it stated in one place that Chicago is in Indiana, and in another gave Illinois.

> When travelling nowadays through Europe with dubious documents, I am getting perhaps excessively sensitive to these questions. You know that MANOLI [Kavetsky, a friend of Bystrolyotov, betrayed by Krivitsky] was searched when he left Holland for France. RAIMOND [Reiss] was also searched. I flew and not only was I not searched but I was not even asked to open my suitcase At the same time another passenger in the same aircraft was searched, probably a Greek or an Armenian or perhaps a Jew. And I had my pockets full of FRITZ's mail.

FRITZ was the codename for Mally's assistant in Holland and clearly the discovery of his papers would have been extremely embarrassing. However, Mally's passport problems did not prevent him from visiting Britain in May 1935 to complete John King's recruitment and in July the Centre noted that Mally and Bystrolyotov had done very good work, and that MAG 'promises to be very important and interesting in the future'.[19]

At the beginning of October 1935, Mally flew to Moscow for six weeks to visit his son, who was ill, and to settle family affairs with his first wife. When he returned to London at the end of November to work with MAG, Bystrolyotov was getting ready to return home.

Mally's first report from London was dated 9 January 1936, and one of his next, dated 20 February 1936 and addressed to an unknown senior officer, gives an insight into how he handled MAG.

> I should tell you that I am extremely busy. Even my hobby, British history, suffers from the fact that I have not enough time. I have to meet him four times a week. Those evenings I am busy. When I receive material, I must read it and take it to P.'s flat. Then couriers arrive with mail which also means work. In the day time I am busy with firms. I visit them in turn. We have bought already three railway trucks with goods and they have to be despatched so I have to get in touch with the carriers. At present I have more favourable offers from Manchester and Liverpool. I shall have to go there for 1–2 days.[20]

Mally's cover, as a trader, buying up old clothes for export to the Continent, took up much of his time and required travel throughout the country, which is why he raised the question of more convenient work. Evidently he envied Alexander Orlov's cover occupation, as a director of the American Refrigerator Company Ltd. 'Could I not join the refrigerator business which Lev ran?'[21]

In the spring of 1936, Mally and his wife suffered from kidney disease, apparently brought on by the hardness of London's water, and in June he asked permission to take some leave. This was granted and two reservations were made for him at the resort of Kislovodsk for the beginning of October. However, Mally's arrival at the Soviet frontier was not uneventful, as is clear from the report of Brigade Commander Ulmar, dated 7 October 1936, submitted to the Head of the Foreign Department, Slutsky.

> On 28 September of this year arrived in Moscow by the Nord Express No. 4, the Dutch subject William Broshard, carrying a false passport and watched by an officer of the Immigration Control Point at the station Negoreloye, Shamrai. Broshard told the Head of the Immigration Control Point at Negoreloye, Danilovich, that he was an official of the Foreign Department of the Chief Directorate for State Security of the NKVD named Mally, and the husband of citizen Razba who accompanied him from abroad and was let through without search at your request. We attach a report from the officer of the Immigration Control Point at Negoreloye, Shamrai.[22]

Shamrai's report repeated Brigade Commander Ulmar's account with this additional detail that Mally and his wife, leaving the station in Moscow, got into a car which was waiting for them and drove off in an unknown direction. Shamrai himself, being in an unfamiliar city without money, was unable to continue the surveillance.

When Mally's leave ended he remained on official business in Moscow and returned to London only in the beginning of January 1937. By May the accumulation of legalization problems endured by both Deutsch and himself compelled Mally openly to admit that 'up to now none of us is firmly established here. Not even STEPHAN. He was again refused a work permit.' Mally tried to establish himself in England more permanently and on 24 May 1937 reported his visit to the Aliens Registration Office where he asked for leave to remain in the country indefinitely. The authorities were prepared to agree on condition that he opened a business in one of the regions most affected by unemployment, so Mally filled in forms and sent them to the Board of Trade. The Centre, fearing that Mally's documents might be checked with the Austrian police, was alarmed and suggested an alternative scheme which required travel to Canada and acquiring a passport there. Mally replied that verification through the Austrian police was unlikely as Deutsch 'frequently meets false Austrians here, former communists . . . take STEPHAN himself, with a real passport. If they enquire about him in Vienna, the answer will be as unfavourable as it would be in my case (he is a well-known communist and I am just a crook). Extremely sensitive and fraught with organizational consequences is your argument that if they make enquiries about me, they may simply say nothing and start to investigate me. But there are many "ifs" here and it is a very academic question.'

Mally took the view that one might just as well assume that he might be discovered during meetings with the legal *rezident* KLIM or that he could be betrayed by one of his agents or be recognized in the street by one of the accused in the Metro-Vickers trial, at which British agents had been prosecuted in Moscow in 1931. 'Without neglecting theory, I hold more with practice,' he argued. 'If one were to act so strictly in accordance with assumptions one would never do anything. There is always ten per cent risk at least and in this case I consider that the risk is no more than ten per cent.'

He rejected the idea of going to Canada on very sound grounds: 'There the quantity of theoretical risk in percentages turns into quality, which makes the danger real. There are already quite a lot of people here who know me as an Austrian.' In concluding his letter to the Centre, Mally made some observations that were to prove fatal:

1. I do not think that the situation is so dangerous that I should flee from here; 2. To go to Canada in order to return here is in my

view impossible and if I consider it impossible it is hardly likely that I can carry it out; 3. If you think that in case of verification the British begin to investigate me without saying anything, this means that you divest yourself of all responsibility for any possible unpleasantness and put the whole burden on me if I remain working here. That is why logically I should put the question to you this way: I ask you to allow me to leave here for home and to discuss every possibility of my further work at home and only at home.[23]

The Centre's answer arrived on 4 June 1937: 'A telegram has been sent to you giving permission to return home. Wire your return route and day of departure.' Mally replied, 'I can leave by ship from France on 5 July directly for Leningrad and be in Moscow on 11th or 12th'. Although Mally had asked to return home for only a few days simply to clarify the legalization issue in a personal interview, he stayed longer and went on leave as is shown by a note about travel documents to Sanatorium No. 1 in Kislovodsk issued to him and his wife. The delay was most probably caused by Poretsky's defection, and when Krivitsky followed suit it settled the question of Mally, who was well known to both of them, being sent abroad. Although it is not known whether Poretsky gave anybody away, the Centre, realizing that Krivitsky was telling the Americans and British all he knew, had to assume the worst.

The tension between Mally and the Centre over his legalization in Britain did not affect his position immediately, but his stubbornness played a role later when he was taken into custody. The exact moment of his arrest is not recorded, but he was probably named in a 'confession' extracted during the purges. Later he was to be accused of links with traitors and defectors, and in March 1938 reports were received from the Paris *rezidentura* on the common views and intentions of Mally, Krivitzky and Poretsky. One, dated 2 March 1938, appeared to implicate Mally.

> It follows from Elsa's words [Elizabeth Poretsky] that she, RAIMOND (Poretsky), GROLL (Krivitsky) and MANN (Mally) and a certain Fedya met in Paris, held pro-Trotskyite conversations and went so far as to agreeing that the death of Stalin was for them the only way out of the situation.[24]

The report was endorsed by Spiegelglas with the words 'Source absolutely reliable' and another dated 10 March 1938 repeated the same theme:

> Elsa relates that LUDWIG [Ignace Reiss] had three friends: Walter [Krivitsky], Mally and Fedya. They met frequently, discussed various

questions together and prepared their defection from the organization. Mally and Fedya returned to Moscow.[25]

Although this information might be quite true – Mally and his
colleagues were people with independent minds and might well
have criticized Stalin and his policies and the NKVD had indeed
'absolutely reliable sources' in Paris – it was not reflected in the
indictment. It was considered dangerous to raise political questions
in such a document and simpler to reduce everything to the standard
accusation of espionage, as had happened in numerous other cases.
This was exactly the offence with which Mally was charged in the
case heard by the Military Collegium of the Supreme Court of the
USSR on 20 September 1938, on an indictment that seemed to rely
on Mally's refusal to go to Canada:

> Grounds for Mally's arrest were provided by the 5th Department of
> the First Directorate of the NKVD which discovered Mally's activities
> harming the interests of the USSR (malicious violation of the security
> rules, disclosure of state secrets, refusal to carry out orders in combat
> conditions).[26]

Clearly Mally's last controversial message had played a part in
his fall, as had his discussions with Krivitsky, admittedly on orders
from the Centre, of his prospects in England including the MAG
case, and the offence he committed by his disclosure at the Negore-
loye border post that he was an intelligence officer. According to
his file, 'Being under arrest, Mally T.S. during the preliminary investigation stated that he was a German spy and in the course of several
years had actively worked against the USSR. About the origins of
his links with German Intelligence the accused stated the following:
in 1917, in a POW camp in the Urals he was recruited to collect
information on Soviet Russia for the Austro-Hungarian headquarters by an officer of the intelligence service, Schonfeld. In
1927, in Moscow, Mally was again recruited for intelligence work
against the USSR by the *rezident* of German military intelligence,
Steinbruek.'

The indictment also contained some other details of what purported to be Mally's espionage activities: 'Contact with the Berlin
Centre of German military intelligence was maintained by the
accused through the above mentioned *rezident*, Steinbruek, through
a special courier, Helwig, and also by direct conversations with an
officer of that service who was known to the accused as Captain
Dietrich.'[27]

These are the only specific admissions of hostile activities given by Mally, or more likely beaten out of him. Everything else in his confession is vague. His experience was shared by around 70 per cent of the NKVD's staff, which handicapped the organization quite disproportionately; it took it years to repair the damage inflicted during the purges. In retrospect, it is clear that Mally played a vital role in developing Moscow's worldwide network of illegals, an organization that went unsuspected in England until MI5 eventually penetrated one branch in what became known as the Woolwich Arsenal case.

Although the KGB's files indicate that not all its members have been identified, there is enough material available to show how the ring operated. The first references to the group are contained in an undated memorandum written by Yevgeny Mitskewich, codenamed ANATOLY, addressed to the OGPU's Chief of the Foreign Department, Artusov, on the subject of creating an illegal *rezidentura* on THE ISLAND. Mitskewitch, a former illegal *rezident* in Hamburg and Italy, had been sent to Britain in 1931, became the legal *rezident* in London in 1932 when diplomatic relations were re-established and remained in the post for the next two years. Internal evidence implies that his report was compiled in the first half of 1933, for Arnold Deutsch and Ignaty Reif were sent to London in the second half of that year. In summarizing the current situation on THE ISLAND, Mitskewich declared that

> There are two intelligence groups 'on ice' in England, of which one is the Arsenal group ... made up of employees of 1) the Arsenal (testing of shells and weapons); 2) Armstrong (tanks, guns, rifles); 3) Furst-Brown (tanks, and armoured steel). A negative feature of this group is that it is led by a prominent member of the local Communist Party. The group itself consists of non-party people ... Reif could be sent to London (without his wife) as illegal *rezident* and only these two groups should be given to him.[28]

Artusov approved Mitskewich's proposal. Reif and Deutsch were sent to London, to be followed in June 1934 by Alexander Orlov as the *rezident* of a newly established illegal group which became known as SCHWED, after Orlov's own codename. Clearly the SCHWED group operated successfully, for there is little to indicate that anything occurred which required the Centre's intervention, and the files consist mainly of letters accompanying intelligence material. However, in the spring of 1939, Deutsch was asked to prepare a memorandum in which he included one of his psychological portraits of the Woolwich Arsenal group's leader, Percy Glading, codenamed GOT:

I met him for the first time at a regular meeting in May or April 1934. He has been a member of the British Communist Party from the time of its foundation and has even been a member of the Central Committee. He attended Lenin courses in Moscow. Up to 1928 he worked in the Arsenal in London. Recently he has started work as secretary to the League against Imperialism. GOT is aged about 38–40 and of proletarian origin. During the war he spread anti-militarist propaganda. He is a devoted communist, courageous, daring, painstaking and industrious. He is also well-read and well-educated. He is a good organizer and writes well. Although he has done illegal work for many years, he has never been able to free himself of his legalistic tendencies. Before I started working with him, he combined his party work with our work. Material destined for us was brought directly to him in the party offices where he kept it. Caution and vigilance were not of great importance to him. He was ready to trust every comrade, even if that person had not been put to the test . . . He did not understand the requirements and specific conditions of our work, although he was always anxious to do much for us. While I was working with him, I insisted that he should observe the rules of *conspiratsia* [security]. I did not meet with him often; once every one or two months. I did not allow him to keep material in his party office. I accepted the people he brought to me, but after that they were not allowed to see him again. We observed all precautions in respect of the people we acquired through GOT. I allowed him to continue his party work but insisted on great caution. He did not know my name, occupation or address. GOT did not agree with my way of doing things and considered that he should give up party work and devote himself entirely to our work. In addition, in his view, work in England should not be carried out by us, foreigners, but by English people. He thought we were overcautious.

When MANN [Mally] arrived in London and later MISHA [unidentified], we changed our tactics in regard to GOT and his proposals were accepted. He gave up his party work and started working only for us. GOT's recommendation became sufficient to trust a person (this is shown by the example of the provocatrice). MANN frequently met with him. They visited each other's homes. GOT even knew who MANN had been previously (during GOT's trial it turned out that the provocatrice even knew that MANN had been an Austrian officer. This she evidently learned from GOT).

GOT is an honest and good comrade and ready to make any sacrifice. He is very careful with money and in general a blameless person who leads an exemplary family life. If we had adhered to the old tactics he would probably not have been found out. In August or September 1934, GOT introduced me to ATTILA.[29]

From that moment onwards, according to Deutsch, the Arsenal group began to grow. An unusual feature of the network was the inclusion of ATTILA's son, codenamed HEIR. Deutsch explained to the Centre how this had happened:

> ATTILA accidentally involved his son in our work. Reif spoke English badly. On one occasion, ATTILA told Reif about his son and asked him if he should involve him in our work. Reif understood something quite different and answered 'yes'. So ATTILA brought his son with him to the next meeting. Reif got very worried when he saw him, and when he heard who he was, he upbraided ATTILA. I met the latter to find out what exactly had happened. It turned out that it was Reif's lack of knowledge of English which was the cause of the incident. The son turned out to be very useful to us, however, and we began to work with him.[30]

MI5's version of what happened to the Arsenal Group was removed from the Security Service registry by Anthony Blunt in 1941, and the papers he copied included a brief summary of the counter-espionage investigation.

> On 14 March 1938, the British subjects Glading, Williams and Whomack were found guilty of espionage and sentenced respectively to 6, 4 and 4 years' imprisonment. Williams and Whomack were engineers working at the Woolwich Arsenal. They were known Communists over many years, but had not been known to be engaged in espionage until the time of their arrest. Glading worked in the arsenal from 1924 to 1928, when he was sacked for Communist activities. Up to March 1937 he was an employee of the League for the Struggle against Imperialism when he left and broke off all legal connections with the Communist Party.

Glading's organization was exposed through the work of Olga Gray, the MI5 agent referred to in MI5's internal files simply as Miss X, who successfully infiltrated the Communist Party in 1931 and between 1935 and 1937 cultivated Glading and several other prominent Communists. In February 1937, Miss X telephoned an MI5 officer and told him that Glading had asked her to rent a flat for him for meetings with his contacts. On instruction from MI5 she agreed and a flat was found in Holland Road. At the end of April, Glading visited the flat accompanied by a man called Dr Peters, whom MI5 later identified as Paul Hardt (actually Mally). The purpose of the visit, in MI5's view, was to look at the flat, meet Miss X and approve Glading's choice. In May 1937, Glading suggested to Miss X that she should leave the firm where she was working as a typist, learn photography and work at the flat. In

August 1937, Glading brought a Mr Stevens to the flat; he was later identified as Willy Brandes, an OGPU agent. Glading said that Stevens's wife would come to the flat twice a month to do photographic work, starting in October, and early in that month the Stevens couple brought a Leica camera and photographic equipment to the flat and took trial photographs of a map of the London Underground. On 21 October Mrs Stevens brought an enormous blueprint to the flat which was photographed in parts; Miss X learned that this was the blueprint of a naval gun. Surveillance established that Mrs Stevens took the blueprint to Hyde Park Corner where she met her husband and another man to whom she handed the blueprint, wrapped in a newspaper. This other man was George Whomack. At the beginning of November Glading said that Mr and Mrs Stevens had returned to Moscow, and they left England on 6 November for Paris. The following month Glading collected the camera and, according to Miss X, worked with it at home. On 12 January 1938 he told Miss X that on 15/16 January he had to do special work and photograph a complete book. On 16 January surveillance established a meeting between Glading and a man to whom he handed a parcel wrapped in a newspaper, and who was identified as Charles Munday, an assistant chemist at the Arsenal. On 21 January Miss X rang MI5 and reported that Glading had just left the flat and was going to Charing Cross Underground station, where he was to meet a man at 8.15 and receive material to be photographed. Special Branch officers watched this meeting and, as soon as the material had been handed over, arrested both men. The second man turned out to be Albert Williams, and the material passed consisted of documentation on a pressure apparatus from the research department of Woolwich Arsenal.

A search of Glading's flat revealed much interesting material, in particular a film of a *Manual of Explosives* and the blueprint of an aircraft design. Photographic material was also found at Williams's flat. George Whomack and Munday were arrested on 29 January 1938. Whomack was found to be in possession of a suitcase with a double bottom which he used to remove blueprints from Woolwich Arsenal. At their trial Glading, Williams and Whomack pleaded guilty. Munday pleaded not guilty and it was decided to release him.

Blunt's notes on Glading's MI5 card mention that his personal file started in 1922 with a report on his official Communist and trade union activities, with a reference in 1927 to his alleged connection with the Soviet intelligence organization of Kirchenstein, through a man called Messer. The first reports from agent M-12,

Olga Gray's codename, started in 1933, and later Glading was in contact with agent M-3, whom Blunt identified as Tom Driberg, a possible link to the Air Ministry. The Glading file consisted of reports from M-12, notes on his official activities, intercepted correspondence and accounts of his movements. It appeared that Glading was an extremely suspect individual though the material did not reveal anything directly compromising, leading MI5 to conclude:

> Investigations carried out after the completion of the Glading case have thrown light on Soviet military and naval espionage in Britain in 1937. The British subjects who were used were all members of the Communist Party of Great Britain. They all ceased open Party work as soon as they were recruited for the espionage group. Other British communists apart from those mentioned are strongly suspected of also belonging to this group, but it proved impossible to obtain evidence. It is interesting to note that although Glading was undoubtedly the organizer of this group of Communist sub-agents, he was not free to run the group and recruit agents as he thought fit, but was under control of the foreign resident in Britain, except for a period of two months immediately before his arrest ... As an example, Miss X did not get permission to continue the work and did not know its nature until she had been seen and vetted by Paul Hardt, alias Peters [actually Mally]. The way in which Glading obtained military and naval material for the USSR was extremely simple. His sub-agents worked in various departments and places such as the Woolwich Arsenal. In the evening they took the blueprints home with them, handed them to Glading who immediately photographed them and then returned them the same evening. The sub-agents, evidently, were able to put the blueprints back in their place the next morning without arousing suspicion. It is absolutely clear that the Soviet Embassy had nothing to do with the financing of the Glading organization or the transmission of the intelligence material to Moscow. It is known that because Brandes' successor did not arrive in the beginning of January, Glading became worried about how to transmit the material which he had received during the previous two months.[31]

The Woolwich Arsenal case proved a considerable success for MI5 and, much to Moscow's embarrassment, established a definite link between Soviet espionage and the CPGB. At the end of his six-year prison sentence Glading, disgraced and stripped of his CPGB membership, moved to China where he eventually died.

CHAPTER VII

Burgess and Blunt

Although it is rarely acknowledged by observers, the roles of Guy Burgess and Anthony Blunt within the Cambridge Ring-of-Five were almost indivisible. Each was complementary to the other, with sometimes one, then the other, taking the lead.

The recruitment of Guy Burgess at the end of 1934 marked a significant moment in the development of what was to become known as the Cambridge network; the next two years were spent cleansing Philby, Burgess and Maclean of their Leftist connections and laying the groundwork for their penetration of Britain's establishment, in particular the institutions that had been targeted by the Centre. Maclean acquired a post in the Foreign Office in October 1935 and started passing classified diplomatic documents to his controller, Arnold Deutsch, while Philby was still experimenting with a pro-German magazine and Burgess had joined the BBC.

There is no evidence in the network's surviving files that any consideration was given to expanding the organization, but there is a report written in December 1937 by Abram Slutsky, Chief of the NKVD's Seventh Department, for Nikolai I. Yezhov, entitled *About the Work of our Underground Rezidenturas in England* which refers to recruiting at British universities.[1] Certainly Theodor Mally, then the illegal *rezident* in London, discussed the issue while on leave in Moscow during the second half of 1936, for in his later account, dated 23 May 1938, he mentions that he had asked Deutsch about the 'technical line' (scientific and technical intelligence) in preparation for his visit to Moscow in the autumn. Doubtless Mally would have raised the issue of the 'political line' at the same time, but not with Deutsch because he already had the details at his fingertips. Certainly protracted discussions did take place in Moscow at this point because Mally records that when he returned to London he and Deutsch 'began to activate new possibilities in the political line', in particular 'information from SOHNCHEN, MADCHEN and EDITH' (Philby, Burgess and Edith Tudor Hart).

The key figure during this period was Guy Burgess who, according to Deutsch's perceptive psychological profile recorded in his file, by virtue of his sociable character had an astonishing ability 'to become acquainted with almost anyone'. Similarly, Alexander Orlov had observed that, bearing in mind that 'the majority of this country's most polished sons are pederasts', he was 'a cultural pederast' who could exploit 'the mysterious laws of sex in this country'. Certainly this predatory homosexual possessed great charm and his upper-class background gave him an impressive social entrée, even if his personal habits appalled many who met him. However, his Soviet contacts were evidently undeterred by his proclivities, and he was given perhaps the most difficult intelligence task, that of talent-spotter and recruiter. Having accepted the assignment with alacrity, Burgess wrote a report for the NKVD on the prospects of recruiting students at Oxford and Cambridge, building on the proposals already submitted by Orlov and Deutsch. His first approach was to Anthony Blunt, then teaching history of art at Trinity College, Cambridge, an old friend with whom he asserted he had conducted a homosexual affair. Although Blunt had no access to secret information, Burgess considered him of inestimable value as someone in a position to pick out students whose ideology would make them sympathetic to his political views and who, by their family origins, would be well-suited for a career in government service, perhaps even in the Foreign Office or the intelligence services.

By the beginning of 1937, Blunt had already started his experiments with Marxism, applying its political principles to history and interpreting art according to the tenets of historical materialism. However, despite his considerable ideological fervour, he never joined the Communist Party, and his conversion to Marxism was both gradual and idiosyncratic, as he explained in his highly personal account of his life, submitted to the Centre in February 1943. This fragment is of considerable importance because it represents the only candid autobiographical material Blunt ever wrote.

> I was born in 1907. My father was an Anglican priest and from 1912 to 1921 was British chaplain in Paris where we lived. My mother came of a family of Indian civil servants who had for a long time been connected with government service in India and also with the East India Company. I have two elder brothers, one in business and the other a schoolmaster at Eton. My father died in 1929 and my mother is still living near London. My other relations I rarely see.
>
> From 1918 to 1926 I was at school in England and in 1926 I went to Cambridge where I read mathematics and then languages. In 1932 I was elected to a fellowship at Trinity College and stayed there

doing research until 1937. I then came to London and got a job at the Warburg Institute, a German refugee research institute from Hamburg. At the same time I lectured for the Courtauld Institute of London University in the history of art, and finally I became deputy director of it in the beginning of 1939.

In September 1939 I joined the army and was given a commission in the Intelligence Corps. In December 1939 I went to France in charge of a Field Security section. I came back in June 1940 and after a few weeks joined MI5 through my friend Victor Rothschild who was already working there. For a time I worked in D Division under Colonel Norman and then as personal assistant to Brigadier Allen, and in March 1941 I managed to get myself transferred to B Division, first as personal assistant to Captain Guy Liddell, and then running a section on my own on diplomatic problems under Dick White. There I still am.

I do not think anything in my career is of interest before 1934, when I first came in contact with Party members. Up till then I had been an ordinary Cambridge intellectual – an 'art for art's sake' type, with no interest in politics at all and even an active [dis]belief that the arts – in which I was genuinely interested – had any connection with active life or politics at all.

In 1933 I went abroad for the greater part of a year. My fellowship allowed me to study elsewhere than in Cambridge. This year I spent mainly in Italy and south Germany working by myself studying architecture. I came back to Cambridge, however, for an examination in January 1934 and found that the intellectuals whom I had known before I went away were all coming under the influence of Communism. Guy Burgess who had been almost my closest friend before I went away had joined the Party and James Klugmann, who had been a brilliant student of mine and also a friend, had also joined. I was only in Cambridge a week or so at this time, and was not affected by what I saw beyond a vague surprise at finding so many intelligent people joining the Party.

When I came back in October, however, things were quite different. Events which took place in Germany had begun to penetrate even my intellectual isolation, and I was becoming dimly aware that my own position wasn't quite satisfactory. In this state of mind I found myself in constant contact with members of the Party whose whole outlook was totally different from mine. At first I could see no arguments for their views but gradually I came to feel that apart from their attitude towards politics – about which I still felt completely unable to form any opinion – their views on subjects which I understood such as history, and above all my own subject of history of art, were not only interesting, but even provided a real basis for

understanding the subject correctly and in a scientific manner. This
feeling gradually grew inside me also owing to the influence of Guy
Burgess, Klugmann, John Cornford and others belonging to this same
group. So I became fully convinced in the correctness of the Marxist
approach to history and to the special subject in which I was interested. Naturally when I was becoming acquainted with the Marxist
approach to different subjects, I also listened to various discussions
on political topics of the contemporary situation and gradually
became convinced that the Marxist point of view in the given matter
made sense. I know this is already outdated but I am speaking about
the way my personal consciousness changed. In spite of the fact that
I still feel that politics is a difficult subject for me, my views have
changed entirely and I realized the importance of understanding politics not only for practical purposes but also as a necessity for my
own specialist studies.

By this time I was seeing almost entirely the left-wing students in
Cambridge, and came to be regarded as very close to them in sympathy. Many people in fact thought that I was a member of the
Party. Actually I was only once asked to join by Roy Pascal a member
of the group of dons who had joined the Party. Fortunately, just at
the moment the obvious suggestion was made, I did not accept,
giving as my excuse that there were still too many points about
which I was not really clear and that I did not want to commit myself
till I had thought them out. During my last years at Cambridge
roughly from 1935 to 1937 I knew a great many of the Party
members among the students. Apart from those mentioned above
the following occurred to me: Brian Simon, Michael Straight, John
Cairncross, Leo Long, Matthew Hodgart, Charles Rycroft, John Sim-
monds, John Madge, Peter Newmark, John Waterlow. And among
dons, Maurice Dobb, Roy Pascal, George Thompson, Bernal Wad-
dington and his wife. My contacts with all these people were entirely
in the general intellectual field rather than over strictly political issues.
I used to attend and lecture to the various student societies which
were started by these men, but always on literary or historical subjects. These lectures or discussions were clearly Marxist in approach
and I was therefore commonly thought to be a sympathizer though
I know from things I heard later that the tougher Party members
such as Klugmann thought I was hopeless and would never get any
further. This opinion was partly formed after I had started to do our
work and was trying to combine the difficult task of not being
thought left-wing and at the same time being in the closest contact
with all left-wing students in order to spot likely recruits for us. As
you already know the actual recruits whom I took were Michael
Straight and Leo Long. John Cairncross I was asked to contact and

did so for Guy Burgess, but I was never officially told whether he was actually taken and he knows nothing of my activities. Apart from these direct recruits there are others who know about my activities and whom I know. Kim and Litzi in circumstances about which you know, Goronwy Rees with whom I was put in touch at the time of Munich when Guy Burgess thought we might all be scattered, and should therefore be in a position to make direct contact if necessary, when we were out of contact with you at the time. Goronwy thinks that I stopped working at the time of the Russo-German treaty at the same time as Guy Burgess; Brian Simon, in circumstances which you know in order to remake contact with possible students; Edith I know by name only, and she knows mine. I believe that through her my name is also known to Bob [Stuart] for whom we were all working in your absence. This also I think applies to Guy, Kim and Litzi. I have wondered recently whether there is any danger of Bob ever mentioning any of our names at King Street or at Great Newport Street in front of the microphone, but I do not imagine he would have any cause to do so. As far as I can think for the moment, that covers my activities up to the beginning of the war, since for the two years just before it, after I came to London in 1937, I was almost completely inactive. For the first part of the war I was able to do little that was useful. I went through various courses of training for the intelligence at Minley and Mytchett and gave in the notes I took there. In France I had no contacts until I met Kim, and then he was also out of contact, and my war career did not bring me into contact with anything of interest to us. After Dunkirk however I came back and after a week or two during which I was sent to Dover to help the security people there in the evacuation I was asked by Rothschild whether I would like to join MI5. I agreed to do so and it was originally intended that I should work with him in his counter-sabotage section. Since, however, I was in the army, the military part of the office claimed me and I was put to work on the purely military side under Colonel Norman and Brigadier Allen. It is not easy to define the work done in this department since it covers a wide range of miscellaneous subjects which are not very obviously related. Allen is head of C and D Divisions. The business of C Division is to check all people who apply for jobs in which any degree of secrecy is involved. One section of it deals with the applicants for the Intelligence Corps. Others with applicants for employment in civil departments, another with proposed employees of SIS and SOE, etc. It also deals with the question of recruitment of foreigners into the British Army, for example the problem of dual nationals or friendly Germans being employed elsewhere than in the Pioneer Corps. It is a particularly badly run division since its members are incapable of interpreting the information which is at their disposal, and that information is in addition rather scanty. The only precaution taken when an applicant's name comes in is to put the name through the registry and see if we have anything recorded about him. If not, the candidate is automatically cleared. If there are papers the officer dealing with the case will see if they contain anything serious. In many cases the papers will indicate some kind of political activity and the officers of C Division are perhaps less politically educated even amongst other members of MI5. They often therefore make the most surprising decisions which later have to be withdrawn. It is important to remember in this context that MI5 cannot prevent a government department from employing a man. They can only advise against it and if the department chooses to take the responsibility for not taking MI5's advice, there can only be a protest. I myself was, I imagine, a case of such disagreement for in an episode known to you but which I should have mentioned above, you will remember that when I was doing a course at Minley I was sent for by the commandant, Colonel Shearer, and told that he had received orders from the War Office that I was not to be employed on intelligence work. As a result I left Minley and came to London to await orders. After a day or two I was sent for by Brigadier Martin who was Deputy Director of Military Intelligence and given a long interrogation. He told me that they had received reports that I was 'connected with communism' and had been to Russia. I gave a long explanation of my position saying that my interest was purely in the intellectual side of Marxism and that I had studied it mainly in connection with my old historical studies. After a long talk he said that he would think the matter over and let me know what I was to do. A few days later I got a letter telling me to go back to Minley for the next course. This was I think due partly to the intervention of Dennis Proctor [a senior civil servant who was later to become Permanent Secretary at the Ministry of Fuel and Power] who knew Martin and gave him a favourable report of me. I have never yet fully fathomed the truth of this incident. The original decision not to employ me must have come from MI5 and was no doubt transmitted through MI-1(a) who deal with postings to Minley. I imagine that Shearer, who was very kind over the whole thing, probably raised my case with the DDMI. He therefore sent for me and after the interview presumably decided that he would not take the advice of MI5 but would employ me all the same. This he was perfectly entitled to do.[2]

Although details of the precise date and place of Blunt's recruitment do not survive in TONY's file, it is clear that Burgess did the greater part of the work and that Deutsch conducted the conversation in which the final approach was made. In a series of impressive biographical portraits written by Deutsch about his illegal agents, Deutsch confirms that 'MADCHEN [Burgess] in the beginning of 1937 acquainted me with TONY'.[3] In a letter from Mally to the Centre dated 29 January 1937, he refers to

> Anthony Blunt, codename TONY. He has already been recruited by us as a talent-spotter. I have reported detailed data about him.[4]

Since none of this detailed data survives, it can be assumed that Mally delivered it to the Centre in person when he visited Moscow in 1936, but Deutsch's perceptive account fills in some of the gaps:

> TONY is a typical English intellectual. Speaks very highly-flown English. Looks very feminine. A pederast. MADCHEN says that with TONY it is congenital. He is very educated and clever. Communism for him is based on theory. Has several works on Marxism in the history of art. Is considerably steadier and more rational than MADCHEN. He is a simple person and without big pretensions. Can control himself, is cold and a little mannered. Is to a lesser degree connected to the Communist Party than MADCHEN. He would hardly give up his career for the sake of our work. He understands well the tasks he is to do for us and is ready to help us. He has a large influence on students.[5]

Blunt's operational activities for the Soviets in the period 1937 to 1939 were probably very limited, judging by the very general entries in his file, and this view is borne out by Blunt's own account in which he admitted: 'Describing my work in the period from 1937 to the beginning of the war I can say that I did almost nothing.' He had

> tried to fulfil a rather difficult task: to create the impression that I didn't share left-wing views and, on the other hand, to be in the most close contact with all left-wing students in order to select people necessary for us.

One of those he recruited successfully at that time was Michael Straight, codenamed NIGEL, the son of an American millionaire close to President Roosevelt, who in 1983 published his version of events in his autobiography, *After Long Silence*. Another recruit was an exceptionally able second-year scholarship student, Leo Long. Codenamed RALPH, Long later confessed to MI5 in return for immunity from prosecution. Blunt also talent-spotted John Cairn-cross (MOLIERE), who wrote *An Agent for the Duration* shortly before he died in October 1995. Both RALPH and MOLIERE were to become extremely useful during the war when they joined different branches of British Intelligence. As for NIGEL, he returned to the

United States and, at the request of the local *rezident*, went to work for the State Department, although he did not accomplish as much as the Centre had hoped.

The principal reason for the lack of activity in London during the critical pre-war period was the continuous interruption of the *rezidentura*'s work caused by the recall to Moscow of *rezidents* and agents during the purges. In the autumn of 1937, Arnold Deutsch's permit to live in London expired and, his attempts to renew it failing, he was obliged to withdraw. Order was only restored in December 1940 after Anatoly Gorsky, codenamed VADIM, was finally installed at the embassy as the new *rezident*, following the temporary closure of the legal *rezidentura* the previous February. In the meantime intermittent contact with Blunt was maintained by Burgess, a necessity because Gorsky worked entirely alone, under cover as a cipher clerk, and had no time to meet individual agents. Indeed, when initially operating in London as KAP, before his appointment as *rezident*, Gorsky had been obliged to remind the Centre of Blunt's existence. Echoing Burgess, he wrote that 'TONY is quite a reliable person, an indispensable recruiter and talent-spotter [who] knows not only all the smallest details of MADCHEN's work with us but with STEPHAN's (Deutsch's) knowledge, typed MAD-CHEN's summaries for us. MADCHEN pointed out to me that TONY has recruited a person for us who very soon will pass examinations and will probably work in the NOOK [Foreign Office],'[6] a reference to Leo Long, who was destined to join the Directorate of Military Intelligence at the War Office.

As Blunt sensed the approach of war with Nazi Germany he pressed the Centre regarding the possible change in his official status at the Courtauld Institute, and thereby in his role as recruiter. In a letter dated 10 August 1939, Gorsky reported that TONY was seeking advice about how he could be of the most use in the event of war, suggesting two possibilities: firstly, that he enlist as an officer in the Territorial Army, and secondly, that he join the military intelligence staff. Gorsky was informed that 'since there was no personal contact with TONY it was difficult to give concrete instructions to him, but his going to work in intelligence would be preferable'.[7]

Evidently British Intelligence took the same view of Blunt's abilities because he soon received a letter from Major M.H. Brooks, on behalf of the Director of Military Operations and Intelligence, which ordered him to report no later than 1430 hours on 16 September 1939 at Minley Manor, Mytchett, in Surrey for an intelligence course. After completing the course, Brooks wrote, Blunt would be commissioned into the Intelligence Corps.[8] This solved the problem of how Blunt could insert himself in Britain's intelligence establishment, but no sooner had he begun his training at Minley than he experienced his first operational crisis. Gorsky was informed in a message from Guy Burgess, who acted as an intermediary, that on 26 September Blunt had been withdrawn from the intelligence course by Colonel John Shearer:

> I was this morning summoned by Colonel Shearer, the Commanding Officer at Minley, and told that he had received orders from the War Office that I was on no account to be used in intelligence of any kind. He did not show me the letter but told me that no reason was given but that the orders were absolutely categorical.[9]

Although the reasons for the recall were not given, Gorsky reported that Blunt himself had suggested two: perhaps MI5 had received information about his Communist views in the past, or it had become known that he was a homosexual. Burgess, when handing over his friend's message, asked for instructions. In his opinion, if Blunt remained passive, this might be interpreted as an admission of guilt.[10]

Several days later, as Blunt recounted in his autobiographical sketch in 1943, he was summoned to an interview with Brigadier Martin, the Deputy Director of Military Intelligence at the War office, where he found that his first guess had been correct. 'There was a long talk between them,' Gorsky reported to Moscow on 3 October, 'at which Martin announced that TONY had been recalled from the intelligence school because allegedly he had been connected with the Communist organization at university, and besides had gone to the Soviet Union and had written Marxist articles.'[11]

Blunt did not conceal from Martin that when he was an art critic for the *Spectator* he had theorized about the application of Marxism to the history of art. This, Blunt supposed, might have suggested to someone that he must have held the same political viewpoint. However, at the conclusion of 'a long and difficult conversation carried on under extreme strain', Martin said that he would think over the impression Blunt had made on him ('impressions which I may say are favourable,' recalled Blunt) and would enquire about him at Trinity College.[12]

Soon afterwards Blunt produced his notes of his meeting with Martin:

> Martin asks: 'What do you think the effects will be of the Soviet Pact on conditions inside Germany?' Blunt responds: 'Well, it seems to me to destroy all hope of a working class movement against the

regime.' Martin: 'Working class movement?' Blunt: 'Yes, left-wing, working class movement. I mean what are they to do now that they find that the country which claims to be the representative of Communism is in alliance with the regime that they hate?' At one point we came back to the problem of what I had read about Bolshevism for which in answering I had always substituted Marxism and I said that I had mainly read the historical works of Marx, particularly those on Nineteenth Century French history. We eventually came back to the problem of how the report [questioning Blunt's loyalty] could have been formed and I then led off with Lord Lee [of Fareham]. Blunt: 'Well, it occurs to me that this sort of thing has happened to me once before when I was being considered for a post at the Warburg Institute. Lord Lee protested against my appointment on the grounds that I held left views politically. I don't know what he was basing his views on but I imagine it was mainly Cambridge gossip, although there is another possible reason. I was for a time a journalist. I was actually art critic on the *Spectator* and I tried in my articles to work out the applications of Marxism to art history but I know that these articles gave a great deal of offence to many people and that some of them drew the conclusion that because I held these intellectual views I must also hold the political views of the Marxists.' Martin: 'Well, I want you to realize that we have to be very careful indeed in intelligence and that what has been done was probably done in excessive zeal and I hope therefore that you will not feel that you have grievance.' Blunt: 'No, certainly not. I was above all mystified.' Martin: 'Well, I hope that the mystery has been cleared up. The problem for me is how are you going to fit into our intelligence?' Blunt, slightly puzzled by the question: 'In what way do you mean?' Martin: 'Well that's what I want to know from you.' Blunt: 'I suppose my only qualifications are linguistic.' Martin: 'You know German?' Blunt: 'Yes, but French is really my better language.' Martin: 'Ou est-ce que vous avez prié votre Français? Where did you learn your French?' Blunt: 'Mainly in Paris.' Martin: 'What were you doing there?' Blunt: 'I lived there. My father was chaplain at the embassy church for nearly ten years, chiefly during the last war.' Martin: 'Where does he live now?' Blunt: 'He's dead. He died ten years ago.' Martin: 'I am sure he would turn in his grave if he thought you were doing subversive work or perhaps I am a little traditional in this way, I mean about respect for one's forebears. Did you know any of the French Communist leaders?' Blunt, perhaps rather too hastily: 'No.' Martin: 'There would be nothing discreditable in knowing them.' Blunt: 'No, of course not. I imagine that people like Tores are very good people.' Martin: 'Do you know what is happening to the Communist Party in France now?' Blunt: 'No. Not at all.' Finally,

Martin said, 'Well, I should like a little time to think over the impressions of you I have formed, which I may say are favourable and I hope you won't mind perhaps coming here again for another talk.' One point that Martin particularly caught was the fact that I was a fellow of Trinity, i.e. he will certainly make enquiries in Trinity about me. This I think can only be to the good. The upshot of the whole interview was that I think it went well but one must add to that the immediate corollary that if it had not gone well Martin would have certainly been clever enough to have given me the impression that it had gone well. This account is, as you will realize, made up from what I can recall of a long and difficult conversation carried on under extreme strain. It is therefore in no sense as photographic as it may appear at first sight.

It was at this point that Burgess intervened and arranged for his friend (Sir) Dennis Proctor to visit Martin with the aim of finding out what he thought about Blunt, and if necessary to exert some influence. Proctor subsequently confirmed that the brigadier had formed a very good opinion of Blunt and that he had recommended his return to Minley Manor because his withdrawal had been a misunderstanding. On Burgess's instructions Proctor had told Martin that 'all decent people have if not left-wing views, then at least left-wing friends'.[13]

Burgess reported his suspicion that information about Blunt had originated from an MI5 source at Trinity, and identified the economist and homosexual (Sir) Dennis Robertson as the most likely candidate: he had earlier refused to act as a referee for Kim Philby when he had wanted to join the Foreign Office. Knowing Robertson well, Blunt was convinced that he might have reported him, even though they were close friends. He recalled having seen Robertson lunching with a staff officer, and had noted that afterwards Robertson's behaviour towards himself had been somewhat odd.

Following Proctor's meeting with Martin, Burgess, who had been very nervous, was filled with optimism and concluded in a personal note to the Centre that the crisis was over. 'May I, (1) on behalf of the Party, congratulate A.B. on passing the ordeal (2) thank HENRY (Gorsky) for his calm advice and right analysis at the moment when I was excited and very much in the wrong.'

Blunt's own account of this harrowing experience was written for the Centre, which must have expressed some scepticism that an academic with his doubtful antecedents could successfully worm his way into the heart of the Security Service. Clearly Blunt was anxious to provide a comprehensive explanation of what had happened, and to let the Russians know his progress up MI5's hierarchy.

Considering that his MI5 colleagues Guy Liddell, Dick White and
Victor Rothschild believed him to be their faithful friend, Blunt's
conversational style of betrayal is truly breathtaking.

One thing is, however, mysterious. When I eventually joined MI5
my name was put through the registry in the ordinary way by Rothschild. He told me that the only records were an intercepted postcard
from Maurice Dobb to *Left Review* suggesting that they should print
an article of mine, and mention of my name on a list of those visiting
Russia in 1935. (This incidentally fits with the facts mentioned to
Martin.) These he did not consider important and they were ignored.
But if MI5 had at this time recommended that I should not be
employed there should among the papers under my name be somewhere a letter to that effect. If so this should have appeared when
my name was looked up in 1940. I do not however believe that it
did because I am sure that Rothschild would have mentioned it to
me, and moreover there would then have been more difficulty about
my employment. There seems to me only one possible explanation.
The letter would have been in a file with a number which the secretary
doing the look up would immediately recognize as being simply an
application for employment from the number without seeing the file.
She may therefore have said that it was not worth sending for it as
it would not contain anything of importance, not realizing that it
contained a letter recommending non-employment. This is only a
guess and I have never wanted to go further into the matter on the
grounds that I do not want to call attention to the problem at all. I
have however taken the precaution to mention privately and in a
half-joking way to Liddell and White that C Division once recommended that I should not be employed. I did this partly because they
both know all about my past contacts with the party, and also
because I want if ever challenged on the subject to be able to say
that I had not concealed the fact that I had been turned down, but
had on the contrary mentioned it to my bosses.

I reported fully on the first part of this incident through Guy
Burgess at the time but I am not sure if I ever wrote down the last
part since most of it took place while I was almost out of touch.

To return to the functions of C and D Division. C Division has
been covered. D Division deals generally with military security. D1,
D2 and D3 are the sections which cover the security of certain factories which have secret contracts. As far as I can understand they
are run in a very mechanical manner. The principle is that in each
factory a security officer is appointed and he receives a booklet of
instructions from MI5. These booklets give general instructions
about anti-sabotage precautions, fencing, guards, etc. In addition the
MI5 officers make visits to the various factories and discuss the

problems with the security officers on the spot. But there are so few in number that they can only visit any one factory about once a year, and there is little doubt that the actual security regulations are not generally applied with any efficiency. Rothschild, whose job is primarily the investigation of alleged cases of sabotage, but who is also naturally interested in counter-sabotage precautions, has tried to make them more active, but without success. As a result he is himself organizing a scheme for testing out the security of factories by having Field Security men trained to try and get into factories which are supposed to be securely enclosed. He has also tried to make the D officers concentrate on the factories which really matter, i.e. those which are bottle-necks or which are peculiarly liable to sabotage, but without success. D Division also refuses to have anything to do with utility undertakings as not being their business, so Rothschild is now organizing schemes for their security. In fact he is now doing a great deal of the work which they should be doing themselves.

D4 is in charge of travel control. This means primarily the direction of the security officers at the ports who are becoming of increasing importance. But in addition it means the control of visa and exit permit applications.

D5 is administrative and D6, which used to be called DuD, is the section for liaison with the War Office and with the Home Forces. It also deals with all miscellaneous cases of military security which need investigation.

After nine months of work in this department I was transferred to B Division. The original plan was that I should be personal assistant to Liddell. This did not work well as he is not the kind of person who can have assistants since he always does all the work again himself when they have prepared it for him. I came therefore gradually to do more and more things for White who is the direct head of the German counter-espionage. For a time I was still nominally with Liddell, and I still have certain jobs which he gave me to do for him, such as the directing of B6.

White asked me to investigate the question of diplomatic communications which had not up till then been studied systematically by MI5. Each country section was naturally interested in its own particular diplomats but there was no section to study the problem as a whole. I had therefore to start from the beginning. First I had to find out what mechanisms already existed, and then what could be found or invented. The existing ones were nearly all in the hands of SIS. For instance the breaking of ciphers by GC & CS is in effect directed by SIS and the opening of diplomatic bags is also in their hands (though the people who do it are nominally censorship servants). The listening to embassy telephones is also done by SIS. The

reason for all their doing these things which seem on the face of it
to be more for MI5, especially bags and telephones, is that SIS is
technically under the Foreign Office and diplomats are supposed to
be primarily of interest to the Foreign Office. My first job – and by
no means my easiest, was to persuade SIS to let MI5 see the material
which they had which was of interest to us. By managing to see their
old files I discovered that there was a mass of material of the greatest
interest from the counter-espionage point of view which we had never
seen. Eventually after a lot of struggles which are not interesting, I
have got things on to a basis that SIS really must let us see what we
want, though this was only achieved by showing them that we could
give them in return a great deal that they wanted.

That is to say, I soon found that by using mechanisms in the hands
of MI5 I could get a lot of material which SIS could not get. For
instance, in the matter of bags, I found that by using the officers
which we have in ports we could get hold of many bags which were
being carried out by couriers. In some cases it was possible to take
the bag because the courier had not obeyed the traveller's censorship
regulations; in others it was possible to persuade the courier – extraordinary though it may seem – to put his bag in the care of the
security officer at the port rather than leave it in the hotel overnight.
This method works particularly well with the Spaniards and Portuguese who go out from Poole or Bristol to Lisbon. We also arranged
that certain allied couriers who were sent to the Patriotic Schools
[in Wandsworth, a screening centre for recently arrived refugees]
should have to give up their bags for safe keeping while they were
there. In this way we managed to cover a very large field which had
been entirely closed to SIS.

I also began to develop the idea of having agents in embassies.
When I took this question up I found that altogether MI5 had one
agent in the Japanese embassy, and I think one in a South American
legation. In addition we were in contact with one Rumanian ex-
diplomat. (Before the war we had had much better contacts in the
German embassy.) The first step was to get control of one of the
servants agencies, and fortunately Hunt's was found to be possible
– through one of Maxwell Knight's people. [Knight was MI5's star
agent handler: he controlled Olga Gray in 1938.] Later the International domestic agency was also one used but this has now been
dropped.

Hunt's is used entirely through Maxwell Knight's section. The
details are all carried out by Dickson and Gladstone. The usual
process is as follows; She [Hunt] has built up a certain group of
servants, mostly people she knew before and she could get hold of
through friends. These are planted, as opportunity offers. What usu-

ally happens is that she rings me up and says that, let us say, the Argentine embassy are looking for a housemaid and asks me if I am interested. I say yes or no according to the interest in the embassy and the suitability of the post offered. Certain jobs are almost useless. For instance, a housemaid in the ambassador's house as opposed to the chancery. Others, such as the position of the man who burns the waste paper are obviously ideal. One way or another we have a constantly changing series of people in certain of the embassies. In some cases we only leave them there for a short time and then take them away if we find they cannot get anything of interest. In others we have got people who constantly get us really good stuff, for instance in the Spanish embassy. The useful material they get is of different kinds. Our best agent of all, who is a secretary and not a servant in the Spanish embassy, gets us cipher tape, clear versions of cipher telegrams, drafts of the ambassador's reports, private letters, notes on dinner parties and visitors, and general gossip about the members of the embassy. Others only get us the torn letters from the waste-paper baskets, but even these are sometimes of interest. The immediate project I am working on is to get a good agent in the Swedish legation about which we are still badly informed. Our results with the Swedish bag have been very disappointing. We have seen about half a dozen – we are actually examining one now – and so far they have produced absolutely nothing of importance. They only show that the Swedes all break the rules about carrying private and business letters in the bag. Apart from servants we have also organized a number of agents of other kinds in embassies. I have already mentioned the secretary in the Spanish embassy, Villaverde's secretary, and we have certain others of the same type but none nearly so good. The Turkish military attaché, for instance, but she is quite useless since the Turk is very silent and careful, burning every trace of secret paper or cipher material. The most active section in this respect is the Spanish and South American section which has managed to make contact with several diplomats whose names at various times I have given to you – Brugada in the Spanish embassy for instance, a man in the Spanish consulate, etc. Apart from Brugada these are not of much interest as they are not taken on the basis of working against their own country but only against the Germans, or sometimes against other South American countries. I cannot for the moment give a complete list of all of these but I have reported their names to you as they occurred. In addition to these more or less useful activities against embassies I have also had to spend a good deal of time on measures of general security which have not been very productive. For instance, when I began on this job no-one had paid any attention to the question of the movement of diplomats, except for the watching of members of the Soviet embassy by B6, and I had to organize arrangements to have some idea of what they were doing. For ordinary diplomats we are still very badly placed and unless we have some special reason to suspect them, e.g. the case of Menendes in the Portuguese embassy whose name came up on ISOS [the codename given to decrypts of Abwehr hand cipher wireless traffic] as a German agent, we do nothing in the way of following them. It has been possible to do a little more in the case of service attachés who are naturally regarded as more dangerous. It has been arranged that service attachés are not allowed to move from London without first notifying their intention to do so to the Foreign Office. They are also required to indicate the route which they follow if they live outside London. In fact it is hard to do much more than to watch them and to see that they follow these regulations as the police are not very active in this sort of job and are in addition always frightened of a car with the letters 'CD' on it. As for activities in connection with the Soviet embassy, I have already given you every scrap of information which has come to my attention. I will therefore only summarize it here. Before June 22nd a good deal of watching was done by B6. This was originally directed towards following members of the embassy but this proved too difficult and it was decided to try and identify those who visited the embassy rather than follow members of the embassy when they went out. The theory was that in this way we might identify people who carried information into the embassy. After June 22nd however it was decided that the watching must be dropped. This was done probably because it was thought that if it was discovered that we were watching the embassy it might damage relations, and also probably for another reason: after June 22nd it was said that large numbers of Party members visited the embassy and [Harry] Hunter who used the same men on the embassy as he used on party members was frightened that the latter might recognize his men if they saw them hanging about outside the embassy and that they might therefore become suspicious. For this reason, but above all for the other political reason stated above, watching was stopped, except for a period when at the special request of Swinton [Lord Swinton, Chairman of the Home Defence Security Executive] it was put on again to see what members of the party were actually visiting the embassy. For this short period it was done for two or three days a week and not every day. Since then B6 has not been working on the embassy at all. They have of course been active on various jobs of watching our people, especially in the Green case, but that I have reported to you in detail.[14] Apart from the functions described above I have spent a good deal of my time arranging for various kinds of most secret documents to come through me. I get in the ordinary course of my job the deciphered diplomatic telegrams, the diplomatic telephone conversations, and the product of the various agents in the embassies except from the agents run by the sections themselves. That is to say that I see primarily what comes from the servants. In addition, I have established a claim to see ISOS, although in fact it has nothing to do with my work and I have managed to get myself into a position where I can get a certain amount of operational information from Lennox's section[15] on the grounds that I have to watch for leakages in the diplomatic channels which I watch. I have also managed to get myself into touch with Robertson[16] who runs the double agents over the question of putting over false information through diplomatic channels. In this way I can usually get an idea of what is actually planned and what is being put across as cover. I have also made myself a sort of liaison officer for Shillito[17] in London and do all sorts of odd jobs for him which give me the opportunity of talking to him about his work. In this way he is usually ready to tell me far more than is really necessary about his cases. He is forced to tell me a certain amount because he often has to apply to me for the use of B6. In general however he is well disposed and in fact tends to talk far too much. I have also got myself into a position of doing a good deal of liaison with other departments, particularly with the Foreign Office, the War Office, SIS, GC & CS and Censorship.

Burgess's erratic behaviour during Blunt's hazardous entry into MI5 was partly in consequence of another crisis which was unfolding almost simultaneously, concerning his old and trusted friend Goronwy Rees. Codenamed GROSS, Rees had been recruited by Burgess in 1938, but he had refused to co-operate after the Ribbentrop–Molotov pact the following year. In an undated report to the Centre Burgess had used the excuse of the *News Chronicle*'s opposition to the treaty as a pretext for severing his connection with Rees and had 'told GR that I agreed and intended to stop working for the Party. Thus we have freed ourselves from GR (Goronwy Rees) and at the same time have provided ourselves with the fact that he thinks I don't work for the Party and comrades any more. The crisis has showed in fact that he was no Marxist at all, but from the Seventh Congress on he began laying his criticism on thick.'[18]

On 14 October 1939, Blunt was reinstated by the War Office and made a fresh start at Minley Manor, having received an apology for what was described as an unfortunate misunderstanding. When he finished the first induction course he was placed on a second, more specialized, course on 20 November. Throughout his period at Minley Manor, Blunt collected training material for his controllers and recorded the lectures delivered by military intelligence and Security Service personnel.[19] Of great interest to Moscow was the first detailed structure of Britain's military intelligence establishment, dated 17 November 1939 and passed via Burgess.[20]

In preparation for a transfer to France with his Field Security section of the Intelligence Corps, Blunt provided Gorsky, through Burgess, with half of a ten-franc note, which would be used to identify his Soviet contact abroad. It was also arranged that in Blunt's absence on the Continent, Burgess would act as the Centre's link with RALPH (Leo Long). However, because of the uncertainties of the military situation on the Continent and the difficulties in locating Blunt, the Centre eventually decided, in a note dated 7 February 1940, against contacting Blunt in France and suggested instead that Gorsky should meet him in London.[21] A further undated note from the London *rezidentura* mentions Blunt being in Boulogne,[22] a fact apparently reported to Gorsky by Philby who, in September 1980, recalled his encounter with Blunt:

> I came to Boulogne where the chief of a field security section was Anthony Blunt. There were many refugees in the town and panic often arose. Once he called me on the phone and said that German parachutists were near. Since there were no other officers in town Blunt took upon himself the organization of defences from what was left of the troops. Soon it emerged that there had been no parachutists whatever.[23]

The London *rezidentura* was closed down in February 1940, and in the *History of the London Rezidentura* there is only a single short entry:

> On the orders of the People's Commissar Comrade Beria the *rezidentura* in London was closed down and KAP [Gorsky] was recalled to the Soviet Union. The reason for closing the *rezidentura* was, allegedly, disinformation given by agents.[24]

The real reason was Stalin's continuing purge of the NKVD, combined with a degree of paranoia in Moscow regarding the reliability of the sources in London. Gorsky, of course, was entirely above suspicion, having been in the relatively humble post of cipher clerk at the height of the purge which had already cost the life of his first *rezident*, Adolf S. Chapsky (alias Second Secretary 'Anton Shuster'), who had been recalled in 1937, while his successor Grigori B. Grafpen (alias Attaché 'Gregory Blank') was sent to a labour camp. The purge had decimated the NKVD and as the leadership gradually realized the implications it began to rebuild the Centre's efficiency. One of the first manifestations of the restoration of good sense was the transfer in August 1940 of Aleksandr Korotkov, now apparently fully rehabilitated, to Berlin, where he resumed contact with Arvid Harnack, and at the end of the year Gorsky was sent back to London as VADIM to revive the local agents.

Gorsky's first task was to find Blunt and on 28 December he reported that he 'had come into contact with TONY who made a good impression on him'. This was their first direct encounter, and Gorsky noted that Blunt now held the rank of captain on the General Staff, his cover for the Security Service, and had acquired access to military intelligence documents, including information from agents about the Red Army, and could visit MI5's famous archive, known as the registry.[25] Quite why Blunt took it upon himself to penetrate MI5 can only be guessed at. Was he looking for a legitimate wartime role, or was he simply seeking to serve the Soviet cause all the better? The most likely explanation is the latter, bearing in mind Blunt's consistent commitment and his very highly developed sense of discipline. Certainly he had remained close to both Philby and the irrepressible Burgess, and they would not have advised him to make any other choice, for all three were equally devoted to their secret purpose.

In January 1941, Blunt passed the first MI5 documents to Gorsky, among them a complete copy of the debriefing of Walter Krivitsky, the GRU illegal who had defected in 1937 and betrayed the Foreign Office cipher clerk Captain King (MAG). Under interrogation Krivitsky had also compromised another key Soviet source, Henri Pieck (COOPER), and had warned of another leak in the Foreign Office which the NKVD supposed was either STUART (Donald Maclean) or LISZT (John Cairncross).[26] Naturally this document describing the defector's debriefing was of supreme importance for Moscow.

The following month Blunt moved into B Division, the Security Service's counter-espionage branch, where he worked briefly as a personal assistant to the Director, Captain Guy Liddell MC, and then switched to a small unit headed by Dick White which concentrated on foreign diplomatic missions in London.[27] An analysis compiled by the Centre in April 1942 reviewed the activities of MI5 and SIS in this field during October and November 1941, based on Blunt's information:

1. The interception of German Intelligence communications between Turkey–Hamburg, the Ukraine–Sofia, the Crimea–Sofia.
2. German Intelligence data received by the British from other

countries, principally Poland and Sweden, including cryptographic information and the use of microdots.
3. Data about the deployment of German and Japanese troops.
4. Physical and technical surveillance of the Soviet embassy and
   military mission in London, their telephone lines, and personnel
   including the names of the watchers.

Having assessed TONY's material, Moscow concluded that it 'presented value, although all the work of MI5 and of the intelligence
services is not yet reflected in it. TONY's and RALPH's (Long's)
material is mixed and it is difficult to say who has access to
what.'

The Centre's enquiry was answered on 29 October 1942, when
Moscow was informed that 'TONY worked in B Division of the
HUT, in sub-division B2, which dealt with the most secret information which did not go to other departments. His main work was
the distribution of deciphered diplomatic telegrams, the analysis
of intercepted diplomatic mail, and the processing of telephone
intercepts. In addition the section dealt with the movement of
foreign diplomats, handling agents in foreign embassies and the
development of new methods of opening diplomatic mail and communication with GC & CS.' Specifically, Blunt dealt with the disposal of waste paper from diplomatic premises, liaison with the
Czech counter-intelligence service and HOTEL (SIS) in relation to
the arrival of its agents to THE ISLAND (Britain). The reason for
this multiplicity of responsibilities was apparently MI5's chronic
shortage of staff. Blunt's key role was later described by Boris
Kreshin, codenamed BOB, who took over supervision of the Cambridge ring from Gorsky in 1942, and was known to them as
'Max':

> TONY is a thorough, conscientious and efficient agent. He tries to
> fulfil all our tasks in time and as conscientiously as possible. TONY,
> by the way, is the opposite of MADCHEN [Burgess] both in character
> and in his attitude to his duties to us. TONY is thoughtful, serious,
> will never promise if he knows about the difficulty or impossibility
> of giving an answer to this or that question.[28]

All the Centre's information about Blunt suggested exceptionally
fruitful co-operation, and one reference in Kreshin's report to the
interception of German wireless traffic proved to be prescient. This
highly secret topic was the subject of a note from Blunt in April
1942 in which he summarized the progress achieved through ISOS,
the decryption process applied to Abwehr hand ciphers, and known

by the initials of a unit named after its head, 'Intelligence Service Oliver Strachey':

> ISOS and diplomatic intercepted documents can't be taken out. However, as to diplomatic documents, sometimes I take them out, but ISOS, never. ISOS could be taken out, but with a certain risk. I often keep ISOS for the night, but then it is necessary to arrange regular photographing.

Blunt went on to suggest that he should remove entire batches of ISOS intercepts so that Gorsky could assess their importance and determine whether they would assist Soviet efforts to decipher the enemy's signals. Clearly Blunt had seen an opportunity hugely to increase his supply of information to the Centre; a reply, sent on 26 June 1942, requested a detailed account of MI5's work and the role of the subsection in which he worked, as well as a comprehensive study of the rest of the organization.

This desire to learn more about the work of the London *rezidentura* demonstrated that the Centre had begun to recover from the damage inflicted by the purges. In Moscow the relevant unit, the 3rd Department of the NKGB's First Directorate, was headed by Lieutenant Elena Modrzhinskaya, a strong-willed woman with a rational, analytical mind who was permanently preoccupied with the threat posed by MI5. She recorded on the file: 'TONY is connected with Shillito, chief of the Russian section of HUT, and says that HUT practically does not work against us.' Obviously the Centre was anxious about security, and that meant taking an interest in MI5's surveillance of Soviet citizens in Britain, with a special emphasis on measures taken to watch the *rezidentura*. Once Elena Modrzhinskaya had taken over the British Department she raised this issue frequently, but in her opinion she never received a completely satisfactory reply from London about her many suspicions. Only Blunt in MI5 or Philby in SIS could give definitive answers to the Centre's persistent queries, and the lack of comprehensive replies served to create a crisis of confidence. Moscow found it impossible to accept the Cambridge ring's assurances that neither MI5 nor SIS was planning any anti-Soviet operations, and the *rezidentura*'s reluctance to press the issue allowed members of the ring inadvertently to make suggestions and behave in a manner that had the effect of confirming the ever-vigilant Modrzhinskaya's worst fears.

The first sign of the developing crisis can be detected in a message to the London *rezidentura* dated 26 August 1942, devoted to BOB's (Kreshin's) supervision of the Cambridge ring. He was reprimanded for an 'insufficiently attentive and watchful attitude towards agents'

statements and behaviour', and several further suspicions were identified, one of which was Burgess's improbable suggestion that his
immediate superior in MI5, Kemball Johnston, would be a suitable
candidate to approach. Burgess had been in contact with MI5 since
1937, a link that had been approved by Deutsch, but now gave rise
to suspicion:

> SOHNCHEN's (Philby's) and TONY's suspicious understatement of the
> work of British Intelligence against us, MADCHEN's offer to recruit
> Johnston and also 'the existence of communication and contact
> between SOHNCHEN, TONY and MADCHEN'.[29]

Coinciding with this rebuke was another communication 'about
the work of HOTEL' which complained that 'in spite of the large
amount of information, there is little to show about HOTEL's work
against us'. It was to become a constant theme.

> Statements: SOHNCHEN's about HOTEL's weak activity against us
> and TONY's about the absence of HUT's work against us on THE
> ISLAND are suspicious. They do not mention being ill-informed,
> which proves the absurdity of it.[30]

The Centre also gave the *rezidentura* examples of what it alleged
was TONY's 'insincerity', including the very dubious fact that not
a single Soviet intelligence officer ever figured in any of the surveillance data he passed over. This, the Centre calculated, was highly
unusual, particularly as 'HUT actively cultivates Yugoslav and
Swedish missions, but not us'.[31]

Curiously, the negative opinion developing about the Cambridge
ring was not endorsed by everyone at the Centre, for a memo dated
October 1942 recorded:

> From TONY's materials received with the latest few shipments, it is
> seen that HUT conducts active cultivation of Soviet citizens on THE
> ISLAND, the Soviet colony is being approached by agents, telephone
> tapping is being conducted, surveillance is established.[32]

Kreshin met Blunt for the first time on 23 June 1942, but because
of the unreliability of the diplomatic courier, who took up to three
months to reach Moscow via the Far East, his report was probably
out of date by the time it was received at the Centre. Kreshin stated
that he had asked Blunt directly about British counter-intelligence
operations directed against the Soviets, and had been informed that
the MI5 section responsible for this activity was headed by Hugh
Shillito, who was based at Oxford. Blunt had asserted that MI5
had no agents inside the Soviet Embassy, and that surveillance had
been restricted to individual callers at the embassy, but even this

modest coverage had been discontinued. Only telephone tapping had been maintained, so he claimed, explaining that the Home Defence Security Executive headed by Lord Swinton had decided, after Hitler's invasion of the Soviet Union, that all MI5's efforts should be concentrated on the Nazis. Swinton's view, endorsed by the Security Service, was that the Soviet target could wait until after victory over Germany, and this had become official policy. During a further meeting on 16 October 1942, Blunt explained to Kreshin that he did not have access to information about very important agents, nor an opportunity to cultivate members of the government, but from what material he could see, there did not appear to be any sign of anti-Soviet operations. The first indication, Blunt insisted, would be found in MI5's surveillance reports, but there was absolutely nothing, so he remained 99 per cent certain of his opinion.[33]

The MI5 documents supplied by Blunt to Kreshin tended to reinforce his view. The Security Service worked with hopelessly inadequate resources and the surveillance section, designated B6 and headed by Harry Hunter, had a staff of just thirty-six watchers. Following his introduction to Hunter, Blunt sent in a long typed message in which he identified by name the watchers who had been deployed so successfully in the Monckland–Macartney case in 1927[34] and against the Woolwich Arsenal spy-ring that had been headed in 1938 by Percy Glading.

I have had quite a long talk with Hunter about the method which he uses in watching; but it is difficult to set out anything very precise about it as his methods are very unscientific and depend above all on the experience and the patience of his men.

Hunter himself has been doing this kind of work since at least the early twenties, and from what he told me I had the impression that he had done something of the sort during the last war. In the early days he had only a very few men for the job and did a good deal of it himself, e.g. in the Macartney case. In the years before the war he built up a somewhat larger organization and produced two really first rate watchers, Hutchie and Long. who did the main work in the Miss X–Glading case. They are still his best workers though a third, Tonkey, who has joined him much more recently is also regarded by him as first rate. These three are those who do all the really ticklish cases, which means in effect the cases connected with the party. All of them by now have a good knowledge of the chief members of the party, especially those who are believed to be connected with underground activities. They have all been used in watching King Street and also in work on the embassy when watching was still carried out there.

In addition to these experts he has a number of men who are competent but not so skilled. The only one whom I know by name is Woodhouse. These men, who seem to number about a dozen, are used for the less difficult jobs, e.g. cases for Blg, B4, etc. and are quite capable of following anyone who is not very much on his guard. They are not good enough however for cases of people who are really looking out for watchers.

The rest of his men, who make up the total of about 38; he has recently sent away about 5 as he had too many men not used for anything but for enquiries, e.g. in hotels, in which Hunter has certain good contacts, or at private houses which they usually approach under the cover of making enquiries about fire-watching or some other routine matter. These men are not really trained and are not generally used for watching of any kind.

The process of recruiting is usually through a personal recommendation from some contact of Hunter's, or by recommendation of Special Branch or some other section of the police. In the case of men used for lower grade work they are sometimes sent to him by the recruiting office of the Field Security Police. If they find a candidate who has no language qualifications, or has not the necessary educational level. Such men would be used for enquiries unless they showed a particular ability for watching, in which case they could be transferred to the watching part of the section.

Hunter's method of training is rather primitive. He gives the new men lectures on the lines of the notes which are already known to you, but he relies almost entirely on practice. The new men are sent out almost immediately on minor jobs accompanied by more experienced watchers, from whom they learn the methods in the actual process following selected persons.

Clearly the Centre found it hard to accept Blunt's verdict that the famous MI5 operated with such limited resources, to the extent that observation was limited to officials of neutral embassies in London who could act as proxies for the German Abwehr, particularly those of Spain and Portugal who were judged by MI5 to be particularly susceptible to the Nazis. As well as the physical surveillance, these diplomatic premises were also the subject of microphone cover organized by Mrs Grist of A5. In addition, MI5 had penetrated the Spanish Embassy with several agents, and had paid close attention to the Swedish Embassy where the air attaché, Flight Lieutenant Frank-Rutger Cervell, had come under scrutiny. As for telephone tapping, Blunt claimed that MI5 had a capacity to cover a maximum of only forty lines, and there was very little scope after office hours.

With access to the registry, and his wide circle of homosexual friends, Blunt must have been almost too much of a good thing for the Soviets. Certainly he did not disguise his sexual inclinations, as is clear from this text in which Blunt reveals the relative paucity of MI5's agents, and identifies his homosexual partner. After describing a scandal in the Swedish embassy, Blunt listed some of MI5's agents:

1. Mrs Susan Maxwell, wife of Colonel Somerset Maxwell MP, who was recently killed in Libya. She was originally a contact of the Czech agent Brochbauer who worked for Czech Intelligence and through them for us. Later on I took her on myself and we worked together. Her value is that she knows some of the Swedish diplomats. Her position is very curious. She used to have a boyfriend there called Knut Wijk from whom she got a certain amount of gossip for us. In about March 1941 the minister told her that he was to go back to Sweden. This was partly the result of an intrigue against him from other members of the legation who were jealous of him because he was better off and better paid than them. Mrs Maxwell took the opportunity of getting from him while he was rather embittered with his own people a note on various cipher telegrams which had come into the embassy recently and also a piece of cipher tape. Wijk's particular rival in the legation found out about the report but not the tape and told the minister. There was a fearful scandal but Prytz was anxious to cover it up and in the end made Wijk go back to Sweden at once and leave the service. As a result of this Mrs Maxwell's position was very difficult as it was known that the note was in her handwriting. However, in spite of this she remained on good terms with Carlbom who was almost more English than Swedish and also Aminof. From them she still occasionally gets items of interest. Recently however her most useful function has been to clear up the case of Brochbauer who, we discovered, was being utterly indiscreet and using methods which were quite impossible. As a result of this he has been liquidated and is now back with the Czech Brigade. It may be necessary to intern him later.
2. Lady Dalrymple-Champneys, wife of Sir Weldon Dalrymple-Champneys, who is permanent under-secretary at the Ministry of Health. She is useful only in one way, namely through her contact with the Egyptian Ambassador, but she is only able to get gossip from him. She moves in a circle where she also meets a number of undesirable people, like Prince Letislan, men such as Busch and also Queen Geraldine of Albania. In general however she is not useful.
3. I used to see an agent called Miss Foster Haal who is secretary to the Turkish Military Attaché, but I have now handed her over

to Brock who deals with Turks. As stated above, she is not much use.

4. Jack Hewit, my boyfriend, about whom we spoke. He was brought up to London to try and contact a man named Father Clement Russell, an ex-British Union of Fascists Roman Catholic priest who is supposed to be pro-German. So far we have not got any definite evidence about him, though there is little doubt that he is still entirely Fascist in sympathy. On the other hand I do not believe that he is either active or powerful. I think he is lying low and praying that the Germans will win the war. He is homosexual and it was hoped to get in touch with him and his circle in this way. In addition Hewit is being used to contact a new agent, Mrs Newman, who keeps a public house called the Dover Castle, off Portland Place where all the Swedish Legation go. I have only just taken her on but she will clearly be able to give me good gossip about the legation, and also to help me get an agent in the legation. I am at present planning to get either the porter, Myhill, or the boy who burns the paper, Bowen. I shall be getting on with this next week. I hope in this way possibly to get hold of some cipher material.

5. Ustinoff, or U35. You have already had a full report about him. I see him rather less at present since our dealings were mainly over the Brochbauer reports. But White is going away for a few weeks and I shall have to deal with a good deal of the contact for him. In any case I can always see him on personal grounds. I think that I once mentioned that he had a sub-agent in the Dutch forces who was in the entourage of Prince Bernhard, and whom it is hoped to use after the war. I have now discovered that his name is Sevat, his father is an art dealer like U35 and I gather that White has plans for developing the connection through the art-dealing business after the war.

In addition to those agents with whom I deal more or less directly, there are others whom I control through Burgess. These are: Eric Kessler, about whom you have already had full reports. Revai, who was taken on recently with the idea that he could give us information about foreign journalists here, Hungarians generally, and also about Swedes as he has the representation of a Swedish paper in England. So far we have not made very much use of him. Pollock, a friend of Burgess, who has been used to make contact with one or two characters such as Brooks, Wachenfeldt, now dropped as uninteresting, and Hiddeduss.

MI5's apparent weakness did not mean that there was no anti-Soviet work at all, conceded Blunt. In fact it was done in a round-about way, through active penetration of the CPGB which, historically, had been the principal Soviet vehicle for espionage and manipulation by the Comintern. This had been demonstrated on several occasions, most recently in the Woolwich Arsenal case where the insertion of Olga Gray into the Communist apparatus, close to Harry Pollitt, had proved so effective as a counter-intelligence measure. Blunt explained that covering the CPGB was the responsibility of David Clark's section, designated F2, which concentrated on tracing the links between the CPGB and the Soviet embassy, and that one of his subordinates, Miss Ogilvy, was particularly assiduous in this work although to date nothing incriminating had been discovered. A microphone concealed in the CPGB's headquarters in King Street had proved very useful, and had helped identify as a CPGB source a secretary in MI5's registry who had expressed much interest in the dossiers kept on the Party's membership.[35]

Kreshin's meetings with Blunt were maintained on a regular basis, once a week according to a report to the Centre dated 10 March 1943, and were held in different parts of London between nine and ten o'clock in the evening. Most of Blunt's information was in documentary form, so a further meeting was held the following morning when the material could be returned. Over a period of two years, Kreshin came to know Blunt quite well:

> Usually at meetings TONY is very apathetic, he comes very tired and forgetful. He speaks very little about his life and he strongly dislikes when this matter is touched on. He is very reserved and in this respect is the opposite of MADCHEN, although they are great friends. TONY is very little interested in political matters, only seldom touches upon them, and only about current events at that. In this respect one has to urge him on sometimes but his answers are primitive, a very weak response to the simplest of political questions is perceptible. The only favourite topic of conversation at meetings is architecture. This is his favourite subject, which he gives all his time to. In spite of his being busy in the HUT he continues to write articles on architecture, to lecture and so on. Partly this explains his weak interest in political life. TONY comes to meetings very punctually. Sometimes he is nervous, but not very strongly so. He may be nervous but he has such a colourless, typical English face, that it is hard to notice it. When he is nervous, he drinks.[36]

In describing the material supplied by Blunt, Kreshin noted that most were MI5's own internal documents, personal files on people targeted for cultivation, wireless intercepts from GC & CS, codenamed RESORT, diplomatic telegrams and German intelligence reports from the Eastern Front, papers obtained by MI5 agents from diplomatic missions, copies of illicitly opened diplomatic mail, weekly summaries of German intelligence radio intercepts, routine military intelligence summaries, codenamed CASINO, MI5 reports on immigrants, telephone intercepts and surveillance reports on suspects. In addition, Kreshin also listed numerous personality profiles of Blunt's MI5 colleagues, including Hugh Shillito, Miss Ogilvy, Dick White and the Director of B Division, Guy Liddell. Indeed, Blunt's references to the last-named were so frequent that the Centre assigned him the codename LIN, although nothing sinister can be extrapolated from this common expedient. Undoubtedly Liddell was indiscreet in his dealings with Burgess and Blunt, whom he trusted completely, particularly when he complained in January 1944 that MI5 had failed to install a single microphone inside the Soviet embassy, but indiscretion and trust were his only crimes.

The Centre's assessment of Blunt's material can be judged from an estimate dated 12 April 1943 which highlighted Moscow's interest in the intelligence summaries from CASINO (military intelligence) about the situation in certain countries and on the Eastern Front; about German intelligence radio networks in the Balkans, and in the Near and Middle East; lists of German and Japanese agents; MI5 reports on CPGB members and a survey conducted by Millicent Bagot of F2(b) about the cultivation of the members of a GRU ring known as the Robson–Gibbons group (about which nothing has ever been published); and an investigation of another low-level GRU case, that of a man named Green, conducted by Hugh Shillito which revealed MI5's methodology, including the use of bugging equipment that had exposed six of Green's fellow conspirators.[37]

The Centre took a special interest in MI5's techniques and objectives, and Blunt's surveillance summaries allowed the *rezidentura* to take appropriate counter-measures. Indeed, as a consequence of advice from Blunt in 1942 and 1943, three important sources in London, codenamed KORONA, VALET and VITYAZ, were temporarily placed on ice because Moscow thought it insecure to use them.

MI5's embarrassing discovery of a CPGB source inside its own registry prompted an internal investigation of Security Service personnel with suspected Communist links, causing Blunt to wonder whether his own early experiments with Marxism and the history of art would re-emerge and embarrass him. However, his close personal knowledge of the staff conducting the enquiry, Shillito, Ogilvy and (Sir) Roger Fulford, gave him confidence and allowed him to exercise some caution. In an undated note in 1943 he mentioned that Shillito 'and Fulford told me also that they were absolutely sure that the Communist Party still has an agent inside MI5.

Burns has heard through the microphone "our girl" there being referred to. Therefore it is supposed that there is either a secretary or somebody else in the registry who works for the Communist Party. It is good that it is a girl they speak about.'[38]

On another occasion, noted in April 1942, Blunt learned that a microphone had been installed in the flat occupied by the flatmate of Elizabeth Shield Collins, who was then married to his old university friend Brian Simon. Blunt promptly severed his connections with them, fearing that he might come up in one of their recorded conversations as someone who had sympathized with the Communists.

Moscow's interest was not limited to the domestic scene in Britain and the Centre was particularly keen to learn more about plans for Allied military operations in Europe and the long-awaited Second Front. On 12 April 1943 the London *rezidentura* received this query about a tip from Blunt concerning Italy which had been confirmed by the GRU, codenamed the NEIGHBOURS:

Will the invasion of Italy be conducted on a large scale or will the main operations be conducted in the Balkans with the aim of moving towards Poland and meeting the Red Army from the West? Contradictory information is spread by the British themselves. Judging by TONY's data it is done according to a plan which has been worked out beforehand, and the British in reality prepare operations against Italy and spread other variants with the aim of disinforming the adversary. The variant of invading Italy coincides with the NEIGHBOURS' data: the capture and holding of Sicily which is considered the first step in bringing Italy out of the war.[39]

Although Blunt had no direct access to this kind of strategic information he kept Moscow's request in mind, and later extracted the relevant information from Marcus Hayward, an MI5 Deputy Director, who had indiscreetly mentioned that the invasion of Italy was scheduled to commence on 8 September with Operation AVALANCHE, a landing near Naples, and BUTTRESS and BAYTOWN further south. Blunt promptly passed this nugget on in a message dated 4 September 1943.[40]

Much of the strategic information supplied through the London *rezidentura* came from enemy wireless intercepts via Blunt and John Cairncross. Blunt had announced his access to ISOS in April 1942[41] and had also relayed ULTRA decrypts from Leo Long (RALPH), causing Moscow to attach the highest importance to this new material, as can be seen from a Red Army intelligence estimate dated 25 May 1943, and signed by Lieutenant-General Ilychyov, on the eve of the Battle of Kursk:

The agents' information about operational orders of the German command on the Soviet–German Front received from you is very valuable and in most cases has been confirmed by other sources or actions conducted by the Germans on the Front. In particular, the information received over the past two or three months exposed a number of important measures taken by the German command which included: (a) regrouping of the 4th Airfleet, and the beginning of mass bombing of our railways on the Voronezh–Rostov line, about which our command was warned several days in advance; (b) The structure of the 1st and 4th Tank and the 6th Armies, the forming of Army Group KAMPF in the Kharkov–Belgorod sector, the forming of Army Group A in the Crimea and the Caucasus; (c) The forming of the 5th and 15th Airborne Divisions, the transfer of units of the 22nd Airborne Division to our front; (d) Substitution of Operation TOTENKOPF on bringing out troops from the Caucasus for Operation NEPTUNE on further holding of the Taman bridgehead and measures connected with this; (e) Creation of a test group of anti-tank planes in the Bryansk direction and other information.

Ilychyov concluded by expressing his belief that the transmission of similar material 'in future is necessary and highly desirable',[42] about as great a compliment as possible from the Red Army, and one repeated to the NKGB's Chief of Intelligence, Pavel M. Fitin, from the Deputy Chief of the General Staff, Lieutenant-General V.I. Kuznetsov. This rare praise encouraged the head of the 3rd Department, Colonel Gaik Ovakimyan, to send a token of his gratitude to TONY and LISZT in the form of £100. Ovakimyan's recommendation was accepted by the NKGB Chief Vsevolod N. Merkulov,[43] Blunt responded on 10 June 1943:

It is difficult to say how proud I feel that the work which I have been doing has been of value in the struggle against Fascism in which we are all engaged. Compared with the heroic tasks which our comrades in the Red Army are performing at home, the work which we are doing here seems trivial but the proof that it is worthwhile will, I hope, provide a stimulus to producing better results. That greater possibilities of useful work will develop I have no doubt, but this will give me renewed energy for pursuing them since I now have positive evidence that the work is valuable.

With the benefit of hindsight one can see that the events of 1943 proved the foundation of a definite turning-point in the course of the war, not just one of military significance for the Red Army, but one which was to have a global impact. It also had the benefit of encouraging agents and sources, and preventing the NKGB hierarchy from taking hasty decisions.

Despite what had been accomplished in military terms, the Centre's relations with the Cambridge ring suffered a setback in the spring of 1943, following an incident with an agent codenamed ABO, as was subsequently recounted by Philby in 1980:

> Once, on my own initiative, I decided to recruit an agent, a Henri Smolka, an Austrian who was the correspondent of the right-wing *Neue Freie Presse*. In spite of working for the magazine, Smolka was hundred percent Marxist, although inactive, lazy and a little cowardly. He had come to England, taken British citizenship, changed his name to Harry Smollett and later had headed the Russian department in the Ministry of Information. I asked him to pass me, on a personal basis, any item that might be of interest, and we arranged that if he had something worthwhile to give me he would take two cigarettes out of a pack, one for me and one for himself, and hold them in the shape of the letter 'V'. We did so several times, and he gave me some really good material. In 1941 [*sic*] I introduced Smollett to Guy Burgess, but six months later he mentioned this recruitment to Gromov [Gorsky]. For acting without official permission I received a severe rebuke.[44]

This account coincides with the explanation offered by Philby to Gorsky and Kreshin in 1943, although in his original version he had given a few more details. He had recruited ABO at the end of 1939, but had lost contact with him while he was in France, resuming it only upon his return in 1940; in any case, Philby had been isolated from the Soviets while the *rezidentura* was suspended until Gorsky came back to London in December 1940. In March 1941, Gorsky forbade any further use of ABO, as his information had been judged to be of no value, but Philby disagreed with this decision, not least because ABO had just been appointed to a new post at the Ministry of Information. A private conference was convened by Philby with Blunt and Burgess, and they concurred that henceforth ABO should be handled by Burgess, who had an excuse to meet him on official business. For his part, Blunt checked ABO's MI5 file, and Burgess passed off ABO's information to the London *rezidentura* as his own. When the *rezidentura* finally displayed some interest in reviving ABO, the trio convened another meeting and agreed to own up to the deception.

Philby's recollection in 1980 of the ABO episode, which he considered mildly amusing, had caused pandemonium in the *rezidentura* and the Centre. Who was Smollett? Might he be a counter-intelligence plant? What was the extent of his knowledge about the Cambridge ring? These were the anxieties that preoccupied Gorsky in London and Ovakimyan in Moscow. Blunt too was challenged because he was close to Burgess and considered more reasonable and reliable. In a note dated 22 April 1943, Blunt responded to the cross-examination with what had really happened: In the spring of 1941, Philby, then based in St Albans, had raised the issue of passing Smollett on to Burgess because he could not get into London often enough to meet him. Blunt, Burgess and Philby had discussed the problem and acknowledged that because of his position in the MoI, Smollett would be useful 'for our work. We came to the conclusion that in this case we should refuse existing rules', by which he meant that they intended to keep Gorsky ignorant of the true situation. 'Guy established contact with Smollett and, as far as I know, got a number of tips from him, owing to which he managed to get very valuable information from other sources.' Blunt had no doubts about Smollett's loyalty, for otherwise Philby would have been exposed, but, when Gorsky renewed his interest in Smollett, he recognized that 'not to tell the true state of affairs would be dishonest' and 'it was better to reveal everything'.[45]

The situation was regarded as serious because Philby had originally consulted the *rezidentura* over the possibility of recruiting Smollett, and Gorsky had advised against it. Thus the trio had defied the *rezident*, who was furious enough to ask the Centre to break off contact with them. Kreshin had refused to support him, concerned that Burgess might turn up at the embassy or even approach the CPGB for help. Fortunately, immediate disaster was averted by the GRU's high regard for Blunt and Cairncross, which was communicated to London.[46] This was followed by a message to London, dated 14 June 1943, which began with the admission that 'our former statements about the unreliability of the majority of probationers from SOHNCHEN's and MADCHEN's group have been confirmed by the ABO incident'. However, the Centre vetoed Gorsky's proposal of 'a break' with the disobedient agents and directed that 'we should as before receive material from them, primarily about the Germans ... Our task is to understand what disinformation our rivals are planting on us.' The Centre further recommended a serious conversation with Burgess to explain that he and his friends had jeopardized the entire Soviet operation. Curiously, Moscow authorized continued contact with Smollett, but forbade the acceptance of any information from him unless it had been specifically authorized by the *rezidentura*.[47] This ambiguity can only be explained by the Centre's apparent recognition that, if the operation had been compromised, no further damage was likely to be sustained, and whatever information was forthcoming ought to be used to Moscow's advantage. Alternatively, it might be interpreted as someone's decision not to kill the goose that was laying such golden eggs.

Gorsky's dramatic confrontation with Burgess took place on 20 July 1943, when the latter admitted to some serious mistakes and promised not to repeat them. The standing of the Cambridge ring was restored, but not for long.[48] New suspicions were aroused by a telegram intercepted by Bletchley Park from the Japanese Ambassador in Berlin, which was copied and passed to the NKVD by Kim Philby. The final paragraph of the text, which the Centre believed contained vital information that was to Britain's disadvantage, was missing from the version delivered by Philby, who explained that GC & CS had failed to decipher it all. This prompted a seven-page memorandum on the Cambridge ring, addressed to Vsevolod Merkulov, Head of the NKVD, and entitled 'About our work with agents SOHNCHEN, MADCHEN, TONY, LISZT and STUART'. This damaging document was based on another report, dated 17 November 1942, by Elena Modrzchinskaya which was an analysis of the information produced by the London *rezidentura*. This initial study suggested that the Cambridge ring was nothing more than an exercise in disinformation, but nevertheless was somewhat ambiguous. Modrzchinskaya opened with the entirely reasonable statement that 'when the British know that this person or that is an agent of a foreign intelligence service, they do not subject him to repression but use him, often unconsciously, as a conduit for disinformation. According to existing data, at present in Britain active work on disinformation is being conducted, the co-ordinating centre of which is the XX Committee of the British Intelligence Services which unites representatives of the various branches of military intelligence, the Secret Intelligence Service and the Counter-intelligence Service.'

Naturally one would like to know the nature of the 'existing data' to which Modrzchinskaya referred: the answer, of course, had to be the very sources that she so distrusted as channels of disinformation, as being incomplete, selective and tending to conceal information about British anti-Soviet operations. The files make it clear that she had no other sources to rely on, which rather undermines her labyrinthine interpretation. This basic contradiction was articulated by an endorsement dated November 1942 on a memorandum by an intelligence chief whose signature is indecipherable: 'The memorandum absolutely fails the tasks set by me and already explained in detail.'[49]

Modrzchinskaya's memorandum remained buried until October 1943, when Philby was judged not to have passed on the crucial part of the Japanese Ambassador's telegram, thus giving her analysis new weight. As a result, yet another report was commissioned into what were perceived by some as the suspicious events associated with the Cambridge ring. This paper began with a bleak denunciation:

> The group of sources SOHNCHEN, MADCHEN, TONY, LISZT and STUART, according to all the data, is known to the British Intelligence organs and works with their knowledge and on their instructions.
>
> There are reasons to believe that SOHNCHEN and MADCHEN even before their contact with us were sent by the British Intelligence Services to work among students with left-wing sympathies in Cambridge.

This interesting proposition was supported by the assertion that 'TONY is politically indifferent, SOHNCHEN and MADCHEN make politically incorrect judgments.' It was also 'difficult to suppose' that, moving among students well-disposed towards Communism, the sources had not come under the scrutiny of British Counter-Intelligence, or that details of 'this group' had not reached the ears of MI5. Therefore,

> to all appearances, they had been connected with the British Intelligence organs since before we recruited them and before the beginning of their official work in British Intelligence. Nor can one suppose that the British would entrust such responsible work to people who in the past had been connected with the Communist Party without first checking on them and ensuring their loyalty. Nor can one suppose that in such a busy period of contact with the Soviet Intelligence Service the sources could not have fallen under the surveillance which is conducted against all Soviet personnel in Britain by Counter-Intelligence.

Thus Modrzchinskaya impugned the professionalism of the London *rezidentura*, even though the Centre must have known her charge to be baseless because none of the *rezidentura*'s staff had featured in any of the routine MI5 surveillance reports supplied by Blunt. Undaunted, Modrzchinskaya continued her critique: 'The following facts speak in favour of the supposition about the connection of these agents with British Intelligence before their connection with us, and supports the opinion that they were planted into our network by the British: SOHNCHEN and MADCHEN come from the families of prominent British intelligence officers.' In reality, of course, Burgess's stepfather, Colonel John Bassett, as a professional soldier had only the most peripheral connections with intelligence, while Philby's father had served briefly in the Indian Intelligence Bureau. 'TONY and MADCHEN had visited the Soviet Union', in 1934, a visit 'certainly not unknown to the British Intelligence organs'; and 'MADCHEN had met the British *rezident* Wickstead on the instructions of Pears, the chief of intelligence of the British mission to the Kolchak headquarters.'

But were Wickstead and Pears really the master spies the NKVD had taken them for? Certainly Professor Alexander Wickstead, a longtime English expatriate resident in Moscow whom Burgess met on his 1934 trip, was no British agent, but actually a committed Marxist and admirer of the Soviet system. However, in the small world of the British élite which predominantly had attended just two universities, it was perfectly possible to have entirely innocent contact with people judged by the Kremlin to be dangerous. Even the most tenuous connection with Admiral Aleksandr V. Kolchak would have been calculated to arouse suspicion, even though he had been shot by the Bolsheviks in February 1920. Formerly Commander in Chief of the Tsar's Black Sea Fleet, he had played a key role in the Allied intervention in the Russian Civil War, his name revered by the Whites and loathed by the Communists.

The 'suspicious understatement' regarding British Intelligence efforts against the Soviets mentioned by SOHNCHEN and MADCHEN also featured in Modrzchinskaya's analysis. 'Not a single valuable British agent in the USSR or in the Soviet embassy in Britain has been exposed with the help of this group,' she complained, 'in spite of the fact that if they had been sincere in their co-operation they easily could have done.' The possibility that such agents never existed did not occur to the author, who found it sinister that 'the large amount of valuable documentary material about the activities of our adversary, which this group gives to us, does not conflict with the interests of the British and serves only as evidence of the value of these sources.'

MADCHEN and TONY were accused of seeking 'in every possible way to perform the function of talent-spotters and recruiters for us, trying to plant the qualified British Intelligence officers Scafe, Footman, Johnston into our network'. Clearly the proposition that men of the calibre of David Footman and Kemball Johnston could be approached to spy was regarded in Moscow as preposterous. Besides, MADCHEN 'suggested that he should be sent to do recruitment work for us to Oxford and Cambridge'. Modrzchinskaya also condemned TONY for 'incomprehensible carelessness concerning

security' and because he 'continues to pass over to us original documents' instead of photographing them. During the past year he had
filled 327 rolls of film, and had never failed to bring at least a
hundred documents to each meeting, but in noting these impressive
statistics, Modrzchinskaya expressed the view that Blunt's lack of
photographic skill was nothing more than a ploy to allow MI5 to
develop an alternative strategy at a later date.

Naturally Modrzchinskaya interpreted the ABO incident in the
worst possible light, together with MADCHEN's offer to murder
Goronwy Rees. This latter episode is one of the most astonishing
in the history of the Cambridge ring, not least because it was interpreted as yet another deliberate provocation intended to entrap the
network. It is now clear that Guy Burgess really wanted to kill Rees,
whom he saw as a potential threat.

At a meeting held at the beginning of July 1943, Burgess unexpectedly raised the issue, thought to have been settled months earlier,
of disconnecting Goronwy Rees, codenamed GROSS and later FLIT,
from the other members of the Cambridge ring. He confirmed that
Rees knew about his co-operation with the Soviets, and Blunt's,
and suggested that since he might let the cat out of the bag, he
ought to be 'removed'. This was the subject of a report from the
rezidentura dated 9 July, which was immediately characterized by
the Centre as an outrageous provocation mounted by either MI5
or SIS. At a subsequent meeting with Gorsky on 20 July, held
specifically to discuss ABO, Burgess again returned to the potential
problem presented by Rees saying that he was a 'hysterical and
unbalanced person' who had not betrayed Burgess and Blunt
because of 'personal friendship and attachment' but was capable of
doing so 'at any moment', which meant that they were living under
'the sword of Damocles'. In Burgess's opinion 'the only way out of
the situation was the physical liquidation of FLIT'. Since he was
personally responsible for Rees's recruitment, Burgess declared that
he was prepared to take on the task himself.

When Modrzchinskaya examined this proposal she concluded
that 'in the light of our suspicions about MADCHEN his offer concerning FLIT deserves most serious attention since the British Counter-Intelligence Service, as was seen from the interrogation of
Krivitsky, studies the question of our using methods of liquidation'.[50] Once again, Modrzchinskaya overlooked the NKVD's
source for its copy of the Krivitsky interrogation – an MI5 document
supplied by Blunt.

In retrospect it is clear that Burgess's romantic enthusiasm for
espionage and his position in British society were not always under-

stood by the Centre's analysts, working from long-distance. Burgess's work for MI5 and SIS, which he had only initiated on instructions from Deutsch, caused endless suspicion and this cast a shadow across the entire Cambridge ring. Based in Moscow, Boris Kreshin came to the view, minuted on 17 March 1940, that Burgess 'was and is an Intelligence Service agent',[51] because of his inexplicable behaviour and his request for a passport under another name to be used in the case of exposure. However, once he had been given the opportunity to work with Burgess in London, Kreshin changed his mind and in June 1942 reported that

> the most difficult task for every one of us is to give this or that characterization to MADCHEN. Before I came here and before I came in contact with him I had a certain prejudice, like every one of us who knows him by material and not personally. MADCHEN has produced a far better impression on me than that which I got from materials and characterizations at home. His distinguishing feature in comparison with other agents I meet is bohemianism in its most unattractive form. He is a young, interesting, clever enough, cultured, inquisitive, shrewd person, reads much and knows much. But at the same time with these qualities he is untidy, goes about dirty, drinks much and leads the so-called life of the gilded youth ... He is well grounded politically and theoretically ... in conversation quotes Marx, Lenin and Stalin.[52]

In support of the view that Burgess must be genuine, Kreshin cited the moment when he had asked him to return some already photographed documents to Blunt. 'He became very frightened and flushed, was excited as though not himself and all but trembled. I had to calm him down and say that I hadn't expected such cowardice from him. This incident is very characteristic from the psychological aspect. If he were an *agent provocateur* he would have absolutely nothing to fear.'

Kreshin and Gorsky elaborated on this theme in a message to the Centre dated 25 October 1942:

> MADCHEN is a very peculiar person and to apply ordinary standards to him would be the roughest mistake. Having become convinced of this here on the spot as a result of all our experience with MADCHEN we cannot cite a single concrete fact which would absolutely indisputably testify to MADCHEN being a double agent.[53]

One is bound to wonder whether Burgess ever realized he had fallen under the *rezidentura*'s suspicion; as a sensitive individual, he must have sensed some unease. In the beginning of April 1943, just as the ABO affair was being discussed with Philby and Blunt,

Burgess himself had confided to Kreshin that 'he had gained the impression that the comrades treated him, TONY and SOHNCHEN with a kind of mistrust and that he did not understand it'. Kreshin had brushed the comment aside, putting it down to Burgess's 'imagination', an overreaction to his surprising assertion that the British were not mounting operations against the Soviets, statements that 'were incomprehensible and, it is quite clear, cause surprise on our part'.[54] Burgess quickly latched on to this remark, as Kreshin described:

> MADCHEN said that in connection with this the following conclusions could be made, namely (1) the British do not work against us; (2) the British know about the organization and they feed just that information which does not touch on matters of work against us; (3) that SOHNCHEN, TONY and MADCHEN may be double agents. Analysing these questions MADCHEN said that if the British knew about their work with us neither TONY nor SOHNCHEN could occupy such jobs in such establishments. Proceeding from this the first conclusion remains: the British at present do not conduct the above work against us.[55]

Kreshin avoided being drawn into such a delicate discussion and answered that he could not speculate and was solely interested in more concrete information. The memorandum continued its pursuit of the double agent theory, noting that

> The British are interested in the continuation of this group of sources for feeding disinformation through them, planting other agents of theirs and having the opportunity to carry out a provocation against the Soviet Intelligence Service at any advantageous moment. We are interested in retaining this group of sources in order to discourage the British from looking for our other agents by our refusal to make contact with them; and also because this group of agents nevertheless gives valuable information about the German adversary.[56]

Thus the report concluded that the link to the Cambridge ring should not be severed, but a new approach to supervising its operations should be adopted.

The whole of the memorandum about the Cambridge ring reflected the author's one-sided attitude to the agents in London, and his prejudices are very evident in his analysis which ended on a rather ambiguous note. Of course, all intelligence agencies regularly conduct independent audits on their sources to double-check on their reliability, a standard procedure for ensuring the continuing security of operations and the integrity of the sources themselves; but this study was an attempt to understand the inexplicable by someone who had reached an opinion before the evidence was assessed. His tendency to assume the worst can be seen as an attempt at self-protection, and perhaps an erroneous application of the classic assumption that the adversary is cleverer and stronger than oneself. The trips to the Soviet Union made by Burgess and Blunt are seen as missions on behalf of British Intelligence to contact the local British Intelligence representative, and no consideration was given to their true motive, simply a desire by two Communist sympathizers to visit the birthplace of Socialism. As for Burgess's suggestions for recruitment, and Philby and Burgess's involvement with ABO, these were surely examples of the sources seeking to fulfil their role as well as possible, even if they were a little unskilled and over-zealous for their own good.

As for the proposed liquidation of Goronwy Rees, this was probably nothing more than an attack of panic by Burgess, tormented by his conscience and anxious to protect himself and Blunt against the threat of exposure. The report's author never tried to see Burgess in terms of an ordinary person seeking to rid himself of the sword of Damocles by a method more prevalent in fiction and the cinema. Indeed, by 1945 the situation had changed dramatically:

> Now, when several years have passed and we have had the opportunity to become convinced of his honesty, his offer to liquidate FLIT can be explained by nothing else but HICKS's unbalanced character and the usual sense of fear of being exposed.[57]

(HICKS was yet another codename for Burgess.)

The original author was never able to identify precisely what disinformation had been peddled by the Cambridge ring, although the report emphasizes what was considered a deliberate under-estimate of MI5 and SIS operations against the Soviets. In reality, of course, MI5 did not work directly against the Soviets or the embassy staff, as Blunt had confirmed, but had kept the CPGB under scrutiny. As for SIS's activities, they had been handicapped by the Head of Station's transfer from Moscow to Kuibyshev with the rest of the foreign diplomats (where conditions were hardly conducive to anti-Soviet operations, as Philby had already pointed out), and were constantly the subject of intensive surveillance by the local security apparatus. Certainly neither Philby nor Blunt had attempted to conceal British liaison with their anti-Soviet Czech and Polish intelligence counterparts, and finally there was the disclosure of ISOS, and the very admission that ULTRA even existed. That would have been an astonishingly high price to pay for the potential advantage of planting agents in the Soviet network, particularly when one considered that five members of the Cambridge ring held posts in the most sensitive parts of the British establishment.

Having read the memorandum, and recognizing the very high value of the material already supplied by the Cambridge ring, Vsevolod Merkulov made an entry on Burgess's file in which he 'cautioned against premature conclusions and suggested checking more thoroughly on the sincerity of this group of sources in working with us'.

Despite Merkulov's caution, the Centre sent a directive dated 25 October 1943 to London ordering the *rezidentura* to take great care in handling the group in the future. It referred to the breaches of discipline committed by Philby, Blunt and Burgess, and drew attention to the unpalatable fact that each knew about the other's activities.[58] As for the diplomat Donald Maclean, Modrzhinskaya had been unable to make any kind of a case against him, and therefore had concluded that he had been manipulated unwittingly by the others. This crisis in confidence was to be settled by, of all people, Philby.

Together the Centre and the *rezidentura* undertook a classic check to verify the authenticity of the Cambridge ring's information by comparing it with similar material acquired from other sources through independent channels. The results of this searching enquiry was submitted by Pavel Fitin, Chief of Intelligence, to Merkulov on 22 August 1944:

> In the process of carrying out your instructions of 13 October 1943 about the check on the sincerity of SOHNCHEN, MADCHEN, TONY, LISZT and STUART, the sources of the London *rezidentura* working with us, we gave SOHNCHEN instructions to get information on co-operation between the Ministry of Economic Warfare and the Soviet service. On 13 June 1944 we received through SOHNCHEN the HOTEL file N95670 about 'Contact and Co-operation between the British and Soviet Intelligence Services'.

The comparative analysis then noted that analogous material had been obtained from another independent and reliable channel and that when it was examined it was found that 'the text of the separate documents fully coincided'. In particular, a list of British documents used in the study were attached:

> Telegrams N1507–1511 in which the question of the worsening relations between the Ministry of Economic Warfare, Special Operations Executive and the NKVD is looked into; A study of the case of Erich Vermehren, an Abwehr officer who had defected to the British in Turkey; About the refusal of the British to hand over

Vermehren's interrogation notes to our organs; About the anti-Soviet activity of German Intelligence in Turkey; About NKVD suspicions regarding SOE's Swedish-based operations against the Baltic countries; A study of the case of a Hindu, Bkhagat Ram, and his unjustified detention in India.[59]

As well as these top secret SIS documents, Philby also passed on many files, 'the contents of which rules out any premeditation on the part of the Intelligence Service to pass them over to us through SOHNCHEN'. Singled out was a document dated 3 July 1942 in which the Deputy Chief of SIS remarked that 'we mustn't make mistakes, we can't trust the Russians in the same way as, let us say, the Czechs or the Americans or give them information which can betray an important or sensitive source or allow officers of the local unit of Soviet Intelligence to obtain information about our organization somewhere.' In another paper, dated 17 July 1942 and headed *Co-operation with the Russians*, its author wrote that 'our policy concerning co-operation with the Russians is the following:– We cannot cooperate with them openly, in order not to compromise ourselves ... we have an opportunity to break off this so-called cooperation at any moment without damaging ourselves.'

As well as these documents, which were more politically sensitive than operationally awkward for SIS, the report acknowledged that other evidence from sources unconnected with the Cambridge ring endorsed the authenticity of Philby's material. Pavel Fitin's final summary concluded:

> Taking into account that sources are connected with each other and each knows about the connection of the other with us, the received proofs of the authenticity of material passed over to us by source SOHNCHEN positively characterizes the work of this group in general.[60]

'Good', scribbled Merkulov on 22 August 1944, authorizing further 'contact with this group with even more care'. That ended the long period of suspicion which had undermined Soviet confidence in the reliability of the Cambridge ring. From the Soviet files it is clear that the NKVD made a colossal miscalculation, based mainly on Soviet ignorance of British society, overlaid with a baffling certainty that the British intelligence agencies must have suspected Philby, Blunt and the rest, when in fact each enjoyed total trust. It took two years for the Centre to dismiss the proposition that the Cambridge ring was an elaborate device invented by 'the competitors' and in at least one regard, the British approach to Soviet espionage had been justified. By concentrating MI5's limited resources on the CPGB, rather than the embassy, it succeeded in breaking the important Woolwich Arsenal case in 1938, achieving a counter-intelligence triumph. Surveillance on the embassy would not have led the Security Service to Percy Glading and his fellow conspirators, whereas penetration of the CPGB had yielded impressive dividends.

The debate about the trustworthiness of the Cambridge ring was conducted at the Centre and inside the London *rezidentura*, so none of the members ever realized the scale of the doubt that had tainted their activities. Blunt, for instance, never received any hint of the crisis and nothing compromising was said on this topic at any of his scheduled meetings which continued to be conducted according to a regular routine. Indeed, his usefulness grew as he gained in seniority inside the Security Service. In the autumn of 1943 he was appointed MI5's representative on various inter-service Whitehall committees dealing with strategic deception, a position that allowed him to advise the Soviets on the crucial subject of the Second Front. In a message dated 15 September 1943, Blunt described the role of the Bevan organization, headed by Colonel John Bevan, who was in charge of co-ordinating deception plans for the invasion of Europe. Blunt joined the sub-committee known as TORY, which drew up a report in October 1943 for the Chiefs of Staff on the measures required to deceive the enemy about the Allied landings in France and later worked on SHAEF's deception scheme for the Mediterranean.

In May 1944, Blunt was attached to Noel Wild's planning group and handed the Soviets the Cabinet paper written by Sir Findlater Stewart on the precautions taken to protect the security of the invasion. On 26 May he passed on a copy of the entire deception plan for OVERLORD and, on 3 June, three days before D-Day, he met his controller and disclosed details of an imaginative deception scheme intended to convey the impression that General Mont-gomery had been posted to the Mediterranean in anticipation of an invasion there. In an operation codenamed COPPERHEAD, an actor who bore a close resemblence to Monty was flown to Gibraltar, supposedly for a high-level conference. That the general's presence had been spotted by German agents became clear when Bletchley Park intercepted an enemy signal reporting the news, and according to Blunt, further confirmation that the deception had achieved its objective was obtained from a German double agent under MI5's control who was instructed to determine Monty's whereabouts. His reply simply stated that he was not in London, thereby adding collateral to the German evidence. This episode was followed on 7 July 1944 by Blunt's gift of a comprehensive account of MI5's B

Division's role in deception and, in particular, the use of double agents.

Blunt's productivity as a Soviet agent was prodigious: files on the most esoteric topics were copied and handed to the *rezidentura*.[61] Typical was a summary of MI5's efforts aimed at the Swedish Embassy in London. On 29 October 1943, Blunt reported that a very accurate German analysis of British aircraft production had fallen into British hands, which had caused consternation in London. MI5 suspected that the information had been compiled by a neutral service attaché and the Swedish air attaché named Servell had become the subject of intensive surveillance which had included the tapping of the embassy telephones, the recruitment of a source in the building, and the interception of the Swedish diplomatic bag at a special centre in Aberdeen. The evidence suggested that Servell had been responsible for the leak, and that he had relied upon gossip from an indiscreet American air attaché and a certain Captain Kenely Bartlett, a director of an aircraft company. Blunt recommended that he should deliver a sharp warning to the US air attaché, Colonel Tamar, and that Bartlett should be sacked immediately, without explanation, but MI5 was worried that this would compromise their sources. Instead a microphone was installed in Servell's flat and in Bartlett's office.[62]

Predictably, the Soviets were fascinated by MI5's procedure for inserting listening devices. Blunt explained that upon an officer's recommendation Guy Liddell endorsed an application which was then passed to Brigadier Jasper Harker, MI5's Deputy Director, for approval. Having gained his initials it went to the Home Secretary for a warrant which, if signed, was sent to Sir Raymond Birchall at the Post Office, and to the Foreign Office if diplomatic premises were involved. Once sanctioned, the technical work was undertaken by an MI5 officer who arranged for the target's telephone service to be disrupted, and then had his own personnel masquerade as repairman to install a microphone inside the instrument itself.[63]

Blunt also volunteered a mass of information about Dr Erich Vermehren, the German intelligence officer who had been persuaded to defect to SIS in December 1943 in Istanbul. A devout Christian, Vermehren gave SIS's Section Ve a wealth of information about the Abwehr's operations in Turkey which fascinated the Soviets. Another of the files he compromised was a summary of German Intelligence activity in the Baltic, as well as a memorandum on the wireless equipment issued to Abwehr agents which disclosed details of a new code, known as 111/333,[64] which had been brought to London from Lisbon by a spy named Hvesterling.[65]

Among the other crown jewels copied by Blunt, who had now received promotion to the rank of Assistant Director in B Division were: details of the cultivation of the Turkish Ambassador in London by an MI5 agent designated W/69; Shillito's monthly report for the Prime Minister on CPGB activity; a progress report on the penetration by agents of the CPGB branches in Sheffield, Glasgow and London;[66] details of conversations with Guy Liddell about B Division's current operations.[67] Blunt's key position inside MI5's counter-espionage branch gave him access to numerous other organizations through his inter-departmental committee work, including the Imperial Security Committee headed by Sir Herbert Creedy and the Home Defence Committee chaired by Sir Findlater Stewart. Altogether, Blunt gave the Soviets a total of 1,771 documents between 1941 and 1945, the most active period of his espionage.[68] Of this vast collection, only two volumes survive in Moscow's archives: one is entirely devoted to ISOS intercepts and the second is largely concerned with a single case, that of a Russian White Guard known as EMIGRANT B.

On 15 September 1944, when the end of the war was already in sight, Blunt attended a meeting with the *rezidentura* and explained that he proposed to return to civilian life, but that he had received an assurance from Guy Liddell that the Security Service would maintain contact with all its former staff, hold regular meetings and arrange annual training sessions.[69] One of the first to leave, in April 1945, was David Clark, formerly of F Division, who went straight to a post in the Conservative Party's Central Office.[70] Kemball Johnston left on 25 July and in October Blunt reported that Shillito had been succeeded by an officer named Spencer.[71] Blunt himself took up the prestigious appointment of Surveyor of the King's Pictures on 28 April 1945, but remained working for one or two days a week at MI5.[72] During his remaining period with the Security Service he undertook two important missions, to the home of the Duke of Brunswick in Germany in August 1945 to select works of art connected with the history of Britain and, although officially demobbed on 6 September, he flew to Rome on 19 September, on an MI5 assignment that lasted three weeks, to undertake a trawl through the archives of the Italian security and intelligence services.[73] Although apparently mundane, this mission proved exceptionally valuable to the Soviets who received confirmation that their source inside the pre-war British Embassy codenamed DUNCAN had also been in the pay of the Italians (see Chapter Five). Furthermore, it was clear that DUNCAN's duplicity had become known to the British.

Shortly before the end of hostilities in Europe the Centre started to consider rewards for its most valued sources, and Fitin was instructed to recommend individual agents to Merkulov for special recognition. Among the British sources deemed to have made a particularly important contribution to the victory was Philby, who was to be granted an annual pension of £1,500, with £1,200 each for Burgess, Blunt, Cairncross and Maclean.[74] However, before submitting his nominations, Fitin asked the London *rezidentura* to talk to the members of the Cambridge ring and in May Kreshin cabled Moscow: 'All PROBATIONERS have refused pensions because it would be difficult for them to explain the existence of large sums of money.' Instead the sources suggested that they be compensated for their operational expenses, and this was accepted.[75] The reward demonstrates how their status had been restored in the Centre's estimation. Burgess, of course, had been denounced by Elena Modrzhinskaya as a very dubious source, and in the first half of 1944 Moscow had complained that he had supplied very little in the way of documents, merely plenty of reports in manuscript which 'present great interest but the information is based on hearsay and is badly processed'. By October 1944, Merkulov had authorized the payment of a bonus of £250 to Burgess,[76] who had become much more productive. Having left the BBC on 3 June, he had joined the Foreign Office's Press Department, apparently with some help from the London *rezidentura*, the exact nature of which remains tantalizingly secret; it seems that Maclean's departure for the United States was the catalyst for advancing Burgess's career. After his appointment to the Foreign Office Burgess supplied 4,404 documents, out of a total of 4,605 for 1941-5, only exceeded by John Cairncross who is credited with the delivery of 5,832 papers from the Foreign Office, Bletchley Park and SIS during the same period. In contrast, Philby's file shows he sent 914 documents. Maclean supplied 4,593.[77]

During the period 5 May to 3 June 1944, Burgess kept his desk at the BBC while installing himself at the Foreign Office. On 30 May he took the opportunity to extract the first of a series of classified papers, a Ministry of Economic Warfare decision, regarding the Ministry's internal reorganization dated 18 April 1944, to transfer responsibility for economic intelligence to the Foreign Office.

Burgess's arrival at the Press Department marked a turning-point in his clandestine career and the Centre was overwhelmed by the breadth and abundance of papers now available to MADCHEN, now known as HICKS. His productivity was so large that on 2 December 1944 the *rezidentura* was asked 'whether HICKS uses sources unknown to us because information received from him is wide in scope and deals with a variety of questions'.[78] London reassured the Centre that the Press Department received virtually all the Foreign Office's output. In August this was particularly evident when Burgess achieved something of a coup by supplying telegrams from Duff Cooper MP, then the British representative on the French Committee of National Liberation in Algeria. In a six-page message, addressed to Anthony Eden and dated 30 May 1944, Cooper had suggested the creation of a strong Poland to counter-balance the Soviets, with a Western bloc of countries to act as a buffer. Eden's reply, on 25 July, insisted that Britain's post-war policy must be based on co-operation with the Soviet Union, a sentiment confirmed by the Centre through other channels.

In August 1944, Burgess received permission from the head of his department to take documents home at night, and this resulted in the *rezidentura* reporting on 1 September that 'MADCHEN has for the first time brought a large number of authentic materials. We have photographed ten rolls of film, six of them decrypted telegrams.' Kreshin noted that at their meeting, 'MADCHEN had become intensely and noticeably nervous. This is normal', no doubt recalling his reaction when asked to return MI5 documents to Blunt.[79]

The idea of Burgess handling original Foreign Office papers caused some anxiety in Moscow and in October 1944 the *rezidentura* was reminded that 'such removal is dangerous for the agent' and told that the source should 'concentrate attention on strategic and big issue information'. Despite the caution, Moscow was obviously delighted by what Burgess had achieved, as disclosed on 24 October 1944: 'In the recent period, in the course of only several months, MADCHEN has become the most productive source . . . now he gives most valuable documentary material.'[80]

The Centre's fear about the drunken Burgess walking around London carrying secret papers was not unfounded, as Kreshin reported on 4 March 1945, describing 'a rather unpleasant incident':

Recently I have been meeting HICKS in the street. But on 4 March it was raining and HICKS suggested going into a pub for a short while. We went inside where we spent no more than fifteen minutes. Having left the pub I noticed that he was not coming out. Setting the door ajar I saw that HICKS was picking up materials on the floor. Without entering the pub I waited in the street until HICKS came out. He announced that when he had approached the door the ZAKOULOK [Foreign Office] materials had fallen out of his briefcase onto the floor. The telegrams had fallen face downwards and nobody paid attention because the door was screened from the pub by a curtain.

Only one telegram had become dirty. HICKS claims that he thoroughly inspected the place and not a single document remained on the floor.[81]

Kreshin delivered a lecture on personal security, but when Burgess returned to collect the copied documents, with his briefcase tied up with string, he dropped them again. 'It was good that there was no one else in the lavatory and the floor was clean,' he commented.

As well as having to cope with Burgess's inherent lack of security, the *rezidentura* dealt with other hazards. In November 1944, Burgess informed Kreshin that Goronwy Rees had been offered a job by David Footman in SIS's Political Section, designated Section I. He was concerned that Rees might blab about his former association with the Soviets, and together he and Kreshin constructed an elaborate alibi in case Burgess was ever challenged. Burgess was to say that he had approached Rees on behalf of GRENADIER (the codename for Lawrence Grand, who had founded and headed Section D, the SIS sabotage unit), but, to conceal that organization's existence, he had claimed to be working for the Communist Party. However, rather than take the risk of relying on this rather lame explanation, Burgess talked Footman out of employing Rees in SIS, and reported this success to Kreshin in March 1945.[82]

Burgess had always enjoyed a close relationship with MI5 and had even run an agent, codenamed SWISS, on their behalf. His move to the Foreign Office did not end the link, as was demonstrated by a request from Kemball Johnston, writing from PO Box 550, Oxford, the postal cover address of MI5's wartime headquarters at Blenheim Palace. He was seeking information about one of Burgess's new colleagues, Frank Ashton-Gwatkin, a senior diplomat who was supposedly connected with an Austrian, Anton Bon.[83] According to Johnston, 'Ashton-Gwatkin conducts far from angelic activity in the Foreign Office'; this assignment gave Burgess an opportunity to remain in contact with the Security Service, though doubtless it occurred to him that one day he might be in the same position as Ashton-Gwatkin.

At a meeting held on 11 August 1945, Burgess expressed optimism about the recent Labour Party election landslide and explained that two of his friends, the Labour MPs Hector McNeil and John Strachey, had been given junior ministerial appointments in the Foreign Office and the Ministry of Aviation respectively. Burgess intended to cultivate McNeil, but all plans were suspended following a meeting on 20 September at which an agitated Burgess delivered 'an exceptionally urgent message from Philby' who wanted a rendezvous the following day.[84] Apparently Philby had called on him at the Foreign Office and had given him an envelope to pass on to Boris Kreshin (MAX) the same evening; he cautioned Burgess to take exceptional care, which was why, unusually, he had not brought any Foreign Office documents with him. Kreshin, of course, recognized that such an unprecedented breach of tradecraft indicated a crisis: his judgement was correct, for the envelope contained Philby's account of the intended defection in Istanbul of a NKGB officer named Konstantin Volkov.

The recent defection of the GRU cipher clerk Igor Gouzenko in Ottawa, followed by this unexpected development in Turkey, led the Soviets to suspend most of their operations in London until the end of 1946. Minimal contact was maintained with Blunt, who was considered out of danger because he was at the Courtauld Institute, and Philby, whose position in SIS gave him the best possible vantage point from which to monitor MI5's enquiries into Gouzenko's testimony.[85] On 17 January 1946, Kreshin reported that 'In STANLEY's [Philby's] opinion, the situation is not quite favourable yet and it is better not to establish contact with HICKS in the meanwhile.' Philby gave similar advice about Blunt, and in October 1946 the Centre directed the *rezidentura* 'to break off contact with ATHLETES [agents] completely for a while' and to work on the basis that contact would be resumed sometime in the future.[86]

Despite the official suspension of operations, the Cambridge ring remained in existence. In May 1946, Blunt passed a note via Philby reporting the imminent arrival in London of Michael Straight who, he said, 'in principle remains our man' although his views were now at variance with the Communist Party, and especially with the CPUSA.[87] Blunt also held two meetings, on 16 September and 9 December 1946, at which he relayed some important information including details of MI5's recent reorganization, received from friends still inside the organization, and data from Leo Long (RALPH) about the Intelligence Division of the Control Commission for Germany, where he now worked.

Meanwhile Philby had been active, reporting on a recruitment pitch made by an SIS officer named Merick to a Soviet Army officer, and news of his own posting in January 1947 to Istanbul. For his part, Burgess was appointed Hector McNeil's personal assistant from 1 January, and in a note dated 9 December, passed by Blunt, he described how he could exploit his new position by gaining access to the kind of documents used to formulate Britain's foreign policy.[88] The Centre was sufficiently impressed by what Burgess had accomplished that Kreshin was made personally responsible for translating his communications and, on the order of General Petr V. Fedotov dated 9 January 1947, the number of people initiated into the HICKS case was limited to four or five. Security was so tight that even typists were excluded from access to his product.

Burgess took his isolation badly, or so Blunt reported, and it is ironic that he achieved the pinnacle of official access at a moment when the Soviets could not risk direct contact. For a man of whom Arnold Deutsch had said that the essence of his existence was his clandestine work for the cause, it can be imagined that the solitude must have been hard to bear. On 6 January, in a letter signed JIM, he wrote to MAX (Kreshin) expressing his delight at 'the wonderful news from FRED [Blunt] that there is a definite possibility of resuming contact soon'. To understand how Burgess was consumed by his secret life, one can turn to some of his earlier correspondence. On 16 September 1946 he wrote:

> I am writing with a pencil because (1) I am trying to write this only in the last moment before my meeting with FRED in the evening (2) I am writing in the lavatory and in such a place an inkpot is unsafe from any point of view.[89]

In fact contact with Burgess was resumed early in 1947 following special permission granted by the Minister for State Security, Colonel-General Viktor S. Abakumov. On the suggestion of Fedotov, the meeting was to be used to obtain information about the forthcoming four-power conference of foreign ministers in Moscow, and to introduce Kreshin's replacement in London, Mikhail F. Shishkin, codenamed ADAM, who was to operate under press attaché cover at the embassy.[90] The meeting took place on 5 March, and Burgess's documents proved so useful that Abakumov authorized a bonus for him of £500.[91]

During the suspension of operations Blunt acted as a go-between for Burgess and Philby, and he continued his role during the subsequent periods, from June to October 1947, and between February and March 1948 when contact was broken again.[92] Thus, unexpectedly, Blunt was restored as a key player in the Cambridge ring, photographing Foreign Office documents for Burgess, as was agreed with Shishkin at a meeting on 20 January 1948. He was invariably alone in his apartment on the top of the Courtauld Institute in the evenings and was therefore free to use a camera, a second-hand Leica with which he soon became adept.[93] At a meeting on 20 December 1948, 'ROSS [Nikolai Rodin] told JOHNSON [Blunt] that the Paris treaty photographed by him came out perfectly.'

On 22 March 1948, Blunt reported that MI5 had stepped up its surveillance of Soviets and had intensified its telephone tapping at the embassy, including installing a microphone into the military attaché's handset.[94] Blunt's information came from indiscreet Security Service personnel, as he explained in terms which were less than complimentary about the ineffectual Director-General Sir Percy Sillitoe:

> Dick White is too correct in his manner and will never gossip on matters connected with work like Guy Liddell or Robertson. Hollis is also correct and almost hostile. John Marriott sometimes talks, but he isn't overfond of me ... With good contact with Liddell and Robertson I think I will be able to get information about MI5 activity interesting enough for us ... Guy Liddell is Deputy Director but, taking into account that the Director himself is only a puppet he, in essence, is in the know of all current affairs and issues.[95]

Blunt's other sources included David Boyle, an SIS section head and the Chief's adviser on interception, who had approached him for help in developing new techniques for opening diplomatic mail and had disclosed details of a secret wireless intercept centre in Cairo which read Arab diplomatic traffic;[96] and the head of MI5's B4 section, Colonel T.A. Robertson, the mastermind of the wartime double agent operations, who consulted Blunt on anti-Soviet projects. Indeed, in January 1948, Blunt reported that Robertson had confided that 'the difficulty is that we can't clear up anything about Russian espionage' and asked him to let him know if any useful ideas occurred to him.[97] On 9 January 1949 and again in May, Blunt described how Malcolm Cumming, a senior MI5 officer, had asked him for permission to use a room in the Courtauld Institute to hold meetings with agents recruited inside various Eastern Bloc embassies in London. Naturally, Blunt agreed with alacrity and handed the keys of a room on the ground floor to MI5's Leslie Jagger who gave access to his colleagues George Leggett[98] and Norman Darbyshire. When Shishkin suggested that this MI5 operation might inhibit the copying of Burgess's documents, Blunt assured him that his possession of the Leica was entirely justified and that no one could enter his room while he was at work with his camera. By September 1949, at least one meeting with a foreign MI5 agent had been conducted at the Courtauld.[99]

Although the Cambridge ring's operations had been restored, danger still lurked. On the evening of 21 January 1949, Blunt and Shishkin's temporary replacement that day, Nikolai Rodin (or Korovin), codenamed ROSS, were stopped in Montagu Square and questioned by two detectives. They searched Blunt's briefcase, which contained a package of Burgess's Foreign Office files he had not yet had time to photograph. Fortunately the documents were wrapped in brown paper, and the policemen made only the most cursory examination, but they kept a note of Blunt's name, claiming that their patrol was entirely routine in response to an increase in crime in the area.[100] The Centre immediately imposed restrictions on contact with Blunt, but these were relaxed once Moscow was satisfied that the incident had no sinister connotations. Indeed, a few months later, in August 1949, Burgess had much the same experience: he was stopped when carrying a parcel containing towels belonging to his club. He took the opportunity to find out why the police asked his name, and discovered that the sole purpose was in case the member of the public concerned lodged a complaint about his treatment, news that served to reassure Blunt and the Centre.[101]

Burgess's standing at the Foreign Office was high, and the fact that he continued to be trusted was shown on 15 March 1948 when Hector McNeil asked him to report anybody suspicious on the staff. Nevertheless Burgess exercised greater care in contacting the Soviets, and restricted himself on this occasion to handing over the text of the Brussels agreement on the Western European Union, and a record of McNeil's conversations with the Belgian Foreign Minister, Henri Spaak.

On 22 March 1948, Blunt produced the key to a safe in Burgess's office and asked the *rezidentura* to make a duplicate. At his next meeting Burgess explained that the safe was used to store MI5 and SIS documents which only the Foreign Secretary Ernest Bevin, Hector McNeil and (Sir) Orme Sargeant (later head of the diplomatic corps) had access to. The keys were kept by the relevant private secretaries, McNeil's being (Sir) Fred Warner. Burgess never explained whether Warner had lent him his key, but as he too was a notorious homosexual and one of Burgess's favourite drinking companions, the Centre decided that he had probably been the source. In May Burgess returned the duplicate to Shishkin, explaining in a note that 'the key fits exceptionally well and is returned herewith. My chances of using it are very small. I wish greater success in this respect to somebody else.'[102] Apparently SIS and MI5 sent their classified briefs to Bevin and McNeil in small yellow boxes, and although Burgess was often alone in the room where Warner kept the boxes, the risk of his opening them was too great. A key had been stolen from one of the ministers and, although it was returned two days later, the incident had served to heighten security and the locks had changed.[103]

The failure over the yellow boxes was more than compensated

by Burgess's success in copying Foreign Office papers concerning the United Nations General Assembly meeting held in Paris in the autumn of 1948, complete with the draft resolutions and the Cabinet's instructions for the British delegation.[104] Korovin took them straight to the Soviet Foreign Minister Andrei Vyshinsky, and met Burgess, who had accompanied McNeil to Paris, under the Arc de Triomphe.

In April 1948, Burgess started planning the next stage of his career, mindful that the usual two-year rotation of Foreign Office personnel meant that he would have to leave McNeil for another post, perhaps abroad.[105] While McNeil advised that he should consider the Far East Department, which promised to focus on developments in Korea and China, the Centre was anxious for him to try for the General, American or Northern Departments. On 12 October Burgess outlined his prospects:

> I won't do my duty if I don't tell you that I am going to work to this department with completely different opportunities in comparison with those I had while working with Hector. It is true that I am being transferred there with his support and that he has spoken to Dening and Caccia, chief of the Personnel Department, and given a recommendation and asked to give me important work. It is true but it will not mean very much. Still, we shall see. I suggest; (1) My being cautious and even timid in this respect until the opportunities become clear. (2) Using to the maximum on a personal basis the contacts and friends, Fred, Hector and co. I know that suggestion No. 1 will be approved.[106]

Burgess's confidence was well-justified. The Centre took the personal security of agents extremely seriously, and had demonstrated its commitment to Burgess in the past. Between 6 November and 11 December 1947, when the four great powers were meeting in London, Burgess passed 336 Foreign Office documents to the *rezidentura* and earned warm praise from Vyacheslav Molotov, who asked whether even more material could be made available. When the situation was explained to him he insisted that Burgess should not be endangered, and even authorized the payment of a £200 bonus to Burgess, £100 to Shishkin, and £50 each to two of the *rezidentura*'s technical officers who had been initiated into the case.[107]

Burgess went to work in the Far East Department on 1 November 1948, but remained in close contact with Fred Warner who obligingly provided him with copies of various NATO documents. Burgess had them copied by Blunt and the exposed film was promptly passed to Korovin. On 22 December Burgess gave his first detailed account of his new post, and provided some flattering character profiles of his colleagues. The supervising Under-Secretary was (Sir Esler) Bill Dening, a career diplomat who had made his reputation in Indonesia a few years earlier. The head of the department, (Sir) Peter Scarlett, was described as 'quite an ordinary man, typical of an English gentleman'; Burgess was friendly with him and had visited his country home.

> I can't say anything about other officials except that it has proved possible to establish excellent personal relations with them, owing not only to my abilities but also to the lucky chance that almost all of them like myself have been to Eton. Things of this kind have great importance.

Only the assistant head of the department, (Sir Frank) Tommy Tomlinson, was 'an exception' and 'an interesting contrast'. Tomlinson 'likes to consider himself an Etonian among radicals and he likes me as a radical among Etonians'. Apart from outlining the functions of his new department, Burgess explained that in future his access to classified papers would be limited to those directly related to the Far East but, with the exception of top secret documents, he would be able to produce an even greater volume than hitherto.[108] As Korovin subsequently reported,

> He at once advanced the idea of passing over to us at every meeting still larger bundles of documents than those he had passed over up to now, and he asked to buy a suitcase for this purpose.[109]

The New Year of 1949 proved eventful for Burgess, not least because of a period in hospital after he had been thrown down some stairs by Fred Warner while engaging in a friendly wrestling match at some London drinking club. This incident was disclosed to the *rezidentura* on 1 March 1949 by Philby, who was on a brief visit to London and had explained that Burgess was in Ireland, recuperating at his mother's home. However, Philby warned that Burgess's drinking was getting worse, and another embarrassment might lead to him being sacked from the Foreign Office. Exactly a week later, on 7 March, Philby reported details of a car accident in Ireland, following which Burgess had been arrested on a charge of drunk driving, and announced that his mother would return him to London very shortly.[110]

In November 1949 yet another incident occurred, this time during Burgess's annual leave which he had chosen to take in the notorious homosexual resort of Tangier. Before leaving London he had

obtained introductions from the author Robin Maugham to the
MI5 representative in Tangier, Kenneth Mills, and to the SIS station
officer in Gibraltar, Teddy Dunlop. Unfortunately, while they were
drinking together on the Rock, a furious argument erupted about
the social psychologist Franklin Frazier, which developed into a
violent row over Franco's regime, which Dunlop and Mills supported. Thoroughly inebriated, Burgess then 'taught Mills a lesson'.
This had resulted in a complaint to the Foreign Office from SIS
alleging that Burgess had addressed the two men as MI5 and SIS
officers, but Korovin reported that Burgess had protested that there
had not been any indiscretion as the confrontation had not occurred
in the presence of outsiders.[111]

The Centre was alarmed at this unexpected crisis, particularly
when Blunt explained that SIS had been itching to put the knife
into Burgess ever since an episode that had taken place some time
earlier. Apparently Goronwy Rees had once tipped off Burgess
about the imminent arrival of Alex Halpern from the United States.
Halpern, who had served with British Security Co-ordination in
New York during the war, was a lawyer who had been Kerensky's
private secretary in Petrograd before the revolution and supposedly
had interesting information. Burgess had seized the opportunity to
invite Halpern to lunch and then circulated a memorandum
throughout the Foreign Office based on his conversation, in which
he mischievously identified Halpern as the source and added that
SIS would probably conduct a similar debriefing. Naturally SIS had
been infuriated by the way Burgess had hijacked their man and
compromised his identity, and this episode had rankled long
afterwards.[112]

Astonishingly, Burgess survived the Gibraltar fiasco, but clearly
he was falling apart and his increasingly erratic behaviour was manifested in his failure to warn of the storm clouds gathering over the
atom spy Klaus Fuchs. At the end of September 1949, shortly before
his departure for Washington DC, Philby had warned Burgess of a
joint Anglo-American decryption programme which had started to
break some of the Soviet wartime wireless traffic, including signals
that referred to NKVD sources. One, apparently codenamed
CHARLES, had received special attention from the counter-
intelligence analysts who were closing in on Klaus Fuchs. The news
had only reached Philby after his last meeting with Shishkin, held
on 21 September, so he had entrusted this vital information to
Burgess. According to Philby, the Americans had worked on the
Soviet traffic for years, with minimal success, but GCHQ had
recently achieved impressive results.

All this was reported by Burgess to his new Soviet contact, Yuri Modin, on 10 February 1950, eight days after the arrest of Fuchs had been announced in London. Burgess recalled that he had included Philby's tip in a personal note which had been photographed by Blunt, together with other documents, and then handed to Modin.[113] Naturally, the Centre was alarmed, particularly when Shishkin confirmed that Philby had said nothing about the decryption effort when they had met on 21 September. Certainly Modin had received three rolls of film from Blunt on 11 October, but when the pictures had been developed they had been found to be over-exposed and out of focus. As for Burgess's personal note, it had mentioned nothing about CHARLES.

At their subsequent meeting, on 25 October, Burgess had promised to re-copy the documents, and on 7 December had produced 168 documents, totalling 660 pages, but no personal note.[114] Thus a combination of Blunt's error and Burgess's forgetfulness had ensured that the warning about Fuchs had failed to reach the Centre. Burgess had said nothing to Modin, and Philby had been out of contact while he settled into his new post in America. The Centre was painfully aware that Fuchs could have been exfiltrated in September or even December 1949, and at the very least he could have been briefed on how to resist an MI5 interrogation, although at that late stage there was little the *rezidentura* could have done as it had been out of touch with the spy since mid-1949. As events turned out, MI5's interrogator, Jim Skardon, skilfully manipulated Fuchs into making an entirely unnecessary confession, which ensured his subsequent conviction at the Old Bailey and a long prison sentence.

According to Modin, reporting their meeting on 10 February 1950, Burgess reacted with 'calm and composure' to the news of the nuclear physicist's arrest, but accepted that a mistake had been made. The Centre immediately suspended contact with Burgess and Blunt for six weeks, but Burgess failed to turn up at the next scheduled rendezvous, on 20 March 1950 and to the back-up meetings.[115] However, at the beginning of April he left emergency signals for Modin and contact was restored on 17 April, not with Blunt but with Burgess. 'Instead of YAN, PAUL came to the meeting without materials,' reported the *rezidentura*, which submitted a lengthy report on the crisis to Moscow, by courier rather than cipher. Apparently Burgess had not attended the meetings in March because Philby (STANLEY) had been summoned to London by SIS to discuss the Fuchs affair.[116]

STANLEY asked to communicate that the Americans and the British had constructed a deciphering machine which in one day does 'the work of a thousand people in a thousand years'. Work on deciphering is facilitated by three factors: (1) A one-time pad was used twice; (2) Our cipher resembles the cipher of our trade organization in the USA; (3) A half-burnt codebook has been found in Finland and passed to the British and used to decrypt our communications. They will succeed within six to twelve months. The CHARLES case has shown the counter-intelligence service the importance of knowing the past of civil servants. Although STANLEY is trusted, Vivian [see below] considers that STANLEY's past is not entirely clear. A role in establishing STANLEY's past may be played by his first wife who is somehow connected to the CHARLES case. STANLEY, PAUL and YAN consider that the situation is serious. A long meeting is needed to discuss it. The meeting has been arranged for 15 May.[117]

Modin was instructed to calm Burgess at the meeting on 15 May, and to arrange a further meeting with Korovin for 4 June. Modin's meeting with Burgess was 'businesslike' and he was 'very calm, self-possessed, unhurried'. When he offered to give Korovin at the next meeting a bundle of Foreign Office documents about the recent conference of the three foreign ministers, Modin forbade it.[118] The second meeting, with Korovin, was held in a quiet suburban park and lasted six and a half hours. The marathon length was accounted for by the Cambridge ring's anxieties about the threat posed to them by the new decryption machine. This, of course, was the latest generation of GCHQ's computers, then completely unknown to the wider public, which had only recently become familiar with relatively primitive automated data processors and card sorters. Korovin admitted that mistakes had been made in Soviet cipher procedures, but tried to reassure Burgess that the errors had been limited and had only occurred in wartime. He insisted that no 'supermachine' existed capable of cracking the Soviet codes, but events were to prove him wrong. In fact the combined Anglo-American effort had produced a series of partial decrypts, code-named VENONA, which eventually were to expose the Cambridge ring.

The most immediate worry was Philby's safety, and Burgess relayed to Korovin that Blunt had explained how, during the period in 1940 when the ring was out of direct contact with the *rezidentura*, communications had been maintained through Edith Tudor Hart who had passed the ring's information to Bob Stuart of the CPGB. Blunt recalled that during his conversations with Litzi Philby she had mentioned the desirability of recruiting an atom scientist, and he had gained the impression that she had found a suitable candidate. He was worried that if her nominee had been Klaus Fuchs, he might compromise her under MI5's interrogation. If that happened the entire network would be put in jeopardy, but Korovin had assured Burgess that Fuchs was entirely unconnected with Litzi. Nevertheless, Burgess himself was in considerable danger, and he said that, according to David Footman, it was Colonel Valentine Vivian, the head of SIS's security section, who was behind his persecution. Fortunately Guy Liddell had ridiculed the Gibraltar incident, but Burgess feared that Vivian had been listening to Goronwy Rees who was entirely capable of whispering about Burgess's past political unreliability. Although the two men maintained good personal relations – Burgess was godfather to one of Rees's four children – he judged that Rees could easily take such a step to deprive him of access to British secrets. However, Burgess felt that Rees would be reluctant to do anything more than hint, for fear of endangering his own lucrative position as a consultant to SIS's Russian and German sections. On the other hand, Vivian might be keen to get even with Footman who had openly sponsored Burgess.

Certainly Burgess enjoyed many protectors in the Foreign Office, principal among them being Hector McNeil, Bill Dening and Gladwyn (later Lord) Jebb, and he recognized that he had survived the Gibraltar affair 'because my friends proved to be stronger than my enemies'. In support of this self-evident proposition, he cited a hitherto undisclosed incident which centred on a draft document he had glimpsed. The memorandum, dated 9 May 1950, concerned his imminent appointment to Washington DC, and on 17 May he had been informed officially of the termination of the internal enquiry conducted into SIS's complaint about Gibraltar. 'Thus', observed Burgess, 'I have no doubt about the firmness of my position.'

Finally, Burgess explained to Korovin that his role in Washington would be one of co-ordinating the affairs of the Far East Department in anticipation of opening an embassy in Peking, a development which would require the transfer of a diplomat with first secretary rank from the embassy in Washington. Before Burgess bade Korovin farewell, he returned to his preoccupation about exposure:

Before leaving for the USA STANLEY [Philby] asked PAUL [Burgess] to communicate to us his personal request for granting him political asylum in the USSR in case of obvious danger. PAUL added that essentially it was also a question of granting asylum to him, PAUL. YAN [Blunt], like STANLEY and PAUL, was strongly alarmed by recent

events but showed no signs of cowardice and made no hasty conclusions. In PAUL's opinion, if serious danger threatens, YAN will
commit suicide. PAUL said that YAN's moral qualities are not like
STANLEY's and PAUL's. STANLEY and PAUL think themselves politicians who have gone through the hard school of life, know what
struggle is and know they should achieve their aim. PAUL considers
YAN a good comrade, entirely devoted to our cause, but the spirit
of an intellectual which is characteristic of YAN's profession is still
firm in him, and this spirit makes him accept the inevitable and he
doesn't mobilize for the struggle.

Dismayed by Blunt's gloomy prognosis, Korovin asked Burgess
to point out the senselessness of his frame of mind, and to persuade
him to 'abandon all thoughts of suicide'. Burgess, Philby and Blunt
'can certainly count on our help,' insisted Korovin, but when he
announced that further personal meetings would have to be suspended, Burgess replied that he 'saw no signs of danger' and said
that he was ready to resume passing documents, either originals,
on film or in the form of personal notes. Korovin declined the offer
and provided a new procedure for establishing contact, concluding
the meeting on an optimistic note:

> PAUL was in a good mood. He came to the meeting sober. He thanked
> me for a long time for my conversation with him and asked to assure
> the centre that everything was all right with him and that he would
> wait for instructions about passing over material to us.

This meeting was something of a milestone and it was not until 1
July 1950 that Ivan Chichayev and Mikhail Shishkin had prepared
'a summary of ROSS's talk with PAUL'. Its conclusion, endorsed by
the London *rezidentura*, was:

> Taking into account the absence of any dangerous signs concerning
> THE FIVE to conduct the prearranged meeting with PAUL in the first
> half of July at which to arrange for a meeting with YAN in a month's
> time for receiving materials. In future to receive documents from
> PAUL and YAN only on undeveloped film and at personal meetings.
> To give consent to the rezidentura's suggestion about continuing
> work with PAUL and YAN and to receiving materials from them.[119]

On 1 July it was Burgess, not Blunt, that came to the arranged
meeting and, in accordance with instructions, he came empty-
handed. Instead he gave a verbal account of the war in Korea and
said that he would be departing for the United States on 28 July.
At his next meeting, held on 8 July, he passed over a film of Foreign
Office papers and received instructions on how to establish contact

with the Soviets in Washington DC.[120] On 30 July Modin met Blunt
and questioned him about some of the issues which the Centre had
asked the *rezidentura* to clarify. Blunt recalled, for example, that
in 1939 Burgess had gone abroad briefly and had passed Goronwy
Rees over to him, confirming that Rees was definitely in a position
to compromise Blunt. He expressed the view that Rees certainly
had not forgotten this episode, which had lasted for some weeks,
but doubted that he would blab. Burgess's worries on this topic
were, he asserted, unfounded. Similarly, Leo Long was too much
in awe of Blunt as his mentor to make trouble for him, and Michael
Straight could be put in the same category. His sole concern was
that Bob Stuart might be indiscreet in a room bugged by MI5, in
case he had a knowledge of anyone else in the network beyond
Edith Tudor Hart. Modin summed up the meeting with Blunt in
these terms:

> YAN remarked that if danger of exposure arose he would try to flee
> to Paris or would commit suicide. The thought about suicide in the
> case of extreme necessity has appeared in his head because of his
> feelings towards his mother who, according to his words, will be
> able to get over his suicide but won't be able to get over his exposure
> and imprisonment. YAN announced that his whole position testified
> to 'bourgeois individualism', but added that he would hardly be able
> to act differently and resolve to begin a new life.[121]

Burgess's departure to America brought his extraordinary partnership with Blunt to an end, although the pair remained in touch
by letters containing hidden prearranged signals. However, this was
by no means the conclusion of Blunt's role as an active member of
the Cambridge ring, although he later concealed this part of his life
from his MI5 interrogators. From his unlikely vantage point in the
Courtauld Institute, Blunt monitored developments inside MI5 and
did his best to protect the interests of Philby, Burgess and Maclean.

A brief review of the highly sensitive information Blunt delivered
to the London *rezidentura* about MI5's postwar operations demonstrates the degree to which he exploited old friendships inside the
Security Service and encouraged his contacts to be indiscreet. Shortly
before his departure he prevailed upon a subordinate to compile a
comprehensive list of all MI5's agents placed in diplomatic premises
in London. Reluctantly he did so, imploring Blunt to destroy the
document as soon as he had read it. Naturally, Bllunt passed it
straight to his contact. Even the most mundane of items, such as
the report from a German agent named Popov in September 1945
about the Soviet mission in Stockholm, was routinely conveyed to

the NKVD with the minimum of delay. Others were more significant: in January 1948 he had reported that John Marriott had told him that MI5 had failed to break any Soviet ciphers or to open any of the embassies' diplomatic bags. In March Guy Liddell had told him about the creation of a secret committee to supervise the development of bacteriological weapons. In December 1950 he had identified John Shaw as the head of MI5's new overseas branch, and in February 1951 had warned that Tommy Harris, formerly of MI5 but now employed by SIS, was to use his wartime double agent GARBO to penetrate the new East German intelligence organization. Not surprisingly, this particular project had foundered instantly. Undoubtedly, the damage inflicted by Philby, Burgess and Blunt can only be described as colossal, and on a much greater scale than has ever been publicly admitted. (See Appendix I for transcripts of documents passed to Moscow by Anthony Blunt.)

CHAPTER VIII

The KLATT Affair

One of the greatest mysteries of the war surrounds the huge espionage network masterminded by the German spy codenamed KLATT by the Abwehr. He is of considerable importance, not just because of the doubt that surrounds his very extensive operations, which seemed to stretch across the Soviet Union and into the Middle East, but because of the uncertainty that exists even today regarding precisely who he was working for. Was he an Abwehr double agent, did he work under Soviet control, or was he an independent operator? Even the Americans, for whom he worked in Austria after the war, could not fathom the extraordinary tale of the spies known as MAX and MORITZ who preoccupied a large part of the British signals intelligence organization for much of the war and baffled some of the best analytical brains ever gathered together in one place, Bletchley Park. As an example of how the NKVD came to rely on information from Philby, Blunt and Cairncross to solve their own intelligence problems, it has no equal.

The first transmissions from MAX and MORITZ were intercepted by GC & CS between December 1941 and March 1942. More than 260 of MAX's messages were copied and the contents, decrypted through ISOS, suggested that MAX was collecting information on the Russians, while MORITZ, who had sent forty reports during the same period, ran a network concentrating on the British.

According to the KLATT files in the Soviet archives, Bletchley Park won the race to intercept and decrypt radio traffic exchanged between what was referred to as the 'KLATT bureau' in Sofia and an Abwehr unit in Vienna, and this was conveyed to Moscow by the London *rezidentura* in the form of a report dated 24 April 1942 and entitled *Luftmeldekopf, Sofia*:

The role of the Luftmeldekopf, in future SCHWERT ('SWORD') in the collection and transmission of intelligence is of considerable importance and interest but the organization and its methods remain unclear. SCHWERT communicates to WAGNER (Major von Wahl) in

Vienna for further forwarding to the 1-Luft branch of the Abwehr in Berlin quite a considerable number of intelligence reports concerning Russia and the Near East. The person responsible for this material in Sofia is a certain KLATT. Reports marked MAX originate from areas behind the Russian front, along the line from Leningrad and down to Rostov and Kerch, from Novorossisk to Batumi, from Georgia, Azerbaijan, Armenia and from Iran, Iraq, Tehran, from districts near Mosul, Baghdad and Basra, and also Kuibyshev, Astrakhan and from the west coast of the Caspian. Another group of reports marked MORITZ covered Egypt, Libya, Palestine, Syria, Cyprus, Iraq and Iran, and finally there is one report from IBIS in Turkey.

Attached to the British report was a map dated 12 April 1942 marked with the locations and frequencies of the component parts of the network and headed 'Sources of MAX and MORITZ Reports'. The highly classified document showed the impressive extent of the German organization and indicated that the most productive transmitters were sited at Soviet ports along the Black Sea. The British noted that the volume of MAX's reports had been gradually but consistently increasing, as had MORITZ's, which were not quite so plentiful. 'In the four months from December 1941 to March 1942, 260–300 such reports were received, the total number being 30% to 50% higher.'

The British analysts had been particularly impressed with the speed with which the network operated, observing that 'Some reports from Novorossisk, Rostov, Sevastopol, Kerch, from the Moscow area, Tblisi and Batumi were received by SCHWERT on the very same day the events took place.' Others were forwarded by SCHWERT to Vienna in the course of one, two or three days following the events described in them. A case in point was a fire at an installation in Maikop, near the Black Sea, which was reported 'not only on the day of the fire, but even before it had been put out'. As regards the accuracy of MAX's and MORITZ's information, there was only circumstantial evidence to suggest that 'it is quite convincing', considering that German aerial reconnaissance could easily verify the authenticity of the intelligence, and 'only one case is known when a report was the subject of doubt'. The very fact that the organization was continuing to expand was, in the opinion of the authors, an indication that the 'information supplied by SCHWERT is considered valuable'. Also remarked on was the absence of any data in the texts regarding sources or their methodology. All organizational matters had been omitted, although the content implied that the reports contained 'eye-witness data, and were not borrowed from staff reports, intelligence summaries, newspapers, radio broadcasts or hearsay. Nor were they obtained by the interception of Russian signals.'

The analysts acknowledged that, on the basis of the speed with which the organization exchanged information, 'these reports are transmitted by radio all the way or most of the way to Sofia. The natural conclusion to be drawn from this is that there are several dozen single-operating agents equipped with radio transmitters in all the districts from which the reports are received. It is difficult to imagine how such a mass of agents could have been deployed there and maintained in areas where the Russian Army, Navy and Air Force conduct operations.'[1]

Another puzzle mentioned was why the organization sent their reports to Sofia, for example from Moscow, Kursk and Batumi, when it would have been far easier for a portable wireless transmitter to communicate with a German station located just behind the front line. The analysts speculated that perhaps the Abwehr had constructed a powerful control station, maybe located in Novorossisk, which tasked the German agents and relayed their replies.

Soon after the completion of the first British report which initiated the lengthy Allied investigation of KLATT, cryptographers at Bletchley Park broke the key to KLATT's traffic with Berlin to reveal some of his sources. One identified was a certain Captain Samoylov, who supposedly had been at Stalingrad and, after the amputation of his leg, had undergone radio training in Kuibyshev with a man named Lang. Meanwhile GC & CS continued to monitor the Abwehr's Sofia–Vienna link and, when KLATT moved to Budapest, the Sofia–Budapest–Vienna circuit. The resulting Abwehr intercepts were passed to Moscow by Anthony Blunt (TONY) and John Cairncross (LIST).

The Centre knew from the members of the Cambridge ring that a Joint Signals Intelligence Committee had been formed in London to evaluate and co-ordinate the interception of the Abwehr's wireless traffic, and learned that it was composed of representatives from Section V of SIS, Major Felix Cowgill and a counter-intelligence specialist named Ferguson; Guy Liddell, Herbert Hart and (Sir) Dick White from MI5; Colonel E.F. Maltby and Kenneth Morton-Evans from the Radio Security Service (RSS); and (Sir) Denys Page and Leonard Palmer from GC & CS. The committee's secretary was Hugh Trevor-Roper (later Lord Dacre) and it met weekly. At its 35th meeting, held on 22 October 1942 with Major Malcolm Frost of MI5 also present, Kenneth Morton-Evans gave a presentation on the comparative importance of different Abwehr wireless channels, stressing that limited resources required the development of a priority list, on which VII/23 (Sofia–Vienna) would figure. According to the minutes of the meeting, Guy Liddell asked whether 'the Russians have succeeded in the interception and decryption of this particular channel'; in response Captain Ferguson, Denys Page and Kenneth Morton-Evans confirmed that 'no technical, radio-telegraphic or cryptographic information had been communicated to the Russians'. The RSS and GC & CS representatives suggested that sharing this information would enable the Russians to monitor the traffic and would not interfere with British decryption of other Abwehr circuits. However, Ferguson pointed out that 'the initial policy of SIS consisted of conducting this liaison in the form of a bargain, in the hope of obtaining intelligence from the Russians, forcing them to share information'.[2] This view was sharply criticized by the rest of the committee which recommended that the material relevant to VII/23 should be handed over. In reality, of course, Philby had already intervened, and had despatched the following report to alert the Soviets to what was afoot:

SERVICE VII/23

I understand that the ISOS schedules and cypher keys for the above service (Vienna to Sofia) have been, or shortly will be, handed to the Russians. There is, however, a very interesting catch in this. A few days ago this service was changed from book (transposition) cypher to machine cypher, which works, of course, on an entirely different principle. It is clear, therefore, that the cryptographic material which the British intend to give to the Russians will enable the Russians to solve only the book material, viz. the traffic which was transmitted before the change took place; it is quite useless for the solution of the traffic sent by machine cypher. As you know, the traffic sent in book cypher is known as ISOS, and the traffic sent in machine cypher is known as ISK. It is for the present at any rate a settled principle of British cryptographic policy to give the Russians nothing about ISK.

It may be of some interest to you to know that, at the present time, the German Abwehr machine cypher is solved much more easily and rapidly than the Abwehr book cypher. Once the principle is understood, the material can be turned out without difficulty, whereas the book cypher can, by various artifices, be made very difficult indeed.

I was present at a recent meeting with Commander Denniston who is in charge of the diplomatic and commercial side of GC & CS. He [was] asked about Russian cryptographic achievements. It was clear from his answer that he knows very little about it. He merely said that he did know that in 1939 the Russians were about a fortnight ahead of the British in respect of the Japanese cypher (I do not really understand what this implies, but it is clear that the Russians were slightly better than the British).

Incidentally, as you probably know already, the British are also cracking the cyphers used by the Japanese Military Attaches in Europe. This material is known as ZIP/JYA in British cryptographic circles. There may soon be talk of sharing some of it with the Russians.

SIS was soon to learn much more about KLATT courtesy of Mirko Roth, a Yugoslav Jew holding a German passport in the name of Michael Rat and using the alias Imre Roth, who turned up in neutral Portugal. The Yugoslav chargé d'affaires in Lisbon informed the British Embassy that Roth was a German agent, but apparently he was willing to work for British Intelligence. In a subsequent interview at the embassy Roth explained that after the Serb massacre at Novy Sad in January 1942 he had fled to Budapest with his wife and child, where he had established contact with the Abwehr in the hope of leaving Europe. In the middle of October 1942 he had been sent to Sofia, where he had learned more about the local Abwehr organization, before his arrival in Lisbon in December, on a very general intelligence-gathering mission, equipped with a recipe for making secret ink. Details of Roth's interview at the Lisbon embassy were passed to the London *rezidentura* by Kim Philby in March 1943.

Since last meeting I have discussed at length with various people interested in the famous Max and Moritz leakages. It is the unanimous opinion of those who have been working on the details of the Moritz case (Hudson-Williams, Trevor-Roper, Gilbert Ryle, Herbert Hart, etc.) that Cowgill's theory of cryptography in Sofia, which I described in my last report is wrong. The chief arguments against it are as follows:–
  (i) On occasion Moritz has been asked to watch certain activities in Alexandria. This indicates the presence of an agent, not the interception of wireless traffic.
 (ii) On occasion ISOS has mentioned Moritz's 'sub-agents' which again indicates an agent at work.
(iii) ISOS traffic referring to Moritz has been read for many months now. If Moritz did refer to cryptography, that would almost certainly be reflected at some point in the ISOS. (It should be mentioned that where the Germans do resort to cryptography, eg in Las Palmas, it is mainly reflected in the ISOS traffic.)

(iv) Mirko Rot, who knows quite a lot about the Sofia Abwehrstelle, knows nothing of a cryptographic unit there.

(v) To sum up, there is not a shred of positive evidence to suspect the existence of a cryptographic unit in Sofia; and there are certain positive indications that Moritz is an agent, viz a person.

Incidentally, Cowgill made a fool of himself with this theory. He induced RSS to write a letter to [the Director-General Sir David] Petrie strongly supporting the cryptographic theory. This letter was produced at the RSS meeting on 25.3.43 and was greeted with general derision. Even Hudson-Williams who was representing Section V at that meeting, was forced to discredit the letter, and disown the views expressed in it. As Patrick Reilly, Personal Assistant to CSS, was present at this meeting, it is clear that he must have gathered the worst possible impression.

While the cryptographic theory is discredited, it appears that the theory that Max and Moritz reports represent false information put out by the Russians is still quite strongly held. As a result the MI5 representatives on the RSS Committee have evolved the following plan:– It should be hinted to the Russians that the British intend to make use of Mirko Rot for certain purposes of their own; but the British at the same time express concern as to whether the use of Mirko Rot by the British would perhaps damage Russian intelligence interests. It is hoped that, by threatening the Russians with the use of an agent of the Sofia Abwehrstelle (and consequently disturbing any game they might be playing with the Abwehrstelle), the British might force the Russians to disclose some of those games. This line, of course, depends on the assumption that the Russians are in fact playing games (Max and Moritz games) with the Sofia Abwehrstelle.

The above plan is being put up to CSS by the RSS Committee. I do not know whether or in what form CSS will approve it; but I will try and keep you informed. (Incidentally, it will be almost impossible for the British to use Mirko Rot since he spread his story all around Lisbon, particularly in the Jugoslav Legation circles; and it is most likely that his journey to England and subsequent imprisonment is already known to the Germans.)

Meanwhile MI5 had compiled a much larger dossier, amounting to 114 pages, on the self-confessed spy to which Anthony Blunt had access. It showed that Roth had been allowed to enter Britain on 22 February 1943, but after six days at the Prince of Wales Hotel in De Vere Gardens, Kensington, he and his wife were arrested by Special Branch detectives accompanied by Jim Skardon and Herbert Hart. Under interrogation, Roth identified three other Abwehr agents, one of whom named Haggar was subsequently arrested in Egypt and disclosed his knowledge of KLATT, whom he named as

Richard Kauder. He also provided details of Kauder's mistresses in Sofia and Budapest, and explained that KLATT had operated semi-independently of the Abwehr in 1941 until the organization's development had been completed and had received official recognition from the Germans. Roth commented that KLATT was now so important that the Vienna Abstelle depended almost entirely on his network. The MI5 file included a short description of 'The Main Functions of the Abstelle' which was collecting information from Russia and the Near East:

> Daily at 8.00 am and 3.00 pm the wireless station receives messages directly from Russia. The information contained in these signals is of great operational importance and was communicated shortly after the reported events took place. In recent months the information almost entirely concerned operations near Stalingrad and was of great value to the air force.

According to Roth's friends, these radio messages had led to the Russians suffering great losses, and some of them had come from a White Russian émigré based at the Soviet Embassy in Sofia who had a brother or near relative serving on the Soviet General Staff. This spy in Sofia, who was alleged to communicate to the Abstelle through another agent known as IRA, had been responsible for copying Soviet Embassy reports as well as compromising Comintern agents in Bulgaria and Romania who subsequently had been arrested. The spy in the embassy had travelled to Russia in late 1941 or early 1942 to recruit the officer on the Soviet General Staff who in turn was alleged to have supervised an entire network of agents equipped with wireless transmitters. In addition to the material relating to KLATT, Roth also volunteered details of Abwehr activity in Turkey and the Near East. MI5 attempted to check Roth's information, and on 10 March 1943, Hart's B1(b) section sent an internal memorandum to a colleague, (Sir) Helenus Milmo:

> I am sending you a copy of my report where the references to highly sensitive sources contained in paragraph 15 have been omitted. I suggest sending a copy of the report to V35 (whom I have informed orally about the essence of the matter) so that he can show it to HARLEQUIN [a former Abwehr officer working for the British]. The latter would either have to give a written estimate of the case or, if he likes, discuss it with me or V35. Possibly we may point to the circumstances that appendices A and B are considered by us to be extremely important and that HAGGAR, as it emerged after his arrest, was a German agent in Egypt. It is highly desirable that HARLEQUIN should give his opinion on Roth's story and his mission.

When HARLEQUIN examined Roth's tale he expressed serious doubt about the ingredients of his secret ink, which were a cherry liqueur with a few drops of lemon juice, and his supposed Abwehr task of organizing propaganda in favour of the Hungarian regime. Roth's case was studied by J.C. Masterman of MI5's B1(a), who pointed out that 'his value to us is based almost entirely on information about the Sofia Abwehrstelle and Abwehr personnel'; he concluded that he was probably holding back information and therefore unsuitable for use as a double agent. 'I cannot see what we can gain by making him a XX agent. It seems to me it will be another difficult channel which we will have to feed without being able to count on any useful results.' Accordingly Roth was sent to MI5's detention centre, Camp 020, for further interrogation, with SIS entertaining the possibility that if he had been rejected by the XX Committee, he might be usefully deployed against the Soviets. Doubtless SIS considered the possibility that KLATT was nothing more than a complex Soviet deception scheme designed to misinform the Nazis. While such a proposition was supported by the extent of the network and the speed with which it appeared to work, it was undermined by the authenticity of the organization's information. From a professional intelligence standpoint, if the material was known to be bogus, one could predict not only Russian actions, but the German reaction, so much depended on establishing the nature of KLATT's network. Ideally, SIS wanted the Soviets to declare whether KLATT was one of theirs:

> We intend to get information from the Russians concerning MAX's organization and, in particular, whether or not this organization is under Russian control. The plan consists of announcing to the Russians that we intend to use Roth as a XX agent but that, quite probably, he may betray us and tell the Germans what information was given by him to our intelligence service ... We are afraid that if the Germans are informed about our knowledge of the existence of MAX's organization it might undermine the Germans' trust of it. In connection with this we suggest refraining from action until the Russians disclose the facts to us. Of course, to implement this we must not report the fantastic story Roth told us about his connections with the Abwehr because the Russians will never believe if they learn about this story, that we seriously intend to use Roth as a XX agent, so many questions being overlooked by us. As to whether more favourable results will be achieved if we first give the Russians ISOS, and only then give them Roth's dossier and his story of obtaining a visa to Britain, I prefer the former because it will strengthen the

Russians' trust in us if they are given the real goods from the very beginning.

This report coincided with a memorandum addressed to Patrick Reilly, the personal assistant to the SIS Chief (Sir) Stewart Menzies dated 15 March 1943, which mentioned that the idea of playing Roth's card in a game with the Russians had been discussed at an inter-departmental conference where MI5 had been represented by Herbert Hart. Doubtless this was a regular meeting of the Joint Signals Intelligence Committee, and another memo, written by Reilly and addressed to Felix Cowgill, suggested that only the part of Roth's story directly concerning the Russians should be conveyed to them, as 'the CSS is not inclined to use the Roth information with the aim of attempting to gain data about MAX and MORITZ from the Russians'.[3]

In the event, nothing was officially disclosed to the Soviets about Roth, and the NKGB noted that 'Roth's testimony has not officially become the property of the Soviet Intelligence Service', a view endorsed by the Soviet signals organization which commented that 'material handed over by the representative of the British Military Mission in Moscow, Cecil Barclay, contains only the most general information' and noted that 'material obtained by agents of the First Directorate of the NKGB shows that the British possess far more detailed information about the organization and work of the German signals intelligence service, and signals counter-intelligence, than Cecil Barclay reported.'[4]

The Soviets subsequently voiced their dissatisfaction with the quality of the information officially supplied by SIS through the liaison channel. In September 1943, Kim Philby told IGOR of the London *rezidentura* that his section's representative in Moscow, Cecil Barclay, codenamed 95500, had reported that two handbooks compiled by Section V describing Abwehr activity in Bulgaria and Romania had been handed to Russians who had criticized them. Major O'Brien, the head of Section V's Soviet and Balkan sub-section, observed that the Russians had claimed there was nothing new in the documents, and that details of German operations against the Soviets had been omitted deliberately. In particular, the Russians had protested that the British must know much more about KLATT than they were letting on. As O'Brien admitted, the handbooks were more than two years old, and SIS had indeed accumulated a wealth of information about KLATT.[5]

SIS had harboured two concerns about sharing intelligence information with the Soviets. The first was one of security. No disclosure

had been made in 1943 when GC & CS solved the Abwehr's
machine cipher, codenamed ISK. Instead of sharing everything, SIS
had passed over some selected decrypts relevant to Europe. Secondly, by the summer of 1943 the British had concluded that KLATT
was not a Soviet exercise in disinformation, and therefore there was
no point in sounding them out on the subject. This view had been
reached following an extraordinary stroke of luck. On 25 June 1943
the SIS officer 18700 informed his colleague 89700 that agent 18701
had received information from a Hungarian based in Istanbul named
Andre Georgy about Abwehr operations in Sofia. Georgy had met
18701 because he had volunteered to work for the British, and had
asked for two wireless transmitters which he intended to take to
Sofia. Both 18700 and 18701 considered Georgy to be 'almost
certainly an agent provocateur' but some of his information had
been assessed as 'possibly correct': in the part relevant to KLATT he
had described the organization, named its membership, listed their
functions, detailed their communications system and confirmed that
KLATT ran an agent inside the Soviet General Staff. Significantly,
he had named HAGGAR as a German source in Egypt and had
insisted that he had been operational until as recently as two months
ago.

In retrospect it is clear that much of Georgy's story, which covered
ten pages of an SIS summary, was true, for KLATT had moved to
Budapest, apparently with the consent of a high-level conference
headed by the Abwehr chief Admiral Wilhelm Canaris, which took
place in Sofia on 21 July 1943. Furthermore, Georgy had correctly
identified the Abwehr's new codename for KLATT's information as
BULLY.

Part 12 of Roth's SIS summary proved to be of special interest
to the Soviets because it described how at 'the end of July there
was great alarm [in Sofia] because of the fear that the White Russian
General Anton Turkul had fallen into enemy hands in Italy and had
compromised the secret of MAX's reports'. KLATT, Lang and the
chief of the Abwehr's I-Luft, Lieutenant-Colonel Kleinstuber, had
hurried to Vienna and Rome to get Turkul out of Italy to Budapest,
a task they accomplished successfully. General Turkul, the summary
noted, 'works with particular zeal against the USSR' and 'has a
long record of espionage'. Thus SIS opined that 'we must suppose
that MAX's intelligence system was either built by Turkul's friends
or, at least, with his knowledge and advice.'[6]

With information of this kind the British dispelled some of the
myths surrounding KLATT and became more willing to accept his
organization as genuine. This was the view expressed by Major

Millend at the 65th meeting of the Joint Signals Intelligence Committee held on 31 July 1943. His report was printed in full in an appendix to the minutes and prefaced with the comment: 'The aim of this report is to make clear whether MAX's material continues to remain valuable and whether the disinformation theory may be given up as the explanation or a partial explanation of MAX's intelligence.' Millend noted that a previous discussion on this topic had taken place on 8 April, when MAX's warning of a Russian advance near Novorossisk and on the Taman Peninsula had been confirmed. A comparative analysis of German and Soviet troop movements in the Kursk–Orel region, and signals intercepted on the VII/23 channel, indicated that 'MAX's recent reports entirely confirm the earlier conclusion, made on the basis of studying MAX's reports for the periods 1 November 1942–15 March 1943, which claimed that MAX's information had been confirmed by operations.' However, Millend revealed that two of MAX's reports had been untrue. One related to the despatch of Soviet assault troops to Egypt, and the other concerned the hesitation of the Soviet military command caused by information that the Germans had abandoned plans to launch an offensive. Millend thought these two items could be overlooked, and advised the committee

> (1) It is absolutely obvious that the German intelligence service and operational departments appreciate MAX's reports highly. It is quite possible that these reports are the most effective form of tactical reconnaissance received by the enemy. (2) MAX's reports during the last four months do not confirm the earlier theory about deliberate disinformation, so it would now be sensible to abandon the theory.[7]

Although much more of MAX's radio traffic was intercepted after 1943, when he changed his codename to EDELWEISS and then OLAF, the British opinion about him remained the same. The only question remaining, then, is how did the Soviets react to the unpalatable disclosure that KLATT supposedly was haemorrhaging authentic secrets to the Nazis? With the help of Philby, Blunt and Cairncross the Centre learned exactly what the British had discovered about KLATT, and the NKGB's Second Special Department was assigned the task of intercepting the Abwehr's Sofia–Vienna wireless link in the autumn of 1941. The Soviet cryptographers finally broke the German cipher in July 1942, judging it to be a 'letter cipher of a comparatively simple system',[8] although the British decrypts leaked via the London *rezidentura* probably gave the code experts invaluable assistance. Either way, the Soviets mastered the Sofia–Vienna and the Sofia–Budapest circuits entirely independently of official help from Bletchley Park.

While the NKGB concentrated on KLATT's wireless traffic, the military counter-intelligence service known by its Russian acronym of SMERSH trawled the Balkans for members of KLATT's organization. However, it was only after the Red Army had occupied Bulgaria, Hungary, Czechoslovakia, Austria and Germany, and hundreds of captured Abwehr officers had been interrogated, that the Centre concluded its own lengthy investigation.[9] After enquiries lasting two years, a sixty-one-page report, *Memorandum on the KLATT-MAX Case*, submitted by the MGB to Stalin in July 1947, recorded that the NKVD had initiated its own search as soon as the first decrypts had been received from the London *rezidentura*. The content of the messages was cross-checked and this analysis showed that only an insignificant amount of MAX's information was authentic. A longer study of his traffic between the middle of 1942 and January 1945 revealed that only 8 per cent of the material was genuine.

The NKVD also reported that its own highly effective radio monitoring had failed to identify a single unauthorized wireless transmission from the Soviet Union to Bulgaria, so it felt justified in its belief that KLATT could not have received his information directly from inside the Soviet Union. But if this was the right judgement, where had KLATT obtained his material, and where had the vital 8 per cent of real information originated? This was the subject of the report to Stalin which, while KLATT himself was in American hands in Austria, relied on the interrogation of his Abwehr colleagues and the testimony of his second wife Gerda Filitz. KLATT himself was positively identified as Richard Kauder, born in Vienna in 1900 to a Jewish family, but baptized a Catholic. At the age of twenty-eight he had worked as a life insurance agent, and then had managed the estates of a local aristocrat, Baron Tavonat. Following the *Anschluss* in 1938 he had emigrated to Hungary where he had operated on the black market selling visas to Jewish refugees. Opinion about precisely when Kauder had come into contact with the Abwehr differed. Lieutenant-General Hans Piekenbrock, the head of Abwehr-1, thought that he had approached the Abstelle in Sofia in the summer of 1941, armed with reports about the Soviet air force. However, the head of Abwehr-3, Lieutenant-General Franz-Eccard von Bentivegni, thought KLATT had been recruited in 1939 in Budapest by the head of the Vienna Abstelle's counter-intelligence branch, an officer named Schmalschleger, and had worked on penetrating a channel of couriers run by the Polish intelligence service.

Either way, Kauder certainly had moved to Bulgaria in 1940 and had joined the Abwehr's KriegsOrganisation-Sofia. Another source suggested that KLATT had been hired in Vienna in 1940 by Lieutenant-Colonel Wahl-Welskirch, who had gained his release from a prison sentence for currency offences.

The Bulgarian police had a record of the arrival in Sofia of KLATT's principal aide, Ilya Lang, on 10 October 1940, and what became known as the 'KLATT Bureau' was definitely operational soon afterwards, answering directly to the Vienna Abstelle. This arrangement baffled the NKVD analysts who could make no sense of it, although from their own research they were satisfied that KO-Sofia, and its successor, the Abstelle Sofia, headed by Otto Wagner, codenamed DELIUS, was entirely isolated from KLATT and had minimal knowledge of the network. 'They were at odds with one another. DELIUS did not support KLATT in any way, had nothing in common with him, tried to compromise him and drive him out of Sofia. Moreover, KLATT warned his staff that they should not associate with Germans because DELIUS was watching them.'

In the autumn of 1943, KLATT moved to Budapest, probably as a result of pressure from DELIUS, leaving only a small wireless station in Sofia which he directed during occasional visits from Hungary. While in Budapest KLATT acquired official Abwehr status and was designated *Luftmeldekopf Süd-Ost*, but in reality his only source was a transmitter in Istanbul, and his staff had very little to do because KLATT preferred to process the information personally before it was relayed to VERA, the Abwehr station in Vienna. He went to tremendous lengths to promote the appearance of great industry, but all the cars, the staff and the inactive wireless sets were simply a sham intended to cheat the Abwehr. So where had KLATT acquired his information? Early in 1945 he had been questioned about this by an Abwehr official named Klausnitzer, who asserted that he had 'received intelligence information mainly from three sources: VIGO, alias Dr Willie Getz in Istanbul; from his radio operator Arnold Dalisme in Ankara, and from IRA, alias Lang'.

According to his OGPU and NKVD dossiers, Ilya F. Lang, alias Ira Longin, was a former Tsarist army officer who had emigrated in 1920 and was closely associated with General Turkul, a character well known to the NKVD as having been in the pay of the Japanese and German intelligence services back in the early 1930s. He had been spotted attempting to infiltrate agents in the Soviet Union in 1937 and therefore had earned himself a large file.

Having identified KLATT's main sources, the NKVD was anxious to check on the British reference to Lang's accomplice in the Soviet embassy in Sofia, and through him to trace the spy on the Soviet General Staff. Extensive enquiries showed that Lang could not have had such a contact in the embassy, which suggested that the other agent was also a fiction. The British had also deduced a possible source in the communications of a Soviet front-line headquarters, but after a prolonged investigation conducted on the authority of the Minister of Defence Nikolai Bulganin and the Deputy Minister of State for Security, Selivanovsky, the NKVD again came up with nothing.[10] As for the one-legged Captain Samoylov identified by SIS, it was determined that no such person existed.[11]

Under interrogation by the Russians KLATT's wife Gerda Filitz recalled that upon his return from Vienna her husband had been in low spirits and had told her that he 'had been reprimanded for the fact that Lang had passed dud information about the Soviet army and cheats'. Another member of the KLATT Bureau, named Sturm-Schneider, said that on one occasion he had seen Lang dictate to a colleague, Eva Hamernik, while reading newspaper cuttings. Finally, a *Sicherheitsdienst* agent named Willie Getz, codenamed KAUFMAN, said that before the war Lang had passed anti-Comintern information to Milan which he alleged had come from a White Russian intelligence organization.

The NKVD concluded that the small proportion of KLATT's information which was authentic had been gleaned by Lang from Russian émigrés who had interviewed Soviet PoWs in the refugee camps on behalf of the Germans. It was also suspected that KLATT might have cultivated contacts inside foreign embassies in Sofia, and even the British thought it likely that the Swedish Embassy might have relayed information from its Embassy in Moscow. Finally, there was the strong possibility that KLATT had actually acquired some of his data from the Germans themselves, like the White Russian émigré Vasilyev who had bought material about the Soviet air force from a German intelligence officer named Brauner for 7,000 levs. He had then corrected it using newspaper articles and, using his own experience in the First World War and his imagination, had fabricated a plausibly detailed report on Soviet plans for an invasion of the Crimea. When questioned, Vasilyev had remarked that the Germans had been snowed under with intelligence reports of varying reliability, so deceiving them was quite a safe undertaking. Although he was unconnected with KLATT, Vasilyev's ingenuity and enterprise had borne a strong resemblance to MAX's efforts. Clearly the White Russian émigré community in Europe had acquired years of experience in the manufacture of fake intelligence.

KLATT's source in Turkey, Willie Getz, was traced by the British and he admitted that he had relied for his information on White Russians and a few diplomatic contacts. SIS and the NKVD concluded independently that MAX was not a single individual, but simply a generic term to cover information which purported to have come from inside the Soviet Union. The official view espoused by MI-14 in 1943, that MAX had been useful to the Germans, persuaded SIS to approach the Russians in October 1943 with a summary of the MAX traffic, but to their astonishment MAX continued in operation until February 1945. The post-war British interrogation of KLATT's surviving team led SIS to conclude wrongly that

> the MAX reports were a Russian-controlled operation based on the penetration of the White Russian circles which purported to supply KLATT with his intelligence. KLATT's principal source himself admitted that the MORITZ reports were 'pure smoke' concocted in Sofia as an additional lure for the Abwehr.

The one surprise about the entire KLATT affair is that he managed to dupe the Abwehr for so long. General Piekenbrock mentioned during his interrogation at the hands of the Soviets that KLATT had come under suspicion several times for fabricating intelligence, but since the Luftwaffe never complained about his reliability, he had not been the subject of any rigorous double-checks. Eventually suspicions about KLATT had strengthened, and he was arrested by the Abstelle Vienna in February or March 1945, together with some other members of his organization.[12] One, Valentina Deutsch, made a statement to the MGB, saying that 'when, after my arrest in February 1945, I was interrogated by the Gestapo, they demanded evidence about KLATT's intelligence activity and told me that KLATT was an adventurer, a cheat who had cost Germany big money.'

The fact that KLATT was paid huge sums by the Abwehr is a clue to his motivation, which may also have been self-preservation. Certainly, as a Jew, he could not have sympathized with the Nazis, but doubtless he saw an opportunity to enrich himself and save his skin. He enjoyed an expensive lifestyle, although the same could not be said of Lang who was an altogether more modest individual. Whatever had driven them to build such an elaborate charade, they unwittingly served the Allied cause and, with the benefit of hindsight, it seems most unlikely that any Allied deception scheme could have been maintained against the enemy so comprehensively and for so long.

In this remarkable case, with the Allies equally intrigued by KLATT, the Cambridge ring was able to give the Centre the kind of invaluable intelligence that had a direct impact on the Red Army's

prosecution of the war, but Allied interest in the KLATT affair continued long after the war. As we have seen, the MAX and MORITZ
traffic was the subject of the most intensive study conducted by
MI-14 and SIS's Section V, and in the spring of 1943, MI5 sent an
analyst to Cairo to undertake a joint analysis with SIS of the intercepts. This was the precursor to Cecil Barclay's delivery, in October
1943, of a summary to the Russians, which elicited no response.
According to the official history of British Intelligence in the Second
World War, 'Post-war interrogation of the members of the Dien-
stelle KLATT left little doubt that the MAX reports were a Russian-
controlled operation based on the penetration of the White Russian
circles which purported to supply KLATT with his intelligence.'[13]

That the Germans relied upon KLATT's source codenamed MAX
is unquestioned, and it is equally certain that the Abwehr believed
he had given genuine advance notice of no fewer than four separate
Russian winter offensives. Certainly the Russians did develop an
extensive military deception scheme, codenamed MONASTERY,
according to General Pavel Sudoplatov of the NKVD, but their MAX
was actually Aleksandr Demyanov, an experienced Soviet penetration agent codenamed HEINE, who entered the scene much later
and succeeded in duping the Abwehr over a long period, under
the supervision of William Fisher.[14] His view is contradicted by SS
General Walter Schellenberg who recalled that MAX's network was
run by 'a German Jew, and he conducted its activities in a manner
that was unique':

> The work of this man was really masterly. He was able to report
> large-scale strategic plans as well as details of troop movements, in
> some important cases down to divisional level; his reports usually
> came in two or three weeks ahead of events, so that our leaders
> could prepare suitable counter-measures – or, should I say, could
> have done so if Hitler had paid more attention to the information.[15]

General Reinhard Gehlen, then head of the intelligence branch of
Foreign Armies East, described MAX as 'the office controlling the
Abwehr agents in Moscow' and characterized it as a source 'that
must have been genuine'.[16]

Precisely who KLATT was working for, and where he acquired
his information, has been a subject of much discussion since the
end of the war, but the consensus was reached on evidence from
KLATT himself who, ever ingenious, sought American financial support for his agents operating in Eastern Europe.[17] However, this led
him into conflict with the Soviets and in January 1946, following
his attempted abduction in Salzburg, Kauder was taken into a

lengthy period of protective custody by the Americans at the Camp King interrogation centre at Oberursel, accompanied by General Turkul and Ilya Longin. Here the trio were cross-examined by Arnold Silver who also obtained testimony from Colonel Wagner, then a prisoner of the French at Bad Widungen. According to Silver,[18] Kauder eventually confessed that his principal source had been Joseph Schutz, an Austrian friend based in Vienna who had originally introduced him to General Turkul. Apparently Kauder had begun to suspect in 1941 that Schulz was himself operating under Soviet control, but had not dared share his opinion with either the Abwehr, in case he was handed over to the Gestapo, or, after the war, with his new American employers for fear that their supply of dollars might dry up.

Kauder was also questioned on behalf of SIS by 'Klop' Ustinov,[19] who established from Kauder that shortly before the end of the war Schultz had admitted that he had been a Soviet agent since 1939, and that the entire network had been a vast exercise in military deception, although neither Longin nor Turkul had realized the truth. By mid-1947 the Americans were convinced that Kauder had worked unwittingly as a wartime conduit for Soviet disinformation, and he was released with his two companions. He was last seen in Salzburg in 1952, offering the CIA access to an extensive network of agents behind the Iron Curtain. As for the Soviet archives, there is no evidence to support Kauder's claim that Schultz had been a Soviet agent, so it is likely that Kauder was simply covering up for himself and Turkul.

CHAPTER IX

The Vegetarian

In 1937, after his return from a long official visit to the USSR which had started the previous year, and part of which had been spent on holiday on the Black Sea coast, his first vacation in two years of work abroad, Theodor Mally and his assistant Arnold Deutsch began to expand their agent network on the same principles adopted for the recruitment of the first members of the Cambridge group.

If Philby had played the main role in the first network, Guy Burgess and Anthony Blunt, with whom contact had been established in January 1937, were the main actors in the second. Working in Cambridge as a lecturer on the history of art, Blunt initially recommended his former pupil, John Cairncross, who was by then already working at the Foreign Office, and was therefore regarded as a promising intelligence source.

At the end of February 1937, the consummate charmer Guy Burgess visited Cambridge for the sole purpose of meeting Cairncross, who had been invited for the weekend by Blunt. The first encounter took place on the last Sunday of February 1937 and turned out to be the start of a long acquaintanceship, described by Guy in his report of 1 March 1937; it sheds as much light on the author's character as it does on his subject:

> Cairncross: I befriended him and we returned to London together. I asked him to give me a ring and to come and see me. He came yesterday evening and spent the whole evening with me. It seems to me that I managed to interest him in my person. That is already clear from our conversations. He promised to come again.
>
> Cairncross is 23 years old, he comes from a lower middle class family and is of humbler origin than I. He speaks with a strong Scottish accent and one cannot call him a gentleman. He studied at Edinburgh University, the Sorbonne and Cambridge (for one year). He was easily accepted for government service. He is a lower middle class intellectual (from a theoretical point of view he is well developed). I had long talks with him on French and English ideas, on French history etc. From discussing these questions we moved to

politics (I pretended to be a supporter of Kautsky [the German Social Democrat theorist], we spoke about revisionism, super-imperialism, conservatism and Marxism). I formed a few preliminary opinions about him. For what reasons did he join us? He was led by purely cultural considerations, in contrast to social and radical ones.

In his view Marxism, from a cultural point of view can contribute to the solution of theoretical problems and he discussed these questions with us from that angle. He was never a member of the party in the real sense of the word, but I think that we should work with him and involve him, though I am inclined to think that it would not be entirely without danger to approach him directly, at least until such a time that TONY [Blunt] or another party member has taken him in hand.

He is a typical petit bourgeois who always thinks that he can achieve a great deal in bourgeois society, in particular, in the department where he is now serving. If he were still at Cambridge, the task would be easier, but even now not everything is lost. This is, to some extent, confirmed by his attitude to the party. He says, for instance, the following: 'It is true, I have abandoned this now (i.e. active membership), but in a theoretical and spiritual sense I shall always remain on the side of the party.'

But, generally speaking, he is well set up and very pleased that he is working there. I don't want to say with this that he has been consciously bought. That would not be true (so far) and it seems to me that there is still time to bring him over to us. So far he is still quite direct and open (he talks continuously and tells you the truth about everything, beginning with Augustine and ending with Aldous Huxley).

He belongs to that category of petit bourgeois who is intoxicated with his own success, with the fact that he could raise himself to the level of the British ruling class and has the possibility of enjoying the luxury and delights of bourgeois life. He achieved this, however, by working for six years without any holidays or leisure time. His Presbyterian background instilled ambition in him and it was his dream to get into the Foreign Office at any price. But he did not only work, he also developed spiritually. After 5 years of academic work he came spiritually to Marxism. Cairncross: 'What else could I do? I had already become a convinced person. To start working for the party would have meant for me abandoning all I had been trying to achieve during 6 years. I don't know what to do in the future. If I had come to the party earlier, I would probably have abandoned all my endeavours – but I could not do this when the goal was already so near.' The situation, therefore, is not at all hopeless for us. It seems to me that if we say to him that he can have the one and the other, i.e. both the party and the Foreign Office, he would start working for us.

I think, however, that neither I nor A.B. should put ourselves at risk in this case, because his personal and social maturity conceals a danger. He has never had the time or the money to enjoy life, he has always suppressed himself and denied himself everything for the sake of the future. Now he is close to the goal. Though I think we may count on his goodwill, nevertheless his personality is fraught with many dangers and all this is not without a certain risk. We can only accept this risk if the acquisition of such a man as he is of such importance that for its sake it is worth sacrificing me, A.B. or somebody else.

It seems to me that the only way out of the situation, though I am afraid it may be difficult to implement this, is for an open party member to approach him, whom we could fully trust and who would be used for this one case only. This would somewhat reduce the risk which exists if I or A.B. were to act directly.

Cairncross, I think, would agree, at least at the present time to pass on to me everything he knows. He feels no respect for the British Foreign Office or his colleagues.[1]

This penetrating analysis of Cairncross's personality and state of mind, combined with Burgess's practical comments, persuaded Mally and Deutsch to take his advice and, taking advantage of the independence allowed an illegal *rezident*, Mally set out his plan for Cairncross's recruitment in a letter to the Centre dated 9 March 1937:

We found a way of approaching C. without M. [MADCHEN] and T. [TONY]. A former party organizer in Cambridge who is now working in Paris will speak to him in such a way that we shall in no way be involved. His name is Klugmann.[2]

James Klugmann had known Philby, Maclean and Burgess at Cambridge, and Deutsch had met him in 1936 in Paris through his acquaintance Olga Halpern, when he was working as secretary of the International Students' Organization against War and Fascism. However, operational contact with him was not established until the beginning of 1937, as Deutsch recalled in his 1939 notes, presumably for the sole purpose of recruiting Cairncross. Klugmann wanted reassurance through a source he trusted, the CPGB's Percy Glading, codenamed GOT. 'Before agreeing to give us any help, James asked that a responsible party functionary should give his consent to this. That is why GOT introduced MANN [Mally] and me to James in April 1937.'[3] Assessing Klugmann, Deutsch commented:

James is a party functionary who devotes himself entirely to the party. He is a quiet and thoughtful man. Modest, conscientious, industrious and serious. Everybody who knows him likes him and respects him. He exercises great influence over people. As a person he is honest and beyond reproach. Responsive and attentive to comrades. Ready to bring any offer for the sake of the party. A good organizer. Very careful with money. Never takes anything for himself. Outwardly shy and reserved. Strict in respect of women. Pays no attention to his appearance. He can do much for us if we are recommended to him by Harry Pollitt or Tores. He is known to the British police as an active communist. He is used to legal work and therefore incautious. But if his attention is drawn to this he will act as required.[4]

Because of Mally's departure from London in the summer of 1937, followed by that of Deutsch in the autumn, the hope that Klugmann 'could do much' was unfulfilled, but this delayed recruitment of Cairncross by Klugmann was more than enough to earn him a place in the history of intelligence. Of particular interest are Klugmann's remarks about Burgess and Maclean, made in the spring of 1937, which demonstrate their skill in concealing their true situation. Of Maclean, Klugmann wrote:

At one time he was a party member but since he joined the diplomatic service two years ago he has broken off all relations with the party and even avoids old comrades as if he were ashamed of the fact that he has gone over to the bourgeoisie. It would not be without risk to approach him and tell him that the party counts on him.

On Burgess. 'He is the most clever and capable of them all. He has distanced himself from us, because his family relations have enabled him to move in high society: ministers, lords, bankers. He is friends with such people as Victor Rothschild. Without wanting to he still thinks on Marxist lines. It would be worthwhile to capture him because if he became an enemy he would be a dangerous enemy.'[5]

Details of Cairncross's recruitment are not available in the documents, but there is a short message from Mally to Moscow on file, dated 9 April 1937: 'We have already recruited Cairncross. We shall call him MOLIERE. We have been able to manage things in such a way that neither M. (MADCHEN/Burgess) nor T. (TONY/Blunt) was endangered. For this Klugmann was used who came over from Paris twice. MOLIERE went to Paris once. He gave Klugmann his agreement to work, but knows, of course, only half of what we want from him. So far his only contact is Klugmann. We shall take him over from him by the end of May.'[6]

Everything went according to plan. Towards the end of May Deutsch went to Paris, where Klugmann introduced him to Cairncross, as Mally reported to the Centre on 9 June 1937. 'We made direct contact. He was very glad that he could make contact with us and not feel himself cut off from the party.' Mally also added Cairncross's opinion of Maclean (codenamed WEISE), with whom he worked in the same department of the Foreign Office. 'He knows from his Cambridge days that WEISE also was a Party member and he says that although WEISE had become a complete snob, he nevertheless maintains a "healthy line" in his work which shows that he has retained Marxist principles in his subconscious. What is more, he is of the opinion that WEISE has the best brains in the Foreign Office.'[7]

This independent opinion was undoubtedly of value to Mally, as a security measure both for Maclean and for the rest of the network, and Maclean was later instructed to be more careful. The Centre responded to Mally's message on Cairncross's recruitment and the establishment of direct contact with him with a short approval in a letter dated 19 June 1937: 'MOLIERE – this is a great achievement.'[8] Congratulations were premature, for in Deutsch's view a great deal of work had still to be done. In a message dated 24 June 1937, he informed the Centre that 'I have met him once. Before I met him his convictions were of a politically deeply pessimistic nature since he was politically completely cut off and very dissatisfied with his work. Hatred for his social environment which behaved very untactfully towards him. He drew the following conclusions for himself: they won't keep him for long and that soon he will have to start looking for another profession. He was very happy that we had established contact with him and was ready to start working for us at once.'[9]

Deutsch reported that he had tried to persuade Cairncross to remain in his job, socialize with his colleagues and 'create the impression that he had accepted his fate'. For this reason and also because there were other alternative sources in the Foreign Office, Deutsch wrote: 'we do not receive any material from him for the time being and we keep him in reserve.'[10]

In trying to understand the nature of the conflict between Cairncross and his Foreign Office environment, Deutsch concluded that 'he is no doubt very intelligent, proud and ideologically on our side. His opposition towards his environment clearly has its origin in his convictions. This feeling of opposition puts him outside the ranks of his environment.' Maclean also commented on the situation, as was reported by Deutsch: 'MOLIERE is very intelligent, but works badly and is mainly careless. This is because he considers himself more clever and better than all the others. WEISE thinks that MOLIERE's position is very weak but that for the time being they will keep him in his job.'[11]

Cairncross's status in the Foreign Office continued to remain uncertain and in October another alarming report reached the Centre from Paris, where Deutsch had gone because he had been unable to stay in London without the proper papers. Once in France he had organized contact between the *rezident* in Spain, Alexander Orlov, and Kim Philby: 'WEISE [Maclean] arrived here a few days ago and told me that MOLIERE would be transferred to another department as they are, apparently, not satisfied with him.'[12] With Deutsch's departure, contact with Cairncross, as with the London *rezidentura*'s other sources, was broken off for a considerable time, and there was no news until September 1938 when a short message was received from Maclean, through a woman codenamed ADA, to the effect that Cairncross had been transferred to the Treasury on 1 October 1938.[13] Cairncross's reappearance was largely due to the omnipresent Burgess, who had reported through the new *rezident* in Spain, Leonid A. Eitington, whom he met in Paris. Burgess had made contact with Cairncross since he regarded the latter as a 'novice and I was afraid that he might drop out altogether, feeling isolated' and 'also because he has at his disposal the very best information imaginable on Czechoslovakia'.[14]

Eitington, arguing that 'the relations between MADCHEN and John are such that in spite of the prohibition they remain in touch anyway', asked the Centre in a letter dated 22 October 1938 to give permission for contact between Burgess and Cairncross so that documents could be received from him.[15] But it seems from a report by the temporary *rezident* in London, on 10 March 1939, that Cairncross had supplied some Foreign Office papers through Klugmann:

In August – September 1938, LISZT [Cairncross] worked in the special 'crisis' group of the Foreign Office and had free access to documents on Munich. When he heard about his transfer to the Treasury, he took these documents with him and passed them at once on to us. In September 1938, LISZT saw in the Foreign Office a report from a British agent in the USSR on the unpreparedness of the USSR to render military assistance to Czechoslovakia. Among those in the Foreign Office who advocated an agreement with Hitler were a) the Ambassador in Berlin, Henderson, and b) the Ambassador in Paris, Phipps.

According to Gorsky, Cairncross was not kept very busy in the Treasury and was preparing a monograph on English literature during the French Renaissance; he noted that 'MAYOR [Klugmann] has made arrangements with LISZT for further meetings with us in London'.[16]

Gorsky's appointment to London meant taking over the legal *rezidentura* from SAM (Grigory B. Grafpen, alias Blank), who had been arrested on 29 December 1938 and sentenced to five years in a labour camp. Thus Gorsky was faced with the difficult task of guiding the *rezidentura* through the chaos of the purges which eliminated 70 per cent of the NKVD. With the forced departure from London of Mally and Deutsch, their illegal network also ceased to exist, and 'the golden decade of the great illegals' had come to an end. Of the very few who survived the purges, such as Deutsch, none could act alone, without the supervision of experienced colleagues, or with the freedom they had enjoyed hitherto. Instead, the intelligence department began to fill up with a new generation which, inevitably, had little knowledge about living abroad or working underground.

As Gorsky took control of the *rezidentura* and the organization built by Mally and Deutsch, becoming the focus of intelligence-gathering in London, he was assisted by the psychological profiles of the members of the Cambridge and Oxford groups written by Deutsch at the Centre's request in the spring of 1939. Of Cairncross, Deutsch observed:

He is 25–6 years old. He studied in Cambridge and was a not very active member of the Communist Party there. He passed the entrance examinations for the British Foreign Office, achieving first place thanks to his outstanding erudition. In November 1936 he started work in the Foreign Office. MOLIERE comes from a Scottish lower-middle-class family – religious people who because of the difficult life they lead are very hard-working and thrifty. The Scots hate the English. MOLIERE inherited some of their characteristics. He is pedantic, industrious, zealous and thrifty. He knows the value of money and how to handle it. He is modest and simple. When I met him the first time and took a taxi this was an event for him – it was the first time in his life he had ridden in a taxi. At the time I established contact with him he lived in a cheap furnished room in a working-class district of London, although he was already working in the Foreign Office. He is very well educated, serious and a convinced communist. He at once expressed his readiness to work for us and his attitude to our work is extremely serious. He is very interested in all our party, practical and theoretical problems and he grasps a great deal. He is avid for knowledge. Every time I met him, he brought with him a list of the most varied questions and explained that he was asking them not because he doubted the justice of our cause but because certain things were not clear to him.

He is simple, sometimes naive and rather provincial. He is very trusting and finds it difficult to hide his views. In the Foreign Office he was considered left wing even before I met him. This was because he did not hide his opinions on certain political questions. Although he realizes that he should not openly show his support for the Communist Party, he could not refrain sometimes from airing his left-wing views. Outwardly he is very modest and kind. His attitude to women is normal. He is disciplined and cautious. He trusts us absolutely and we carry great authority with him. Since he did not have any experience, he decided in the beginning against taking any documents with him. I managed by working on him to put this right and he started to provide documents. It was the same with WEISE [Maclean] at first, but when he saw, step by step, that everything went all right, that we were careful and that we were particularly concerned about his well-being, he overcame his indecision and later became sometimes even careless. In respect of MOLIERE we could have achieved the same, but I left and he remained without contact. It should be said that the indecision on the part of both WEISE and MOLIERE is not due to cowardice but rather to inexperience and the newness of this business. MOLIERE is a lively and warmhearted person. He loves France (this is, in general, true of Scotsmen, in contrast to the English who hate France).[17]

Anatoli Gorsky was left to himself in London with a good dozen sources who were unknown to him. Having received news that the arrangements for meeting Cairncross had been agreed on, the Centre hastened to give instructions to establish personal contact with him and find out whether 'he could supply, as MADCHEN [Burgess] says, the report on the talks between Mussolini and Chamberlain'. Another question which interested the Centre was the information received from Cairncross, through Burgess in September 1938, on the presence of an important British agent inside the People's Commissariat for Foreign Affairs (NKID), who was alleged to be working as 'head of a non-territorial department' and from whom British Intelligence had received three reports, the most recent dated August 1938, concerning correspondence exchanged between Stalin and Edward Beneš. The Centre wanted to know what else Cairncross knew about this British source which Moscow codenamed TEMNY ('Obscure').[18]

On 25 April 1939, eleven days after receiving the Centre's enquiry, Gorsky reported that he had met Cairncross who was working as assistant to the head of the Treasury section supervising the Post Office, the Stationery Office and some other government departments. He sometimes had access to the accounts of the Secret Intelligence Service, the War Office and military intelligence, and he kept in touch with his Foreign Office colleagues, particularly with the heads of the Central European Department, (Sir) William Strang, of the Southern European Department, Edward Ingram, of the Northern Department, (Sir) Laurence Collier, and others, a total of sixteen altogether. Among them was Henry Hankey of the Central European Department, the younger son of the Minister without Portfolio, Lord Hankey, who soon was to be of great service to Cairncross. The latter was also acquainted with a White Russian émigré called Nina, a veteran SIS agent who knew several officials at the Admiralty.

When asked about TEMNY, Cairncross could say nothing new apart from the fact that he was not sure that the agent who had supplied the information on the correspondence between Stalin and Beneš and the agent who passed on Litvinov's report at the Politbureau meeting were one and the same person.[19]

Cairncross's humble and at first sight not very interesting post soon turned out to be vital, granting him access to a mass of secrets. As the source and controller of the British government's finances, the Treasury must know of its commitments at home and abroad, and accordingly receives all the most important defence, Foreign Office and intelligence documents. Traditionally the Chancellor of the Exchequer has always enjoyed a Cabinet status similar to the Secretary of State at the Foreign Office, and by Whitehall standards his staff has always been exceptionally well-informed.

In June 1939, Cairncross demonstrated the extent of his access when he obtained secret documents during his chief's leave and passed them on to Gorsky. Among them were Committee of Imperial Defence reports on illegal activities in Germany; a memorandum on the creation of the Ministry of Information; on propaganda in a future war; a minute from the Director of the Imperial Bureau of Communications, Sir Campbell Stuart, to the Home Secretary, Sir Samuel Hoare; a letter from Hoare to Chamberlain; and an agent report on the situation in Germany.[20]

Subsequently work with Cairncross went so smoothly and productively that Gorsky did not bother to give details of their meetings to the Centre, but merely reported what he was sending with the next mail to Moscow. On 10 July 1939 he sent a batch of defence material which had been circulated to the Treasury, and a fortnight later some fascinating documents on the establishment and offices of the Security Service; on the construction of a chain of secret radio interception stations; and details of the Government Code and Cipher School. In this illuminating material SIS was mentioned as 'the Admiral's organization', a reference to its Chief, Admiral Sir Hugh Sinclair. It also disclosed that MI5 was located in the west wing of Romney House in Marsham Street, Westminster, and had a permanent establishment of 150 in 1938 which might be increased by a further fifty. Information was also received about the SIS branch run by Lawrence Grand, a great enthusiast for illicit propaganda, for whom Burgess was then working. On 10 August Cairncross passed the secret minutes of the Committee of Imperial Defence, items on reserves of raw materials, on the Ministry of Information, instructions on the evacuation of government departments and other papers, amounting in all to nine rolls of film. At the end of 1939 he supplied two War Office directories which showed that a certain Peter Fleming, who had been in the USSR as a foreign correspondent for *The Times*, was working for MI-1 at the War Office, and that Iverach McDonald, who had also been in Moscow for *The Times*, was working for MI-7. The Centre's only disappointment was the unanswered question whether the two journalists were really career intelligence officers, or whether they had been called up and were serving in military intelligence during the war only.[21]

At about this time the Centre was also puzzled by information from Cairncross on the subject of SIS which appeared to contradict other sources. While lunching with Lord Hankey's son, then a Third Secretary at the Foreign Office, he learned that the Soviet ciphers had not been solved, and that SIS's most valuable source was a man in the People's Commissariat for Foreign Affairs. However, in September 1939 he reported that the British were reading Soviet traffic, having received help from the Poles. Cairncross also told Gorsky that, according to a secretary working at the Admiralty, the British knew about the statements made by Marshal Voroshilov on the Anglo-Soviet negotiations. Naturally this caused some alarm, enough for Gorsky temporarily to stop sending enciphered material, and required thorough investigation.[22]

In February 1940, Lavrenti Beria decided to close the London *rezidentura* and when Gorsky reached Moscow he reported that Cairncross would 'in the near future become (or already has

become) the personal secretary of the Financial Secretary to the
Treasury, Captain Harry Crookshank MP, if before that he had not
managed to get more interesting work, such as personal secretary
to the Minister without Portfolio, Lord Hankey, who was charged
with particularly secret tasks by the Government and headed the
activities of the Committee of Imperial Defence'.[23]

Returning to London at the end of 1940, Gorsky re-established
contact with his sources and was pleasantly surprised to find Blunt
employed in MI5 and Philby working for SIS. On Christmas Eve
he brought the atheists in the Centre a wonderful Christmas present,
reporting that Cairncross had been promoted and 'is now working
as secretary to the man I had proposed already at the beginning of
the year that he should seek employment with' (Hankey). He was
already providing SIS reports, contained in incoming and outgoing
Foreign Office telegrams, War Cabinet minutes, reports from the
General Staff on the course and the prospects of the war, and a
mass of other data, the volume of which led the *rezident* to complain
that there was too much to transmit in cipher.[24]

During 1941 the total number of intelligence items provided by
Cairncross reached 3,449, a figure exceeded only by Donald Maclean who passed on 4,419 documents, and the list of papers received
between January and May 1941 takes up eleven pages, mentioning
among many others reports in April and May a telegram from
Anthony Eden to the Foreign Office on a conversation between
Hitler and King Paul of Yugoslavia on the invasion of the USSR; a
telegram from Lord Halifax on a conversation with Sumner Wallace
(of the US State Department) on the same question, and an extract
from an SIS bulletin, dated 4–11 May 1941, on German plans in
respect of the Soviet Union.[25] Naturally, only the most urgent
reports were sent to Moscow by telegram; most of this information
went by diplomatic bag, for example a consignment accompanied
by this letter from Gorsky dated 31 May 1941:

> We are sending 60 films with material from LIST: Foreign Office
> cryptograms, weekly SIS, Foreign office and General Staff bulletins;
> 2 reports from the commission of the BOSS [Lord Hankey] on the
> results of an investigation of the counter-intelligence service with the
> characteristics of leading members of the staff and the functions of
> individual sections; a report on radio measures against night
> bombers; a report from the commission of the BOSS on means and
> methods of bacteriological warfare; documents from the Y Commit-
> tee (a special committee on cipher security).[26]

The value, variety and volume of the Cambridge group's information, which reflected the interesting posts to which the members had been appointed, was considered suspicious by some in Moscow and gave rise to misunderstanding at the Centre. These concerns prompted directive N 4411 which was sent to London at the end of 1941, together with a questionnaire which Gorsky ignored until he received a reminder on 15 March 1942:

> About LIST. It is so far not clear to us in which way LIST obtains such a quantity of material and why his boss who is not even a member of the government has access to such top secret intelligence documents as, for instance, Eden's memorandum of 28 January, Lord Swinton's memorandum on COMPATRIOTS [the CPGB]; copies of Baggallay's telegrams from Kuibyshev, etc. We have already put a number of questions to you in regard to work with LIST, MADCHEN and SOHNCHEN a.o. We await your detailed answer to these questions. Once more we request to inform us by post where LIST is at present working, in which way he obtains the material and passes it on to you, where and how this material is photographed . . . What is the situation in respect of LIST's call-up into the armed forces?[27]

Gorsky's initial failure to answer these queries was undoubtedly a mistake and justifiably gave rise to further questions from the Centre. Indeed, it is remarkable that they had not been put earlier, clearly a reflection of the disorganization handicapping the NKVD resulting from Stalin's purges of 1937 and 1938. Additional difficulties arose at the outbreak of war in Europe when the *rezidenturas* in the occupied countries were closed down, and further time was needed after the Nazi invasion of the Soviet Union to reorganize the service for wartime. In 1941 the Third Department of the First Directorate of the NKVD was headed by Yelena Modrzhinskaya, who took over the supervision of the London *rezidentura* and undertook a personal study of all the Centre's files on former and active sources (see Chapter Seven). Although she reached several incorrect conclusions, these were subsequently put right. As for Cairncross's work for Hankey, Gorsky relayed his answer to Moscow:

> In the course of my work I have access to the FO telegrams, War Cabinet distribution (Distribution B) which I can keep or return (after my master has seen them) as I will. Of course I return the great majority and retain only a few really interesting ones and those which affect subjects he is interested in. I also see a large number of SIS reports, but these must be returned, usually after a lapse of three days. Further, the following documents are circulated to us: Weekly Reports of Operations by the Chiefs of Staff; Weekly Reports on Enemy trading by the MEW; Weekly Summary by the Foreign Office;

the daily reports on bombing by the Home Security Department and the daily War Cabinet Record of Operations and Intelligence. The value of these you will be able to judge from specimens submitted.[28]

Somewhat later Gorsky explained to the Centre how Cairncross had become secretary to Lord Hankey. As it turned out there was nothing miraculous in this: it all came down to the benefits of vegetarianism:

The whole story of how LISZT became personal secretary to BOSS was thought out by us and implemented under our direction although at the very end, when he started to work for BOSS, I was not here. I have already reported this story in detail to Comrade K. and, in brief, it comes down to this. At the end of 1939 in a series of conversations with LISZT we gave him to understand that his future job with Crookshank would hardly be satisfactory for us and that he should try to find something more interesting from our point of view. We were aware that questions were being asked in Parliament about the function of BOSS's son, who acted as his personal secretary. The government then gave assurances that BOSS's son would be dismissed from his job . . . In view of this we drew LISZT's attention to the desirability of his getting the job of personal secretary to BOSS since the latter was exercising exceptionally interesting functions in the War Cabinet and the Committee for Imperial Defence.

Having set ourselves this goal, we began, together with LISZT, to look for ways and means of achieving it. We decided to try and make use of the good relations which existed between LISZT and one of BOSS's sons from the ZAKOULOK [Foreign Office] days and which we knew about. LISZT pointed out that BOSS was an enthusiastic vegetarian and looked with great approval on modern young men who were also vegetarians. Through his son, LISZT also discovered that BOSS frequently visited the Vega vegetarian restaurant near Leicester Square.

After it had been established when BOSS went to this restaurant, often accompanied by his whole family, including the son with whom LISZT was friendly, we instructed LISZT to become a devoted vegetarian and to frequent the restaurant, as far as possible, at the same time as BOSS. LISZT carried out our instructions and this simple scheme led to BOSS finally noticing 'this modest young man who apparently was a fanatical vegetarian', which was not unusual in a restaurant that was rarely full. It so happened that one day BOSS drew his son's attention to LISZT whereupon his son told him that he knew LISZT and then introduced him to his father. In this way the acquaintanceship was established and LISZT succeeded in creating a favourable impression on BOSS.

In conversations with BOSS's son, LISZT hinted a few times at his wish to work for his father. For several months nothing happened and then I went on leave. After my return from leave, at the end of 1940, LISZT told me that our scheme had succeeded completely, since BOSS, under parliamentary pressure, had been compelled to dismiss his son as his personal secretary and release him to the Army. On his son's recommendation, BOSS had asked the Treasury to put LISZT at his disposal and this had been done.[29]

The Centre's worries concerning Cairncross's call-up for military service were far from groundless. At the beginning of 1942, Gorsky had reported that he should have been drafted on 15 January, but Lord Hankey had asked for a postponement until March. When Lord Hankey left his post, Cairncross's call-up was again postponed until 1 May 1942 so he could acquaint his new chief with the current affairs of the office. On 7 May Gorsky relayed the last lot of material from Cairncross's old job, and noted that Cairncross would most likely be exempted from military service and transferred to KURORT, the NKVD's codename for Bletchley Park.[30]

In anticipation of Cairncross's imminent call-up, he and Gorsky had devised a plan similar to the vegetarian scheme and Gorsky, being cautious rather than superstitious, only reported the details after it had been successfully implemented. On 9 June 1942 he informed the Centre that in the course of his work with source PAUL, an unidentified spy who worked at Bletchley Park, he had established the structure and staff of KURORT and, in particular, that the training of personnel and the expansion of this service in wartime was entrusted to Colonel F.W. Nicholls. 'In the course of his professional duties, LISZT became acquainted with Nicholls and by rendering small services (hastening the processing of additional estimates, introducing him to BOSS) established friendly relations with him. During lunch at the Travellers' LISZT complained to Nicholls that he would soon be called up by the Army where he would be unable to use his knowledge of foreign languages. Nicholls started to persuade him to come and work in KURORT. After he received his call-up papers, LISZT told Nicholls about this, remained in his unit for one day and was then put at the disposal of the War Office which conditionally demobilized him and seconded him to KURORT. Formally LISZT is not in military service and considered a civilian employee of a military organization.'

Gorsky also reported that the KURORT school in Bedford, where Cairncross was sent for special training, was preparing two types of specialists, civilian for SIS and the Foreign Office and military for the War Office. He assumed that inasmuch as Cairncross's

Russian was not very good, he would probably be trained for work with the German language. The training would take between one and six months.

In Moscow, the report written by Gorsky (VADIM) was received with mixed feelings: on the one hand, there was satisfaction that the holy of holies of British Intelligence had been penetrated, on the other, there was displeasure at the London *rezident*'s failure to keep the Centre informed of his activities. Gaik Ovakimyan, the Chief of the 3rd Department, underlined in his own hand Modrzhinskaya's minute on Gorsky's letter: 'One cannot consider normal the practice, introduced by VADIM, when we hear about the schemes implemented with agents only in the last instance and even then with considerable delay.'[31]

Cairncross started work at GC & CS at the beginning of August 1942 and, as he had anticipated, acted as an editor/translator in the German section. At the end of October Gorsky summed up the first results, reporting that he had received from him two volumes of the secret training manual on deciphering, a guide for the reading of the German Enigma key codenamed TUNNY and a description of a machine constructed by the British to read the Luftwaffe's cipher traffic. 'In spite of the fact that Cairncross worked in one room with several other people he succeeded in taking with him numerous documents. In his words, the British were interested, in the first place, in what was happening on the Western front and only in the second place processed material emanating from the Eastern front.'

In his letter Gorsky touched briefly on Cairncross's motives for collaborating with Soviet intelligence. He considered that they were a combination of 'our ideology and Anglophobia', noting Cairncross's enthusiasm and recalling how, when working in the Treasury, he had insisted on daily meetings. Describing the personal qualities of this source, the *rezident* referred to his extraordinary linguistic abilities: perfect knowledge of French, German, Spanish and Italian, as well as being able to read and understand texts in Swedish, Norwegian and Russian. Gorsky wrote that Cairncross was also a music-lover: Liszt, Schubert, Schumann, Beethoven, Verdi and Bizet were his favourite composers. 'He was very touched when I presented him with a complete set of records of the *Cavalleria Rusticana* opera as this is one of his favourite musical works.'[32]

The material which Cairncross could pass to Gorsky, he copied out by hand, but frequently he took it from a disposal box where copies to be destroyed were kept. 'There are several thousand documents at a time in the box, and taking a small quantity of them from time to time represents therefore, LISZT states, no danger.'[33]

By the summer of 1943 the intensive work with texts led to a deterioration of Cairncross's eyesight and he sought a transfer to another SIS section where the strain would be reduced. On 1 June 1943 he was relieved of his work as a translator and sent on two weeks' leave. On his return he was transferred to the V(g) sub-section of SIS's counter-intelligence branch, located in Harry Lane, St Albans, and earmarked for transfer to Ryder Street, St James, on 18 July 1943. Cairncross's immediate superior in V(g) was the author Graham Greene, who was referred to by the Centre as LORAN. However, they did not work together because the head of R5 first sent Cairncross for a training attachment to V-03 which was responsible for studying German counter-intelligence organiza-tions on German territory. In V-03 Cairncross worked with William Steedman, a former Passport Control officer, who went through the German intercepts and selected what he needed, then Cairncross registered them. Gorsky reported that 'LISZT is also responsible for the destruction of intercepts. When he started work there was a heap of old intercepts. He destroyed them [evidently registered their destruction], burnt some and passed about 1,500 on to us.'

V-03 had information on the location of German military coun-ter-intelligence stations working against the Soviet Union, the Ast (Abwehrstelle) Ostland in Riga, Bureau Cellarius in Finland, Ast Ukraine and Rovno with substations (Nebenstelle) in Odessa and Nikolayev, Ast Warsaw, Krakow, Poznan. Gorsky reported that 'LISZT will supply a short résumé of contents for our evaluation' and by 15 May this had included material regarding the Abwehr on the Russian front; a memorandum on German Intelligence dated 26 September 1942; the internal code used by German Intelligence, supplied on 19 January 1943 and 9 March 1943; the file in SIS's Central Registry on the surveillance of A. Dyakeli and his organiz-ation in Turkey linked to German Intelligence.[34]

Cairncross was not kept long on V-03 and in September 1943 was, in his own words, 'lent' to V(e), the subsection responsible for the Balkans and the USSR, concentrating mainly on the Balkans. The move was a disappointment to Moscow. He saw only one item connected with the Soviet Union – a telegram sent to Cecil Barclay, the SIS representative in Moscow, informing him, on the basis of German intercepts, about the reorganization of the NKVD, the separation of the Special Department known by the acronym SMERSH from the Counter-Intelligence organization. There was also a file, *The work of the Abwehr in the USSR*, containing some useful, if one-year-old, data on agents.

Section V(e) was headed, according to Cairncross, by Major O'Brien, a sixty-year-old war veteran who spoke Arabic, German and French and was personally acquainted with Churchill. The officer responsible for the Soviet Union was Trevor Wilson, who worked directly under the Deputy Head of the Section, Captain Guthrie, and his assistant was Captain Hutton, who had been transferred to SIS from MI5. The acting Deputy Head of the Section, Harry Hudson Williams, was the liaison officer between SIS and radio intelligence, as well as supervising the SIS station in Istanbul.[35]

In November 1943 the new *rezident* in London, Konstantin Kukin (IGOR), who had replaced Gorsky in June of that same year, informed Moscow that Cairncross would probably soon return to section V-03, noting: 'As before he continues to work for us with enthusiasm and to show initiative.' However, Cairncross's transfer from one section to another temporarily reduced the quantity of information he could transmit. While 1,454 documents were received from him in 1942 and relayed to Moscow, in 1943 they dwindled to just 94. The greatest of Cairncross's achievements was the passing to Soviet intelligence of the Luftwaffe's decrypted signals, which played an important role in the Battle of Kursk in 1943. Other items provided at the Centre's request included details of radio channels used by the German High Command and the Abwehr and, in October 1943, Cairncross disclosed valuable information about Operation ULM, a secret landing by German ski troops planned for the Eastern Front.[36]

In 1944 the quantity of information provided by Cairncross rose to 794 documents, but in August he was transferred to SIS's political branch, Section I, where he became responsible for the processing of all information on Germany and its Eastern neighbours. Although at that time reports were received from Blunt, Philby and Cairncross himself, indicating that the British had stopped decrypting Abwehr radio signals on the Eastern Front and were concentrating their efforts mainly on the Western Front, Cairncross nevertheless continued to have access to some very interesting material. In October 1944 he transmitted a special SIS report, dated 28 October, on Himmler's instructions to set up a Nazi underground resistance organization, an item reproduced from memory by a British source in Germany. Soon afterwards Cairncross also supplied an SIS survey on the USSR which covered the period 1939 to 1944 and included correspondence with the SIS Head of Station in Moscow.[37]

On the eve of the November holidays, the anniversary of the October Revolution, the Soviets rewarded Cairncross for his 'long and useful' work with a gift of £250. It was handed to him on 31

October 1944 with expressions of gratitude, and Cairncross wrote a short note to the Centre, signing himself by his operational pseudonym:

I am delighted that our friends should have thought my services worthy of recognition and am proud to have contributed something to the victories which have almost cleared the Soviet soil of the invaders. I am sorry that the past 18 months have been a lean period. I am not without hope that affairs may take a turn for the better. The premium presented to me is of the most generous nature, and I shall try to express my gratitude for it by redoubled efforts in the future. James Roberts[38]

In January 1945, Cairncross heard that the Treasury had asked SIS to return him, so he asked his Soviet contact how he should react. The *rezident* suggested that agreement should be given to this transfer since, in his view, Philby sufficiently covered the work of SIS. At the Centre the Head of Intelligence, Pavel M. Fitin, wrote 'agree' on the *rezidentura*'s message, but SIS thought otherwise and Cairncross was retained for several more months. This delay enabled him to report at a meeting on 5 February 1945 that the British had intercepted and decrypted a telegram from the Japanese Ambassador in Berlin to his Foreign Ministry to the effect that the Germans were preparing to launch a counter-offensive in the East within the next two weeks, which, in their view, should decide the outcome of the war. It would be launched from two areas, one of which was Pomerania, and Himmler had been appointed Commander in Chief at the Eastern Front with Guderian as his Chief of Staff.[39]

Another interesting item supplied by Cairncross was the news of the British interception of Soviet radio telephone conversations which, he maintained, was conducted by Commander Dunderdale's section which included a man who monitored the Moscow–Yakutsk–Kysyl radio relay channel. Apparently, SIS planned to expand the monitoring to the whole of the Soviet Union.[40] Before he left SIS in June 1945, Cairncross succeeded in getting details of British agents in Finland, Sweden, Denmark, Spain, Portugal and South America. The Centre evaluated this information as very important and gave instructions to thank Cairncross and give him a present.[41]

On 25 June Cairncross started work with the rank of Principal in the Treasury section dealing with War Office estimates, where he routinely handled documents from the Ministry of Supply and the Home Office's Civil Defence branch, and served as secretary of the Treasury Disposal Committee. There is no record of how the value of the documents he supplied was rated, but certain information he received through his connections was particularly appreciated. For example, SIS's Commander Wilfred Dunderdale told him that the Poles had broken the Soviet Air Force ciphers and he also heard that the British had obtained information on preparation of the testing ground for an atom bomb in the area north of Yakutsk, and on the construction of a new radio station there.[42]

Contact with Cairncross was broken off on 22 October 1945, immediately following Igor Gouzenko's defection in Canada, a suspension that was anticipated to last only two or three months, but in fact became nearly three years. In December 1947, Burgess reported that Cairncross's position had improved because Sir Stafford Cripps had been appointed minister, and this prompted the *rezidentura* again to suggest a renewal of the contact. The Centre eventually agreed, although contact was not re-established until 11 June 1948 because Cairncross, as he later admitted, had forgotten the arrangements and responded only to an emergency call. However, at the next meeting, held in July 1948, he started to pass documents.[43]

As Cairncross worked in the department dealing with War Office personnel, he had access to the Army, Navy and Air Force lists, which were considered especially valuable by the Centre, as were War Office documents on the requirements of the armed forces and Civil Defence in personnel and on pre-mobilization measures, as well as the *Technical Intelligence* bulletin. Cairncross did not have direct access to material relating to the development of an atom bomb, but he was able to report that a good friend, George Oram, headed the section dealing with defence supplies, and he did have access to this kind of information. However, to protect him, the Centre forbade him to borrow any material from Oram.[44]

At a meeting on 24 January 1950, Cairncross brought with him, as the *rezidentura* reported, a large quantity of valuable files, accompanied by a personal note: 'I have been appointed Treasury representative to the Western European Union which means that all military documents of the Union will be or should be sent to me. Most of them are of considerable interest. I am already transmitting the old documents. I shall be working under Humphrey Davis (from my old section), but will do a lot of work for E.G. Compton. At present I am sitting in the same room and sharing the same drawer as Oram who is dealing with atomic energy, military research and development. Finally I have partly access, which, in time, I hope, will be full, to all documents and minutes of the Defence Committee.'[45]

The meeting in February 1950 was also marked by the passing of 'a large quantity of important documents' and, as the *rezidentura* noted in the accompanying letter: 'One can judge from the documents passed by KAREL [Cairncross] at the meeting on 21 February 1950 that documents of the highest secrecy pass through his hands. KAREL's new appointment opens to us great possibilities for acquiring interesting material. Among the papers passed by KAREL are a few files related to the atomic problem. In as far as can be judged from the remarks in the margins of these documents, they belong to Cairncross's friend Oram, with whom he evidently shares a safe.' Among this same lot of papers were also documents on bacteriology.[46]

In July 1950, at the start of the Korean War, Cairncross supplied government documents dealing with the influence of events in Korea on British interests and foreign policy in the Far East, and an assessment of the war dated 5 July 1950.[47] In August 1950 another batch of documents was accompanied by a note from Cairncross that caused consternation at the Centre:

I regret that I have to report that my relations with Compton are becoming so strained that I am not at all sure that I can keep this job if the appointment which I now hold will be given a higher grade.[48]

Cairncross's fears were confirmed when he heard upon his return from leave in September 1950 that he had been transferred to the foreign currency control section. 'As I feared, the appointment which I held has been upgraded and has been given to one of my colleagues. I hope, however, to get a job in the Ministry of Supply where I shall be dealing with re-armament questions.'[49]

Naturally Cairncross's transfer and the implied reduction in his access to classified material concerned the Centre, but it was reasoned that if he had fallen under suspicion he would be denied access to any secrets, a point the *rezidentura* put to him. He replied that 'the bad relations with Compton came about only because of the latter's despotic character and his fault-finding, and that the only reason why he was not kept in this job were his bad relations with Compton'.[50]

Everything happened as Cairncross had anticipated and he was transferred from the Treasury to the Ministry of Supply, where he started work on 1 May 1951. The idea of a transfer had been mooted by the Personnel Department and not by Cairncross, and at a meeting on 4 June 1951 he told the Soviets he was working in the planning section where he was dealing with questions related to the land forces.[51]

Although the disappearance of Burgess and Maclean had not yet become widely known to the public at the time of this meeting, the event was the subject of speculation by 23 June and on the assumption that it was necessary to discuss this issue with Cairncross with a view to protecting his security, the *rezidentura* asked the Centre for instructions on what he should do if he felt he was in jeopardy. The Centre replied that Cairncross should be told that the defections represented no danger to him, and that if he were questioned he should answer that he knew Maclean from his time at the Foreign Office and Burgess as an acquaintance whom he had not seen for at least eight to ten years. In case of real danger of arrest, Cairncross should leave the country.[52]

From the file it remains unclear precisely how much knowledge Cairncross had of the rest of the Cambridge ring. He might have guessed about Blunt, and on one occasion when they were colleagues in the Foreign Office, he had asked Maclean if he 'was still in touch', although whether he meant with the CPGB or the Russians is uncertain. Maclean had pretended he did not understand the query, and later received instructions to keep away from Cairncross.

At the meeting on 23 June Cairncross arrived in a good mood and was very calm, proof of his composure being the large parcel of secret documents he carried. As predicted, he asked about Burgess and Maclean and, having heard the Centre's explanation, said that 'he was now ready for any talks with counter-intelligence'. He recalled that he had met Maclean a few times in 1937 and 1938, at the Travellers Club where they had greeted each other, but had never shared a table. Burgess, of course, knew about Cairncross's links with the Soviets, and they had once lunched together at the club, but had seldom met since 1943. Cairncross supposed that in checking on the backgrounds of civil servants, MI5 could discover his Communist past, and in that eventuality he would try and explain it away as a passing youthful flirtation which had been followed by disappointment. Although such a discovery could affect his position, the worst that could happen would be a transfer to non-secret work.

Cairncross also gave a detailed account of his new job in a Ministry of Supply section headed by John Horsefield, one of whose deputies was Elizabeth Ackroyd, and he acted as her assistant and dealt with armament questions. The section received papers from the War Office, the Joint War Production Committee, the Committee on Production Capacity and other government departments including the Chiefs of Staff Committee and the Cabinet, and these were the documents Cairncross brought to the meeting.[53]

Exactly a month later Cairncross again passed a large quantity of most important documents and announced that as everything was quiet he intended to go on holiday in the middle of September 1951.[54] The documents he supplied were considered so important that they were reported to Stalin, and his attention was drawn to the fact that in June and July 1951, 1,339 pages of documents were received, many of them suggesting that the British rearmament programme had been completed. In a report to Stalin sent by the Head of the Committee on Information, Valerian A. Zorin, on 7 August 1951, he mentioned that the total had reached 1,339 photo pages of English text and tables. Of special importance was a report from the Central Statistics Office on the actual production of various types of weapons and military equipment from April 1948 till March 1951, and the planned military production up to March 1954.[55]

Despite the defections of Burgess and Maclean, Cairncross retained his composure, bringing new documents to a meeting on 20 August 1951. He reported that all was quiet at work, but the blow fell at the beginning of September when he was summoned by MI5 for an interview with Arthur Martin. Most of his questions had been anticipated, so Cairncross was ready to answer them, and the conversation boiled down to whether he knew Burgess and Maclean. Cairncross said only that they were acquainted, and had occasionally greeted each other. Had Cairncross been involved in the Communist Party? No, as a student he had shared the Party's views on Germany, but his opinions now were totally different from those he had held when he was young.

After the interrogation Martin showed him a letter, addressed to him and sent before the war, which started with the words 'With fraternal greetings' and contained information on relations between Hitler and the Italians. Cairncross denied that he had ever received such a letter, and asserted he could not think who could have sent it. In any event, he claimed that at the time he was working at the Foreign Office so a letter of this kind was entirely normal.

Cairncross also told his Soviet contact that he had destroyed his photographic equipment, which he had kept at home, and the next meeting was fixed for January but, because Cairncross made a mistake in the time, it did not take place until March 1952.[56] On 3 March he arrived without any material and reported that in December 1951 he had again been questioned by MI5, this time by a young officer who talked quietly and politely, in contrast to Arthur

Martin's aggressive and insistent tone. His questions had concentrated on the origin of the letter, so Cairncross said that from a number of clues, such as the abbreviation 'Mr' before the Christian name of the addressee, the crossed downward stroke of the 7 and the expression 'With fraternal greetings' he deduced that the letter had been written by a foreigner who was a member of the Communist Party, but he had no acquaintances of this kind.

Cairncross reported that two weeks earlier he had been returned from temporary loan to the Ministry of Supply to the Treasury, which had suffered some sharp staff reductions, explaining that his relations with the woman for whom he worked had been strained. He had noticed no signs of being followed so the next meeting was fixed for a month later, but on 6 April the *rezidentura* saw his danger signal. In spite of the *rezidentura*'s desire to find out what had happened, the Centre forbade a meeting[57] so contact with Cairncross was broken off and Soviet Intelligence remained ignorant of his fate. A check in the telephone directory established that he was still living at his old address, but he was not mentioned in the Civil Service List. A review of a book by Cairncross was noticed in *The Times Literary Supplement* of 11 January 1957, and some light was thrown on the situation by a report from Philby dated 4 August 1959 in which, quoting Blunt, he said that 'when Guy's flat was searched MI5 found among other things a handwritten memorandum containing intelligence information. Investigation of the handwriting led to Cairncross and he came under serious suspicion. He was able, however, to show that this was merely a memorandum from one civil servant to another and that it had no connection with any foreign power. I doubt whether this explanation fully satisfied the authorities, but, apart from dismissing him from the Treasury, no further steps were taken.'[58]

Having been warned by MI5 that to remain in England would risk prosecution, Cairncross took his German-born wife to Geneva where they worked as translators for various United Nations agencies. Later, after working in the Far East for the UN Food and Agriculture Organization, they settled in Rome. When, in November 1979, Cairncross heard that Blunt had been exposed publicly as a traitor, he anticipated similar treatment, and the following year he was identified as a member of the notorious Cambridge Ring-of-Five. Avoiding media scrutiny, he fled to France and completed his memoirs shortly before his death in October 1995. According to his version of events, he had been coerced into helping the Soviets, and had never compromised Allied atom secrets. As we shall see, this was far from the full story.

CHAPTER X

Atom Secrets

In 1938 the 10th section of the NKVD's Fifth Department was given responsibility for the collection of scientific and technical information and in May 1940 it was headed by Leonid R. Kvasnikov, a graduate of the Institute of Chemical Engineering who had worked in the security service since 1939. He had just returned from a mission to Poland, lasting several months, where he had been attached as an intelligence officer to the commission for resettlement in the eastern part of the country, occupied by the Red Army. His contact with the German authorities, principally the Gestapo, had filled him with grave forebodings of the imminent war. One of the Gestapo officers, who had made no effort to disguise Nazi aggression towards Russia and was proud of the 'new order', had readily organized a trip to Berlin. In the capital of the Third Reich, Kvasnikov's opinion that Hitler would not confine himself to the conquest of the former German territory he called 'Lebensraum' was confirmed, and he concluded that sooner rather than later the Führer would direct his tanks even further eastwards. Upon his return to Moscow, where he received a severe reprimand for his unauthorized trip to Berlin, Kvasnikov took charge of the scientific and technical intelligence section which had been badly depleted during the years of Stalin's purges, a period when one discovery had followed another in nuclear physics, and considerable advances were made in the military use of atomic energy.

In 1939 the Frenchman Frédéric Joliot-Curie, the Hungarian Leo Szilard, working in the United States, and other physicists were working on the emission of free neutrons as a result of the disintegration of Uranium-235 nuclei, and were predicting the possibility of a chain reaction which would release colossal amounts of energy. In the autumn of that year the Soviet physicists Georgy Flyorov and Konstantin Petrzhac discovered the spontaneous disintegration of U-235, while Yakov B. Zeldovich and Yuli B. Khariton in Leningrad determined the magnitude of the enormous energy freed in this process. Kvasnikov monitored these scientific developments and, seeing the military potential, prepared a questionnaire to collect the relevant information. This was despatched to the countries he considered most likely to be engaged in the military application of atomic power, and although the text of the questionnaire and the date of its despatch are not preserved in the files, Kvasnikov recalls that it 'was not sent to the US because there was nobody to send it to, Ovakimyan having been detained by the American authorities'. This comment fixes the date to the middle of 1941, for Gaik Ovakimyan, the illegal *rezident* in the US under Amtorg cover since 1934, was been arrested in May 1941, and deported in a prisoner exchange two months later.

The first to react to the questionnaire was the London *rezidentura*. On 25 September 1941, VADIM (Anatoli V. Gorsky) reported that on 16 September a meeting had taken place in London of the Uranium Committee, a Cabinet sub-committee, at which it had been concluded that:

> It is quite feasible to develop a uranium bomb, especially if Imperial Chemical Industries (ICI) undertakes to do this in the shortest possible time. The representative of Woolwich Arsenal, Ferguson, stated that the bomb fuse could be constructed in a matter of months.

Gorsky's telegram contained certain scientific and technical information suggesting that the development of the atom bomb was already in progress in the USA, and concluded with a report that 'the Chiefs of Staff, at their meeting on 20 September 1941, had taken the decision to start on the construction of a plant in Britain for the manufacture of a uranium bomb.' On 3 October 1941 he despatched another message on the work of the Uranium Committee which contained information on the proposed magnitude of the critical mass of uranium in the bomb, and the problems connected with the industrial separation of U-235 by gas diffusion. The full report, delivered to the London *rezidentura* by John Cairncross, was sent by courier and in translation consisted of seventeen pages of most valuable data. The subsequent encoded reports to the Centre were prepared by Vladimir B. Barkovsky, then aged twenty-eight, who had graduated from the Moscow Lathe and Instrument Institute in 1939. He had been selected by the Deputy Chief of Intelligence, Pavel A. Sudoplatov, for work in Britain immediately after he had graduated from the School for Special Assignments, a facility set up in 1938 to train a new generation of intelligence officers to replace the heroes of the 'golden decade' at the end of the 1920s and the first half of the 1930s who had been purged by Yagoda and Yezhov. Barkovsky remembers how Gorsky summoned him late in the evening, presumably immediately after he returned from his meeting with Cairncross although he did not disclose his source, and ordered him to prepare short résumés from the original English material. Barkovsky was, of course, unfamiliar with the subject of the reports and he worked hard throughout the night to understand what it was all about.

Barkovsky's initiation into atomic secrets in the autumn of 1941 was also his introduction to a small circle of privileged intelligence officers who are now known as the atom spies. The experience determined his further career in the service, and became his lifelong interest. Within six months of his sleepless night poring over the first reports he was sufficiently familiar with atomic theory to be able to run other sources of information, but before that there were still some serious obstacles to overcome.

Leonid Kvasnikov recalls that Lavrenti Beria, the head of the NKVD, was always suspicious of atom research intelligence, apparently convinced that the intention was to lure the Soviet Union into enormously expensive but unproductive work. He was encouraged in this view by scientists to whom the material had been submitted for evaluation, who considered that although it might be possible to develop an atom bomb, it could only be accomplished in the distant future. The names of the experts to whom Beria turned for advice were unknown to Kvasnikov, but he supposed that they were physicists languishing in the NKVD's concentration camps. Even when the atom project made progress, Beria never lost his suspicion and Kvasnikov remembers that once, when he submitted new material on 'the atom problem', Beria said: 'If this turns out to be deception material, down you all go into the cellars!'

In February 1942 the Plenipotentiary for Scientific Affairs of the State Committee for Defence, Sergei V. Kaftanov, heard from the GRU of the capture in a raid on the Ukrainian town of Taganrog of a German officer named Vandervelde who had been found to possess an exercise book filled with incomprehensible notes. Experts who studied the pages concluded that they were of considerable value because they indicated that work was in progress in Germany on a military atomic project. Kaftanov reported this to the State Committee for Defence, and it was this German interest that finally convinced Beria of the feasibility of developing an atom bomb, prompting him to submit the information received from the London *rezidentura* to Stalin.

The NKVD prepared a memorandum in March. Apart from the descriptive element, this paper contained proposals for what the

Soviets should do next, suggesting that a consultative body on atomic problems should be set up and attached to the State Committee for Defence, and that prominent experts should be allowed to study the NKVD's material so that it could be evaluated and exploited. The first draft of the memorandum preserved in the files was never signed by Beria; according to Kvasnikov, the suspicious head of the NKVD was forced to submit another version to Stalin, on much the same lines, but this has been lost.

The Soviet physicist Georgy Flyorov, who had volunteered for the armed forces at the beginning of the war and was attending a course at the Air Force Academy in Yoshkar-Olu, had always been convinced of the possibilities offered by atomic energy, and he confided in Igor V. Kurchatov, a member of the Committee for Defence, as well as the Director of Kazan's Physical-Technical Institute, A. F. Yoffe. In May 1942, Flyorov found himself in Voronezh and, browsing through scientific literature in the university library, noticed that foreign publications on atomic issues had disappeared. This was a clear sign that research in this field had become classified and he wrote another letter to the State Committee for Defence raising the question of developing an atomic bomb. His second letter, which contained the sentence 'It is essential to manufacture a uranium bomb without delay', was passed on to Stalin and coincided with Beria's submissions and those made by Kaftanov. Flyorov's timely intervention hastened the decision to tackle the problem of building a Soviet atomic bomb, and consequently the collection of relevant intelligence. On 26 November 1942 a special questionnaire was sent to New York, and another went to London two days later, containing instructions to assess the chances of acquiring new sources. It so happened that the day after receiving the questionnaire, Gorsky was able to report that Professor James Chadwick, together with three young scientists, had left for Canada to work on the atom project.

In order to carry out their new task, the NKVD set up a special substation in New York, for scientific and technical intelligence designated 'XY' and headed by Kvasnikov himself, by now a great enthusiast for the atom project. His immediate subordinates were Anatoli A. Yatskov, Semyon M. Semyonov and Aleksandr S. Feklisov; during the war years Vladimir B. Barkovsky and Pavel D. Yerzin were directly responsible for the collection of atom intelligence in London. Gorsky, the *rezident* in London who had received the very first uranium bomb papers, said to Barkovsky, 'You are an engineer, you deal with it', but in 1943 he was replaced by Konstantin M. Kukin, who not only supervised the operations on the atom problem but, according to Barkovsky, played a key role himself.

The Centre's work on the atomic problem, codenamed ENOR- MOZ, was supervised by the the Head of the 3rd Department of the NKVD's First Directorate, and later by the Deputy Head of Intelligence, Gaik Ovakimyan, while a staff intelligence officer, Major Yelena M. Potapova, was directly responsible for the pro- cessing and translation of all the material; at certain stages she was assisted by an officer of the 3rd Department named Andrei Graur. According to the file, Yelena Modrzhinskaya, Dmitri F. Ustinov and Cohen were initiated into certain purely operational aspects of the case, and Ovakimyan reported on all operational questions and intelligence material received directly to the Head of the First Direc- torate, Pavel Fitin. Through him or the Head of the NKVD, Vsevo- lod N. Merkulov, all the material reached Beria who co-ordinated the entire project.

Outside the NKVD only three civilians knew about the collection of atom research intelligence: the Deputy Chairman of the Council of People's Commissars and People's Commissar for the Chemical Industry, Mikhail G. Pervukhin, his personal secretary, A.I. Vasin, and the physicist Igor Kurchatov. The concentration of the NKVD's efforts brought its first results in the beginning of 1943 when Bar- kovsky established contact with a valuable source of information on atom research in Britain known only as 'K'. The Centre had learned of 'K' in December 1942 when the *rezidentura* reported that a Communist sympathizer had passed a detailed report on atom research in Britain and America. The unnamed scientist intended to send the material to the CPGB but it had been relayed to the Soviets, which suggested that the scientist had been ideologically motivated. With ENORMOZ in mind, Gorsky had asked the Centre for permission to establish direct contact with this source and when approval had been given Gorsky asked his contact to meet the scientist again and ask him to agree to a meeting with a Soviet intelligence officer. In a letter to the Centre dated 10 March 1943 the *rezidentura* reported on the meeting with 'K'. 'At first he hesi- tated, saying that he would have to think it over and that he saw no need for meeting anybody since he had already written all he knew about the atomic problem. Later in the conversation his atti- tude changed and he said that he hoped it would not be an English- man since his English comrades were very careless. Finally, after assurances that everything would be properly organized, he said that he would be glad to meet our comrade.'

The meeting took place in January 1943 at a tube station, and after the usual signs and passwords had been exchanged, the scientist was judged to be straightforward and friendly, although obviously nervous. The meeting lasted more than an hour and a half, during which nothing was called directly by its name, but '"K" knew with whom he had agreed to cooperate,' concluded the *rezidentura*.

When Barkovsky met his new source for the first time he was asked whether he understood nuclear physics and, upon receiving an unsatisfactory reply, the scientist said that he wanted his contact not to be just a transmitting channel, but to understand what it was all about. He urged the intelligence officer to study *Applied Nuclear Physics* by Pollard and Davidson. Barkovsky took his advice, and was grateful to 'K' for insisting on this as the American textbook turned out to be a great help to him in running his source.

'K' passed on the secret material to which he had direct access and, being of a daring nature and something of an adventurer, he took what was kept in the safes of his colleagues. Barkovsky recalls that he handed over the impression of a key of which a duplicate was required. It was too dangerous to have this done in a local shop, and it would take too long to send the impression to the Centre: the wartime diplomatic bag had to travel via the USA and the Far East, taking months to reach Moscow. However, as a young man Barkovsky had been a sixth-grade fitter, so he did the job himself and made duplicates that fitted perfectly:

> As a result of the decision taken by us we manufactured a copy of the key for 'K' and worked out arrangements for meetings so that we can contact him three times a week in London without prior notification.

The volume of documents reaching the *rezidentura* considerably increased, comprising British and American originals, the latter being passed to the British in accordance with the Anglo-American agreement on atomic co-operation. Among them, noted Barkovsky, were various American documents, apart from those officially passed on, which bore signs of having been secretly photographed. The number of these copies, apparently obtained illicitly by the British, increased towards the end of the war when the Americans considerably reduced the scope of their co-operation.[1]

'K's importance as a source is confirmed by a reference to him in an internal NKVD memorandum entitled 'On the composition of the agent network for ENORMOZ of the First Directorate of the NKVD of the USSR (as of August 1945)':

During the period of his co-operation with us he supplied an enormous quantity of most valuable, genuine documents in the form of official American and British reports on the work on ENORMOZ and, in particular, on the construction of uranium piles.

Describing 'K's relationship with the NKVD, Barkovsky noted in a letter to the Centre that he had been motivated by ideology, and was scrupulous when it came to money: '"K", as before works for us with enthusiasm, but still turns down the slightest hint of financial reward. Once we gave him more to cover his expenses than he had asked for. He showed his displeasure and stated that he was suspicious of our desire to give him financial help. He asked us to stop once and for all our attempts to do so. In view of this, we fear that any gift to him as a sign of gratitude for his work would have a negative effect. "K" is completely unselfish and extremely scrupulous in regard to anything that might appear as "payment" for his work.'

Another of the London *rezidentura*'s sources, codenamed MOOR and run by Barkovsky, passed on information about the separation of U-235 and on the efforts made by the Americans and British to find new deposits. A third ENORMOZ source in Britain was KELLY who, like 'K', passed on important documents and in June 1945 supplied more than 35 reports and scientific correspondence on atom bomb developments.

Having started the ENORMOZ project in the autumn of 1941 with John Cairncross's reports, the London *rezidentura* continued to be Moscow's main source of Allied atom secrets at least until the end of 1944, as confirmed by an assessment entitled *A Plan of Measures for the operational exploitation of the ENORMOZ agent network*, prepared for the NKGB leadership and dated 5 November 1944:

> 2. In Britain. The positive results which have been obtained in the exploitation of the ENORMOZ agent network as a whole have come mainly from the London *rezidentura*. . . In spite of the participation in the work on the ENORMOZ problem of a large number of scientific organizations and scientists in America, according to most of the information reaching us from agent sources, cultivation there is slow which is why the greater part of information on that country does not come from the *rezidentura* in the USA but from the *rezidentura* in Britain. On the basis of information received from the London *rezidentura*, the Centre has repeatedly sent guidelines on its work to the New York *rezidentura* and also sent a trained agent. The New York

rezidentura has, however, not fully taken advantage of these possibilities. During the whole period of the work on ENORMOZ, they have recruited only one agent and his access is limited.

An example of such guidelines, prepared on the basis of 'K's material and sent to the US, is a letter from the Centre dated 27 July 1943 and listing target atomic weapon facilities:

1. The group of Professor A. Compton, the head of the entire MANHATTAN project in the Research Committee for National Defence, where regular reports are received on the results of the work of all research and project groups.
2. The Columbia group of which Professor Danning and Professor Urey are members.
3. The Chicago group.
4. The California group.
5. The Kellogg Company.

Even in 1945, when the 'XY' sub-*rezidentura* in New York had acquired a number of sources, London's importance remained undiminished and in a report in August 1945 to Vsevolod Merkulov, the People's Commissar for Security, the Chief of Intelligence, Pavel Fitin, praised the *rezidentura*:

Extremely valuable information on the scientific developments of ENORMOZ reaches us from the London *rezidentura*. The first material on ENORMOZ was received at the end of 1941 from LISZT [Cairncross]. This material contained valuable and highly secret documentation, both on the essence of the ENORMOZ problem and on the measures taken by the British government to organize and develop the work on atomic energy. This material formed the point of departure for building the basis of and organizing the work on the problem of atomic energy in our country.

In connection with the reception in Britain of American and Canadian material on ENORMOZ, in accordance with the exchange programme of technical information, we are receiving material from the London *rezidentura* which throws light on the state and course of the work on ENORMOZ in three countries: Britain, the USA and Canada.

Vladimir Barkovsky, who is the best informed KGB officer on the history of the Soviet bomb, discriminates between the information obtained in the USA and in Britain up to the end of 1945: 'In the USA we obtained information on how the bomb was made and in Britain of what it was made, so that together they covered the whole problem.'[2]

Apart from scientific and technical information, the London *rezi-*

dentura also reported on the way the bomb development work was organized in Britain. The Centre learned that this work had been started by the Committee for the Military Application of Uranium Disintegration (MAUD), subordinated to the Ministry of Industry and later to be entrusted to the Department of Scientific and Industrial Research (DSIR), headed by Professor Sir Edward Appleton and supervised by the Lord President of the Council, Sir John Anderson. Within the DSIR, the Directorate of Tube Alloys was formed, headed by (Sir) Wallace Akers, the research director of ICI. The *rezidentura* also reported that the work on rapid neutrons was conducted in Liverpool by Professors Chadwick, Fish and Joseph Rotblat, and on the separation of isotopes by Professor (Sir) Franz Simon, while in Cambridge Professors J.B.S. Haldane, Lev Kowarsky and Allan Nunn May concentrated on slow neutrons. It was also said that some of the scientists had been moved to Canada, together with Professor Chadwick and Niels Bohr, who had escaped from Denmark with the help of SIS. According to a report from Philby dated 20 November 1945, British Intelligence had also set up a new section known as TAL (Tube Alloys Division) to disseminate information on atom research undertaken abroad, principally in the Soviet Union. Headed by Commander Eric Welsh RNVR, formerly the head of SIS's Norwegian section, it was located at SIS's London headquarters in Broadway, Victoria. Philby's illuminating report served to remind the Soviets that it was essential to surround the work being carried out in the Soviet Union with the strictest secrecy.

Meanwhile the 'XY' sub-*rezidentura* in New York experienced, in the early stages, considerable difficulty in approaching those who had access to information about the atom bomb because the nuclear physicists assigned to the MANHATTAN project were located in a number of strictly guarded facilities, far beyond the reach of the New York *rezidentura*, and they very rarely left the compounds. However, after much persistence, sources were acquired at all the key atom research centres in North America, and the breakthrough was achieved with the help of an important reorganization in Moscow.

In July 1943 the Head of the 3rd Department of the NKGB's First Directorate, Colonel Ovakimyan, prepared a memorandum for the Head of the Security Service, Vsevolod Merkulov, while the Chief of Intelligence, Pavel Fitin, submitted a more detailed paper on 11 August 1943 together with a review of work on the atom problem. Both documents recommended handing over all the work on ENORMOZ to the NKGB's First Directorate, a proposal prompted by the need to co-ordinate and concentrate all the relevant intelligence. The principal recommendation was to transfer the GRU's sources to the NKGB, and Merkulov minuted his approval on 13 August, noting that the GRU Chief, Leonid Ilyichev, 'does not object in principle. You should arrange a meeting with him to discuss the details.' This solution proved to be timely because, soon after the conversation between Merkulov and Ilyichov, the secret lines of the NKVD and the GRU accidentally crossed in London, a muddle caused by Klaus Fuchs.

At the beginning of 1943 the London *rezident*, Konstantin M. Kukin, had reported that when checking a list received from 'K' of people working on ENORMOZ, his attention had been drawn to Klaus Fuchs, a refugee who unexpectedly turned out to be an illegal member of the German Communist Party. According to 'K', Fuchs was working on rapid neutrons at Birmingham University and when the *rezident* investigated, he learned that Fuchs was known to Jurgen Kuczinsky, codenamed KARO, a German refugee from before the war. However Kuczinsky, who was not a formal agent, categorically refused to talk about Fuchs and behaved so strangely that it was concluded that he knew Fuchs was working for the Soviets. Kukin asked the Centre to check on Fuchs, an enquiry that, at the end of November 1943, revealed that Fuchs had been a GRU agent since August 1941, when he had been approached on Kuczinsky's recommendation.[3] General Ilyichov also reported that Fuchs was expected to leave for the USA imminently, together with a group of other British nuclear physicists, and that arrangements for meeting him in New York had been made already. In January 1944, in accordance with the agreement to share atom sources, details of these rendezvous arrangements were sent to the NKGB.

The agreement between the NKVD and the GRU conceals more than it reveals, but indicates that each case would be handled separately, depending upon the operational requirements. During the period of his co-operation with the GRU, Fuchs passed on a number of theoretical papers on the fission of the atom and the construction of a uranium bomb which were sent to the plenipotentiary of the State Committee for Defence of the USSR, Sergei Kaftanov, and later to the Deputy Chairman of the Council of People's Commissars, Mikhail Pervukhin. A list of the reports received from Fuchs shows that the first were received in Moscow on 22 and 30 September 1941, while Cairncross sent material to Moscow on 25 September and 3 October. After an interval, Fuchs became active again in May 1943, only six months after 'K's original tip.

Contact with Fuchs was made in the United States on 5 February 1944 by Harry Gold, an 'XY' agent who in turn was run by Anatoli

Yatskov. The arrangements for their meetings at the front door of the Henry Street Settlement in New York, worked out by the GRU, were so good that they remained effective as a contingency plan in case contact with Fuchs was lost in the US, or if he unexpectedly returned. However, the *rezidentura*'s agent must have looked a little strange, hanging around the door of a well-known Jewish charity organization, holding in his gloved hands a third glove. Later this glove was changed for another identifying object which would attract less attention.

Immediately following their initial encounter Gold reported that Fuchs was 'about 5ft 10 in., thin, pale and his behaviour was very reserved at first; this is a good sign. K[laus] is well but not fancily dressed. Obviously he has worked with our people before and he is fully aware of what he is doing. Also he is apparently one of us in spirit.' Fuchs volunteered information about the exchange of scientific data between the British and the Americans and noted that 'The two countries had worked together before 1940. Then there was a lapse till 1942 and, even now, K[laus] says, much is being withheld from the British. Even Niels Bohr, who is now incognito in this country as "Nicholas Baker", has not been told everything.'

Gold met Fuchs in New York on a number of occasions, as is well documented elsewhere, but on 5 August 1944 he failed to come to a meeting, and on 11 August contact was lost when Gold could not make the rendezvous. Fuchs probably missed the first meeting because he was getting ready to leave for 'Camp Y' in New Mexico, where the first atom bomb was under construction, and contact was not re-established until 21 February 1945, at the home of Fuchs's sister in Cambridge, Massachusetts, in accordance with the agreed contingency plan. On this occasion Fuchs handed over some very important material, and made a request: 'K[laus] does, however, want one thing; when we enter Kiel and Berlin in Germany he wants the Gestapo Headquarters there to be searched and his dossier (which is very complete) destroyed, before it should fall into other hands. I told him we would try to do this, if at all possible.' Fuchs had always known that his Communist Party membership in Germany before the war would have been noted by the ubiquitous Gestapo, and he was anxious that, if discovered, details of his previous political activism would compromise his status and his security clearance in England.

For their next meeting Gold travelled to the national park, as the NKGB called the prohibited zone around Los Alamos, and returned to New York on 11 June 1945 with more valuable data, including the news that the first bomb was to be tested on 10 July. Their last encounter in America took place on 19 September 1945 when arrangements were made for meetings in England after Fuchs's return. The next was scheduled for the first Saturday in December 1945 at 8pm in Mornington Crescent, north London, but it never took place because all operations were suspended in November as a result of Igor Gouzenko's defection in Canada. Clues provided by the GRU code clerk alerted MI5 to the activities of the Cambridge-educated physicist Allan Nunn May, and almost simultaneously the FBI began an investigation based on a confession volunteered by Elizabeth Bentley in August 1945. Nunn May, who had supplied Colonel Zabotin of the Soviet Embassy in Ottawa with uranium samples and other atom secrets from his wartime research post in Montreal, was arrested at London University in March 1946. By then Bentley, formerly a key member of Gaik Ovakimyan's illegal network, had named eighty members of her organization, thereby forcing the Centre to suspend operations everywhere.

The Centre monitored Gouzenko's betrayal through Kim Philby in London, who received regular briefings on the defector's disclosures. In his report of 18 November 1945 he described the Nunn May investigation:

> Gouzenko, cipher clerk of the Zabotin organization, has been given the codename CORBY. MI5 has established four planned meetings of May with his London contact. These meeting were fixed for 7, 17 and 27 October and 7 November. Neither May nor any of his contacts appeared at these meetings. In London they are of the firm opinion that May, as well as other agents from the Zabotin network, were warned of the impending danger. According to MI5, May has not put a foot wrong from the time he arrived in England. He did not establish any suspicious contacts. He does not show any signs of being afraid or worried and continues to work quite normally on his academic research. Bearing this in mind, MI5 came to the conclusion that May was a tough customer who will not break down under questioning until he is confronted with fresh and convincing evidence. The matter was postponed indefinitely for serious political considerations. It is not only a question of friendly relations with the USSR, but also of the future control over atomic secrets.
>
> Attlee intends to discuss the CORBY case with Truman and Mackenzie King ... The interested departments (MI5, FBI and RCMP) fear that the decision will be contradictory or such that it cannot be carried out since (1) it will require the simultaneous arrest of all the suspected persons in the United Kingdom, Canada and the USA (this

exceeds the possibilities of the RCMP which can only cope with six of them); (2) it will require the arrest and questioning of the suspects without any publicity (this is, in practice, also impossible since relatives and friends will start enquiries etc); 3) it will require the arrest and subsequent trial of the suspects (the available evidence is not sufficient and the case may have to be dropped).

The arguments prepared by the Foreign Office for Attlee show an increasing tendency to take energetic steps. They argue in favour of arrest and interrogation and, where possible, prosecution of the suspects, the recall of Zabotin and the Soviet Ambassador in Canada and a sharp protest to the Soviet Government. They don't insist particularly on wide publicity of this case but are of the opinion that fear of publicity should not stop us from taking action.

Some indications show, however, that the Canadians and Americans are less enthusiastic about this and may resist the Foreign Office.

After the Centre's suspension of operations in September, the London *rezidentura* avoided contact with Fuchs, so his fate remained unknown until August 1946 when Kukin was instructed to send an officer to the rendezvous, simply to observe whether Fuchs turned up. He was ordered not to approach Fuchs or talk to him as the Centre only wanted to make sure that he was alive, in good health and adhering to the arrangements for the meeting. Kukin entrusted Pavel Yerzin with this mission and although he went to the rendezvous at the appointed time, he did not see Fuchs. It is possible that he went to Mornington Crescent NW1, but there is another street in Houslow, west London, with the same name, so he asked the Centre to check on the exact meeting place.

The Centre's reply was overtaken by events because Fuchs himself made independent contact through two channels, via some German Communist émigrés and through his links with the British Communist Party. Neither channel was directly linked to Soviet Intelligence, and although they were conscious of Party discipline there was a risk that they might be indiscreet about his request, particularly in front of other individuals who could easily be MI5 agents. Alternatively, they might inadvertently give away Fuchs's secret by mentioning his name near hidden microphones, installed by MI5 to eavesdrop on Communists.

The German channel consisted of three people, the first of whom was Jurgen Kuczinsky's wife, her husband having already returned to Germany. She was on the point of following him home so she had directed Fuchs to Hanna Klopstock, another German émigré who, in turn, approached the leader of the German refugees in Britain, Hans Zibert, and he got in touch with the Soviets. Kuczinsky's wife knew about the circumstances in which Fuchs started co-operating with the GRU, but it was not clear whether she had told the story to Klopstock and Zibert. In any case, the danger of Fuchs being compromised clearly existed and Kukin felt that he should immediately be contacted and warned of the need to be circumspect.

The warning would have come too late, for at a meeting with Yerzin, Hans Zibert passed on a message written down as dictated by Hanna Klopstock which included Fuchs's place of work, the Atomic Energy Research Establishment at Harwell in Berkshire, his telephone number, Abingdon 620, extension 73, and details of Fuchs's story of how during his earlier stay in England he had been in contact with ALEKSANDR (the GRU officer Simon Kremer, operating under diplomatic cover in London) and, after Kremer left, with a girl who lived in Oxford. While he was in America he had remained in regular contact, but this had been broken off in the autumn of 1945 immediately following the arrest of Dr Allan Nunn May. He had explained that in London he was to come to Mornington Crescent Underground station, which he did on a number of occasions, but his Soviet contact did not turn up so he had decided to get in touch with the Soviets through Jurgen Kuczinsky. He did not tell Kuczinsky's wife why he needed her husband, but she gave him Hanna Klopstock's address and it was to her that he told his story. He also said that he worked at a secret facility under surveillance of British counter-intelligence, and that it would be impossible to get in touch by telephone. Klopstock arranged a further meeting with him in London, but in the event she could not go, because her child was ill and she was unable to leave him.

Already too many people knew about the Fuchs case, although Hans Zibert, himself an experienced Party member who had been involved with the Party since school, said he was sure of Hanna Klopstock's reliability. After his graduation from the Kassel Academy in philosophy, pedagogics and psychology, Zibert had taught in Kassel's working-class districts, but had been sacked for agitation and was arrested by the Gestapo in 1933, sent to prison and later to a concentration camp. Upon his release in 1935 he had headed an illegal Party organization, acting under cover of an association for the care of young delinquents and invalid children, but this was discovered by the Gestapo in 1936 and he had fled to England.

While the Centre checked up on the background, nothing was done until the spring of 1947 when Jimmy Shields, an employee of CPGB's Central Committee, with responsibility for links with Communist émigrés, approached Zibert through Party channels.

Without going into details, as Zibert explained, he said that 'a comrade, working at the *Daily Worker*, had given him a message to be conveyed to our Party group that "a man from Edinburgh wishes to see big Hanna".' This comrade from the *Daily Worker* turned out to be Angela Tuckett, an old friend of Fuchs who had got in touch with her through her sister, who lived in the country. It was clear to the Centre and the *rezidentura* that Fuchs, having been unable to get in touch with the Soviets through Hanna Klopstock, was persistently but cautiously trying to renew contact through other acquaintances. The Centre decided to stick to the decision taken in September that, in case Fuchs was being watched by MI5, a regular intelligence officer should not go to meet him. Ovakimyan and Kukin suggested that contact with Fuchs should be established through Hanna Klopstock.

On 31 May 1947, Hanna met Angela Tuckett, who told her that Fuchs had suggested that they should meet at 14.30 on 19 July in Richmond Park; he was unable to fix an earlier date because of his work and holidays, including a visit to his brother in Switzerland. The instructions for the meeting given to Hanna Klopstock were simple: she should explain that contact had not been re-established because of the dangerous situation; ask him not to try and make contact through third parties; pass new instructions for meetings (once every three months); not accept any material; and find out Fuchs's ability to travel in order to arrange meetings on the Continent.

When Hanna Klopstock met Fuchs at half past two on 19 July he arrived in his own small car, and together they drove through Richmond to Hampton Court where they walked in the park. Klaus told her that he had been to Switzerland to visit his brother Gerhard and to Germany to see his father, whom he intended to bring over to England to live with him. At Harwell he headed the Theoretical Mathematics Department, a very responsible job, and his relations at work were so good that he was sure he was beyond suspicion. Finally, Hanna passed on the arrangements for the next meeting, which was to take place on 27 September in a pub opposite Wood Green tube station. The password would be the question, 'Do you know big Hanna?'

Fuchs gave her his photograph so his unknown contact might recognize him and asked for a contact address in Paris, as a contingency plan. He also said that if contact was lost again, he could be reached through his elder brother Gerhard, whom he considered absolutely reliable. If an urgent meeting was necessary before 27 September, he would send Hanna a postcard signed 'Bill'.

Soon after this meeting, Hanna Klopstock and Hans Zibert left for East Germany and thus the German channel of communication with Fuchs disappeared. Jimmy Shields of the CPGB did not know the name of the 'man from Edinburgh' while Angela Tuckett probably thought the reason for the meeting between Hanna and Klaus was Party business, since she had no reason to suspect any Soviet involvement. Although the danger of an accidental leak was ever present, contact had been re-established successfully and it was up to Aleksandr S. Feklisov, the new deputy *rezident* who arrived in September 1947, to build on what had been accomplished.

Feklisov had returned from the USA to Moscow in October 1946, retaining his diplomatic cover by working in the Ministry for Foreign Affairs. In May 1947 he started to prepare for his London assignment as deputy *rezident* with responsibility for scientific and technical intelligence, working in the evenings so as to avoid alerting his Ministry colleagues to his true task. After contact with Fuchs was re-established by Hanna Klopstock in July he was urgently recalled from leave at a Black Sea resort. He left for London on 30 August, having received a briefing from a Soviet nuclear scientist on the atom bomb and in special English technical terms; the scientist also drew up a questionnaire for Fuchs.[4]

On 28 September 1947 the Centre received a short report of Feklisov's meeting with Fuchs, which had taken place the day before, and a more detailed account arrived with the diplomatic bag in October. Feklisov wrote that he recognized Fuchs at once from the photograph he had given to Hanna Klopstock and the passwords had been exchanged in the pub, but the main part of the conversation had taken place during a walk through the local streets. Subsequent meetings with Fuchs were to follow the same pattern and on each occasion Fuchs passed his information verbally. It amounted to the assertion that the British had achieved little success in developing an atom bomb. Apparently the single uranium pile at Harwell had a capacity of 150 watts, but a second was under construction with a capacity of 6 kilowatts, and a 150,000 kilowatt industrial reactor was being built at Windscale in Cumbria (later renamed Sellafield) which would become operational in 1950, its production intended for the manufacture of the first atomic bombs. Fuchs reported that other bomb facilities were being constructed and a production unit was planned at Fort Halstead in Kent, twenty-five miles from London, under the direction of Dr (Lord) William Penney. The slow progress was due to the economic situation and the unwillingness of the Americans to share their secrets.

Fuchs disclosed that the Americans were working on a

Konstantin Kukin (centre), the
London *rezident* in 1943–7, in
conversation at an official
reception with Clement Attlee
MP.

Below: General Pavel Fitin,
Chief of the NKVD's First
Chief Directorate, 1939–46.

Above: Vladimir Barkovsky, wearing
his diplomatic uniform in wartime
London, when he was processing
reports on the development of an
atomic bomb supplied by John
Cairncross.

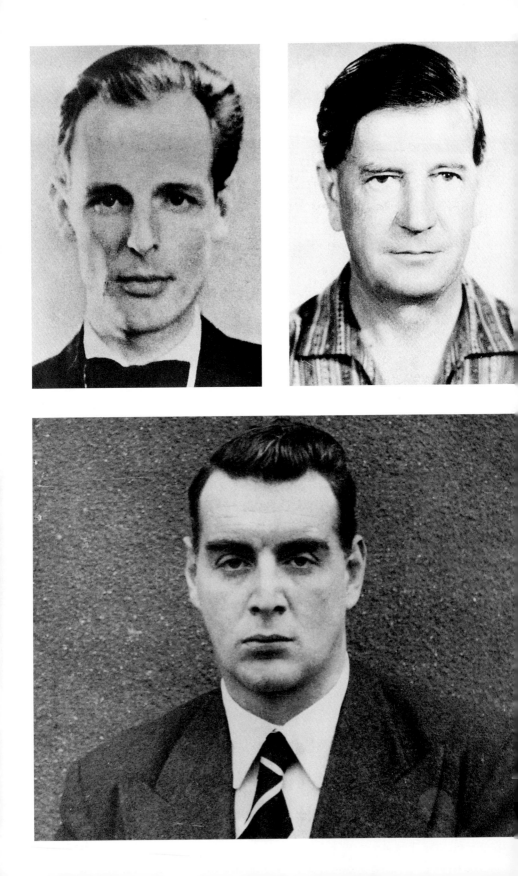

The British spies: *Above, left to right:*
 onald Maclean, Kim Philby, Anthony
 unt, John Cairncross.

 eft: Guy Burgess.

 ight: Edith Tudor Hart, an experienced
 oviet illegal and highly successful
 ofessional photographer, who made the
 st approach to recruit Kim Philby.

Left: Mikhail Shishkin, codenamed ADAM and working under press attaché cover, re-established contact with Guy Burgess in March 1947 and ran him with Anthony Blunt and Kim Philby for three years.

Above: Boris Kreshin, codenamed BOB, who worked under diplomatic cover in London as Boris Krotov and put the Cambridge spy ring on ice in 1945 following the defection of a cipher clerk in Ottawa.

Left: Aleksandr Feklisov, the deputy *rezident* who arrived in London in September 1947, had penetrated the Manhattan Project in the US, and was in charge of all the atomic spies in England, including Klaus Fuchs.

Leonid Kvasnikov, the NKVD officer with a scientific background who was sent to New York as an engineer attached to Amtorg and placed in charge of Operation ENORMOZ, the penetration of the Anglo-American atomic weapons programme.

Sergei Savchenko, Chief of the KGB's Foreign Intelligence Directorate when Klaus Fuchs was arrested.

Left: From left to right: Anatoli Yatskov, Leonid Kvasnikov, Vladimir Barkovsky and Aleksandr Feklisov, pictured in the History Room of the KGB First Chief Directorate headquarters in Yasenevo, just outside Moscow. Together they masterminded Operation ENORMOZ, the penetration of Los Alamos.

Right: Aleksandr Baranov, the attaché from the London *rezidentura* who helped run the spy ring which penetrated the Admiralty's secret Underwater Weapons Research Establishment at Portland.

Right: Konon Molody, the Soviet illegal who ran the Portland Naval Base spy network as the Canadian 'Gordon Lonsdale'.

Left: Vladimir Barkovsky (second left), pictured at the Arzamas Museum, in front of the first Soviet atomic bomb.

Right: Nikita Deryabkin, the KGB officer from the London *rezidentura* who made contact with Harry Houghton at the Dulwich Art Gallery in February 1953 when the Admiralty clerk returned to England from Warsaw.

Harry Houghton and Ethel Gee.
They were finally caught in the
act of passing classified files to
Konon Molody in January 1961,
having been under MI5 surveillance for months.

Harry Houghton's security pass
to the Portland Naval base. He
persuaded Ethel Gee to help him
extract classified information
about submarine detection
systems and sell them to the KGB.

Nikolai Rodin, alias Nikolai
Korovan, with his wife in
London. This legendary case
officer spent two tours at the
London *rezidentura*, in 1947–52
and 1956–61.

superbomb, or hydrogen weapon, at Chicago University where Professors Enrico Fermi and Geoffrey Taylor had in 1946 completed the theoretical work. Fuchs handed over a sketch of the hydrogen bomb's mechanism and explained that the Americans had abandoned the electromagnetic method of separating the isotopes of Uranium-235 because it had proved ineffective. However, they had achieved considerable success with the diffusion method and the process was continuing. He revealed that Canadian factories produced about a kilo of plutonium while American sources produced about 16–18 kilos a year and about 36 kilos of U-235. The Americans had exhausted their stock after Hiroshima and Nagasaki. The current programme envisaged the production of fifty bombs a year, but the uranium installations in Henford occasionally broke down, slowing the work of the chemical facilities at Los Alamos, so Fuchs estimated the American stockpile of bombs at approximately 125 units.

At the end of the meeting Feklisov offered Fuchs £200 to assist in moving his father to England and to pay for the treatment of his sick brother in Switzerland. Fuchs took the envelope with the money, remained silent for a moment, then said, 'We have been given the Nunn May case to read where it says that Soviet Intelligence always tries to give money to foreigners who supply them with information, in order to bind them morally to continue working for them. But I am not afraid of this. On the contrary I take this money to show you my loyalty.' He then asked how much money there was in the envelope. When Feklisov told him, Fuchs extracted £100 and handed it back, saying that his having such a large sum of money might cause suspicion. Finally, Feklisov made arrangements with Fuchs for future meetings in Paris and New York and, in anticipation of Fuchs's forthcoming visit to the US as a member of the British delegation to the talks on Anglo-American co-operation, the next meeting was fixed for 10 January 1948, but he failed to make it. They next met 13 March 1948, in accordance with the permanent arrangements for meetings, when Fuchs explained that he had been unable to attend in January because he had only returned from America three days earlier, and had been fearful of increased surveillance. He had been particularly worried by a remark by one of the security staff that an employee at Harwell was, allegedly, a member of the Communist Party and would be sacked. Fuchs was understandably nervous, kept looking round, stared at passers-by and asked to cross the road in such a way that he could check they were not being followed. Finally, he refused to enter a pub and asked Feklisov to shorten the meeting. In terminating the encounter, Fuchs gave a short report of his trip to the US and emphasized that the Americans did not give his group the opportunity of meeting Professor Taylor. Nevertheless, he had collected 67 handwritten pages of interesting information, which he handed to Feklisov.

Fuchs did not appear at the next meeting, scheduled for May 1948. There was some alarm at the *rezidentura* and in Moscow, for by this time the Centre had been warned that Fuchs was in danger. On 23 March 1948 the *Daily Mail* had published a story by Chapman Pincher claiming that MI5 was interested in three scientists at Didcot (presumably meaning Harwell), because of their Party membership. Apparently their cases had been submitted to the Minister of Supply who was to decide whether they should remain working at the atomic research establishment. Then, on 5 April, there was even more unpleasant news, that Ursula Beurton, the GRU agent who had originally approached Fuchs, had been questioned at her home in Oxfordshire. She told her visitors nothing, but the exact circumstances in which she was interrogated were unknown. Accordingly, the Centre directed that the May meeting should be as short as possible, his contact being instructed simply to accept his material and fix a date for the next meeting. In May 1948 a further *Daily Mail* story asserted that three unreliable employees at Harwell had been sacked, and when Fuchs did not turn up at the May reserve meeting the Centre speculated that Fuchs had been denounced following careless talk by his father, who lived in Germany, or perhaps because his Gestapo file had fallen into British hands. A contingency plan was prepared to spirit Fuchs away to Moscow if he faced dismissal from Harwell and arrest.

However, at a rendezvous held on 10 July 1948, Fuchs explained that he had been unable to attend the meetings scheduled for May because the new reactor was about to be activated and the head of the Atomic Energy Research Establishment had cancelled all leave. He said that since three junior employees had been sacked, as had been reported in the press, everything at Harwell had been quiet; the exchange of information with the Americans was gradually returning to normal and more American material was expected in the near future, apart from information on the hydrogen bomb. Fuchs's personal life was discussed; he said that there had been no change and he was still a bachelor. On being asked by Feklisov if he intended to get married, Fuchs answered that 'in his situation he did not consider it necessary to change this status', adding with amusement, 'That is why I try to avoid falling violently in love.' In spite of this demonstration of devotion to his intelligence work, the

Centre told Feklisov to pay special attention to Fuchs's ideological education, pointing out that Western propaganda was conducted in Germany under the guise of defending democracy and the German people, which was why it was necessary to explain, regularly and clearly, Soviet policy in Germany.

Fuchs missed the meetings planned for August and early October 1948, and appeared only at a back-up rendezvous on 23 October, when he explained that he had been embarrassed by a newspaper article on 20 July 1948 that had reported a ban on press photographs of Harwell's ten leading scientists who had participated in the development of the six-kilowatt reactor. According to the story, the Security Service had imposed the ban because it feared that foreign agents might abduct them if they visited the Continent. This news had prompted colleagues at Harwell to joke that the censorship had been intended to protect Fuchs, who understandably was dismayed by the unwelcome attention. He had decided to take extra care and abandon the August meetings. Nor had he attended the meeting due to be held on 16 October, because of pressure of work, so Feklisov did not have time to deliver the educational lecture recommended by the Centre. Instead the whole meeting was devoted to working out the procedure for an emergency signal, which was to consist of throwing a parcel containing a magazine into the garden of one of the *rezidentura*'s old go-betweens, someone who had been functioning since the days of Arnold Deutsch. The method could also be used for delivering reports. On 9 November Fuchs made a trial run with a parcel with a men's magazine inside, which was delivered to the *rezidentura* the following day.

On 23 October 1948, Fuchs reported that he had recently seen a British Intelligence report on the work of the physics laboratory in Sukhumi on the Black Sea, which mentioned that the German physicist Gustav Hertz was working there, and included a description of the laboratory and a list of the scientific apparatus sent there. In Fuchs's opinion the report had not been written by anyone specializing in nuclear physics, and was more likely to be the handiwork of a technician or a simple workman. He also reported that Britain planned to increase its stockpile of atomic bombs to 200 units by 1957, and at the next meeting, on 12 February 1949 (Fuchs having failed to come to the December meeting because of the Christmas holidays), he mentioned that his friend Herbert Skinner had confided that SIS had established contact with a Soviet scientist from whom it hoped to get atomic data. It was unclear whether the British had already started to get such information, but it had been Skinner who had shown Fuchs the SIS report on the Sukhumi laboratory. Fuchs himself had not seen any Soviet material, but promised to look out for any, and he asked Feklisov to impress on Moscow once more that his information should be treated with the strictest secrecy and only be shown to absolutely reliable people.

On the subject of his security, Fuchs remarked that one of the Harwell staff, a Dr Bletcher, was believed to inform on his colleagues. Fuchs believed that the most vulnerable period of his life in England were the few years after 1936, when he had been living in Bristol and had supported a committee organizing aid to the republicans in Spain. He asked Feklisov to use his name to get in touch with Angela Tuckett, and ask her to go to Bristol and remove any minutes of meetings, or any other incriminating papers in which his name appeared. Neither the Centre nor the *rezidentura* did anything about this request, on the grounds that it required careful consideration: was it worth approaching Tuckett with such a delicate task? It might attract suspicion to Fuchs, and the Intelligence Service could, by removing one danger, simply create another. The removal of papers from the archives, as Fuchs had suggested, would reveal his Soviet connection to Tuckett, at a time when security considerations, following the arrest in New York of Judith Coplon, in the act of meeting her KGB handler Valentin Gubichev, were pre-eminent. Indeed, Coplon's detention had prompted the Centre to introduce new precautions on 12 March 1949:

> In connection with the recent events in TIRE [New York] and in order to avoid a repetition of similar occurrences in other places, it is essential to review most carefully the way meetings with ATHLETES [agents] are conducted and material is accepted. The practice, adopted up to now by certain offices, of organizing meetings in the streets is disapproved of by the INSTANCE [Central Committee] as a stupid way of working, which does not guarantee the security of our people and the ATHLETES. Meetings in the streets should cease as this is fraught with great risk.

The Centre regarded the risk of exposure in London as greater, since the police often stopped people in the street to inspect their papers: it was only a few weeks since Anthony Blunt and Nikolai Korovin had been challenged by a constable in Montagu Square. The directive ended the practice of conducting meetings in the streets but did not suggest an alternative, a matter that would preoccupy the intelligence professionals. Significantly, this was one of the rare occasions when the Central Committee ruled on what was really an entirely operational issue. In response the Centre suggested that street meetings should be replaced by use of a car, or the flat of one of Fuchs's putative girlfriends, or a trip to the Continent where conditions might be more favourable.

Whatever the merits of the ban, it made little sense in Fuchs's case, and the Centre's proposal to introduce an illegal as his handler was not the subject of consultation with the *rezidentura*. For the meeting scheduled for 1 April, Feklisov could not think of an alternative to the existing arrangement, but he discussed the options with Fuchs who rejected the idea of using a girlfriend's flat, because he did not have one, explaining that he had resolved against drawing anyone else into the danger in which he found himself. Expanding on his relationship with Tuckett, at Feklisov's request, Fuchs said that he had not told her anything about his Soviet connections, and she knew him only as a Party member. Fuchs opposed the suggestion of meeting on the Continent as he travelled abroad only rarely, so this left the car, which he said was possible, but only within a radius of 15 to 20 miles of Harwell because of petrol rationing. He did not want to risk buying black market fuel.

Having received a parcel of documents and arranged the next meeting for 25 May 1949, Feklisov said goodbye, as it turned out, for ever: Fuchs never showed up again. Initially this failure caused no concern because analysis showed that out of the eleven planned meetings, Fuchs had come to just six, of which four had been reserves. Later his apparent disappearance caused more apprehension at the Centre than in the *rezidentura* because British press reports, at the end of August and the beginning of September 1949, showed that Fuchs was in good health and was still in his job. He was mentioned by *The Times* on 31 August 1949 as participating at a conference on the 'hazards in atomic research', and also in the October 1949 issue of *Nucleonics*, so the *rezidentura* thought it wiser not to seek any meetings in the next three months and await his appearance. It was assumed that he must have good reasons for not turning up, as had happened so frequently in the past.

The Centre's concerns were caused by events in the US where the FBI were clearly on the track of Harry Gold's contacts. Abraham Brothman's name had been published in June 1949 after Elizabeth Bentley's denunciation to the FBI. The Centre feared the exposure of both Gold and Fuchs, though confident that under interrogation Gold would not say anything compromising; he had not done so when named by Bentley, if only because it was not in his interests to make his guilt worse. However, the NKVD was afraid that he might implicate Fuchs inadvertently because during his last meeting with the New York *rezident*, Anatoli Yatskov, Gold had mentioned having read an article in a July 1946 edition of the *Herald Tribune* reporting the arrest of Fuchs in Britain on espionage charges. Baffled, the *rezidentura* had checked the newspapers for July and other months, but could find nothing. By then it was too late to draw Gold's attention to his mistake because the situation was too precarious to risk contacting him. The fear was that, thinking that he was saying nothing new to the FBI, he might compromise Fuchs. This anxiety led the Centre to instruct New York to arrange a meeting with Gold and tell him that Fuchs had not been arrested, and to recommend that he should disappear and lie low for a while. This rendezvous took place in September 1949 when Gold confirmed that he had been questioned twice by the FBI, in May and June. The first time he had denied having received any secret material from Abe Brothman; on the second occasion the interrogation had been perfunctory and brief, leading him to suppose that suspicions of him had not been confirmed and the FBI would now leave him alone. The Centre interpreted Gold's encounter with the FBI more seriously, fraught with complications, one of which was the possibility that he was under hostile surveillance. Accordingly it insisted that great care should be taken at the next meeting, on 24 October, which was judged essential to ensure Gold's own security and that of Klaus Fuchs. Gold was reminded that Fuchs was still free, and that he knew neither Gold's real name nor his address, but he should invent a cover story to explain their acquaintanceship should this become known. Gold's own disappearance during the period of danger was also discussed. He promised to think about it, but gave no definite undertaking apart from fixing the date of the next meeting for 5 February 1950.

The storm broke on 3 February 1950, when the London evening papers announced the arrest of Klaus Fuchs at Shell-Mex House by Special Branch, and his remand in custody by Bow Street magistrates. He was charged with having transmitted in 1947 to an unknown person information on atomic energy which might be useful to an enemy, and of having transmitted information on research work in the field of atomic energy in February 1945 to a person unknown in the US. The trial was set for 10 February 1950 and similar reports were published in the American press with an FBI statement that 'the British authorities had been investigating Fuchs on the basis of information passed to them by American counter-intelligence' and that 'in this investigation American counter-intelligence had closely co-operated with the British'. The reports also mentioned that Fuchs had admitted the offences.

Much later, new evidence emerged about how MI5 had been alerted to Fuchs and Yatskov, but the Centre's first assessment of the fiasco was based on the premise that he had been given away by the go-between, Harry Gold, in the course of the latter's interrogation. The accusation that Fuchs had transmitted information on the assembly of the atom bomb in February 1945 in the US suggested a strong American connection, and Gold seemed the best candidate. Indirect confirmation came from MI5 which, in the spring of 1949, suddenly became interested in Anatoli Yatskov, the New York *rezident*. He had never worked in Britain, so interest in him could only be explained by the investigation into Gold and Fuchs. Even Fuchs himself was unaware of Yatskov's participation, and the analysts concluded that only Gold, who knew Yatskov, could have mentioned him.

When Gold attended a regular meeting on 5 February 1950, an officer from the New York *rezidentura* checked him and the area for hostile surveillance, but did not approach him in case he was acting under the FBI's control. However, the officer was convinced there were no grounds for suspicion. Gold was ten minutes late, he had indicated by the arranged signal that he was ready for personal contact, and he displayed no signs of nervousness or anxiety. It was felt that if he had been under FBI control the agency would have made sure that he arrived on time, since being late might result in the meeting not taking place at all. The Centre also reckoned that an experienced operator like Gold would never have told the FBI of such a refinement as an additional signal indicating readiness for personal contact. Even under pressure it would have been easier for him to go to the meeting, which then simply would not have taken place because of the non-appearance of his contact.

Although Fuchs confessed at his trial that he had worked for Soviet Intelligence, the Centre wanted to find out how MI5 had traced him, and accordingly meetings were arranged with everyone who could be reached who at any time had participated in his secret life, or had been aware of it. The list was not very long: Jurgen Kuczinsky and his sister Ursula Beurton, Hanna Klopstock and Hans Zibert. Of these only Ursula Beurton, the GRU illegal who had been connected with Fuchs between 1942 and 1943, had left for East Germany after his arrest; she told an MGB official that she had been visited twice in 1947 by MI5, and had been questioned about her former links with Soviet Intelligence. According to Ursula, she had refused to discuss the matter and the officials had showed no interest in Fuchs. As for Fuchs's behaviour under MI5's interrogation, Ursula was of the opinion that 'from a political point of view he turned out to be weak ... his confession was not the result of malice, but of political immaturity.' In her view, the Fuchs investigation could have started after the explosion of the Soviet atom bomb, when a search for Communists might have led to him. Ursula's opinion was quite reasonable, but too vague to satisfy the Centre which was anxious to learn precisely what had happened. In the spring of 1950 it concluded, on the basis of its own intelligence and trial reports:

British Counter-Intelligence started investigations into the Fuchs case in September 1949 on the basis of the following warnings: a) information from the FBI on a leak of atom secrets from the USA to the USSR in the period 1944–5; b) information from Canadian Counter-Intelligence on the discovery of Fuchs's name in the diary of one of the suspects in the May case; study of documents on Fuchs's past, especially those in the Gestapo archives, revealed his membership of the German Communist Party. Earlier vetting of his political reliability, when he was accepted for scientific research work at Birmingham University in 1941, and his behaviour after his return from the USA had given no grounds for suspicion. When, in the USA, he was sent to Los Alamos, he was not vetted at all. The investigation carried out in 1949 convinced MI5 that Fuchs was responsible for the leak of information from the USA, although there was no direct evidence against him and therefore no action was taken. But it was Fuchs himself who hastened events. On 12 October 1949 he approached the security officer at the Harwell atomic research centre, Henry Arnold, and informed him that his father had accepted an offer from the GDR authorities of a professorship at Leipzig University and that this decision would affect his position at the research centre. Arnold did not give an answer straightaway and on 20 October Fuchs again asked him how matters stood. MI5 decided to use these developments to question Fuchs. The interrogation took place in December 1949 and was conducted by an MI5 officer, William Scardon. Fuchs admitted his membership of the Communist Party in the past, but completely denied being a spy. Scardon played on Fuchs's loyalty to his English friends and colleagues and appealed to his feelings of gratitude towards Britain, which had given him shelter and provided him with his life's work. These tactics evidently worked and called forth in Fuchs a psychological conflict. At the end of January he made a full confession of his work for Soviet Intelligence and told everything he knew. On the basis of Fuchs's confession, MI5 established certain specific facts: the name of the man who brought Fuchs in contact with the Soviet representatives, Jurgen Kuczinsky; the name of the first Soviet representative, the secretary of the military attaché, Simon Kremer; the name of the member of the German Communist Party who put him in touch with a Soviet representative in 1947, Hanna Klopstock; the approximate number of meetings and arrangements for contacting representatives of Soviet Intelligence in Britain and the USA, as well as in Paris.

Based on these data, the Centre accepted that under interrogation Fuchs had admitted the transmission of material to Soviet Intelligence and had told the British all he knew about the way it worked. Meanwhile, the search for the source of the original information which put the FBI and MI5 on Fuchs's trail continued. The key turned out to be cryptographic – the decoding by the Americans and the British of cipher traffic that had been exchanged between the Centre and the New York *rezidentura* during the period 1944 to 1945. According to Burgess and Philby, flawed cipher methodology, specifically the mistake of using one-time pads twice, allowed analysts to read fragments of the most secret Soviet communications. Eventually the experts in Moscow were forced to acknowledge that the broken codes, as described by Burgess, in Philby's words, at a meeting held on 10 February 1950, were responsible for providing MI5 with the first lead to Fuchs.

The Centre's reaction to Fuchs's arrest was dramatic, but instead of resorting to the conventional measure of suspending contact with agents and ordering them to lie low, it was decided to carry on as normal so as to give the impression that Fuchs was unconnected with Soviet Intelligence. Moscow was anxious that another suspension of operations would risk frightening and perhaps losing agents, so the Centre recommended propagating the idea that the Americans had invented the Fuchs case in order to deny the British information on atomic energy.

Trying to turn the Fuchs fiasco to its advantage, the Centre attempted to exploit the developing spy mania with the intention of harming the British and American atom bomb programme. The strategy involved casting doubt on the reliability of scientists working on the hydrogen bomb and clearly the scheme bore fruit, as manifested by J. Edgar Hoover's statements that Fuchs was not the only 'Communist spy', and that the FBI was investigating other atom scientists. Among the prominent physicists affected were Harold Urey, Herbert Skinner, Leo Szilard, Cyril Smith, Robert Oppenheimer (whose brother was questioned by the FBI in 1948) and George Gamow. There is no documentary evidence in the archive that this scheme was ever implemented or went beyond the planning stage; but the spy mania heightened the activity of MI5 and the FBI and handicapped Soviet operations. Ironically, Hoover and Senator Joe McCarthy together accomplished much of what had been planned by the Soviets by dragging the most outstanding scientists before the UnAmerican Activities Committee.

Shortly before the trial the Centre considered whether Emil Fuchs should be approached in confidence and persuaded to ask a well-known British defence counsel to take on his son's defence, for which the Soviets would pay. The objective was to seek an adjournment so as to allow a visit to Klaus, when he could be reassured that he would not be left to his fate. The Centre also wanted to find out more about the origins of the joint MI5 and FBI investigation, and hoped that a good lawyer might discover the truth. But the haste with which Fuchs was tried did not leave time to hire defence lawyers and Fuchs pleaded guilty, thereby undermining the entire basis of the plan. Sentence was pronounced on 1 March. In Leonid Kvasnikov's report to the Head of Intelligence, Sergei Savchenko, he explained that the plan had not been implemented, and confined himself to suggesting that Klaus's brother should arrange for an appeal. Savchenko gave his approval, but it never happened because Gerhard Fuchs fell ill and died in January 1951.

On 8 May 1950 the British newspapers had reported that Fuchs was meeting the FBI, and the Centre could only guess what was being discussed, but on on 24 May Harry Gold's arrest was announced. MI5 continued its investigation into the Fuchs case, and in February 1951 the Centre learned through the CPGB that Angela Tuckett had been questioned, apparently to clarify whether she had met Fuchs in December 1946 or January 1947. Angela answered that she could not remember, but evidently MI5 was following up Fuchs's testimony about how he had re-established contact with the Soviets in 1947.

On 15 June 1952 the *Sunday Times* published extracts from *The Traitors* by Alan Moorehead, which included accurate details of the Centre's arrangements for meeting Fuchs in pubs, such as the Spotted Horse in Putney and the Nag's Head in Wood Green, so Kvasnikov drew the obvious conclusion that Fuchs had made a full confession which had been disclosed to the author.[5]

Beria's personal supervision of the Soviet atom research intelligence project came back to haunt him after his arrest in the summer of 1953 when his interrogators proposed to see whether he was responsible for the Fuchs fiasco, and to question his deputies, Bogdan Kobulov and Vsevolod Merkulov, on precisely what information had been transmitted abroad.

Fuchs was sentenced to fourteen years' imprisonment, of which he served nine: he was released in June 1959, a third of his sentence having been commuted for good behaviour. The question of what he would do after his release interested both the British and Soviet security services, and in January 1958 the *Daily Express* reported that MI5 was trying to prevent Fuchs from leaving England, so the Centre asked the KGB's Berlin representative, Aleksandr M. Korotkov, to find out what Fuchs's father knew about his son's intentions. It transpired that he knew nothing about Klaus's release, but he had visited him in prison in the summer of 1957 and found him rather pessimistic about his prospects: he felt he was compromised in Britain and unwelcome in Socialist countries. Emil Fuchs had assured him that he would be well received in East Germany as an outstanding scientist so when, in the spring of 1959, the British press reported that Fuchs would be released early, he announced his intention to go to East Germany to teach philosophy at Leipzig University. Reassured, the Centre took all possible steps, through his father and the German Stasi, to make sure that Fuchs would find work. As an eminent nuclear theoretician it was important to attract him to the East, just as it was essential to deny his talents to Britain. In the end the Stasi's intervention proved unnecessary. Erich Mielke, the Minister of State Security, informed Korotkov that Fuchs's father had approached the Communist Party independently with a plea that Klaus should be allowed to live in East Germany and given citizenship. This request was granted and on 23 June 1959, Fuchs flew to Berlin. In September he married a Central Committee employee, Greta Keilson, whom he had first met in Paris in the early 1930s. He was soon appointed Deputy Director of the Institute for Nuclear Research, and in March 1960 the Head of the Central Committee's Science Department, Hernig, suggested to the Soviets that Fuchs should be invited to visit the Soviet Centre for Nuclear Research in Dubna. Accordingly, he attended a conference of the Learned Council of the United Institute for Nuclear Research as an East German delegate. Between 24 and 31 May 1960 he visited Moscow as a guest of the Soviet Academy of Sciences, and on 28 May Kvasnikov, then the Head of the First Directorate's technical and scientific department, met him in the restaurant of the Hotel Peking.

Over lunch Fuchs told Kvasnikov that after his return to East Germany he had been received by Walter Ulbricht, to whom he had given an account of his Soviet espionage and his arrest. He explained that he sincerely regretted his mistakes, and shortly afterwards he was appointed Deputy Director of the Central Institute for Nuclear Physics and accepted as a member of the Party. During their conversation Fuchs said that the British had received the first clues from the US, an opinion he had formed during his interrogation in 1949 when he had been interviewed by an MI5 official. It had become clear to him that the British suspected him of spying but lacked any direct evidence against him, and in Fuchs's view matters would have been left at that if he had not voluntarily confessed. He explained his behaviour by his serious political doubts about Soviet policy, a consequence of being under the influence of bourgeois propaganda and isolated from sources of accurate information. Specifically, these doubts and hesitations had brought Fuchs to the conclusion that the Soviets were violating the principles of democracy, and that Moscow's attitude to the Eastern bloc was inappropriate. He had begun to think his espionage for the Soviets had been a mistake.

The British had not used any physical methods to extract a confession. They had only brought moral pressure to bear, reminding him of the friendly welcome he had been given as a refugee, and the brilliant scientific opportunities that had been opened to him. In answer to Kvasnikov's question about evidence he had given against any others, Fuchs said that Harry Gold was the only one. He had been shown two American surveillance films in which Gold appeared, the first of which had shown Gold in the street of a small American town, and gave the impression of a man who was under nervous strain who knew that he was being followed. Having seen this movie Fuchs did not admit that he had known Gold, but after viewing the second, which showed Gold in prison, looking as though a great weight had been lifted from his shoulders, Fuchs admitted knowing him and had given evidence against him.

During the investigation Fuchs gave detailed evidence about the data he had supplied to Moscow, omitting only the details of the hydrogen bomb. After his conviction the FBI had visited him in prison and expressed interest in Soviet tradecraft, various scientific and technical questions, and descriptions of individual contacts. Shortly before his release he was visited by an American lawyer defending Morton Sobell, a 'man who had been spirited from Mexico to the US', who tried to persuade Fuchs to give evidence for his defence; after his release the request had been repeated. Fuchs related that the British had tried to persuade him to stay in England, and the Americans were also interested in this. Nevertheless, he had taken the decision to go to East Germany but had said nothing until a journalist named John Clarence, whom he mistakenly took to be a CPGB representative, visited him in prison and induced him to speak about his intentions. Hearing about this the British tried to persuade Fuchs to change his mind but once they realized his decision was final, they opted to release him without publicity.

Fuchs's version tended to support the Centre's own interpretation of what had happened, so Kvasnikov took a tactful line and did not try to press for further information which might have upset him. Fuchs remained in the German Democratic Republic, working on atomic research at Rossendorf, near Dresden, until 1979. He died in January 1988, aged seventy-eight, a member of the Party's Central Committee, having retired as deputy director of East Germany's nuclear physics programme.

CHAPTER XI

Codename SHAH

On 6 October 1951 the Centre issued a directive to all its *rezidenturas* abroad drawing attention to the need to learn more about British and American ciphers. Signed by Yevgeny P. Pitovranov of the Committee of Information, it suggested that anyone with access to Western codebooks should be targeted in the hope of compromising them, their knowledge or their equipment. There was no urgency attached to the message, which was circulated by the diplomatic bag, but it reflected Moscow's concern about the recent reduction in material flowing from the Centre's agents abroad. Guy Burgess and Donald Maclean had fled from London in May, and operations had been suspended in London while Kim Philby underwent an official investigation into his role in their escape. As for Washington DC, the entire country seemed to be in the grip of anti-Soviet spy mania. After years of plenty, Moscow was experiencing a relative famine in terms of intelligence from its two principal target countries, America and Britain.

Coincidentally, as Pitovranov's instructions landed on the desk of Colonel Aleksandr Bezborodov, the *rezident* in Warsaw, he was learning of an extraordinary offer that had been received anonymously by his Polish counterpart. Since 1949 the Centre had banned independent intelligence operations in the Soviet satellite countries and instead had concentrated on developing a close relationship with the host security and intelligence apparatus, which invariably operated as a surrogate. The offer in question had arrived in a white envelope addressed to the private secretary of the Minister of Foreign Affairs and had been sealed with five black wax seals. Inside, intriguingly, was a single sheet of paper marked 'SECRET' at top and bottom in the style used in British communications. In between was a message guaranteed to enthuse even the most cynical intelligence officer:

The secretary to the Naval Attaché at the British Embassy, Warsaw, would, it is thought, be willing to supply any information at his command in return for the following: (a) Sufficient local currency to meet his local requirements. (b) A sum, to be agreed upon, placed to his credit in England. (c) The lease of a nicely furnished flat in a nice neighbourhood, and well heated in the winter. He is attached to the staff of the Director of Naval Intelligence, Admiralty, London, and says he has no particular love for his masters. He is in full possession of all top secret and secret letters from the British Admiralty and also disposes of all mail that is received from the British Admiralty.[1]

Although the letter was unsigned, the author gave his address as Glogera 3/4 and this was visited on 19 January 1952 by a Polish Intelligence officer masquerading as an official of the Ministry of Foreign Affairs. The delay in responding to the offer is probably explained by bureaucratic muddle and perhaps the need to identify the occupant and keep him under surveillance. In any event, the occupant did not admit to the authorship of the letter but indicated that he was willing to act as an intermediary and pass on reliable information from the embassy in return for compensation. He also expressed the view that 'Britain's present rulers had sold the country to the Americans and turned it into an American colony'. Accordingly, Harry Houghton entered the Polish Intelligence books under the codename MIRON.

Houghton's first demand was for £550 to buy a car, and in return he supplied a thick bundle of documents which included the British military attaché's current estimate of the Polish armed forces, the entire structure of the Naval Intelligence Division in London, various Foreign Office summaries and Naval Intelligence papers. However, of principal interest was the naval attaché's codebooks which, Houghton had confirmed, were used by other service attachés elsewhere. All this material was photographed and copies were supplied to Moscow in March 1952, where they were judged to be 'valuable', with the cipher material delighting the Soviet experts. As a result, the Centre asked the Warsaw *rezidentura* to 'draw the attention of the FRIENDS [Polish Intelligence] to the precautions that should be taken to avoid MIRON's exposure', a sure endorsement of his importance as a source.

When Houghton came on stream he made regular deliveries to his Polish contacts, and the procedure became so efficient that the diplomatic mail, which arrived by a special courier plane every Wednesday from Berlin, was often read by the Soviets before it reached its intended addressees as the naval attaché's papers were photographed the same evening. During May 1952, Houghton passed on 715 documents, which included a collection of classified

reference books about foreign navies; some naval intelligence
monthly surveys; a directive from the Director of Naval Intelligence,
numbered NP 6/214 dated 3 April 1952 on the subject of collecting
information about a Soviet torpedo; and instructions from MI-10
about conducting naval technical intelligence. This treasure trove
was followed in July by a further 610 documents, a total escalating
to 1,167 in August. Careful scrutiny of this material disclosed not
only the extent of Britain's knowledge of the Soviet armed forces,
but revealed some of the intelligence methods used to compile the
assessments.

The Soviets were fascinated by Houghton's haul, especially by
a request circulated in July 1952 for information about a Soviet
submarine captured from the German Kriegsmarine at the end of
the war and designated VL/F. The NID wanted details of every
aspect of its performance, endurance and armament, together with
a photograph taken from close range, if possible. Once again, the
data was judged in Moscow as 'valuable' and 'very valuable', and
one item in particular attracted the MGB's military counter-
intelligence branch: a Naval Intelligence weekly summary, numbered 265 and dated 19 March 1952, which suggested that the
British had 'a trusted and approved source' who had described the
construction of a new facility close to quay no. N 15 in Murmansk.
Naturally the First Chief Directorate asked their counter-intelligence
colleagues to exercise discretion in pursuing the source, for fear of
compromising their own source.

In fact Houghton was not endangered by the careless handling
of his product, but rather by the threat of his own withdrawal
made in an unofficial letter dated 1 May 1952 to the naval attaché,
Captain Nigel Austen. Apparently, as an economy measure, the
British were anxious to replace embassy personnel in the Eastern
Bloc who were accompanied by their families, and therefore eligible
for an extra £1,000 hardship pay, with unmarried men. Houghton
was accompanied by his wife and therefore was in danger of being
recalled. To avoid this Houghton suggested that the Polish authorities should intervene, pointing out that two of the three technical
staff working for the service attachés were due to depart shortly
anyway. One, a secretary, had been caught passing information to
the American military attaché, Colonel Schneider, and another had
taken to the bottle and had too many local relationships. As for the
third, Houghton recommended that the Poles should expel him on
the grounds that he had often helped the assistant military attaché
when touring the country collecting intelligence. He also named
another member of the staff, the air attaché's subordinate, who

drank too much and consorted with prostitutes, as another candidate for expulsion. With all the technical staff removed, Houghton hoped to make himself indispensable.

It is unclear from Houghton's file whether the authorities in Warsaw acted on his advice, but when in the summer of 1952 he seemed likely to return to London his case was handed over to the Centre. Poland had neither the experience nor the facilities to run such an important source abroad, and anyway Houghton's access was too wide to interest just the Poles. Accordingly, in September 1952, Houghton was codenamed SHAH and assigned Aleksandr S. Feklisov as his controller, who travelled to Warsaw to meet his new agent and reassure him about establishing contact in London. Following this first encounter Feklisov reported to the Centre that Houghton's

> decision to start co-operating with the Poles formed also under the influence of his political views: disagreement with the policy of the British government and hatred towards the Americans. While still in Britain MIRON told his wife about his intention to earn extra money in Poland. Supposedly he told her that during his stay in Warsaw he would be meeting with representatives of the Polish underground and that for this work he would receive payment in pounds. Now MIRON's wife knows that every Wednesday he goes to a meeting with representatives of the Polish underground. After every meeting MIRON gives his wife thirty to sixty pounds.[2]

At that meeting Houghton had passed over a top secret circular enumerating the dangers faced by British diplomats abroad and describing in detail the various hazards of succumbing to weaknesses that might be exploited by the local secret police or result in blackmail. Houghton certainly acted against the advice offered, to resist apparently friendly approaches from Soviet Bloc personnel, and a signal was sent to the *rezident*, Nikolai Korovin, alerting him to SHAH's imminent arrival, and instructing him to look out for him on the corner of Whitehall and Northumberland Avenue on 1 November at exactly 5.00pm. Houghton drove to London on 23 October 1952, via West Germany and, in spite of a road accident, reached London in time to appear at the appointed place and be recognized by Nikita S. Deryabkin. The same Soviet officer, on the first Sunday of February 1953 at the entrance to the Dulwich Picture Gallery, asked the agreed question: 'Please tell me how I can get to Westminster?' Houghton's improbable response was 'The best way to Westminster is through Washington.' The formalities over, Deryabkin introduced himself as 'Nick, a friend of Roger' and Houghton explained that his situation was entirely secure. On his return from Poland the immigration officers had only expressed some interest in why he had driven through East Germany, whether he had ever visited the Soviet Union, and if he had associated with any private citizens in Warsaw. He had explained that his visit to East Berlin had been necessitated by his wife's illness, and his satisfactory replies to the other questions had left him free to continue his journey. Back in London he had been summoned by H.V. Pennells, head of the NID's civilian staff, who had asked him the predictable routine questions about approaches from the CPGB or Eastern Bloc agents, and Houghton had made the required responses, undertaking to report any future pitches if they occurred.

Deryabkin noted that Houghton's sense of personal security had been confirmed by the offer of a job at the highly sensitive Under-water Weapons Research Establishment at Portland in Dorset, the centre of classified research into submarine warfare and electronic counter-measures. The post was to be an administrative one, as a clerical officer, with an allowance of £90 per annum to compensate him for the conditions of secrecy under which he would have to work. He explained that he would have nothing like the kind of access to classified material he had enjoyed in Warsaw – the centre employed more than four hundred people whose movements were controlled by three different types of passes – but as an experienced intelligence officer, Deryabkin advanced his agent £50 and advised him to take his time before writing off his espionage.

Indeed, at their next meeting Houghton announced that he had gained access to a depository known as 'the safe room' where classi-fied documents were stored, and asked for a miniature camera so he could take pictures. When cross-examined by Deryabkin he out-lined the procedures adopted at Portland. The safe room was super-vised by an official named C.H. Wilkinson, who issued individual documents to members of the staff who signed for them; at the end of each day the interior safes and the room's steel doors were locked and the keys entrusted for the night to the military police. Houghton claimed that for short periods he had exclusive access to the safe room, and Deryabkin did not challenge him on the details:

> It is necessary to note that I still doubt that he correctly gives the post he occupies. Twice I tried to make it clear what his job is, but his answers were vague. Sensing his unwillingness to converse on this subject, I didn't return to it anymore, to avoid being inopportune. I am forming the opinion that MIRON works in a secret department and has access to the safe room.[3]

The issue of Houghton's access to the safe room was to remain unclear to the Centre, for whenever he was asked Houghton replied that his room was nearby and that the person in charge of the depository, a Miss Elder, asked him to take her place when she went to lunch. This unorthodox procedure gave Houghton unrestricted access to whatever documents he wanted, but the 'document to order' service he offered did not, according to Deryabkin, fit in with Houghton's own version of events, so both the Centre and the *rezidentura* retained some lingering doubts about SHAH's reliability. It was suspected that perhaps he was in charge of the safe room, but reluctant to admit it for entirely understandable reasons of self-preservation. Psychologically, this was a well-recognized phenomenon, the wish to keep an ace up one's sleeve to impress one's partner in times of need. There could be no hesitation about the authenticity of his documents, so there was little point in applying any pressure on him. The information was summarized thus in Moscow:

(1) Secret Admiralty orders regarding the Royal Navy, naval weapons and tactics, of sufficient importance to be circulated to the Soviet Navy;
Copies of Limited Confidential Admiralty Fleet Orders (LCAFO) and the more widely used Confidential Admiralty Fleet Orders (CAFO).
(2) Reports of the Royal Navy's tests of NIGHTSHIRT, a device designed to conceal the noise of propellers.
(3) Details of port defences, anti-mine and anti-torpedo precautions in ports.
(4) Correspondence about CHEATER, a device to deflect acoustically-guided torpedos. Temporary handbook on ASDIC set type 170, a description of an acoustic detection system for detecting high-speed submarines, and of the fire control of the Mark 10 depth charge, codenamed LIMBO. Also mentioned are the PENTANE and Mk 30 DEALER-B torpedos.
(5) Description of Type 170 hydrolocators for surface vessels.
(6) Admiralty circular dated 18 March 1954 on torpedo ranges.
(7) Report of the Torpedo Counter-measure Committee
(8) Attack Techniques
(9) New information on Type 170 hydrolocators
(10) Material relating to the chief of Staff, Naval Landing Operations.[4]

In March 1956 the Centre drew up a summary of the material provided by Houghton, listing 4,500 documents supplied between March and November 1952 while he was in Poland, plus ten codebooks, 427 pages in 1953, from the beginning of the summer, 1,927 pages in 1954, 1,768 pages in 1955 and 1,127 pages between January and March 1956. The situation was transformed early in 1955 when Houghton supplied a Subject Catalogue of secret documents stored at Portland which allowed the Centre to draw files at will from a numerical index. This coup so impressed his handlers that Deryabkin was rewarded with the Order of the Red Star on the recommendation of the KGB Chairman, Ivan Serov. As for Houghton, he was given cash bonuses of £500 in July 1957, £400 in December 1955 and £400 in November 1956. Gradually Houghton and Deryabkin slipped into a routine of regular monthly meetings, which were taken over after January 1955 by Aleksandr V. Baranov, a newly-arrived KGB officer under attaché cover at the embassy, in the London suburbs around the A3 main road to Portsmouth. On each occasion Houghton delivered a bundle of documents which were photographed overnight and returned in the morning. His explanation to his wife was that he was earning extra money by dealing in black market penicillin and all went well until December 1956 when Houghton told Baranov about a particularly unsettling incident.

> The port police at Portland detained one of the senior officials, Mr Churchward, at a routine inspection at the dock gates because he had a secret file on him. Churchward had intended to take the papers home to study and probably had no intention of using them illegally. Under interrogation, Churchward had insisted that he had removed the documents without Miss Elder's knowledge, but they were both punished. Apparently Miss Elder had slipped out briefly to the typing pool and had failed to follow the required procedure of appointing a stand-in during her absence. It had been during this period that Churchward had removed the file, which itself was entirely insignificant. No one questioned the source [Houghton] during the investigation since he was uninvolved in the case.
>
> To avoid a recurrence of this breach of discipline, the person responsible for the safe room is now required to lock the outer steel door and take the key with her. If she is on leave or falls ill, Mr Wilkinson will be responsible for the safe room. No one else, apart from Miss Elder and Mr Wilkinson, is allowed access to the saferoom.[5]

This episode cost Houghton his hitherto unrestricted access to Portland's secret documents and, he feared, the financial rewards associated with it. In fact the setback was to be minor in comparison with the development which was the subject of his next personal note, subsequently reported by Baranov:

Since the source wrote the foregoing another misfortune has happened, more serious than everything that has happened up to now. The source has been told that he is being transferred to work in the Portland Docks, to the Chief Engineer's department to occupy a 'Bossy' post. This transfer is a promotion since it carries a larger salary. The source was called to the chief of the administrative department who told him that the Admiralty had chosen the source to appoint him to a vacant 'bossy' post and that the source must set to his duties, starting on Monday 10 December this year. Naturally the source had to express surprise and pleasure concerning this transfer. If the source had not done so it would have provoked undesirable comment since the 'bossy' post is considered a 'tasty morsel'. The source's new post is chief of the personnel department who does not have access to any valuable material except Admiralty CAFO and LCAFO. The Chief Engineer is responsible for repairs of small naval ships and port vessels in the docks of Portland. The docks themselves cannot be compared with the naval docks of Portsmouth, Devonport and Chatham. The source uses all opportunities for the decision about his transfer to be cancelled, however a refusal to accept the new appointment (in view of the increase in salary) would provoke very serious suspicion, since it is quite obvious that no man of sense will refuse a larger salary! The difference in salary amounts to £50 a year which is very little in comparison with the compensation which the source receives from ROGER and from this it is clear that the source takes all measures for the cancellation of his appointment to the new post.[6]

Houghton's strategy to get his new appointment cancelled was to encourage jealous colleagues to protest and the Association of Civil Service Employees registered a formal complaint, which was subsequently rejected by the Admiralty on the grounds that 'there was no one else with sufficient experience for doing the work'.

On 9 January 1957 I was transferred to the new job. My duties are connected with the staff of workers and officials of the docks. As I have already said, I shall apply every effort for getting useful information but the character of my new work limits my opportunities to a considerable degree and I very much regret that the use of which I used to be to you will be or may be somewhat less. I have got good compensation for my work from you and I shall continue to render to you any help which is within my power. Thank you.[7]

To confirm his intent, Houghton enclosed the current LCAFO N117/55 and the telephone directory of the Admiralty Gunnery Establishment, Portland.

One curiosity of Houghton's collaboration with the KGB was the fact that the exercise had been conducted for years under a 'false flag', with Feklisov and his successors pretending to represent Polish Intelligence. The Centre had adopted this deception for fear that Houghton, who had established good relations with his Polish case officer and had full confidence in him, would not agree to a switch of handler at such a critical moment. He had expressed the view that the Poles would not be the subject of the same level of hostile surveillance in England as their Soviet counterparts, and it seemed unlikely that Houghton would have resumed contact in London if he had known ROGER was a Russian. However, this situation changed in the summer of 1957 following the defection of a Polish trade attaché, Richard Relug, which was the subject of press reports in London on 19 August, and severely undermined Houghton's confidence in the Poles, whom he also suspected of developing too close a relationship with the West. As a consequence, the *rezident* in London, Yuri I. Modin, recommended early in September that SHAH be informed that he had been transferred to Soviet control:

The heavy impression which the treachery of the assistant of the Polish Trade Attaché Richard Relug produced on SHAH draws particular attention. From the course of SHAH's conversations with BRON (Baranov) it is clearly seen that SHAH's confidence in Poland had been strongly shaken not only by Relug's treachery but also by the past year's events in Poland. This may seriously affect SHAH's work. In connection with this we consider it necessary to again raise the question about the expediency of ceasing to work with SHAH under the Polish flag. From BRON's previous conversations with SHAH it is seen that SHAH, working with us on a material basis, has no prejudice concerning the Soviet Union. Moreover, he spoke sympathetically of the Soviet Union's struggle for peace. SHAH's only argument against meeting with Soviets was his opinion that the British Security Service watches them more closely than officials of other Socialist countries. We can parry this argument comparatively easily by pointing to the results of our work in London over many years. We believe that SHAH will accept our advice with relief.[8]

The Centre agreed with the *rezidentura*'s recommendation and in October Modin received a directive from the chief of the 2nd Department of the First Chief Directorate, Evgeny Tarabrin:

As a result of a thorough analysis of recent work with SHAH the Centre has come to the conclusion that there are now favourable conditions for transferring him to work under our flag. During the conversation with SHAH on this question it is necessary to explain to him in a friendly way that we did not reveal ourselves to him only so that he should not worry about his fate, since he himself had repeatedly said that the Poles were less closely watched than Soviets. Now SHAH has been able to satisfy himself of the fact that it is quite safe to work with Soviets in London. Explain to him that our meetings with him are thoroughly prepared and we take all necessary measures to rule out the possibility of exposure.[9]

Baranov carried out the Centre's instructions at the meeting with Houghton on 26 October 1957. He explained that neither NICK (as Deryabkin had introduced himself) nor himself were Poles, that both were Russians and all the material Houghton had passed had gone to the Soviet Union. The Englishman was silent for a few moments and then said: 'I must tell you that is not a surprise. I suspected that NICK was not a Pole, and I knew you were not long ago. It was not difficult to make certain. During our conversations I often used Polish idiomatic expressions, to which a real Pole should have reacted. You did not, and you always avoid speaking Polish. You always declined my suggestions about giving presents to my friends in Poland. The Relug incident was yet more proof. I have thought about it a great deal. A few things made me believe you are a Soviet intelligence officer.' The first had been the speed with which he and his wife had received visas for East Berlin where she had received medical treatment. Other Britons had waited months. At the time Houghton had not attached much significance to it, but having reflected upon it afterwards he realized that the Soviets had intervened. Also Deryabkin and Baranov had always shown interest in Admiralty information regarding the Royal Navy: Poland was not a large sea power and probably would not have devoted such resources to data that was not obviously vital to Poland. Houghton had concluded that his information had gone where it was really needed, the Soviet Union.

'Recently this became a serious worry to me,' he confessed, 'but your announcement today is a great relief. I am grateful to you for your frankness.'

Baranov asked Houghton if the conversation had been unwelcome, but was told, 'We should be able to work together even better. Now everything is clear, there are no reasons to worry. We know who is who and what is what. I only wish I had known about this earlier. In Berlin I knew an officer in the British administration who sympathized with you greatly.' Thus the anxieties previously expressed by the Centre and the *rezidentura* proved to have been unfounded, and the measures taken to conceal the Soviet background of Houghton's two contacts unnecessary. Both Deryabkin and Baranov had visited Warsaw to familiarize themselves with the places known to Houghton, but had failed in their attempt to pass themselves off as real Poles, which was not entirely surprising, considering that they had never been trained as illegals. Nor, for that matter, had they realized that Houghton was rather shrewder than he appeared (although, when he later met Gordon Lonsdale, he refused to believe that he could be a Russian).

Houghton had first mentioned his mistress, Ethel Gee, early in 1955. He said that his relationship with his wife had deteriorated to such a degree that he was considering divorce, and he had acquired a lady friend whom he brought to London whenever he met Baranov. Naturally the *rezidentura*'s first concerns were the security implications both on the operation and the source, and he suspected that Houghton had told her rather more than he was admitting, though he claimed he used the same alibi, black-marketeering in penicillin, as he had with his wife. In the spring of 1955 he gave Baranov a brief description of her. Ethel Gee, to be codenamed ASYA, was forty-one years old and worked as a temporary civil servant, third grade. She had no strong political opinions, nor any special educational qualifications, but she lived on a small private income and worked for pocket money of around five pounds a week. 'The source has been in close friendly relations with her almost since he moved to Portland and she is ready to marry the source if he has the opportunity; she has even declared that she would pay £100 to anyone to get rid of the source's wife. The source has said that he will not allow her to do this, although he feels deep affection towards her. She does not know what the source comes to London for, but it is likely that she would help if she knew and received sufficient compensation. There are several facts which support such a statement and it is suggested that the source's knowledge of this woman should be taken into consideration.'

On 15 May Houghton told Baranov of 'his certainty of the fact that Miss Gee would agree to co-operate with us ... once in her office Miss Gee had showed him a secret document and SHAH had said as a joke, "The Russians would also read this with pleasure." Miss Gee had replied, "Well, I'm ready to show it to anyone if I am well paid for it." The talk ended at that and from the tone in which she had said those words SHAH concluded that she could indeed do it.'

The Centre considered SHAH too valuable to risk his exposure, even through the woman he loved, and forbade him even to hint at his clandestine activity. On 26 October 1957, Houghton raised the issue of Miss Gee again and said that he was considering marriage. He was willing to accept his wife's conditions for a divorce but, as he told Baranov,

> this marriage will introduce serious difficulties in our work. My wife didn't interfere with my work. Possibly she guessed about some illegal affairs of mine, but she did not know the essence of the matter and didn't interfere in my affairs. Miss Gee is another matter. We live together harmoniously. It will be very difficult, in fact impossible to conceal anything from her. I want you to help me solve this problem. The best option would be to recruit her for our work (she works in the same establishment where SHAH had worked earlier and has access to drafts of some new secret developments). But I do not know how to do this. I am almost sure that if I tell her openly about my work with you and propose that she should take part, she will agree. But I am not absolutely sure.[10]

Baranov put off dealing with this until the next meeting and in the meantime consulted the Centre. In November 1957, Colonel Tarabrin gave these instructions:

> It looks as though SHAH has told ASYA about co-operation with us and now is trying to 'legalize' this situation by receiving our permission to recruit her for our work. The possibility cannot also be ruled out that in the past SHAH received from ASYA certain secret material and passed it over to us, in particular, drafts of the hydrolocator ASDIC 170, since SHAH himself, in our opinion, could hardly have had access to such material by the character of his work. In connection with this, before deciding the question of ASYA's recruitment, it is necessary to clear up and make more precise the following: (1) Whether SHAH is sure that in the case of a breakdown of the recruitment ASYA will not betray him and won't blab about it to any of her acquaintances, and how he can guarantee it; (2) What concrete help ASYA can give to us . . . (3) Who must conduct ASYA's recruitment – we or SHAH himself.[11]

The Centre took almost a year to consider Houghton's request, doubtless exercising the customary caution shown by an intelligence agency when the initiative for a new recruitment comes from another party. However, in November 1958 consent was given to discuss the matter with Miss Gee, on condition that he did not identify the precise foreign organization with which he was co-operating. On 22 November 1958, Baranov instructed Houghton that if ASYA turned him down, he was to tell her that he agreed with her refusal and would have no further contact with his former friends.

When Houghton did approach Gee in January 1959, her first reaction was relief that he was not meeting other women. Then she refused to believe him: such things only happened in novels and Houghton was not any kind of hero found in literature. Then she was so worried by the danger he was in, she started to cry. Houghton reassured her that he was working in a good cause, and was well paid. According to Baranov,

> Having somewhat calmed down ASYA said that she was not going to be angry with him, did not accuse him and was even ready to understand the aim for the sake of which he had taken the step. She gave a firm promise to keep secret all that she had learned, she won't interfere with his work, but she won't take part – she is terribly afraid of the possible consequences ... All SHAH's logical attempts to convince her of the security and safety of our methods of work haven't yet given any positive results.[12]

At the next meeting in February Houghton passed the following note:

> Unfortunately all attempts to win ASYA over to our side proved unsuccessful. She is terribly afraid of the consequences and, although I have taken great efforts to explain to her how the risk is reduced to the absolute minimum and what precautionary measures are always taken, she hasn't changed her decision. She is extremely fond of money but even the expectation of excellent compensation hasn't made her change her decision ... Earlier I had the impression that ASYA would absolutely easily accept my offer – in fact I was 99% sure of it – I told you so. I consider the situation as a big loss but I haven't yet lost hope, although I must admit that I am bitterly disappointed with ASYA's behaviour.[13]

The problem was solved at Houghton's next meeting, on 17 March 1959, when he handed Baranov a bundle of papers on the anti-submarine Super ASDIC 184, announcing that this had come from Ethel who had changed her mind. Part of her job in Portland's drawing office was to destroy classified documents, and she had simply brought them home and given them to Houghton, who was delighted by this turn of events. His pleasure was shared by Baranov, who was to return to Moscow shortly. The next meeting was conducted by Vasili Dozhdalev, codenamed IVAN but known to Houghton as JOHN.

The Centre's worries about SHAH's continued security were considered at the highest level, and became the subject of a report dated 25 May 1959 written by Aleksandr M. Sakharovsky, the chief of the First Chief Directorate, addressed to the KGB Chairman Aleksandr N. Shelepin. In Sakharovsky's view, the London *rezidentura* had become too successful, the subject of too much hostile surveillance, and he recommended that it would be prudent to transfer the handling of some agents to the illegal *rezidentura* which could run agents without having to comply with the travel restrictions which limited the movement of embassy personnel.

> Taking into consideration the existence in Britain of a number of very valuable agents, contact with whom from the position of the London *rezidentura* is unsafe, I should consider it expedient to pass over some of the agents to BEN's *rezidentura*. . . in the first place SHAH. . . who give(s) valuable documentary information.[14]

BEN was Konon Molody, alias Gordon Lonsdale, who had spent much of his adult life working illegally as a Soviet agent in the West. In his youth he had lived with his aunt in California, he had served as a guerrilla behind enemy lines during the Second World War, gained a degree in international law and was an accomplished Chinese linguist. In London his principal contacts were Morris and Lona Cohen (LOUIS and LESLIE), veteran Soviet agents of American origin who had been implicated in the atomic espionage case in America that had sent the Rosenbergs to the electric chair. Morris had fought in the Spanish Civil War and his wife was a well-known left-wing activist. They had fled New York shortly before they were to be arrested, had been trained as illegals and were sent to England where, as Peter and Helen Kroger, they lived under a quiet suburban cover as dealers in antiquarian books. When Shelepin read Sakharovsky's recommendation, he initialled it with two letters, 'ZA', meaning 'I am for it'. This effectively passed SHAH and ASYA from Dohzdalev's control to that of Molody, who operated in London as a Canadian businessman with interests in vending machines. Molody's arrival in Britain in March 1955 marked the establishment of the first illegal *rezident* in the UK since the departure of Arnold Deutsch in the autumn of 1937. Apart from ADA, who had acted as Donald Maclean's courier in 1938 until he was appointed to the British Embassy in Paris, Britain had been free of Soviet illegals because of a chronic shortage of suitable candidates, a consequence of Stalin's purges.

The CPSU's Central Committee had resolved on 30 June 1954 'about measures on the intensification of intelligence work of organs of the State Security abroad' to build up illegal networks in Britain and the United States, and Molody represented the advance guard. He was introduced to Houghton by Dozhdalev on 11 July 1959, and at their next encounter, on 8 August 1959, Molody 'suggested to SHAH that I should visit him at home and show him how to use a 35mm camera, develop film and so on. SHAH thinks it is a good idea.' In reality Molody wanted to learn more about ASYA: 'I think it will be very important to meet ASYA to make sure of her existence since sometimes I have doubts that she really exists.' Although Houghton had described Ethel Gee, and had received money on her behalf, the Centre had no proof that she was not a creation of his imagination, a device with which to extract more cash from the Soviets.

BEN's encounter with Houghton had not been entirely problem-free:

> SHAH said that my speech and manners had worried him and if JOHN [Dozhdalev] had not personally introduced me he would not have gone to the meeting. I told SHAH that I worked for a long time in North America and this explained my accent and manners. SHAH asked me many questions about the Soviet Union, in particular about pensions and how holidays were paid for, and also asked other questions concerning social insurance.[15]

The Centre expressed some reservations about BEN's proposal to visit SHAH at home, and the issue was the subject of a memorandum dated 29 October 1959 addressed to the *rezident* in London, ROZOV (Nikolai Rodin):

> As you know, in work with SHAH at present BEN appears as an official of our embassy. After BEN took over, SHAH began sounding him out since his style of conversation and accent had put SHAH somewhat on his guard. Besides, at their meeting in August this year BEN suggested visiting SHAH at home with which in principle he agreed. The possibility can't be ruled out that all this could have suggested to SHAH that BEN is an unusual member of our official delegation, for our comrades who worked with SHAH earlier had never put such questions. Since this conversation with SHAH, BEN has repeatedly asked permission to visit SHAH's home, but we have considered it inexpedient to agree before conducting a personal meeting with BEN and discussing with him in detail the cover story for such visit.[16]

Dozhdalev conferred with Lonsdale/Molody on 19 November 1959 and agreed the precautions to be taken before his visit to Houghton's home. This took place early in January 1960, and lasted about twenty-four hours, during which Houghton was taught some elementary photography, and introduced Ethel Gee.

> ASYA knows well who we really are. She's very friendly and talkative, but an awful cook. ASYA had and has at present access to documents of all completed projects which are in her establishment including blueprint copies. She can get a spare copy of the majority of projects which at present are being worked out. The difficulty is that (a) she doesn't know what to take out and (b) how to take them out. In ASYA's office there are two control posts: one, right on the premises

where she works, and the other on the land where her establishment is situated.[17]

Molody gave Gee advice about how to evade the controls, and explained that he would provide a detailed list of items in which he was interested. At his next meeting, held in June 1960, Houghton supplied documents from the 'A/S' index on underwater detection devices, including the 2001 sonar designed for the atomic submarine *Dreadnought*. Although Molody's records are inevitably incomplete, because of the constraints of his role as an illegal, he saw Houghton again on 9 July and 6 August before going on holiday. In fact he missed their next rendezvous, scheduled for 1 October 1960, because he was delayed in Moscow; Dozhdalev went instead and received a roll of film from Houghton, together with an assurance that everything was well with Ethel Gee. When Molody returned to England he met Houghton and Gee on 5 November 1960 near the Old Vic Theatre in London where he received a roll of film. They met again on 18 December, and afterwards Molody reported that Houghton still had not answered some of the questions posed back in August, so he had asked both Houghton and Gee to attend their next scheduled meeting, in January 1961. It was on this occasion that Special Branch detectives closed in and arrested the trio. Almost simultaneously, the Krogers were taken into custody at their home in West London. At their subsequent trial it emerged that the Security Service had kept all of them under surveillance since July 1960, when Houghton's meeting with Molody had been observed by MI5's Watcher Service. The fact that the original tip had come from the CIA was not disclosed.

At the conclusion of their six-day trial at the Old Bailey all five defendants were found guilty of breaches of the Official Secrets Acts. Houghton and Gee received fifteen years, Molody twenty-five, and the Krogers twenty each. Molody was swapped for the SIS agent Greville Wynne in April 1964, and the Krogers were exchanged for the university lecturer Gerald Brooke in 1969. Only Houghton and Gee completed their sentences; they were married upon their release from prison in May 1970 and slipped into quiet retirement. Molody got a cool reception in Moscow, became an alcoholic and succumbed to a heart attack in October 1970. Deported to Poland, Helen Kroger died at home in Moscow in 1992 and Peter survived her for a further three years. Their KGB handler, Vasili Dozhdalev, who was to be promoted to head the KGB's illegals branch, Directorate S, now lives in retirement at his dacha outside Moscow, still very fit and enjoying cross-country skiing.

Postscript

Although the access granted to the KGB's archives represented in these pages is unprecedented, this book cannot be regarded as anything approaching a comprehensive study of the 3rd Department of the First Chief Directorate. There are considerable gaps, the principal being the story of what has become known as the Oxford Group.

While the Soviet spies recruited at Cambridge have now acquired international notoriety, very little is known about the other network known to have been drawn at roughly the same time from Oxford University. Understandably, the guardians of the KGB's archives are sensitive about declassifying anything that might identify members of the organization, especially since they believe that none have been named and some are still alive. Nevertheless, a few items have been released, together with the general assurance that, in contrast to its Cambridge counterparts, it was not marked by any dramatic events. What can be said about these people illuminates the characteristic state of mind and political orientation of British students in the 1930s, and the way Soviet Intelligence made use of this unique social-political phenomenon in order to acquire sources within the British establishment by means which were only pertinent to that particular period.

The contrast between the ideologically very attractive, large-scale social experiment represented by the building of a Socialist society in Russia, on the one hand, and the rise of Fascism in Germany, Austria and Italy, combined with the social and economic crisis in the capitalist West at the end of the 1920s on the other, was conducive to the spread of Communism among students. They constituted the most receptive body of opinion because of both age and intellect, and the Party actively promoted itself among youth. Although Marxism often took on specific, home-grown varieties in the minds of individual students, as suggested in Anthony Blunt's autobiographical notes, its supranational, international component made it easier for them to defy the laws of the society to which they belonged, but which they despised and which, in their view, was already in rapid decline.

As with the Cambridge group, the penetration of Oxford by the Soviets began as a result of the initiative taken by Edith Tudor Hart, a key figure in Soviet espionage operations in Britain, although little has ever been written about her. Born in Vienna in 1908 to William Suschitzky, a radical socialist who advocated birth control and sex education and owned a bookshop in the working-class district of Petzvalgasse, Edith trained as a Montessori kindergarten teacher and in 1925 travelled to England to work as a teacher. Two years later she was back in Vienna, and studied photography under Walter Peterhans at the Bauhaus in Dessau. In 1933, at the height of the political repression, she married Dr Alex Tudor Hart, a left-wing medical practitioner, at the British consulate and they moved to Brixton in south London, then to the Rhondda Valley. As well as being an active member of the banned Austrian Communist Party, she was also a Soviet illegal who had completed two undercover missions, to Paris and London, in 1929.

Upon their return from South Wales, Alex Tudor Hart joined the Republican forces in Spain as a surgeon, while his wife opened a photographic studio in Acre Lane, Brixton, where, after the birth of her son in 1936, she began to specialize in child portraits. During this period, while active in the Workers Camera Club, contributing to *Picture Post* and organizing the Artists against Fascism and War exhibition, she maintained contact with her friend from Vienna, Litzi Friedman, who was by then separated from Kim Philby, and liaised closely with Bob Stuart, who was himself acting as a clandestine link between CPGB headquarters and the Soviet Embassy. She divorced Alex after his return from Spain. In March 1938, a Leica camera originally purchased by her was discovered in a police raid on the home of Percy Glading, who was subsequently convicted of organizing the Woolwich Arsenal spy-ring (see Chapter Six), but when questioned by Special Branch detectives she simply denied any involvement. At that time MI5 had no reason to be suspicious of her, nor any reason to believe that, as a talent-spotter in June 1934, she had cultivated Kim Philby and introduced him to Arnold Deutsch for recruitment.

After the war Edith worked as a commercial photographer and briefly for the Ministry of Education, but her mental condition deteriorated and she suffered a breakdown; her son had already been taken into care. She later opened a small antiques shop in Brighton, and died of liver cancer in 1973, her remarkable espionage role undiscovered.[1]

As a celebrated photographer, Edith enjoyed a wide range of contacts within British society, and her expertise as a recruiter is confirmed in a letter dated 8 October 1936 from the London illegal *rezidentura* to the Centre noting a recent significant success:

> Through EDITH we obtained SOHNCHEN [Philby]. In the attached report you will find details of a second SOHNCHEN who, in all probability, offers even greater possibilities than the first. Edith is of the opinion that [name deleted] is more promising than SOHNCHEN. From the report you will see that he has very definite possibilities. We must make haste with these people before they start being active in university life.

It was only after the return to London of Theodor Mally from Moscow in January 1937 that real work on expanding the agent network in London began, as he described to the Centre:

> About new recruitments. They have been started along two channels: (a) through Anthony Blunt, known to you, who is a lecturer in Cambridge and has already agreed; (b) through [name deleted], also known to you and who has also agreed.

Mally proposed that the 'second SOHNCHEN' should be code-named SCOTT and the London *rezidentura* wasted no time, as he reported by the next mail:

> SCOTT. I wrote to you about him in my last letter. Through him we acquired BUNNY. He has given me about 25 leads. Most of these are raw material, but there are 4–5 among them who have already been studied and on whom we have already started working.

Mally also described briefly the CPGB's status in Oxford and Cambridge:

> In the course of the last five years, about 250 Party members have left Oxford and Cambridge Universities and a considerable number of them are now employed in the Civil Service. Where exactly they are and what they are doing, nobody knows. At present there are about 200 Party members in those universities of whom about 70 will leave this year. Apart from this, there are about 1,300 students who are members of the Left Wing clubs (which have the same platform as us).

Upon receipt of Mally's letter, the Centre became worried about the London *rezidentura*'s activities, and warned it to be more cautious:

> SCOTT and his 25 leads. We are very worried about his activity. All this is too much based on the COMPATRIOTS [the CPGB]. The practice of previous years has shown that this is fraught with great danger. The danger of failure is especially great when we are dealing with groups and not with individuals. Usually, groups of such people

discuss all questions amongst themselves, in spite of all prohibitions, and you, thinking you are dealing with one man only, have all his friends on your hands . . . You should explain this to SCOTT. . . There should be no mass recruitment on any account. From among the many and promising candidates, select the most valuable. Check ten times, do not be in a hurry and recruit only when you have sufficient data. BUNNY's recruitment, for instance, was much too hurried. Bear in mind that all this is not unsubstantiated caution on our part, but that you are running a most valuable network, the preservation of which is a task of the highest importance.

We were very interested in the number of students, established by you, who are sympathetic to our cause. This material should certainly be collected and it would not be a bad thing to keep a regular account, so as to know where these people end up, and in certain cases direct them to institutions which are of interest to us. We think that this should be done in such a way that not every one of them would know beforehand what we want of him. In any case, whenever this is possible, we should cover up our ultimate aim until the last moment. Such a way of proceeding will enable us to build up a reserve of ready leads, which can be developed, as the need arises, into trustworthy and active agents.

In response to the Centre's wish to 'keep a regular account', Mally entrusted the task to SCOTT, who submitted a report in April 1937 entitled *On potential candidates in Oxford*:

The number of student Party members is at present 115. By June this number will increase to 145. I have a list of the future professions of 80 students and will soon get another list of 35 people. Of the above, 32 students will leave Oxford at the end of the next term (June).

SCOTT listed the graduates according to profession, and they included: Civil Service, 17; Scientific workers, 18; Teachers, 23; Army, 1; Law, 5; University lecturers, 7; Business, 2; Politicians, 3; Social services, 1; Doctors, 1; Undecided, 1.

Judging by the experience of the previous 5–6 years, we may expect that 80–90 per cent will remain active Party members. As far as I know, during this period, of about 600 people, only two have betrayed the Party. One became a fascist – the other a Trotskyite. About 60 became passive members or were lost sight of. This can be explained by the fact that either they obtained appointments which were incompatible with Party activity or they were unable to understand the policies of the working class and it was difficult for them to settle down in small provincial towns.

On the whole we have come to the conclusion that the most able people remain loyal to us, a great number of whom become the most capable and responsible among Party members ... Bearing this in mind, if we set about it the right way, we could, within a given period, achieve considerable results. Since we can find people wherever we look for them, it is necessary to have in the University a man who is able, trustworthy and responsible only to us.

On 23 July 1937, SCOTT submitted another report, *On the students in the Party*, in which he concluded that there was a total of 900 students in the CPGB: 150 in Oxford, 200 in Cambridge, 300 in London University and the remainder in provincial universities.

> Cambridge is evidently the most important university. It has a more solid Party organization than Oxford and it is also a larger university. Moreover Cambridge education bears a more special character and the general intellectual level of students is higher than in Oxford. When looking for really good positions, considerably more people go to Cambridge than to Oxford ... A great number of persons who occupy senior positions in government departments come from Oxford and Cambridge. London University is also of great importance, especially as regards to scientists. As I was told, nearly half of the scientists studying at present will enter government service ... If we work cautiously in the universities the risk is not very great. We can be practically sure of always being able to select reliable people.

SCOTT's recommendations arrived at a time when the London illegal *rezidentura* was about to be closed down because of the purges and cover problems, and contact with its sources suspended. Nevertheless, judging by a memorandum written in October 1940, before the return of Anatoli Gorsky to London, a number of people had been recruited using SCOTT as intermediary. When contact with SCOTT was re-established in 1941, new sources were acquired with his help.

Altogether 1937 proved to be something of a watershed for Soviet Intelligence, consolidating its achievements at a time when it was under threat of destruction by the purges. This view is borne out by a remarkable memorandum entitled *On the work of the illegal rezidenturas in Great Britain*, submitted by Abram Slutsky, then the Head of the 7th Department, to People's Commissar Nikolai Yezhov in December 1937:

> Experience of the work of our illegal *rezidenturas* in Great Britain has shown that there exist in that country relatively important circles of left-wing orientated people, who are not Party members but move within the orbit of the Party, are violently anti-fascist and sympathetic towards the USSR. This opens up wide opportunities for using them for our work ...

British intellectuals, especially the young among them, do not find satisfactory ideals in the decomposing capitalist society of Britain and are naturally drawn towards the USSR. They are looking for ways to work selflessly for the furtherance of socialism and the Soviet Union. Our work, demanding such revolutionary selflessness, often attracts to it by its very nature this left-wing, anti-fascist youth, since it corresponds to their ideology and liberates their revolutionary energy. It is our task to earmark, in time, the necessary people and establish contact with them before they compromise themselves in the eyes of the authorities by open revolutionary activity or, at least, isolate them from Party organizations or Party links, if they have already become members and then train them ideologically and operationally.

We have already undertaken this work in Cambridge and Oxford – two outstanding British universities – which supply the senior administrators in the most important ministries (the Foreign Office, the Home Office, the War Office, etc.). We had the opportunity of studying there certain young men, who were pointed out to us by agents, ideologically close to us, and to isolate those of them who were already members of Party organizations from all Party work and Party links and then to recruit them.

It follows from the above that at present we have in Great Britain the foundations of a sufficiently clandestine organization of talent scouts and recruiters of whom each has his potential group of agents. Bearing in mind the difficulties of underground work in Britain, because of the regime governing foreigners and in expectation that this will become even stricter in wartime, we have set ourselves the task of strengthening and widening the existing organization made up of local people, who do not need passports or cover or, of course, to study the language. What these people need most is ideological education and operational and technical training. The purpose of this work is to turn the already existing group of talent scouts and recruiters into operational officers who will lead the groups and act as sub-*rezidents*.

The memorandum ended with recommendations in respect of individual agents, in what country they should operate and what they ought to be taught. As can be seen, Slutsky's memorandum contained proposals for a major reorganization of the work of Soviet Intelligence in Britain: in effect, he proposed to grant considerable, if not full, autonomy to specially trained agent groups, and limit the running of them to general direction, either by the local *rezident*, or even by the Centre via couriers. The intention was to enhance the security of the agent networks, an arrangement that had already been used episodically and in a simplified form during the years when diplomatic relations between Great Britain and the Soviet Union had been severed. This time it was a question of systematic work and such a recommendation could only work if there was complete trust in the English head agents. As is clear from the memorandum, two factors underlay the transition to the new system: one was the current strict immigration regulations in Britain and the other was the expected outbreak of war in Europe.

Stalin's purge of the NKVD prevented the new system from being introduced, so the London *rezidentura* returned to the traditional methods of running its sources through legally accredited officers based at the embassy and the trade mission. This was the tried and tested structure that had produced so many pre-war successes.

The Soviet twin-track arrangement of separate legal and illegal *rezidenturas* ensured that no diplomats were compromised as a consequence of the Woolwich Arsenal case in 1938, the only embarrassment being the lack of insulation protecting the CPGB when Percy Glading was exposed as a major Soviet spy. Indeed, according to the MI5 files plundered by Anthony Blunt (see Appendix I), the Security Service failed to realize the scope of William Euer's organization, and even after the arrest of Captain John King in September 1939 had never appreciated the extent to which the Foreign Office security had been breached by Ernest Oldham. As for Edith Tudor Hart, who was directly responsible for the recruitment of both Kim Philby and the mysterious SCOTT, who is believed by the KGB to have been alive as recently as 1995, MI5 made no progress whatever. The only link established between Philby and Edith, apart from her former husband Alex having been his contemporary at Cambridge, was a telephone call to her home, intercepted in 1951, in which an unidentified caller advised her to destroy the negative of his picture. One of his favourites, with Kim posed pensively smoking a pipe, had been taken by Edith in Vienna in 1933, and amounted to clear evidence of a connection between the SIS officer, then under detailed investigation, and a suspected Soviet spy. In 1951 this would have been almost enough to seal Philby's fate, but he denied ever having known Edith, and MI5 never traced her connection with the photograph.

The KGB's archives demonstrate the very tight control exercised by the Centre, with every aspect of a particular case requiring constant approval by Moscow. For historians, this apparently bureaucratic chain of command, exuding distrust and paranoia, generated a mass of valuable files, internal memoranda, psychological profiles and counter-intelligence double-checks with which to reconstruct an extraordinary, clandestine dimension to espionage war fought between Britain and the Soviets.

Some of the documents passed to Moscow by Anthony Blunt

MI5's Report on Russian Espionage

PAUL HARDT ALIAS PETERS

Only after the arrest of Glading [in January 1938, leading to the exposure of the Woolwich Arsenal spy group] did it became possible to establish that Peters was identical with Paul Hardt, an Austrian born in 1894. It was further established that Hardt frequently visited Great Britain between June 1935 and June 1937, his last stay being for four months. He passed himself off as a representative of Gada, an Amsterdam textile company established in 1933, and through it he conducted some business which in reality was a cover for Soviet espionage.

When Hardt left Britain in June 1937 he did so in a great hurry, without winding up his affairs. He left the caretaker of his flat an address in Paris to which his mail should be forwarded, but by the end of July 1937 the mail was returned and when, in April 1938, the flat was searched about a hundred letters were found. Most of them were not of any interest but one envelope contained a copy of Hardt's bank account with a British bank in Woburn Place, London. Enquiries with the bank showed that on 30 June 1938 Hardt's account amounted to £1,921. In July a cheque for £100 was presented in favour of a collaborator of Hardt in Amsterdam, and in September for £36 in favour of the estate agents managing Hardt's flat.

On 27 February 1938 two cheques were presented at the Midland Bank for £950 and £320 respectively by the Moscow Narodny Bank in favour of the Banque Commerciale in Paris, leaving £36 in Hardt's account. Further enquiries showed that at the end of June 1937 Hardt had left France, having been recalled to Russia where, according to unconfirmed reports, he had been shot in the party purges which at that time were conducted in the Soviet Union. There is no doubt that Hardt was the chief of the political and military intelligence organization of the OGPU which was active in Great Britain from 1935 to 1937.

MR AND MRS WILLY BRANDES, ALIAS MR AND MRS STEVENS

It was established that while in Great Britain Brandes assumed the identity of a French Canadian and pretended to be an agent of a New York furniture firm, as well as representing an American firm selling cosmetic powder. After Glading's arrest the Canadian authorities conducted an investigation to establish if the Brandes held Canadian passports and they determined that the passports had been obtained in 1936 on false grounds, and that they had received Canadian naturalization certificates. The Brandes had been assisted in obtaining these documents by Armand Labis Feldman who was strongly suspected by the American authorities of being a Soviet intelligence agent. In November 1940 Feldman was interned and questioned by the Canadian and American authorities and he confessed that he was a Soviet spy, and that he possessed a Canadian naturalization certificate which had been obtained by deception. He further stated that Brandes was a Soviet agent whom he had met for the first time in America in the summer of 1936, shortly after Brandes had arrived in the USA under the name of William Hopmann. Feldman received orders from his chief, an Amtorg employee, to assist Hopmann in obtaining the documents necessary to be issued with a Canadian passport.

Feldman's wife admitted that her husband's real name was Josef Volodarsky, and it was established that he worked in Britain from 1930 to 1932. In November 1932, Volodarsky committed an offence in London and was fined, soon after which he had left for Russia. In 1934 he went to the USA.

Conclusion
Investigations in the notorious Glading case threw an interesting light on Soviet military and naval espionage in Britain in the course of 1937. All the British subjects involved were members of the British Communist Party but they all ceased to engage in open Communist work as soon as they were recruited in the spy-ring. Other British Communists, apart from those named, are strongly suspected of belonging to the same group though it proved impossible to obtain evidence. It is noteworthy that although Glading was undoubtedly the organizer of this group of Communist sub-agents, he did not have a free hand in directing the work of the group and the recruitment of agents, but was controlled by a foreign resident in Britain, except for two months immediately preceding his arrest. Willy Brandes alias Stevens left Britain in November 1937 and his successor did not arrive before Glading's arrest. Miss 'X' [Olga Gray], for instance, did not receive permission to continue work and did not know the nature of the work she had to do until she had seen and spoken to Paul Hardt, alias Peters.

The way in which Glading received military and naval information for the USSR was extremely simple. His sub-agents worked in various departments at the Woolwich Arsenal. They took blueprints with them when they went home and handed them over to Glading who photographed them immediately and returned them the same evening. The sub-agents were able to replace the blueprints when they returned to work the next morning without arousing any suspicion. When the agents lived further afield, they made copies of the blueprints at the weekend. These were put in a book, which was collected from the Woolwich Arsenal by Charles Munday. This was probably because photographing large blueprints required considerable time.

This shows that Glading gave his sub-agents instructions to take everything they could of importance since in at least one case Glading was not aware of the nature of documents he was to photograph.

It seems that Glading entirely depended on Paul Hardt or Brandes for financial support. Before Brandes left Britain he had taken £300 from his current account, the greater part of which was given to Glading to finance his organization until Brandes' successor arrived in Britain in January. Immediately before Glading's arrest on 21 January 1938, he was in great need of money and was worried about how he could continue working until the new man arrived.

It is quite clear that the Soviet Embassy was not involved in financing Glading's organization or in the transmission of intelligence material to Moscow. Since Brandes' successor did not arrive in the beginning of January, Glading was worried about the transmission of material which he had received the preceding month.

JOHN HERBERT KING

On 18 October 1939 a British subject, J.H. King, employed in the Foreign Office, was accused of having endangered national security, and sentenced to ten years' hard labour. In brief, the facts which led to his arrest were as follows:

In the beginning of September 1939 information was received from a reliable source to the effect that a certain King working in the Communications Department of the Foreign Office was simultaneously engaged in espionage on behalf of the USSR. Investigations showed that in the department in question only one person was employed whose name was King, and this was John Herbert King. It was decided to watch King's movements and since, at that time, he was suffering from exhaustion, he was granted two weeks' sick leave, during which he was investigated. By coincidence, information concerning a Foreign Office employee was received a few days later from a completely different source, named Conrad Parlanti, who reported a Dutchman Hans Pieck with whom he had had a business partnership in 1936. It is probable that Parlanti volunteered to give information because the war had started.

Parlanti's information amounted to the following: He first met Pieck in 1934 through a man named Raymond from the Foreign Office and subsequently they became great friends. After a while, Pieck suggested to Parlanti that he should leave the firm Shop Fitters and start working for him. Pieck was an artist and architect and was ready to provide capital. Parlanti agreed and suggested opening an office in Holborn, but Pieck was against this and an office was found in Buckingham Gate. Here Pieck had one floor for himself and kept one room locked. At first Parlanti paid no attention to this but later became suspicious and found a means of entering the room when Pieck was absent. Inside was a table above which a Leica camera had been fitted for the purpose of taking photographs of what was on the table. He hinted to Pieck about his discovery but did not receive a reasonable explanation.

Later Pieck invited Parlanti to his home in The Hague where he was introduced to Mrs Pieck and he visited several times. On one of his last visits, Pieck unexpectedly told him that he had to go away for a while on urgent business and from then on Parlanti became very suspicious of Pieck, and when the latter was absent again he told Mrs Pieck about his suspicions and asked her to tell him what her husband's real business was. Mrs Pieck opened up and told him that she and her husband and certain other persons were engaged in financial speculation 'to make large profits' and that they were able to operate because they were helped by a man in one of the departments of the Foreign Office in London. This man had access to, and could take from the Foreign Office, secret documents which he passed briefly to her husband to photograph.

When Pieck returned Parlanti confronted him with this information and Pieck more or less admitted that what his wife had said was true. Pieck hinted to Parlanti that this matter had nothing to do with him, but that if he kept silent he would profit from this. Parlanti refused to undertake anything in this matter and soon afterwards broke off contact with Pieck and their business closed down.

Parlanti stated that he did not know who the person in the Foreign Office was, but did not think it could be Raymond C. Oake who had introduced him to Pieck, though he knew that Oake had been friendly with Pieck who, he was convinced, gave Oake money. He thought that the man in question was a colleague of Oake and that he saw him accidentally when, one evening in May 1936, he was with Pieck at the Victoria Hotel in Northumberland Avenue. While they were sitting there, this man entered the hotel and Pieck immediately excused himself and went over to him at the other side of the room. About ten minutes later, Pieck returned to Parlanti who noticed that he was putting something in his inside pocket that looked like documents, with red print on pale yellow paper.

Pieck asked Parlanti if he knew the man to whom he had just been talking and added: 'He has just given me some material.' Parlanti replied that he had only seen the man from behind and therefore could not say if he knew him or not. Soon after that Pieck left the hotel and Parlanti returned to the office in Buckingham Gate where, as he had guessed, the light was on in Pieck's private room. Parlanti was convinced that Pieck had received secret Foreign Office documents and was photographing them. Parlanti was able to give a description of the man he had seen in the Victoria Hotel and this description tallied with that of John Herbert King. Parlanti also said that when he was in Paris in June 1937 he met Pieck there who told him that he had not seen any of his old friends, with the exception of 'my old friend from the Foreign Office' whom he had met at the Brussels Conference.

Following up Parlanti's information, investigations established that only two people from the Foreign Office cipher department had attended the Brussels Conference. One of these was beyond suspicion, the other was John King. Meanwhile, surveillance of King failed to show anything interesting, apart from the fact that he had intimate relations with a Miss Helen Wilky, who lived in Ravenscourt Park and worked with the Chancery Lane Safe Deposit and Estate Company Ltd. King's current account with Mills & Glyn, and Oake's with Barclays Bank were investigated, but they showed no large deposits. It is necessary here to give some information about Hans Henri Christiaan Pieck. He was born in 1895 and was known to MI5 for many years as a Communist and suspected Communist agent. It was also known that he frequently came to Britain on short visits. At the end of March 1938, after the Glading case had been disposed of, information was received from one of our sources to the effect that Pieck had been the predecessor of Paul Hardt (Peters). The report stated that Pieck had been a member of Soviet Intelligence since 1930 when he was sent to Geneva to establish contact with British diplomats through members of the British delegation to the League of Nations. He had remained in Switzerland for about three years and had succeeded in establishing contact at the end of 1935 and the beginning of 1936 with certain employees of the Foreign Office, and regularly received documents from them which he photographed with a Leica in his office in Buckingham Gate. Enquiries about Pieck in Holland in April 1936 compelled the Soviets to break off contact with him and Hardt (Peters) took his place.

The investigation undertaken after this report was received was unable to check any statements contained in it. As soon as Parlanti's information was received, steps were taken to establish contact with the source who had reported on Pieck in March 1939, in the hope that he could provide additional details which would make it possible to confirm King's identity. The source could only add, however, that the man from the Foreign Office who was used by Pieck had a mistress called Helen Wilky. By this time King had returned to work in the Foreign Office and it was decided that the matter should be settled once for all. King and Wilky were questioned and their flats were searched. An envelope was discovered in Wilky's safe at the Chancery Lane Safe Deposit Company which contained Bank of England notes to the sum of £1,300 which Wilky stated she was keeping for King. He explained that he had accumulated this money over several years by gambling. Both Wilky and King admitted that they knew Pieck but King denied that Pieck had at any time shown interest in his work in the Foreign Office. On 20 September 1939 King and Wilky were arrested and eight days later King expressed the wish to see a Special Branch officer in order to make 'a full confession'. The following sets out the substance of this confession:

King met Pieck for the first time in Geneva in 1933 or 1934 and saw him quite frequently while he was there. After that he met him many times in London in the beginning of 1935 and at that time Pieck had an office in Buckingham Gate. He asked King to supply him with information from the Foreign Office. King stated:

Pieck told me that he knew a rich banker in The Hague who could give money to both of us if I could supply Pieck with information which passed between the Foreign Office and various embassies. Pieck and the banker could extract useful information on political affairs from this which would help them to do profitable deals on the stock exchange. Pieck said that if I would do this he would share the profit with me and I agreed. I am not a permanent civil servant and am not eligible for a pension. I felt that in this way I could get some money for when I retire without endangering the security of the state. From time to time I gave Pieck copies of incoming telegrams for example reports on talks between Hitler and Nevile Henderson [the British Ambassador in Berlin] or between Kemal Ataturk and the British Ambassador in Turkey or something of the kind. Sometimes it was eight to nine pages, sometimes three or four, but never more than ten and they were not of great political importance. The telegrams were always deciphered spare copies available in the room.

King said he had met Pieck in various places including his office in Buckingham Gate where in one room there was a table, a lamp and a camera. King said that the telegrams he gave Pieck remained with the latter and it was not necessary to photograph them. Pieck paid him from £50 to £200 at a time. In 1936 Pieck left, having introduced King to a man whose name was Peterson (this man was identified as Paul

Hardt who was mentioned in the Glading case) and they became acquainted in the office in Buckingham Gate. Pieck told King that Peterson would continue the work in his stead and King continued to meet Peterson for a period of about nineteen months, until June 1937, when the latter told him that he would be absent for about a month. King stated that henceforth he neither saw nor heard from Peterson. During these nineteen months, King handed Peterson Foreign Office telegrams in the same way as he had to Pieck and Peterson gave him money ranging from £100 to £150. If Pieck never asked King to obtain codes, Peterson did so on repeated occasions but King swore that he refused and never handed over codes or ciphering pads. All the documents which he passed were decoded already and although King did not remember exactly how much money he received in all, he thought it was about £1,300 from Pieck and £1,200 from Peterson. Two years ago, he gave £1,000 to Wilky and told her that if anything happened to him that money belonged to her. He said that he had not lived with his wife for ten years and had conducted an affair with Wilky since 1933. He stressed that Wilky knew nothing about the source of the money nor the nature of his collaboration with Pieck. He introduced her to the latter but said that she never met Peterson and did not even know about his existence. When King's flat was searched it was found that his current account with Lloyd's Bank, which had been opened in 1913, had been in credit with only a few pounds until February 1936. Between that date and June 1939, however, not less than £3,010 pounds had been paid in, usually in cash. The history of these banknotes was investigated and it was established that most of those found in Wilky's safe had been transferred from the Moscow Narodny Bank (the bank was used by Paul Hardt) to the Rotterdamsche Bankvereniging in Rotterdam and Amsterdam, from Paul Hardt's account to Pieck's. As a result of King's evidence the case against Wilky was dropped and she was released.

Conclusion

This case illustrates the well-known recruiting methods of Soviet Intelligence: selection of people who had access to secret information and who, because of spendthrift habits or for other reasons, were in need of money and could not resist the temptation of making some extra by selling information. Undoubtedly Pieck was sent to Geneva by the Soviets for the purpose of establishing contact with British diplomats attached to the League of Nations. He was described as a man of great charm and a lavish host who easily made friends with plenty of British diplomats. Through these friendships, he had the opportunity of learning about their personal lives and in this way find out who was in financial difficulties and would therefore be willing to sell information.

It is quite possible that King did not even know the country for which his information was destined and there is no doubt that he acted out of purely mercenary motives.

ERNEST HOLLOWAY OLDHAM

In July 1933 information was received from the Foreign Office that Oldham, who had previously worked there, had enjoyed temporary access to the key of the fire-proof room where ciphers were kept. He had evidently made an impression of the key and it was decided that although no official steps should be taken against him, his past and present activities should be investigated. Oldham had worked in the cipher department of the Foreign Office for many years but had retired in 1932. Apart from the fact that in recent years he had travelled frequently to the continent, no other information was discovered. However, he drank a lot, was in financial difficulties and was on the verge of bankruptcy. In September 1933, before any firm incriminating information could be obtained, Oldham committed suicide and the case was closed.

It was not until 1940 that information was received from a reliable source that Oldham had been a Soviet spy since 1930. In that year he had presented himself at the Soviet Embassy and had offered to sell British diplomatic ciphers and other secret documents to which he had access. The Soviets at first refused to have anything to do with him, suspecting that he was an *agent provocateur*, but a few weeks later Oldham reappeared at the embassy and brought with him samples of the material to which he had access. This time, although he still aroused suspicion, it was agreed that he would receive substantial payment for any material from the Foreign Office. Initially Oldham was not given an opportunity to meet Soviet agents in Britain and he had to travel to Paris to hand over the material. However, as soon as the Soviets were convinced that Oldham was not a double agent, they agreed to send somebody to London to collect this material. Since Oldham was extremely nervous and drank a lot it was decided that the Soviet agent sent to Britain to collect material had to monitor Oldham's mental state.

After he left the Foreign Office Oldham continued to receive material from that department by making use of his former position there, and during one of his visits he managed to make an impression of the key to the cipher room. In the end Oldham's nerves gave way to such an extent that the Soviet agent could only induce him to visit the Foreign Office by threatening him with denunciation to the authorities and the cessation of his payment. When it became clear that Oldham was about to break down completely the Soviet agent concentrated on obtaining information from him about the private lives of his colleagues in the hope of finding a future source among them. At first Oldham refused to do this, but after considerable pressure had been brought to bear on him, he finally gave five or six names and one of these was John H. King, who also worked in the cipher department of the Foreign Office.

Conclusion

The principal point of interest in this case is the fact that the Soviet agents had recourse to blackmail in order to obtain information from the Foreign Office and the names of other employees who could become agents in the future. That is how, as is now known, they later succeeded in recruiting John King.

As well as extracting this review, Blunt succeeded in obtaining volume 1 of Pieck's MI5 file, and promised that he would soon get the next volume. In the meantime he summarized the information:

> 1930: The Dutch police considers Pieck to be a communist. 1934: Pieck pays a small sum to Beisman, an arms dealer. 1935: A report from the British Passport office in Holland that Pieck is in Britain. For a few years nothing has been heard of him and he can, therefore, be used for underground work. These reports from the British Passport Office in Holland have been obtained from a certain D.V. Hooper who was in contact with Pieck in Holland. This man lives at 4 Kensington Court. His brother works for MI5. Note on visits to Britain: In 1935 he received a money transfer by telegraph of £200 from Robert Kelly in Paris. In 1938 SIS reports that Hooper is well acquainted with Pieck and was told by him that he had worked for Soviet Intelligence since 1930. He went to Geneva to establish contacts in the Foreign Office. He made the acquaintance of a number of Foreign Office employees. They returned to Britain on various business. In 1935–36 he was able to obtain documents from the Foreign Office. Hooper made a number of enquiries which worried the Soviet representatives who stopped working with Pieck. Later he was replaced in Britain by Peters, who was later recalled and shot. After that Pieck was used to purchase fighter aircraft for the Spanish government. In 1936 he flew to Greece for this purpose and then to Paris where he organized this business through the intermediary of a South American Embassy. Pieck is short of money and goes to London to re-establish contact. Pieck's chief was Walter, recalled in 1937. He went into hiding, however, taking 50 000 florins with him. Walter had his headquarters in The Hague. As a result of this report MI5 made enquiries and sent the following letter to SIS: Paul Hardt left Britain in a hurry on 24 June 1937, leaving behind the following forwarding address: 28 Avenue Friedland, Paris. Later letters forwarded to this address were returned. Two of these letters were

written by a certain R. Danilovich of 156 Stadhouderskade, Amsterdam. This is the address of Gada, the firm of which Hardt was the London representative with an office in Russell Square. Gada had another address: 3 Westeinde, Amsterdam. MI5 supposes that Danilovich is identical with Bendit Davidovich Boorek, born 12 January 1890 who had difficulties with the Home Office in connection with the prolongation of his residence permit in 1920.

Another letter mentions that the £2,000 left in Hardt's bank account here were transferred to the Moscow Narodny Bank. It is quite possible that Peter, who is mentioned by Pieck, is Hardt's pseudonym. According to information from the Swiss police, Hardt returned to Russia on 22 July 1937. They also stated that he was inculpated in the the death of Ignaty Reis [See Chapter Six] (three photographs of Hardt and his wife were enclosed in the letter). The above-mentioned Walter may be the successor of Ulanovsky alias Sherman who was sometimes called Walter. Can Pieck be bought to reveal all he knows?

At this stage the investigation stopped since SIS cut off contact with their agent (Hooper) and did not wish to resume it. In October 1938 SIS reported that Pieck was in contact with the Dutch Economic Department.

On 12 September 1939 Parlanti, Pieck's partner in London, told us that while he was with Pieck in Holland, the latter told him that he regularly photographed Foreign Office documents. It is thought that he uses them to complete various deals. Parlanti met Pieck through Oake who worked in the Foreign Office. Parlanti said that in 1936 Hooper enquired about Pieck. Parlanti stated that Pieck had persuaded him to work with him, but subsequently showed no interest in the work. Pieck had a room in the house which was always locked, but which Parlanti once entered. In the room there was a table and a Leica camera, which Pieck said he used for making pornographic postcards. Parlanti, Pieck and the latter's wife lived in The Hague. Later Pieck was recalled. His wife then tried to start an affair with Parlanti, who refused, however. He asked what she and her husband were doing. She told him that they were in touch with people in the world of finance and that they lived well thanks to the help of a man who worked in the cipher department of the British Foreign Office. This man took away Foreign Office documents and handed them over to Pieck. When Pieck returned, Parlanti questioned him about these facts and Pieck confirmed them. After that Parlanti broke off his business contacts with Pieck. Parlanti stated that he knew Oake and Russel who worked in the cipher department of the Foreign Office, but that neither of them appeared to him to be the man referred to above.

Once Parlanti and Pieck were sitting in his room when a man came in to whom they talked. Then Pieck took some documents from this man and went home. Parlanti followed him and saw that there was light on in Pieck's locked room. Parlanti described the visitor as follows: aged about fifty-three, height five feet and a few inches, thick set with greying hair. Parlanti added that the man who handed over the documents had, in 1937, been sent to the Brussels Conference.

The next time he was interviewed, Parlanti added: In as far as he could remember, when talking about Oake and Russel, Pieck had often mentioned 'my other friend in the Foreign Office' who lived either in Richmond or Campden Hill. He also mentioned another man, who was also linked to Pieck through the International Barter Corporation and the International Trading Company, called Fitzgerald. In Paris Pieck met a man called Basov. Pieck received a letter addressed to Peterson. He was sometimes rung by a man called Simon, whose surname was, he thought, Vries and who lived in Amsterdam and was a friend of Hooper.

Then there is a hiatus in the file and only Pieck is mentioned. The next document is King's interrogation report. It seems to me that at the point where the hiatus occurs in the file, a report was received from Krivitzky which confirmed that Pieck took Foreign Office documents. There is nothing of interest to us in the interrogation report, apart from the following: King was asked whether he knew Kirby and Philip Rosenblit as friends of Pieck. He was questioned on 25 September 1939.

There was an interview with Oake but he said nothing new and confirmed only that Kirby was Pieck's partner. There was an interview with Mr J Russel and Mr R Kinnaird from the cipher department but they did not say anything of interest. In the same way Wilky was questioned, but there were only extracts from the protocol concerning *Major Query*. Helen Wilky was also questioned, and her flat was searched. She lived for a few years with King and Foreign Office documents belonging to Query were found in her personal safe. Parlanti was called in again and he said the following: In 1934 he went to Paris with Stuart Cameron Kirby, an architect and draughtsman, and also met the latter's boss there, Hawes. Parlanti turned to Basov whom he considers to be Pieck's cashier, and Pieck told Parlanti about his admiration for Russia and about his trip there. Parlanti saw two women with Pieck. One was called the Baroness and she was connected with Fokkers. Later Pieck said that they had been arrested as German spies.

The last document is King's confession. It contains details of his first meeting with Pieck in Geneva, arranged by Oake. Already during this meeting Pieck had tried to recruit him and they met again later in England. Pieck told King that he knew a banker who was willing to pay well for valuable information and that if King would help him in this matter, they would share the proceeds. King stated that he handed Pieck copies of telegrams received from embassies, including one reporting a conversation between Henderson and Hitler or between Kemal Ataturk and the British Ambassador in Turkey. These were extra copies. The meetings with Pieck took place in hotels or in his office in Buckingham Gate, and Pieck paid him about £1,500, and Peterson about £1,200. In 1936 Pieck left and handed him over to Peterson who was a Hungarian. He was tall and deadly pale, aged about forty. They continued to meet until the middle of 1937. Peterson was very secretive and he told King that he lived near Marble Arch. He asked King to obtain Foreign Office ciphers for him but King hesitated. Miss Wilky did not take any part in this matter.

Part of the first volume contains Buysman's interrogation report and investigations into his activities in Britain. He clearly was of no interest and was left in peace. I had an opportunity to get the second volume of the investigation report and the following is a short summary: Some facts explain and supplement the above. Remarks on the interrogation of Foreign Office employees show that Helen Wilky's diary was studied and the names appearing there were investigated. £1,300 was found in her safe which belonged to King, as well as documents belonging to Query. These documents were clearly not of interest and were simply kept there. Part of the money was received by King from Pieck and Peterson. Miss Wilky was charged because of the Query documents but later the charge was dropped. Query was the lover of Helen Wilky's sister, Elsie. The next document is a report dated 5 October 1939 on Hooper's interrogation which shows the whole history of his connection with Pieck.

In 1920 he worked in the Passport Control Office in Rotterdam with Harwood and Wood, and was interested in matters connected with communism. 'I was fifteen years old. From 1923 to 1927 I worked in the Consulate. Up to now I have worked for Major Hugh Dalton. In 1927 I was appointed a clerk in the Passport Control Office and again I worked on suspected Communists and collected information on Dutch Communists. Then I was ordered by Commander Fletcher to start looking for agents against the Germans and I succeeded in setting up an anti-German organization.

'In 1935 I became acquainted with Pieck through a lawyer whose name I have forgotten. This happened just before meeting a man called Beck who forged Dutch passports.' In connection with the setting up of the organization International Red Aid, an artist is mentioned who gave assistance. Hooper said this was Pieck.

In 1936 Major Dalton died and Hooper was sacked. Then Hooper met Pieck again who suggested that he should work with him, and his offer was accepted. After a few months it turned out that nothing had been done so Pieck's wife was summoned for an interview. She said that they were supported by people who bought Pieck's works. Hooper became suspicious of Pieck because of his knowledge of two facts connected with the Foreign Office and this suspicion was strengthened by the fact that Pieck received money every month from an unknown source. Gradually Pieck told the whole story, admitting that he worked for the GPU and asked Hooper to help him, who refused. Then Pieck said that because of Hooper's knowledge it had become necessary to reorganize the whole apparatus in Britain forcing Pieck to leave. He was replaced by Peter who spoke English well and had been in America in the first years of the GPU's existence. It was said that the GPU was made up of three departments; the most important had four hundred employees, the second did work of secondary importance and the third operated legally. Hooper tried to convince Pieck that he was a real communist but he was embarrassed by Walter Krivitsky who did not like him. (It is not clear from this whether Hooper really knew Walter or not.) Walter paid Pieck, but received instructions from Paris and it was Pieck's task to concentrate on British diplomats. He tried to become acquainted with the British vice-consul in Geneva, but this came to nothing, though he gained entry into the British colony through Commander John Harvey.

In the end Pieck returned to his wife who was also a GPU agent, and she agreed to his second marriage to Harvey's daughter, who was in love with Pieck. Instead of this, he became acquainted with Foreign Office cipher clerks and through them met King. Pieck was very careful with documents and when he went to Leipzig he asked Hooper to clean out his desk where he found a few papers, including a letter from King. Then Hooper spoke about the penetration of the Foreign Office by GPU agents in 1936. Sometimes King photographed documents in the Foreign Office itself and Helen Wilky was used as a cover address without probably being herself aware of this. Hooper stated that in his opinion, Pieck was again working for GPU, but he remained on good terms with him. He felt that Pieck was leading him into a trap and Hooper was asked if Pieck made use of some other agent. Hooper answered that in the beginning he used Raymond, and this is clearly Enid Harvey's husband. Raymond was paid £300 for which he gave Pieck a receipt. Later he got worried about this receipt and Pieck tore it up in his presence, having previously photographed it. Hooper stated that Walter's surname was Krivitsky and his collaborator was a man called Bruss. Pieck was

instructed to go to Switzerland and kill Reis but he refused. Hooper
mentioned the name Clark, a divorced Englishman living in Rotterdam and working for the Kodak company. According to enquiries
made by us, Harold Clark was one of the intermediaries through
whom some of King's documents passed. Many other things drew
attention to Pieck. We tried to find out more about Clark, but without
success. Our investigations showed that payments into King's
account frequently coincided with Peter's visits to England. In November 1939 Hooper handed us a letter, written by Pieck to Parlanti,
in which he said that he was in difficulties and asked Parlanti for
help. Similarly, Parlanti mentioned Erno Goldfinger (7 Bedford
Square, WC1) an architect who possessed exactly the same camera
as Pieck's. He also had suspicions about the relationship between
the German lawyers Abramovich and Konn (2 Clement's Inn, WC2)
and two people with German names: Bliznyakov and ?, although
they gave no grounds for suspicion.

Bearing in mind the correspondence with Parlanti, a plan was
conceived to lure Pieck into the country so he could be arrested, and
every detail was prepared. Parlanti wrote Pieck a number of letters
inviting him over and Hooper went to Holland to re-establish contact
with him. On his return Hooper reported considerable success and
said that Pieck intended to change his name to Don in case Krivitsky
gave away his real name. Pieck had told Hooper that he had tried
to recruit a Dutchman called Keizer who had been offered a job with
the Dutch military intelligence. When Hooper asked Pieck why he
did not follow Krivitsky's example and write a book, he answered
that he would never be a traitor, however badly he fared.

Vernon Bartlett was also drawn into the scheme to lure Pieck
over here as he was acquainted with him but apparently Bartlett
experienced some pangs of conscience about his role in the con-
spiracy.

Pieck mentioned Miss Macdonald, his former girlfriend in Geneva,
to Hooper and we made enquiries about her but concluded she was
harmless. The same can be said of Goldfinger, mentioned above. The
following document is a letter from SIS, dated 12 May 1940, stating
that Pieck received a visa for France and Britain, but somehow heard
about King's arrest. We learned nothing about Abramovich, Konn
and Machlis. Fitzgerald of Universal Patent, who was a friend of
Pieck, was also questioned but without result. There are one or two
interesting facts in the file but the strangest thing is that although
Hardt was recognized by everyone as an important figure in the case,
no serious attempts were made to keep a close watch on him. His
address was known, although it seems to me that it was only discovered after he had left the country. Anyway, he could have been

found at Percy Glading's home, and a watch could have been put on him. Perhaps the policy was to follow Glading and arrest him so as to frighten the other members of the organization into stopping operations.

After Hardt's departure, much was done to study the evidence and all the inhabitants of his block of flats were questioned thoroughly. Some of his papers and cheques were found and the people mentioned investigated, evidently without results. It is possible that Hardt was not followed systematically, perhaps out of fear that he might notice the tail thus spoiling the game. MI5, as I know, is very careful about such matters and this view is confirmed by the fact that the watch on the embassy was lifted for fear that the sleuths might be recognized by people who had seen them at Party meetings. You once asked if MI5 had photographs of the people connected with this case? They have photographs of Hardt and his wife, and of Brandes and his wife, although I did not see these.

The Philby Reports

One of the most remarkable aspects of the KGB archives devoted to the 3rd Department of the First Chief Directorate is the collection of documents that originated with Kim Philby. Of course, it is hardly news that Philby worked in the Soviet cause and was recruited long before he succeeded in penetrating Whitehall's most secret sanctums. What is astonishing, and still chills the professionals who know the truth, is the sheer scale of his duplicity.

Philby himself only once described his own activities, in his autobiography *My Silent War* published five years after his sudden disappearance from Beirut where he was based as a foreign correspondent for the *Observer*. Apart from a hastily prepared confession for his old friend and SIS colleague Nicholas Elliott, which turned out to be nothing more than a mischievous tissue of lies, Philby disclosed little about his duplicity. In retrospect, one can understand why. At the time of *My Silent War*'s release he had every reason to believe that his fellow conspirator Anthony Blunt had avoided detection. In reality, Blunt was confronted by MI5 interrogators in April 1964 and had accepted a formal immunity from prosecution, but doubtless Philby sought to protect him and the few others who could be put at risk. Among them were the photographer and CPGB activist Edith Tudor Hart whom he had known since Vienna and who had originally introduced him to Arnold Deutsch. She was still living in London even though she had been interviewed by Special Branch detectives in 1938, when the purchase of one of the Leica cameras used in the Woolwich Arsenal case had been traced to her. On that occasion she had simply denied all knowledge of how Percy Glading could have acquired it, and MI5 had pursued the matter no further. Another agent in jeopardy was James Klugmann, the CPGB's official historian who had worked for SOE during the war; and Leo Long, another dormant Soviet agent, then still living quietly in London, having been recruited by Blunt before the war. John Cairncross, by then exiled to Rome, was also in potential danger, and perhaps there were others besides. Accordingly, Philby's book was far less than a candid account of his clandestine life, and his other disclosures, using interviews with Moscow newspapers as vehicles, were nothing more than attempts to gain tactical advantage in the propaganda war that invariably followed some espionage scandal in the West. Whilst the details of Philby's SIS career soon became public knowledge, as was inevitable when his colleagues had included the authors Graham Greene and Malcolm Muggeridge, the depth of his treachery remained obscure. Philby's KGB records, which even he was never allowed to read, make up an impressive series of classified files containing almost every one of the messages he passed to Moscow.

Philby's output was prodigious. This was not a man supplying the occasional tip to assist the Soviet cause, but an incisive, driven intellect dedicated to giving the Russians as comprehensive a picture as possible of how Britain's secret warriors conducted their business. When asked a short question, Philby would type or write in his distinctive manuscript page upon page of explanation. What follows is a selection of the material contained in his dossier, eloquent testimony to the extraordinary dedication of a remarkable individual who must have spent hours every night fulfilling the expectations of his NKVD controllers. It is the very first evidence of precisely what British secrets Philby compromised.

The first text, undated, is a routine message covering various topics that he had selected for transmission to Moscow. It appears to be entirely accurate, although occasionally there is an understandable lapse in spelling. For example, the Nazi identified as the head of the Sicherheitsdienst in Paris was Karl Boemelburg.

PETER BROWN formally a journalist, has been appointed SIS research worker on all Left Wing movements.

BROWN was at one time a student of Balkan social problems, financed by the ROCKEFELLER INSTITUTE. His headquarters were at SKOPJE, where he met DAVID FOOTMAN, about 1928. Then FOOTMAN was British Consul at Skopje. This was before FOOTMAN joined the SIS.

BROWN later became Morning Post correspondent in BELGRADE, but afterwards gave up the Morning Post for REUTER'S. He was caught in Jugoslavia by the war and was captured with the rest of RONALD CAMPBELL's party by the Italians. After a few weeks of captivity he left Italy with the others for England via Spain and Portugal. On arrival here, BROWN was recruited for the SIS by FOOTMAN. He did various odd jobs for the political section, and was then given this definite assignment.

The proposal that BROWN should work against the Left Wing emanated from FOOTMAN, who foresees that, after the war, the main danger to the British ruling classes will come from the revolutionary element. Meanwhile, he argued, the British must not allow their preoccupation with the German danger to obscure this issue.

BROWN has a quick intelligence, combined with a character and appearance that are both Bohemian in the extreme. He dresses abominably: long, straight black hair, bad teeth, dark eyes and is generally rather dirty and unshaven. He is voluble in conversation, tends to spit while talking. For an Englishman his political 'awareness' is rather unusual. He stands about 5 ft 6 ins and is of medium build.

British Strength in East

In mid-September the German SIS station in Turkey (the main German station working against the British in the Middle East) relayed to Hamburg the following appreciation of British strength in that area:
In Libya and Egypt – 150,000 men (all South Africans and Indians)
In Cyprus: 50,000 men (all from New Zealand and Australia)
In Syria, Palestine and Transjordan: 3 Divisions
De Gaulle's total strength (including his West African forces): 20,000
This is rather a curious report. 1) It is somewhat unscientific, in that it mixes up estimates of 'men' with estimates of divisions. 2) It seems to have a certain propaganda bias, vide the great emphasis on non-British troops. But it is not the work of incompetent observers, it is difficult to understand why it was delayed.

Caucasian Nationalists

The political division of the SIS has just circulated the following report from a very sure source.

Member of the Caucasian Nationalist Party (presumably the Caucasian Federal Committee) in Turkey are trying to control the Germans through a certain HALIL HASMAMEDLI, now resident in Berlin, with a view to finding out if steps are being taken to form a Free State of all the Caucasus. The Nationalists propose to send a certain SCHEFI to Berlin to discuss matters.

All the arrangements for SCHEFI's visit, eg visas, etc. were made at the end of September.

German I.S. in France

The following details were told to the British SIS by LEO HIRSCH, the Nazi agent captured in TRINIDAD. Full reports have not yet arrived.
MAJOR BECKER. One of the most dangerous members of the GIS in France. He works directly under Berlin.
Lives: Hotel de Calais, Paris
Office: Avenue Henri Martin, Paris 16
HEINRICH PFEIFFER: Employee of LEO & CO, ZURICH. Important member, GIS.
HENRI BERANGER. Works with DE BRINOD and relays all French information to MAJOR BERMELBERGER, Chief of Paris SICHER-HEITSDIENST.
KARL KITZLER, an Austrian formerly living in Prague is BERMEL-BERGER's private secretary. Both KITZLER and BERMELBERGER are homosexual.
DE HERCKMANNS. Luxembourg art dealer. Lives: St James's Hotel, Rue de Rivoli, Paris. Worked for GIS before the war reporting through AUER of the Embassy.
JAN TOPINKA. Formerly Czech Consular Service in MARSEILLES. Arrested by French in December 1939, then released. Now works for the SICHERHEITSDIENST under the name of DR HANS MEYER, may be in touch with Czechs in London.
DR KNOCHEN, Chief of Paris SS. Age 38, fanatical Nazi and careerist.
  Other agents of the GIS in France are:
WIEDEMANN alias ALESH BRILLIANT, aged about 28. HUTTLER, SOMMER, who is a specialist in religious matters. Gerd THOMA, telephone PASSY 5236 and 5148. Mlle TIRUL GUYON, propagandist for LAVAL. JEAN RALIN, 10 rue CAMBON, Paris, her fiancé. HENRY RUEHL, Manager, Hotel Scribe. JEAN PANAYOTTI, Greek, born Odessa, 15.1.1894. DIAZ and RETZ, both South American journalists. DUTT alias CHAND. Indian. PUNTE ABERASTEIN, Argentine Vice-Consul in PAU. MAJOR RUMPE alias FROHLING, Chief of the Bordeaux Abwehrstelle (He succeeded DR TENGE). Captain BARLEM, alias ANDLER, also of the Bordeaux Ast.

Philby had joined SIS in September 1941, having been recruited from SOE by Dick Brooman-White for Section V's Iberian sub-section, designated V(d). From his previous experience in SOE he had probably gained only minimal understanding of precisely how SIS operated, and his first reports to Moscow from within the organisation are marked by a certain naïveté. Nevertheless, he used his skills as a journalist to observe and to inform the Centre as best he could, using charts to illustrate the way SIS collected and distributed intelligence.

The attached pages represent the actual working of the SIS. In order to assist understanding, a word of explanation is needed.

Chart I represents the course of a message coming in from abroad, the organizations and departments that it actually goes through. The chart is based on the assumption that the message coming in from abroad originates with the contact in Portugal of a sub-agent acting under R J E JARVIS, Passport Control Officer, Lisbon.

Let us call the contact 24134/7. He may be a Portuguese Government official, foreign diplomat, businessman, etc. He is probably unconscious that 24134 (who contacts him) is working for the SIS. But, through indiscretion, his news reaches 24134.

24134, as his symbol shows, is a sub-agent of 24000 (JARVIS) He is probably, though not necessarily, a conscious agent. He will almost certainly transmit the news verbally to 24000.

24000 considers it and decides whether it is urgent or not. If it is he will encipher it and send it by W/T (the transmitter is in the British Embassy) to Section VIII at Whaddon Hall near Bletchley. If it is not urgent, he will have it typed out, with all names and addresses, etc. encoded and send it by the British Embassy diplomatic bag.

If the message arrives by W/T it is picked up at Whaddon Hall and sent by means of a despatch rider to a department known as CODES (This is not to be confused with the GOVERNMENT CODE AND CYPHER SCHOOL). CODES are at Bletchley. If the message arrives by bag it is sent from the FO to Broadway, whence it is despatched by despatch rider to CODES.

CODES decipher the message whatever its origin. When it is deciphered it is sent to either CENTRAL REGISTRY (by day) or to Broadway (for the duty officer, by night). The duty officers are chosen from SIS staff and go by rotation. CENTRAL REGISTRY is a department situated in St Albans, address 'BRESCIA', HOLYWELL HILL. Its head is Captain WOODFIELD and it keeps all SIS records, with very few exceptions.

WOODFIELD is about 58, 5ft 6 inches, slight build, dark hair, bald on top, wears glasses, long narrow face formerly attached for some years to Special Branch. His present official position is Head of Registry.

WOODFIELD by day, and the Duty Officers by night, peruse the messages and decide which sections it is most likely to interest. It will certainly go to the 'G' or 'A' section officer in charge of the territory from which it comes. They get all messages from the particular stations which they are running. Therefore the messages will certainly be marked 'G6' if it comes from Portugal, 'A4' if it comes from France, etc.

Apart from this however the message will probably interest one or more of the circulating sections, ie Sections I, II, III, IV, VI. If its interest is primarily political it will be marked to Section I. If it is also interesting in a secondary sense to the Air Ministry, Admiralty or War Office, it will be marked II, III, or IV as well. Counter-espionage interest would mark it to Section V, economic interest to Section VI. Messages are often marked to four or five sections in their order of interest in the report.

In the case of cables (W/T) each section to which they are marked receives simultaneously a teleprint copy, teleprinted direct from CEN-TRAL REGISTRY for their information only. No section can act on teleprint because it reaches several sections simultaneously and each might take different and contradictory action. For action they must wait for the 'action copy' to come round. There is only one of these and it comes to each section in turn, according to the priority of the marking, each in turn indicates on it the action which it has taken and passes it on. The relevant copy is white paper with mauve ink, the action copy is mauve paper with dark mauve ink.

The message may require no action in which case the message is marked N.A. by all the sections concerned and returned to CENTRAL REGISTRY. The section concerned may, on the other hand, require previous traces on the same subject in which case the message is returned to CENTRAL REGISTRY marked 'CR Traces please'. CR then looks up the traces on the card index, gets out the files in which they occur, and sends the message back to the section interested with the files attached.

The action taken, in the case of most sections, is of two kinds: a) either further information is required from the station abroad which is sent the original message. In that case the section interested sends a minute to the 'G' or 'A' section concerned with the words 'Following telegram (or letter) for 24000 please. Ref your ... of ... (date) ... please investigate, etc. etc.' b) or a station decides that the message is worth circulating as it stands. In that case the material of interest is sent to the FO, Air Ministry, Admiralty, War Office, MI5, MEW or whichever department is the most interested. Once the message is circulated a copy of the material circulated is attached to the original message and both, together with the files, are sent back to Central Registry, where they are carded and filed for future reference. That is the end of the process.

Chart I illustrates a message coming in from a station abroad. Chart II illustrates the course taken by messages going out from sections to stations abroad. Chart III illustrates various special sources of material, ie material not coming from stations abroad, which are a monopoly of Section V. The manner in which such special material is handled is as follows:

There are five classes of special material reaching Section V:

1. ISOS (German Intelligence Service W/T intercepts). These are picked
   up by the Royal Signals School (RSS) address Oakwood (?) Barnet.
   They are picked up, as relayed, in Morse code and are then taken
   by despatch riders from Barnet to the Government code and Cipher
   School (GCCS) at Bletchley. GCCS are not a purely SIS institution.
   It also works for the NID and other Government Departments.

   GCCS decypher and translate these messages and then send them
   on to Section V. Copies are also sent to the Air Ministry, Admiralty,
   MI5 and a very few other organizations. But no action can be taken
   on ISOS without reference to Section V.
2. TRIPLEX (XXX – material extracted from diplomatic bags). I do
   not know quite how these thefts are organized but I think it is either
   by MI5, or in collaboration with MI5.

   Copies of the material are sent to David BOYLE 'B', personal
   assistant to CSS. They also reach Section V through Boyle.
3. BJs (WW – diplomatic W/T intercepts). These consist of intercepts
   of W/T communications between foreign countries and their representatives abroad. The interceptions are done by, I believe, GCCS,
   but I am not sure. The following ciphers have been broken: Japanese,
   Turkish, Italian, French, Egyptian, Portuguese. The Spanish was
   broken but it was changed recently, and the new cipher has remained
   unbroken hitherto. A few South American ones are also read
   regularly.
4. Censorship (XX – postal and telegraph intercepts). These are of a
   more commonplace character, and the existence of this check is
   well-known.
5. Wireless telephony intercepts. International wireless telephony circuits are regularly tapped. I do not know how the circulation of
   these five classes of material is largely controlled by Section V. ISOS,
   XXX and BJs (WW) always go out to other sections in disguised
   form so that the source is disguised. They are circulated to other
   sections (I, II, III, IV, VI) – always in disguise – and also, occasionally, to the administrative 'G' and 'A' sections for transmission to
   stations or agents abroad.

Censorship and wireless telephony intercepts are not so disguised
because the existence of such checks is of course sufficiently well-
known.

Circulating Sections

An analysis of the functions of the circulating sections (numbered thus: I, II, II, IV, V, VI, etc.) shows that the SIS enjoys little power to frame policy. It is in fact a service, serving Governmental departments with information, but with few powers to go beyond this. Of course, the possession of information from sources that are not divulged to other organizations gives a certain power of decision in individual cases. But there is little evidence to show that there is any tendency in the SIS as a body, to exploit that power politically. For example, the Naval Intelligence Department of the Admiralty (NID) works in co-operation with the Naval Section of SIS (Section III). But in the event of any difference of opinion, the view of the NID as representing that of an executive department would normally prevail. Similarly, the Political Section of the SIS (Section I) confines itself to the presentation of information from secret sources. It leaves the formulation of policy to the Foreign Office and the Government.

This subordination of SIS to the executive departments is reflected in its organization abroad. While the SIS representative abroad does not pass his information through the ambassador, he is definitely subordinate to the ambassador in all matters of administration and policy. A protest from the ambassador to the FO will nearly always suffice to secure the reprimand of the SIS representative. In practice, it is usually found that the ambassador whose natural inclination it is to avoid 'trouble' with the government to which he is accredited, keeps a jealous eye on the activity of the SIS and to a great extent hampers its work. Samuel Hoare's support of the SIS today, for instance, is so lukewarm that the SIS is contemplating, under stress of war, the building up of an espionage service quite independent of the Embassy in Madrid. This, according to British SIS standards, would be a revolutionary change. It was to a certain extent due to this friction between Ambassadors and SIS that the principle was evolved that the SIS representative never works against the country in which he is stationed. The PCO at the Hague worked against Germany, the PCO at Riga against the USSR, etc.

SECTION I

The work of this section consists in collating, sifting and circulating the information coming from 'A' and 'G' sections (see previous reports). It consists of Woolcombe, Footman and Pinney. You have seen many examples of its reports and have been able to form a judgement on them. They were piecemeal reports of no great value in themselves as a rule – frequently inferior in value to the work of a well-trained

journalist. The more restricted circulation lists contain reports of no
greater value than the others, only more secret owing to the delicacy
of the source. The foregoing report on the Caucasian Nationalists, for
example, was on a restricted circulation list because its source was
ISOS, not because of its intrinsic importance. In general, the function
of Section I as Footman constantly asserts, is not to present a complete
picture of the political situation in the world, but merely to supply
links that are missing in the picture presented by press reports, FO
reports, etc.

SECTION II

This section performs the same type of work for the Air Ministry. It
passes on to them such information as comes in from 'G' and 'A'
sections that is likely to fill in the gaps left by aerial reconnaissance
and other methods of air intelligence.

The other circulating sections doing the same work for other ministries are: Section III, Admiralty; Section IV, War Office; Section VI,
Ministry of Economic Warfare; Section V is charged with all counter-
espionage work outside the British Empire. It is really a counterpart
of MI5, the boundary between the two being the 3-mile limit. A full
report on Section V follows next meeting.

G SECTIONS

The work of the G sections is pivotal to the whole SIS. It is they that
control the SIS stations abroad (usually, but by no means always,
based on the Passport Control Offices in British Embassies). They are
responsible for the administration of these stations, for the payment
of agents and sub-agents, for recruitment and communications. In
practice they are of course often very largely dependent on the personnel of the stations abroad who, being on the spot, are in a better
position to judge conditions objectively than the G section officers in
London.

The following officers are responsible for SIS stations abroad:

G.2	Captain Taylor	Far East, North America, South America
	R Hoare	Atlantic islands
G.4	Nicholson	Aden, Iran, Iraq, East and West Africa
G.5	Fenwick	Spain & Portugal
G.7	Commander Bremner	Egypt, Malta, Palestine, Turkey
G.8	Major Giffey	Sweden, Finland, USSR

These sections of course deal wholly with neutral or friendly countries, since in hostile countries there is no embassy or commercial organization to serve as adequate cover. Territory occupied by the enemy falls into the province of the A sections, which will be the subject of later reports. The essence of the position of the G sections is that they are based on stations which have official recognition of the countries in which they are situated. E.g. The Passport Control Office in Lisbon or the Evacuation Office in Moscow.

The symbols attached to country stations and agents are adopted systematically. Each country is known by a double figure numeral and the chief SIS representative is known by the numeral of the country in which he works followed by the noughts; eg. Portugal is 24-land, and the Passport Control Officer in Lisbon is called 24000. His agents are known by variations of the final noughts; eg one agent is 24300 and another 24921. Sub-agents run by his agents are known by the agent's symbol followed by a letter; eg, 24300's chief sub-agent would probably be 24300/A. The most important countries are figured as follows:

11	Bulgaria	12	Germany
13	Belgium	14	Rumania
15	Hungary	16	Iceland
18	Turkey	19	Denmark
21	Finland	22	Great Britain
23	Spain	24	Portugal
27	France	29	Czechoslovakia
32	Italy	33	Holland
34	Siberia	35	Jugoslavia
36	Sweden	37	Japan
38	Poland	44	Austria
47	Ukraine	45	USA
75	South America	95	USSR

The agents and sub-agents run by the G sections are of the most varied nature. They are of all nationalities, and are often given symbols, even when they are unconscious agents, there is no attempt made to enrol all British subjects in the intelligence organization. A short time ago, for example, there were 16 agents in Spain working under the Chief SIS representatives in Madrid (HAMILTON STOKES, Third Secretary of the Embassy, 23000 and BENTON, 23400). Of these 3 were British (2 consular officials and 1 businessman), 2 were French, 1 was Polish and the remaining ten were Spaniards. In fact there were more sub-agents operating in Spain and further details will be given later.

The powers of the SIS representatives abroad are severely limited. The station head is under the control of the Minister or Ambassador, and the latter can always limit the activities of the SIS representative if he judges them to be politically dangerous. The only means of redress is to send a protest to the G section under which he is working. The G section then lays the course before the CSS who may deem it important enough to take it up with the Permanent Under-Secretary of State for Foreign Affairs. Unless the case for the SIS is overwhelmingly strong, it is obvious that the Foreign Office will support a cautious Ambassador rather than a vigorous SIS representative. Obviously, much depends on the personality of the CSS. Present indications are that STEWART MENZIES is a weak CSS who is irascible rather than strong.

Communications between HQ in Broadway Buildings and stations abroad are by two means: the diplomatic bag and W/T. The latter is used only for urgent communications, since transmitting time is limited. Most names, addresses, etc. are encoded, though this practice is not by any means general. It is left to the discretion of the sender. The W/T sets used for transmitting and receiving are usually housed in the Embassy precincts.

A Sections

The work of the A Sections is of a different nature. They organize intelligence from hostile countries, and are therefore not based on recognized stations. They are controlled, under CSS, by ACSS, Colonel Dansey, an old cynical and dry personality. Under him, the following officers are placed:

A.1	Major FOLEY (formerly PCO Berlin)	Norway, Germany
A.1a	Lieut. WALSH	
A.2	Col. RABAGLIATI	Holland, Denmark
A.2a	Mr SEYMOUR	
A.3	Mr JEMPSON	Belgium
A.3a	Capt. HENDRICKS	
A.4	Commander DUNDERDALE	
	Capt. HEATH (liaison with Poles)	France & Poland
A.5	Commander COHEN	France, Gilbraltar, Tangier
A.5a	Major CODRINGTON	

These A Sections choose, recruit, train and despatch agents into occupied territory. The methods used vary widely according to the particular problems involved. Men are landed by boat or parachute, or are pushed into occupied territory from neutral countries (in co-operation with the G sections of those countries; eg HAMILTON STOKES runs agents into occupied France from Spain).

Almost all communications are by W/T. Eg the chief British agent in France appears to be stationed in MARSEILLES whence he relays directives to PAU, VICHY and other agents. These agents appear to be largely Frenchmen (not necessarily De Gaullists). In Norway the agents are mostly Norwegians and, so far as I know, never English. There is still a great need for expansion. In France, for example, there is not one single agent employed in counter-espionage work. All information comes from W/T or cable intercepts, and from the US Embassy, or from agents leaving France for neutral countries, eg S. America, and intercepted en route.

The G and A sections are useful mainly as checks and pointers. The vast bulk of intelligence material comes from sources outside the SIS, though most of it passes through SIS.

The Case of USSR

The USSR has been neglected by the SIS for several years. Anti-Communist work in the British possessions has been the preserve of MI5, IPI (Indian Political Intelligence), etc. As far as I can see, the chief Russian expert of SIS, Lt.Col. STEVENS, is dependent almost entirely on the reports from MASON-MACFARLANE which are of a largely hypothetical nature. BERRY communicates to GIFFEY or even if he communicates at all. Certainly, the information on the USSR reaching the SIS has been, in volume, about 5% of the information reaching the SIS on Germany.

ISOS

This (cf. previous reports) consists of the most secret material at the disposal of the SIS. There are four main centres of wireless communication, one in Hamburg, one in Wiesbaden and two (?) in Berlin. The Hamburg centre deals in overseas stations (ie Britain, America, etc.). The Wiesbaden centre deals with all matters affecting the Armistice Commission (it was originally destined for work against France and the Low Countries, just as Hamburg was destined for work against Gt Britain). The main Berlin centre is used for European espionage work (an example of the pedantry with which this distinction is observed is that ISTANBUL – being in Europe – is controlled from Berlin, while ANKARA – being overseas – was run from Hamburg). There have been frequent tussles between Berlin and Hamburg; but the position is further complicated by another Berlin centre which deals almost exclusively with political intelligence of a not very high grade type (cf. messages marked VIII/II previously reported). This is believed, not on conclusive evidence, to be used by the RIBBENTROP bureau as a semi-private racket. There is evidence of struggles between the main Berlin centre run by the OKW [the German High Command], and the Ribbentrop centre. This is presumably a reflection of the Army versus Party struggle.

The cyphers used by ISOS transmissions are of two kinds: a) 5-figure transposition, b) machine. Owing to the danger of capture or confiscation, the machine cypher is used only in areas where it is absolutely safe – in areas safe from raids and risings, eg in occupied territory excluding Norway, Normandy and Brittany. It may be taken for certain that the Germans do not know that their messages are being intercepted by the English.

The conventional signs which head all ISOS messages in the English version are described as follows: The Roman letters at the beginning (eg XIII/II and II/122) are meaningless in that they are invented by the decoders in England to distinguish between the various lines of communication. Thus, the XIII groups are all RIBBENTROP, the I groups refer to NORWAY, and II groups to Spain, etc. On the other hand, the letters and numerals shown thus: ALF on 17250kc have a definite technical significance, ALF being the call-sign, 17250 being the frequency. Most stations have several call-signs and frequencies but, once the principle is grasped, it is easy to follow the variations.

Having given Moscow a brief but comprehensive overview of SIS's internal structure, and identified the principal personalities, Philby devoted himself to compromising as much data as he could lay his hands on. He had no qualms in using extracts from ULTRA summaries and took pains to identify as many people by name as possible.

Extract from Section I Reports

Source 48917 in touch with US Naval Intelligence. US naval representatives in Turkey report that the 'Conservative' factions among the generals (BRAUCHITSCH is its chief, GOERING a sympathizer) aims at a liquidation of the party as a preliminary for a peace move. This faction is against an invasion of the UK but will execute it if a negotiated peace is impossible. The faction is willing to meet US negotiators in ISTANBUL.

German wireless intercepts show that PETAIN told WEYGAND when he last visited VICHY that the Germans had asked for WEY-

GAND's resignation. PUCHEV and BENOIST-MECHINB are intriguing against WEYGAND. According to a memorandum written by a senior official of the German Embassy in ANKARA, Turkish Government circles have set up a secret committee to examine the possibilities of the ultimate incorporation of AZERBAIJAN into Turkey.

In this next document, dated 30 October 1941, Philby briefs his Russian contacts on the level of liaison between the remnants of the French intelligence agencies and SIS. Some of the characters, such as Wilfred 'Biffy' Dunderdale, would already be well known to the Soviets, for he was born in Russia and had joined SIS in Istanbul in 1922. Four years later he had switched to Paris where he spent thirteen years concentrating on developing contacts in the large White Russian émigré community.

The tale about Colonel Dudley Clarke is quite bizarre, and if Philby's version is true it is entirely understandable that the episode was hushed up by the British authorities. Clarke was indeed a key figure in the highly successful and imaginative deception campaign used to mislead the Afrika Korps in Libya, and he subsequently played a vital role in BODYGUARD, the scheme intended to convince the enemy that the Normandy landings would not take place until the autumn of 1944. Previously he had served as military assistant to the Chief of the Imperial General Staff, General Sir John Dill, and was therefore privy to many War Cabinet secrets. Perhaps not surprisingly, there is no mention of this episode in his war memoirs, *Seven Assignments*, published in 1948. After the war he remained unmarried and was appointed director of public opinion research at Conservative Central Office.

Finally, there is some encouraging evidence that for all his skills, Philby was not privy to every secret. He identifies a Spanish diplomat named Brugada as suspected spy. In fact José Brugada Wood, based at the embassy in London, was an MI5 double agent, codenamed PEPPERMINT, as Anthony Blunt helpfully later confirmed.

Contact between the British and French SIS has been maintained since the fall of France.

It is maintained on the British side by A.4 Commander 'Bill' Dunderdale. As you will recall, he runs France for the SIS and also has supervisory functions over liaison with the Polish SIS (whose main operational area is now France).

DUNDERDALE is about 40, 5ft 10 inches in height, thickset, straight black hair, good-looking. He has lived many years in France and is reported to know it well. He is fond of good living, women, etc.

The organization on the French side is not clear to me. It appears that, in time of war, the Deuxième Bureau moves up to the front and plays the role of an operational intelligence force similar to that played in the Dutch Army by the Field Security police. There remains behind in Paris, attached to the Ministry of War, a second organization known as the Cinqième Bureau which corresponds more closely to the British SIS. This Vième Bureau still exists in Vichy under a different name (something like 'Vigilance Committee against anti-regime Movements').

The head of the Vième Bureau is PERUCHE, its codename for the British SIS is VICTOR. Eg, in British SIS terms, 'Information passed to VICTOR' means 'information passed to the Vième Bureau'.

DUNDERDALE's direct contact is Commandant Bertrand, a fat unpleasant character, as silent as an oyster. I do not know how much PERUCHE knows of BERTRAND's activity. But BERTRAND knows a great deal about the British SIS. He meets DUNDERDALE once a month in LISBON. He knows that the British SIS has cracked ISOS, and this is in a way evidence that he has kept the knowledge to himself.

Normal communication between DUNDERDALE and BERTRAND is by W/T. Even ISOS information is passed over to France, although always disguised in a manner that makes it seem that the information was gathered by an agent on the spot. This is to guard against the possibility of interception or betrayal.

This DUNDERDALE–BERTRAND channel of communication is distinct from the channels mentioned in previous reports, eg England to Marseilles and Pau. The latter was purely British agents and operate independently of the Vième Bureau. I repeat that I do not know how far the heads of the Vième Bureau, or the French Government, are aware of these clandestine contacts. This would naturally be kept a secret, closely-guarded even from the British side. But the fact that BERTRAND is allowed to visit Lisbon suggests that PERUCHE, at least, must know something.

Dudley Clarke

The above-mentioned very important member of AUCHINLECK's staff was arrested in Madrid ten days ago, wearing women's clothes. I do not know his rank or title, but his function is Chief of the 'strategic deception unit' attached to GHQ Cairo. DUDLEY CLARKE has under his command three dummy infantry divisions, 1 dummy tank brigade and several squadrons of dummy aircraft. His position is therefore of great importance from the intelligence viewpoint.

There are several mysteries connected with his arrest. DUDLEY-

CLARKE should not have been in Madrid at all. His route was Lisbon–Gibraltar–Malta–Cairo. So far, no reason has reached London as to why he was found in women's clothes. The third mystery is why the Spanish propaganda bureau put out the story that the man arrested in women's clothing was WRANGAL CRAKER, 'Times' correspondent in Madrid. There is no such man. D-C has been released.

The case is being shrouded in the greatest secrecy, but I will try to get more details.

Section V

Section V of the SIS is charged with all counter-espionage outside British territory, its boundary being the 3-mile limit.

It is a comparatively new section in its present form. When France fell it numbered not more than half-a-dozen officers. Recently it has been growing rapidly. At present, its efforts are directed almost exclusively against Germany.

Head of Section V is Major S. FELIX COWGILL, formerly an officer in the Indian Police. He joined SIS in March 1939. His promotion has been rapid. He was introduced to the organization by Colonel VIVIAN, DCSS.

Cowgill is aged 37, about 5ft 9 inches, slight build. He has straight, black hair, worn rather long, large grey eyes set rather close together with deep black marks under them, due to overwork, a prominent sharp nose. His face gives the impression of intensity coupled with a great weariness. He is clean-shaven, but rather dark owing to having a strong beard firmly shaven.

By nature Cowgill is shy and he has few social graces. But his capacity for work is enormous and he tests it to its uttermost. It is no rare thing for him to work from 9.30 am to 5 am the next morning with hardly a break for meals. Although normally quiet in manner, due to shyness, he is combative in his work, always prepared to challenge an office ruling.

COWGILL's chief fault is his dislike of delegation. He keeps all the cases passing through his office in his head, and usually insists on taking all decisions himself. Since his memory is prodigious, he usually acts on it without consulting records, this inevitably leads to a certain number of mistakes. Such a propensity causes him to overlook the need for finding capable subordinates, and it was not until quite recently that the necessity of finding adequate staff was borne in on him. In the IBERIAN section, for instance, things went so far through lack of staff that there is an accumulation of about three months to be worked through before the section can begin to function properly.

COWGILL is married (his wife is a secretary in Section V) and has two children in Canada. He is devoted to all three, but his wife has little private life owing to the intensity with which he works. He drinks very little, but smokes pipe tobacco in prodigious quantities, like Karl Marx.

COWGILL is going to USA shortly. I will let you know the exact date of his departure in due course. The purpose of his visit will be to co-ordinate the work of Section V with that of the FBI or, rather, to extend the co-ordination that already exists. I suggest that COWGILL's activity should be carefully watched. It should have interesting results.

COWGILL's principal assistant is Major E. FERGUSON. Formerly of the Ceylon Police he joined the SIS only last August. His functions are to understudy COWGILL and to take most of the routine office work off his hands. More particularly, he supervises the handling of the most secret material eg ISOS (W/T intercepts), TRIPLEX (diplomatic bag intercepts) etc. 'Handling it' means deciding to whom the information should go and in what form, the form nearly always being disguised in such a way that its origin cannot be traced.

FERGUSON is about 45, 5ft 9 inches, thin with a very small head. His nose is thin, but very prominent. His face is triangulous in shape with a very pointed chin. His eyes are light-coloured (blue? grey?) and he wears glasses. He drinks little, smokes never.

FERGUSON is a prim, painstaking worker but lacks COWGILL's fire and decisiveness. He is somewhat hesitant in manner and thought. In private life he is interested in water-divining. I believe that he is without wife and family.

Under COWGILL and FERGUSON, Section V divides up into regional departments thus: VB1, Scandinavia, Germany; VB, Holland, Belgium, France, North Africa; VD, Spain, Portugal, Spanish Morocco and the Atlantic Islands; VE, North and South America; VA, the rest of the non-British world (eg Turkey, Iran, Africa, Far East, USSR, etc.).

VB1 has two officers attached to it:

a) Captain KEITH LIVERSIDGE. About 6ft, a Yorkshireman, dark, straight black hair, a very prominent nose, very Jewish appearance, bluish eyes, married to LOUISE BROWN, the actress, who is now his secretary.

Before the invasion of the Low Countries LIVERSIDGE worked in Belgium, and was Ib (ie counter-espionage) officer to the BEF, when it marched into Belgium.

b) Mr STEEDMAN. About 29, 5ft 10 inches thin, fair hair, blue eyes, rather an intellectual type. He was formerly attached to the Passport Control Office in Vienna. He talks German more fluently than English. He has a good, sound, scholarly brain. He is of a gloomy disposition and seldom smiles.

By far the greater amount of information obtained by section VB1 comes from ISOS. Whereas in most occupied countries, a great deal of the German traffic goes by courier, despatch rider or even telephone, the long distances and bad communications in Scandinavia make the Germans entirely dependent on W/T traffic. Thus almost all their secret service communications go by W/T and, as they are all transposition cypher nearly all are intercepted and broken by the English. (The Germans dare not use machine cypher in NORWAY, owing to the danger of British raiders capturing the machines.) Likewise, in their advance across the USSR, the Germans have made free use of W/T which has enabled the English to get a good idea of their intelligence organization there (cf previous reports on this subject).

Another course of information is the flow of Norwegians who come over from their homes to Great Britain. They are assembled at LERWICK and systematically interrogated. Those that are suitable are trained and sent back as agents (W/T). Some of these transmitters are on trawlers and fishing smacks, ie constantly on the move. I have the impression that there are not very many of these agents.

Section VB has no opportunities for action as most of its activities are in enemy-occupied territory. The executive organization in all its territories is, of course, SOE (formerly SO2).

VB4 has four officers attached to it:

a) Captain ROBERT MACKENZIE (Baronet) 36, 5ft 6 inches, inclining towards stout, brown hair, pale grey eyes, jovial by temperament, lazy, casual, fond of good living, in peacetime a Lloyd's broker; then personal assistant to MASON-MACFARLANE when the latter was DMI with the BEF. Later he did a few months at WHADDON HALL, near Bletchley, the W/T headquarters of the SIS, then was transferred to Section V. He is in charge of section VB4 and attends personally to France.

b) Mr NICHOLAS ELLIOTT. 24, 5ft 9in. Brown hair, prominent lips, black glasses, ugly and rather pig-like to look at. Good brain, good sense of humour. Likes a drink but was recently very ill and now, as a consequence, drinks little. He is in charge of Holland.

c) ERIC DUVIVIER. 24, fair curled hair, blue eyes, very prominent nose, fresh complexion, 5ft 9in tall, fairly broad-shouldered. He is half, or wholly, BELGIAN. He is clever, hard-working. He is in charge of BELGIUM.

d) FELIX RUSSI (Captain). 45, very dark, small, clipped moustache, fought in the INNISKILLINGS in the last war. Speaks English, French and Spanish perfectly. He is probably of Gibraltarian origin and has lived most of the time since the last war in MOROCCO. RUSSI has only just joined the section and, since he is an almost total moron, will probably leave soon. Meanwhile, he is in charge of NORTH AFRICA.

Section VB4 is probably the worst section in Section V. Opportunities for getting information are few and far between. ISOS in the occupied parts is largely done by machine cypher and is therefore unbroken. The section is therefore thrown back on information from Polish sources and on the result of interrogating German agents caught in other parts of the world (eg LISBON and NEW YORK) and refugees. The Franco-British W/T traffic is largely concerned with operational intelligence and devoted little time to counter-espionage activity.

MACKENZIE, the head of the section, is quite content with this situation, since it means less work for him. He makes little attempt to exploit even the possibilities which do exist.

VD now has six officers attached to it:

a) H.A.R. PHILBY (formerly of SOE, cf previous reports)

b) I.I. Milne. 29, 5ft 9 inches, hazel eyes, brown hair, inclined towards stoutness. A very good brain, though inclined towards inertia. Formerly, in peacetime, employed by BENSON's, the advertising agency. Joined the army when he was called up, summer of 1940; went into the Royal Engineers (driver). Joined Section V in October 1941.

MILNE is now in charge of all the ISOS material for Spain, Portugal and the Islands. His task is to build up a picture of the German organiz-ation in Spain from the internal evidence furnished by ISOS.

c) FRANK B. PARK. 29, 5ft 8 inches, slight build, fair hair, small golden moustache, grey eyes, a shallow face (the distance between crown and chin is unusually short). Carried on a family business in BARCELONA until the Spanish Civil War, when he became an interpreter for the Navy (which was then mainly concerned with the problems of evacuation). PARK is not an intellectual type, but has plenty of solid commonsense. It was he who did most of the research work that led up to the arrest of MIRSCH and GILINSKY at TRINI-DAD. He is now in charge of MADRID, ie counter-espionage in the northern half of Spain. Speaks perfect Spanish, good French.

d) Captain TREVOR-WILSON. 36, 5ft 6inches, prematurely grey, has pale eyes behind glasses, a small greyish moustache, is going slightly bald. His chief weakness is women. His voice is pitched high, and occasionally bursts into a loud laugh. In peacetime he was manager of BARCLAY's bank at Cannes. He was married and divorced, and had one child.

T-W was formerly in SO2 and taught secret inks and ciphers at BEAULIEU. He joined Section V last July and is in charge of SPANISH MOROCCO and southern Spain (ie the area which immediately affects Gibraltar).

e) IVENS, a fruit merchant, about 45. He has only just joined, on the recommendation of Colonel VIVIAN. More details later. He will be in charge of PORTUGAL.

f) DESMOND BRISTOW. 24, 5ft 10 inches, fair hair, long and narrow face, grey eyes. His father owned mines in the RIO TINTO area. He was brought up there. Speaks perfect Spanish. Good athlete and mechanically minded.

BRISTOW is the weak link in section VD owing to immaturity and inferior brain. He has been put in charge, temporarily, of the Portuguese Islands.

Section VD is, potentially, the biggest in scope of all the others, given the present situation. a) the Atlantic Islands are a focus of German naval intelligence operations. b) Iberia, generally, is the stepping-stone for German agents leaving Europe for America and England. c) there are ten ISOS stations operating on transposition, ie breakable cipher. d) there are 10 British intelligence stations in the area: Viz. MADRID, LISBON, GIBRALTAR (controlling southern Spain), TANGIER, PUNTA DELGADA (Azores), HORTA (Azores), LAS PALMAS (Canaries), TENERIFFE (Canaries), FUNCHAL (Madeira) and ST VINCENT (Cape Verde Islands). All these stations provide a certain amount of counter-espionage information.

Apart from all these concrete connections between Iberia and British counter-espionage there are other points to be borne in mind. Most neutral European–American shipping routes pass through Iberia; most airlines and most mail. The BERMUDA censors, for example. have supplied literally hundreds of suspect addresses in the peninsula that have to be watched. Further, Iberia is the base for all German work against us. Finally, the Germans are using Spaniards for work against England, eg diplomats, journalists and merchants. There is, for instance, direct evidence against ALCAZARD DE VELASCO, MIGUEL PIERNAVIEJE DEL POZO, LUIS CALVO, BRUGADA, GARCIA CASTELLO that they are conscious German agents. There is well-founded suspicion against many others.

VB has two officers attached to it:
a) LOUIS CHRISTIE. 47 (?). 5ft 8 inches, stout, grey eyes, brown sparse hair, small greyish moustache. Has been in SIS for many years, starting in ISTANBUL after last war. He is a close personal friend of Colonel VIVIAN, with whom he plays golf. Mental capacity is very low. He has an almost pathological dislike of COWGILL.
b) Captain WRIGHT. 47(?), 5ft 9 inches, thin, haggard face, dark eyes, glasses, dark hair slightly greying. Clean-shaven. Only smokes pipes. Mental capacity on a level with CHRISTIE's. ie very low.

This section is in a very unsatisfactory state. There is a very important station in New York (48000) which controls about 3,000 sub-agents and liaison with the FBI. There is another very important one in MONTEVIDEO (75000) with others in RIO (75200) and elsewhere there are ISOS sections operating in South America, and there is a mass of intelligence material pouring in from the censorship in BERMUDA and elsewhere. Yet, to cope with all this material, there are only two inferior calibre officers. This is a typical example of how COWGILL for all his brilliance and energy, falls down in a detail of administrative organization.

VA has two officers attached to it:

a) Captain MILLS. 47 (?) 5ft 7 inches, greyish hair, slight build, grey eyes, lower half of face slightly out of alignment with upper half. Has been in the SIS for longer than COWGILL and was also senior to him in the Indian Police. Thus a slightly awkward position has arisen, as MILLS is jealous of COWGILL on both counts.

b) Mr HUDSON-WILLIAMS. Professor of Greek. 35, 6ft, dark hair, clean shaven, deep rings under eyes, speaks with a deep drawl.

As well as disclosing the entire SIS internal structure, Philby routinely passed on whatever gossip came his way, and this correspondence illustrates his willingness to exploit any friendship for the cause. A case in point is that of Flora Solomon, a senior Marks & Spencer executive who had employed Philby's second wife, Aileen Furse. After bringing Litzi to London, Philby had separated from her and in September 1940 started to live with Aileen, who bore him three children before their marriage in September 1946. A close ally who may have been approached by Philby to spy for the Russians, Flora Solomon eventually denounced Philby to MI5 in 1962, having been enraged by the pro-Arab bias in his reports from the Middle East for the *Observer* and the *Economist*. In this item Philby refers to information he had gleaned from Flora Solomon, without indicating whether she too had been a conscious coconspirator, and places a new interpretation on the retirement of Field Marshal Sir John Dill, the Chief of the Imperial General Staff.

MARTIN LEES, formerly Chief Geologist of the Anglo-Persian Oil Company, is now an important figure in the Petroleum Department.

He states that the new oil-fields near NOTTINGHAM where drilling began shortly before the outbreak of war, are now yielding 150 tons of crude oil per day. One quarter of this is petrol, one quarter paraffin and the rest Diesel and other fuels.

According to LEES, the dismissal of DILL was very possibly due to miscalculations of the character of Russian resistance. When the German attack on the USSR was launched the War Office estimated Soviet resistance at six weeks (this we already knew). Information to that effect was forwarded to the War Cabinet which decided in such circumstances aid to the USSR would merely mean giving a present of British material to the German conquerors. Accordingly, nothing was done until mid-September, when it became evident that the Germans also had miscalculated, and that help given on some scale to USSR might yield useful results.

Meanwhile, however, three precious months had been wasted. The dissatisfaction due to this mistake was raised loudly by BEAVER-BROOK when he returned from Moscow. DILL, who was CIGS, was the chief adviser to the War Cabinet on all matters of grand strategy, got the blame and was forced to retire. Naturally, the age limit had nothing to do with it.

This, anyway is the view of the Petroleum Department, which is now playing a big part in getting supplies to USSR. They only began in earnest two months ago. The reversal of policy has apparently gone a long way and efforts are now being made to make up for lost time.

FLORA SOLOMON, who is now in frequent contact with ROOTES, one of Beaverbrook's chief advisers, confirms this. The atmosphere of ROOTES's office, she says, is dominated by the aid to Russia campaign. Although very sceptical of big business, she is convinced that the effort is genuine. Such is the degree of political opportunism in Britain today that I see no reason to doubt this.

Naturally the Soviets were tremendously interested in SIS's activities in Russia, and were particularly suspicious of the local SIS representative, George W. Berry, who had previously served in Riga and Vienna. Doubtless the NKVD had identified Berry as a professional intelligence officer long before Philby added his confirmation, but two items show Philby's willingness to compromise Berry, who had moved his station to Kuibyshev with the embassy, and his contacts, in this case a Polish officer. The first is a short handwritten note, the second a longer, typed report of a telegram from Berry.

A new source operating in KUIBYSHEV bears the symbol 95038. There is no clue to his identity beyond the fact that he was expected to leave for Moscow shortly after 20.3.42 (a day or two). On about 15.3.42 he introduced Berry to a Major YATCYNA to whom the symbol 95038/A was allotted. 95038 has reported on conditions in UFA and KINEL. It is just possible that 95038 is a new symbol allotted to either 'PERCH' or 'TROUT'.

Telegrams from Kuibyshev:
CXG 497 of 6.7.42
95038/A's assistant told me privately that a charge of improper behaviour on the part of 95038/A at a local restaurant has been made the pretext for the Soviet demand for his withdrawal from the USSR. 95038/A himself naturally preferred not to indicate this to me. The charges against Kolikowski who is leaving shortly for Palestine, and

against 95038/A's assistant are said to include attempts to collect military information. Above reflects the general deterioration of the Soviet attitude towards the Poles here which is apparent in many other ways. Permission to have Polish delegates in Archangel, Vladivostock and Saratov has just been withdrawn. Search by NKVD was made a few days ago of the Polish delegate's premises at Archangel during his absence from his post. This was reported to the British senior naval officer at Archangel.

CXG 948 of 6.7.42
Co-operation of 95038/A has been rather disappointing. 1) for reasons beyond his control, eg the withdrawal of liaison officers from many valuable observation posts; the most difficult and peculiar conditions under which foreigners have to live and work in this country (without contact with the local population); as well as a deterioration in the Soviet attitude towards the Poles, etc. 2) In minor degree to the fact that he does not appear to possess good qualifications in anything like the same degree as 95038. 95038 is leaving for Teheran, badly shaken.

I understand from 95038/A's assistant that the military attaché will temporarily take over military mission here until the arrival of Roguez, the newly appointed chief. The question arises of selection of suitable person with whom I could continue collaboration. I suggest that 95038's chief in London be consulted.

One item that stands out among the Philby reports is this quite extraordinary account of an investigation apparently conducted by SIS into drug smuggling carried out for some significant names in English high society. Philby explains the background to the racket but makes no mention of how much credence had been given to the allegations of homosexual orgies and black masses. Nor does he say where the original information came from, or what conclusion the enquiry reached. In retrospect it seems entirely unlikely that such misbehaviour could be going on at Leeds Castle, the splendid home in Kent of Olive, Lady Bailey, not least because a fairly regular weekend guest there was Sir Stewart Menzies, the CSS.

As regards authenticity, the people identified in Philby's notes and the charts really existed, even if some of their names sound rather Wodehousian today. Similarly, the nightclubs mentioned also operated during the war, so there is an element of verisimilitude to a rather bizarre tale that links the notorious occultist Aleister Crowley to, of all people, the Soviet Ambassador Ivan Maisky. Quite what the NKVD analysts at Moscow Centre thought of all this is really anybody's guess.

Certainly the proposition that Welsh fishermen were collecting consignments of drugs that had been dropped by parachute into Ireland is really too fanciful to be taken seriously. The very few staff left at the German Legation in Dublin were under constant surveillance by both MI5 and their Irish counterparts in G-2. Perhaps not surprisingly, there is no trace in the open literature of any such activity, so perhaps this story was but one of the many matters that are reported to security and intelligence agencies who are left to judge what weight to give them. In this case, the answer is probably very little, though doubtless Philby considered it worthwhile to alert Moscow to what was supposedly happening in Mayfair circles.

The following is a summary of a report dealing with a complicated racket (which includes drug traffic, prostitution, homosexuality and other vices) organized partly by the Germans with the object of extracting information about the RAF.

There is an organization run by one of the Attachés in the German Legation in Dublin for sending drugs and personnel to England and receiving information and deserters back into Eire. The drugs – cocaine, morphia, marijuana and tijuana – are sent from Germany to Eire probably by parachute. They are smuggled into England by an organization of Welsh fishermen equipped with motor launches. They come in canisters like cigar boxes.

The controllers of distribution outside London are unknown, but it is suspected that the controllers in London are MICHAEL CORRIGAN and HENRY GEY.

The best known distributing centres are: THE MIRAMAR; THE COTTON CLUB; The NUTHOUSE; LE BOEUF SUR LE TOIT; PASTORI's; FRISCO's; The HAVANA; The WELLINGTON CLUB; The STUDIO CLUB, King's Road; PAUL'S CLUB; The CONGA.

Another method is to introduce dubious doctors to healthy clients at the DORCHESTER, GROSVENOR HOUSE, etc. Suspect doctors are Dr McBRIDE, Dr PAUL SAINT; Dr GOMER WILLIAMS; Dr COMTE DE LA VATINE.

The above clubs are frequented by RAF officers who under the influence of drugs, alcohol, sexual orgies or Black Mass are induced to part with information. An important sideline is blackmailing officers, getting them into debt at crooked chemin-de-fer parties.

Personalities mixed up in this racket are: Lady CAROLYN HOWARD, drug addict, always with RAF men.

HAPPY HARBOTTLE of the WELLINGTON Club, who specializes in providing blondes for senior RAF officers (from Group-Captains upwards).

The gaming circles, in order of magnitude of the stakes are: the GREEK SYNDICATE, CHANDLERS, PERCY THOMPSON, SNOOTY PARKER, HARRY MOSS, etc. Typical croupiers are: MICHAEL SELBY, who used to employ KIRA WOLKOFF (Mrs NOEL EGAN); Wing-Comm JOHN HALLET, who is croupier at private parties held at LEEDS CASTLE (hostess OLIVE BAILEY) which are attended by Cabinet Ministers, high officials and undesirables of every kind; VICTOR HARVEY who runs the DEANERY CLUB, now one of the centres of the Black Market organization.

Thugs employed to intimidate victims are: SAM HENRY of the WARDOUR STREET WINE STORES; FRISCO of FRISCO'S Club; VICTOR GARLAND of the HAVANA CLUB; MAX-the-GREEK and a score of others.

Another method is that of blackmailing wives. A Mrs BEAUMONT-NIELSON is the lover of a suspect called S DE TREY. He encourages her to run heavily into debt. As her husband is Vice Chairman of VICKERS and Chairman of both BALDWIN's and the BETHLEHEM STEEL TRUST, DE TREY blackmails Mrs BEAUMONT-NIELSON for information about VICKERS and its associated firms.

Another similar trio is that consisting of MICHAEL SELBY, Mrs LESLIE and Squadron-Leader LESLIE of the Intelligence of Coastal Command. Through this service information has leaked out to SELBY about the 'STARFISH' organization and its unit near WINDSOR (I do not know what the STARFISH organization is).

Mrs BEAUMONT-NIELSON is now living in the house of 'BUFFLES' MILBANKE, who was some months ago in charge of the aerial defences of VICKERS. His girl-friend is PUPE WEIKERSHEIM, daughter of Count WINDISCHGRAETZ. Their great friends are Countess MABEL COLORADO MANSFELT & Countess KNEVEN-HUEHLERS. La MANSFELT is suspected of espionage, formerly at NOTTINGHAM, now at DONCASTER.

Other suspects are: JACQUE POBEREJSKI who supplied information to the Germans before the collapse of France. He was chairman of the firm of Messrs SEMAPE BULLET PROOF COVERING. This firm is still suspect, particularly its presiding manager, M.L. BRAMSON. BRAMSON obtained a position for his brother-in-law in SEMAPE and for his father-in-law in SHORT'S.

SCOTNIKI (Charles KINGSLEY SCOTT) of 28 BERKELEY SQUARE organizes sexual orgies in collaboration with Dr DECAUX of Green Street [Mayfair]. Wing-Commander MOLE, HAPPY HARBOTTLE and HENRY BEY specialize in this type of racket.

Other definite suspects are ANDRE BORZOMENTI, an associate of Sir EDWARD HAREWOOD, Ex-Keeper of the Privy Purse, and Miss ROSE HORLICK. He and Count THEODORE ZICCI are

London's largest purveyors of pornographic literature. There is also a Major ANDRE DINOLI who is certainly a German agent specializing in air-raid damage reports. He is assisted by MINNIE HOGG (CORIS-ANDE of the Evening Standard).

Suspect RAF personnel are: A/C HERRIN (alias PETER PROUD); Sq-Leader DUDLEY WITHERS, Wing-Commander DENZIL FREE-MAN; P/O BIRCH; P/O GERRY MAYO.

Faked passports can be supplied by JASPER ADDIS of ADDIS and EDWARDS, 10 ST JAMES'S PLACE, SW1. ADDIS is a solicitor who acts for all the Black Market gangsters. His clients include PETER MAZZINA (MAUNDY GREGORY's maitre d'hotel) who now runs the MILLIONAIRES CLUB in Cork Street.

This report is accompanied by a series of charts illustrating the inter-connections of gangs and personalities. Curiously enough, MAISKY appears in two of them. Here they are.

Philby's replies to the lengthy Soviet questionnaires are interesting not only because he goes to considerable lengths to provide as much information as he can regarding the issue raised, but also because of what it reveals about Moscow's current knowledge of and deep fascination with the innermost workings of the Secret Intelligence Service. Occasionally Philby chides the Centre by observing that he has dealt with a particular topic on a previous occasion, but gener-ally he makes his replies as comprehensive as he can. At the end of the questionnaire, as in this example, he adds some extra infor-mation which he believes would be useful to the Soviets. The fact that he discusses OVERLORD, the Allied plan for the forthcoming invasion of Europe, shows that he was prepared to take almost any risk to help the Russians.

He was not averse to introducing some humour: at the conclusion of this report he adds 'Rest in Peace' to the news that Harry Steptoe, formerly the SIS Head of Station in prewar Shanghai, has been posted to Algiers. Philby despised Steptoe, an old Far East hand who had been interned by the Japanese and exchanged in Mozambique together with other diplomats after long hardship. Steptoe was later to be appointed deputy head of Section IX, the anti-Communist section that was to prove such an irritant to Philby.

Question: What is CSC, and what is his name?

Answer: CSC is the Controller of Secret Communications. His name is Gambier-Parry. He holds the rank of Brigadier.

CSC's functions are rather complex, since he controls communications other than purely SIS ones. His principal functions are: He carries all SIS communications by W/T throughout the world. He supplies the operators, the equipment, the schedules and expert advice. He also carries the W/T communications of certain Allied secret services which operate under the supervision of SIS. E.g. he carries the W/T communications of the Polish Military Intelligence. He also controls the Radio Security Service (RSS) which is responsible for the D/F-ing and detection of clandestine communications by W/T. He carries a certain amount of SOE W/T communications, and he is also responsible for the transmission of the 'Freedom Broadcasts' organized by PWE. He also carries a certain amount of traffic for the War Office, e.g. he is responsible for W/T communication between London and the British military mission in Moscow. Finally, all GC & CS material sent abroad (e.g. to operational commands) is transmitted over CSC's channels.

Originally, Parry was a servant only of SIS. His symbol was VIII. The SIS part of his organization is still known as Section VIII. This, however, includes only SIS W/T communications, RSS, and such Allied W/T communications as are under the general supervision of SIS. Owing to his origin in SIS, CSC still owes direct allegiance to CSS, and his funds, like the rest of SIS funds, come from the Foreign Office secret vote. But the fact that he also serves other masters gives him a position of considerable independence. His HQ, of course, is at Whaddon Hall, Bletchley.

NB. Parry does not provide the W/T operators for the continent and of Allied secret services. A set operating in Poland would have a Polish operator. That operator would, nevertheless, use call-signs, frequencies, time schedules, etc. provided by Parry.

Parry manufactures nearly all his own equipment, since ordinary commercial equipment has been found not to have the requisite degree of accuracy. Up till a year ago, he also maintained a secret ink laboratory, but I think that has now been transferred elsewhere. It should be added that all GC&CS material that is transmitted by W/T goes, not by an ordinary W/T transmitter, but by telekrypton, which is a transmitting machine, the traffic of which can only be picked up by a corresponding machine at the other end.

Question: What is 'O', and what is his name?

Answer: 'O' stands for operations. His name is Captain Slocum RN. He is responsible for the despatch of agents by sea to their theatres of operations. The details of his operations are not known to me, but I believe that he has for the purpose on hand a certain number of MTB's. Recently, the main theatre of O's operations was the Mediterranean, and Slocum recently spent several months there in person. There he directed the despatch of agents by sea to landing places in Northern

Italy and Southern France; also possible into Dalmatia and Istria. He is now back in this country, whence he is presumably running P1 agents into France. So far as I know, he has no other functions. His principal assistant in Commander Whinney.

Question: What is IIb, and what is his name?

Answer: IIb is Group-Captain Sofiano. He is in charge of all SIS administrative problems affecting the Air Ministry, e.g. the supply of personnel from the RAF for special duties, their pay, allowances, posting, etc. He may also have some intelligence duties in connection with the assessment of air intelligence.

Question: What is CPA and what is his name?

Answer: CPA is Chief Personal assistant to CSS. His name is Commander C. Arnold-Foster. The CSS Secretariat consists of three officers: CPA, PSO/CSS and PA/CSS. PSO/CSS (Wing Commander Koch de Gooreynd) is responsible for all CSS's problems in connection with the Service Depts, GC&CS and Section VIII. PA/CSS (Mr Robert Cecil) for those in connection with the Foreign Office, Dominions Office, Colonial Office and MI5. CPA exercises general supervision over the work of the other two, and he makes a particular speciality of all internal SIS problems on behalf of CSS. E.g. if there were a difference of opinion between Sections I and V regarding their respective responsibilities in respect of underground political intelligence, it would be CPA who would adjudicate in the name of CSS.

NB Arnold-Foster combines the above job with that of DD/Navy. As DD/Navy, he sits on the Board of Deputy Directors, and as CPA he has constant access to CSS. His is probably the key position in the whole organization for those reasons.

Question: What is BCRA, and what is his name?

Answer: BCRA is an organization, not a man. It stands for the Bureau Centralisé de Renseignements et d'Action. It is the combined SIS, SOE and MI5 set up in this country by De Gaulle after the collapse of France. (I wrote you a very long report on its development a few weeks ago.)

Question: What is G2 and what is his name?

Answer: G2 is an organization, not a man. It is the Intelligence Division of the American Army. The Head of G2, General Bissell, corresponds to the British DMI. Every important American command also has a G2 branch. Similarly G3 is the Operations Division, and G5 is the Civil Affairs Division. I think G1 is the Administrative Division, but I am not sure. I do not know G4. G2, Washington, incidentally, controls most of the cryptographic work done in America, and was responsible, in particular, for breaking into Japanese cypher traffic.

Question: What is ONI and what is his name?

Answer: ONI is an organization, not a man. It is the Intelligence Division of the American Navy, corresponding to the Naval Intelligence Division of the British Admiralty. Its head in Washington is, I think, Admiral Schuirmann. The initials stand for Office of Naval Intelligence.

Question: Who was appointed Technical Officer of the Planning Staff?

Answer: Commander Langley RN. Langley was formerly a member of Section 'D' of SIS, which afterwards became SOE. He stayed on with SOE for some time after the split. While with Section 'D', he was in charge of the depot of sabotage materials at Aston (on which I reported at the time). For several months he has been a member of Section VIII.

Question: What does P5 do, and who is the head of it and the R.C.?

Answer: The symbol P5 no longer exists. Commander Dunderdale, who was P5 is now SLC (Special Liaison Controller). When Cohen became CWE (Controller Western Europe), it was felt that Dunderdale, who is an equally senior officer, could not remain an ordinary 'P' officer. He was therefore given the somewhat grandiloquent title of SLC. He is in control of liaison with the Poles and with the dying Service de Renseignements, the old French intelligence service, of pre-war days.

Question: What does P11 do, etc.?

Answer: P11 no longer exists. It was formerly the section dealing with West, South and East Africa, and its head was A.L. Nicholson. Its duties have been absorbed by P2, and Nicholson is now in Section V.

Question: What are the symbols of the representatives in France, Germany, Belgium, Holland, Italy, Hungary, Rumania, Denmark, and where are they located?

Answer: There are no representatives in France, Germany, Belgium, Holland, Italy, Hungary, Rumania or Denmark, although there is a representative for Rumania (I believe) in Istanbul. His symbol would be 14000, and his name, if he exists, must appear on the Mid-East staff list which I gave you recently. In France, Belgium and Holland, there are large numbers of resident agents; many have direct W/T and aircraft communications with the UK, others are contacted via Spain, Portugal or Switzerland. There are no resident agents in Germany or Hungary with direct W/T or aircraft communication with the UK, though there are certain SIS agents in each country who are contacted during their visits to Stockholm, Geneva or Istanbul. The same applies to Rumania, with which SIS has no direct W/T or aircraft communication, though 14000 presumably has a certain number of agents whom he contacts in Istanbul (incidentally, the set taken in by De Chastelain, of which much has been heard during the Stirbey talks, is an SOE set). 36000 in Stockholm, may have direct W/T contacts with agents in Denmark, but I doubt it. In Italy, there are two main 'P' section stations. One has the symbol 32300, the other 32400. Until recently, 32300 was Lt.-Col. Anthony Morris; He has just been recalled. 32400 is Major Bruce-Lockhart, a nephew of the 'famous' Bruce-Lockhart. Both groups are engaged in the penetration of Northern italy. The difference between them is that 32300 co-operates closely with SIM, the Italian military intelligence service, and runs most of its agents in more or less close co-operation with SIM, while Bruce-Lockhart runs his agents 'independently'. In fact, Bruce-Lockhart seems to be heavily dependent on the support of Communist elements around Tedeschi for the provision of agents, etc. 32300 station is in Naples, though it may be moving at any moment. 32400 station was until recently in Bari, but seems to be moving up to Naples also. There is one other SIS station in Italy, the 35600 station at Bari, which is under Major James Miller. This station is interested only in Jugoslavia, and in the penetration of Austria and Hungary from Jugoslav soil. 35600 is strongly pro-partisan in outlook, and has fought a steady fight against those who wish to play with [the Cetnik leader Draza] Mihailovitch. 35600 is not running agents in Jugoslavia without the knowledge of the partisans. All its operations are run jointly with the partisans. All these stations in Italy are under the general control of Captain Bowlby, who is 92000, stationed at Algiers. He is in charge of SIS interests throughout the Mediterranean.

Questions: Who are the heads of P.10, P.5, P.11, P.14, P.15, P.16, P.17, P.18, P.19, P.13?

Answer: P.10 is Hamilton Gordon; P.5 and P.11 have lapsed; P.15 is Major Neave. To the best of my knowledge, all the others have lapsed, and have either disappeared altogether, or have been merged into the new training section, under Major Peters, CSO (T).

Question: Under whom is IX?

Answer: UNder DD/SP, who is Colonel Vivian.

Question: Who are in charge of I, II, III, IV, V, VI, VII, VIII, IX, and to whom are the heads of the sections responsible?

Answer: I is Major Woollcombe. He is responsible in practice direct to CSS. II is Group-Captain Winterbotham. He used to be head of the Air Intelligence section, but gave it up when Air Commodore Payne was appointed DD/Air because he refused to work under Payne. He was then appointed by CSS to control of the security of all 'Ultra' material. Ultra material is all operational intelligence emanating from GC & CS. It is Winterbotham who is responsible for framing the regulations for the secure handling of this information, so there shall be no possibility of leakage. Winterbotham has retained his symbol (II), though this is clearly an anomaly because he has nothing to do with the Air Intelligence section. He is responsible direct to CSS. III is Captain Russell. He is responsible to DD/Navy (Arnold-Foster). IV is Colonel Hatton-Hall. He is responsible to DD/SP. VI is Rear Admiral Limpenny. He is responsible to DD/SP. VII is Mrs Jane Archer. She is responsible to DD/SR. VIII is Gambier-Parry. He is responsible to CSS direct. IX is Mr Curry. He is responsible to DD/SP.

Question: What sections are there in VI and VII, and their heads?

Answer: VI has under him VIa (Roskill) who is in charge of general economic information; VIb (Bruce-Ottley) who is in charge of banking and finance; VIc (Robert Smith) who is in charge of trade questions, imports, exports, etc. None of the three have any assistants. VII consists of Jane Archer only.

Question: Are there P12a, P12b, P1a, P10a, P10b, P10c and what does each section do?

Answer: P12a is Hoare, who is in charge of all SIS stations in the Western Hemisphere. Normally this work should be supervised by P12 (Captain Taylor) but he is an old man and has been very ill recently, so Hoare has been virtually independent. He is responsible to DD/SP. P12b is Walter Bell, who is in charge of liaison with OSS in London. The other sections to the best of my knowledge have lapsed.

Question: Is there such an organization as the Radio Security Intelligence Conference, who are its members and to whom is it responsible?

Answer: There is an inter-departmental committee known as the Radio Security Intelligence Committee, which meets once a fortnight. It is composed of representatives of Section V, MI5, RIS, RSS, GC & CS, the Admiralty, War Office and Air Ministry. This committee discusses any aspect of ISOS and ISK policy that happens to be of interest at the time of the committee meeting.

   The following are examples of the kind of matter discussed: The GC & CS representatives might ask Section V to speed up the interrogation of a German agent in Lisbon on the grounds that he might have information which might help GC & CS to break a new cypher on which they were working; Section V might inform RIS that they had evidence that an unknown W/T transmitter was working from Brindisi and ask them to speed up their attempts to locate it; the War Office representative might ask RSS and GC & CS to concentrate on ISOS services from Turkey, on the grounds that Turkey at that moment was of particular interest; the committee might discuss in general terms the possibilities of speeding up the transmission of ISOS messages to the operational commands, etc. There are all kinds of questions constantly cropping up which need inter-departmental discussion. The only regular item on the agenda of the committee is the question of priorities. There are a vast number of services now being intercepted and read, and it is only possible to concentrate on the most important ones. These are therefore given priority of treatment according to a schedule which is adjusted fortnightly at the meeting of the RSIC.

There is no fixed membership of the committee. Each department sends to the meeting the specialist most competent to speak on the items raised by the agenda. The most usual attendance, however, is as follows: MI5 (Guy Liddell or Dick White and Herbert Hart); RIS (Trevor-Roper); RSS (Morton-Evans and Maltby); GC & CS (Page, Palmer and Twinn); the Admiralty (Cmmdr Euan Montague); War Office (Major Brian Melland, of MI14d); Air Ministry (Flight-Lieut. Casey); Section V (any one of about 18 officers).

The RSIC must lay all its recommendations on matters of policy before CSS for decision. The only thing it can decide for itself is the fortnight's priorities. The recommendations are laid before CSS by the Chairman who varies according to the subject discussed. The Chairman, for instance, might be any one of the officers named above. Perhaps the commonest Chairman is Guy Liddell or Dick White. The meeting incidentally is always held in the MI5 building.

Question: What is the Bland Committee and what are its concrete functions?

Answer: The Bland Committee is a Foreign Office Committee, presided over by Sir Neville Bland, formerly British Minister at the Hague. I do not know its other members. Its task is to work out a blueprint for the post-war organization of SIS. It does not confine itself to matters of policy but is, I believe, devoting its attention also to recruitment, pay, etc. and to the status to be enjoyed by SIS vis-à-vis other government departments. It is rumoured that Bland himself favours the establishment of SIS on an ordinary Civil Service basis, its members receiving regular rates of pay, pension rights, etc. The Bland Committee invites views of all concerned. E.g. Dansey and Vivian are fairly regularly consulted on all matters affecting them. The Committee does not sit continuously. Indeed, its work seems to be of rather desultory nature. I will enquire further.

OVERLORD

I am told by Trevor-Wilson, the Section V representative on SHAEF, that there has been a slight postponement of OVERLORD. D-Day, he says, is likely to be around June 9th. No reason was given. The channel through which this information reached me was, however, slightly unusual and the information may be wrong. It was Gambier-Parry who told Lt Col Gore-Brown, who commands the W/T units supplied by Parry to accompany OVERLORD, and Gore-Brown told Trevor-Wilson.

LOXLEY

The head of Loxley's office is Miss Thomas. She not only supervises the secretarial work of the office, but also manages all the accounts of the expenditure of the secret vote, ie SIS, SOE and PWE expenditure. This amounts to about £10,000,000 (ten million) annually.

Loxley told me that, in his view, the visit of the delegates from Eastern Poland to Moscow should not be taken too tragically. There were signs of a slight detente in the relations between Russia and the Polish Government in London. It was evident anyway that the Russians are playing a waiting game and are unlikely to commit themselves to any definite line of policy until they are surer of what they will find in Poland.

There has been a reorganization of P4 and P10. You will remember that General Marshall-Cornwall was appointed C/Med (Controller/ Mediterranean) as regional controller over P4 and P10. Between C/ Med on the one hand and P4 and P10 on the other there has now been appointed another officer, P/Med. His duties will be to supervise the production of intelligence in P4 and P10 areas on behalf of C/Med.

P/Med will be Commander Bremner, who has been up till recently second-in-command to Bowlby in Algiers. He has been described to me as an 'unemployable naval officer', so the improvement will probably not be very considerable.

Major Wallerstein remains P4, though his functions will clearly be slightly diminished, by the interposition of P/Med between himself and C/Med. Denne, however, has left P10, charge of which has now been assumed by Major Hamilton-Gordon.

Denne has become SPS (Secretary of the Planning Staff and Production Committee). The functions of this committee I have already described. You will find them in greater detail in the batch which I have brought today. A peculiarity of Denne's position, however, is that he retains control of the USSR as a region, which thus becomes split off from P10.

It has at last been decided to hand Vermehren's information (or rather a brief digest of it) to the Russians. This is largely due to the advocacy of Denne, who is keen on pushing the Russian liaison, doubtless for the reason that it will give him greater prestige, if information is forthcoming from the Russians.

Steptoe has arrived in Algiers (RIP!)

This questionnaire gives a further insight into the matters which preoccupied the Centre at a critical time, a few days before D-Day. According to a handwritten note on the original, it was received in Moscow on 30 May 1944, and there are two items worth noting. One is the reference to 'Fred', who is said to be in a position to corroborate Philby's pejorative opinion of his colleague David Boyle. Clearly 'Fred' is Anthony Blunt, who encountered Boyle when they worked together copying the contents of the diplomatic bags of foreign embassies in London.

The second, slightly obscure comment regarding information from 'Vermehren' concerns Dr Erich Vermehren, a senior Abwehr official and devout Catholic, who defected to SIS in Istanbul in January 1944 after a lengthy courtship in which Nicholas Elliott skilfully exploited his deep religious commitment. A public statement was released in Cairo on 9 March 1944, and evidently the Russians were intrigued to know what Vermehren and his wife had given away under interrogation. Although the defection helped to discredit the Abwehr, which was absorbed into Himmler's Reich Security Agency soon afterwards, his debriefing had little strategic significance.

Question: Which section in V deals with Communism in foreign countries?

Answer: There is no section in V today dealing with Communism in foreign countries. VA used to deal with it, but ceased to do so on the formation of Section IX. The present position is that Curry deals with all Communist problems abroad, while sub-sections of V merely watch developments in their areas, leaving all the practical work to Curry.

NB Cowgill is seizing every opportunity to disparage Curry's work, on the grounds that, at the moment, it is a study of purely academic interest. Vivian, though in principle willing to support Curry's efforts, realizes that Curry is totally lacking in the force necessary to pursue the study with success. The result is that, whereas Curry constantly attempts to put questionnaires on Communist problems to Section V representatives abroad, Cowgill consistently blocks these enquiries on the grounds that his officers have more immediate problems on hand.

Question: What is the function of VA sub-section?

Answer: VA is responsible for counter-espionage activity in the Western Hemisphere, in the Far East and India. VA is Major S.H.H. Mills. Mills is the oldest member of Section V, having worked for SIS for over ten years. He has, however, lost all his influence. principally owing to laziness and lack of drive. The Far East will shortly be taken away from him, as a new section is to be formed when the war against Japan gets properly under way. The Western Hemisphere is of a dying interest from a Section V viewpoint, since there is no considerable German espionage problem there. The work consists of problems arising from the relations between SIS and American agencies such as the FBI, OSS, G2, etc. India is looked after principally by IPI and VA serves simply as a postbox for information of interest to IPI from SIS sources.

Question: What does VQ do?

Answer: VQ no longer exists. It was Mrs Archer, before the formation of Section VII. The symbol was then given to Captain Graves, the administrative officer of Section V. He left Section V some months ago for the army, since when the symbol has been in abeyance.

Question: What does RP mean?

Answer: RP was the officer in charge of Recruitment of Personnel. The symbol has, however, lapsed, and the officer responsible for the recruitment of personnel is now called Admin (R). He is Hayward. 'Personnel' in this connection means secretaries and clerks only. He is not concerned with the recruitment of officers or agents.

Question: What does Section 'B' do?

Answer: 'B' is David Boyle. He is the representative of CSS in all matters of censorship. He is also responsible for the distribution and for the security of all TRIPLEX (XXX) material, viz, material extracted from diplomatic bags. He is also in charge of censorship of all correspondence of a private nature sent by SIS by diplomatic bag. Boyle is an exceptionally nasty person (as Fred will tell you). His principal characteristics are snobbishness and stupidity, redeemed from the lowest level only by a certain crafty cunning. In peacetime, he was CSS's stockbroker, so he has a considerable personal pull in the office.

Question: What does section 'H' mean?

Answer: 'H' is Colonel Henniker-Heaton. He is in charge of the press section of SIS. He is in liaison with the Ministry of Information and with the press direct. His principal function is to influence the press in the sense of omitting items of information that may leak from SIS to the press.

Question: What does CEO mean?

Answer: CEO means Chief Executive Officer. This was Captain Ridley RN. Ridley was in charge of all SIS administration. He is now, however, subordinated to Air Commodore Peake, who is DD/Admin.

Philby's willingness to share the secrets of D-Day, risking tens of thousands of lives, is quite remarkable, as is his candour in mentioning those who had indiscreetly confided in him. In this text he identifies Victor Rothschild, MI5's scientific expert, and Marcus Hayward, MI5's main deception planner, as his principal sources for information about the invasion. One curious aspect of this material is his continuous reference to the First United States Army Group which actually did not exist. In reality FUSAG was nothing more than a notional military formation which had been invented for the purpose of giving MI5's double agents apparently authentic units to report. The scheme, codenamed FORTITUDE, was intended to suggest to the enemy that a large army was being assembled in East Anglia in readiness for an assault on the Pas-de-Calais within a couple of weeks of the landings in Normandy which, it was hoped, the Germans would interpret as a diversionary feint calculated to draw the enemy's armoured divisions away from the real objective. After the war examination of captured documents and interrogation of prisoners demonstrated that the deception had been entirely successful, and it would seem that Philby, who clearly had not been briefed on the detail of FORTITUDE, was also taken in.

OVERLORD

HQ 21st Army Group has moved to Portsmouth. The Section V units attached to it reached Portsmouth on 15.5.44. The OSS units to be attached to FUSAG (First US Army Group) went to Bristol early in May for training.

The following armies will take part in the invasion of France: 21st British Army, 1st Canadian Army, 1st US Army and 3rd US Army. In the early stages, 21st Army Group will direct operations, and for that purpose will have under its command, in addition to the British and American armies, one American army. According to present plans, when the other American army reaches France, the two American armies will combine to form FUSAG parallel to and separate from 21st

Army Group. Gossip in SHAEF and 21st Army Group circles, however, has it that Montgomery is making a bid to gain command of all the Allied forces operating in France.

According to Marcus Hayward, the first wave of the Allied assault will comprise seven divisions, four of which will be British and three American. Tomas Harris confirms this, saying that it is hoped to land on the first day three divisions, on the second day two divisions, and on the third day two divisions; thus making seven in all for the initial assault. Harris also states that the shipping scarcity makes it impossible to land bigger forces simultaneously.

'Y' day, the date of embarkation, is May 30th or 31st. The attack will take place as soon as possible after that date. The governing factor of the actual date of the attack will be the weather.

Hayward confirms that considerable concern is felt at the prospects of breaking through the 'rail-barrier' which the Germans have erected along the water line. He says that this barrier consists of concrete blocks, bristling with steel bars, like railway tracks. This barrier has been called by the British 'element C'. It is presumed, however, that it will be possible to tear chunks out of it in the preliminary air assault. The dilemma with which the Allies are faced is that, in order to ensure its destruction, the air assault would have to be started too early, viz. enough to give the enemy adequate warning of the point of attack. It is therefore doubtful to what extent the necessarily short initial bombardment will damage it. (You will recall also that Rothschild told me that craters caused by air bombardment would be almost as embarrassing to landing craft as the barrier itself.) Aerial bombardment will also help to eliminate minefields, since the detonation of aerial bombs under water touches off mines over a wide area.

The invasion will be assisted by a number of gadgets of an ingenious type.

Rothschild told me of a monster which has been nicknamed 'Pluto'. Pluto is a vast petrol tank (?60ft by 60ft), which has a huge length of steel tubing wound round it. Rothschild tells me that, according to ordinary standards, a steel tube that can be wound round anything is a scientific impossibility, since the outer edge of the tube must be longer than the inner edge. In spite of this, he tells me, these difficulties have been overcome and the steel tubing does actually wind and unwind. The idea is that Pluto is towed across the Channel, and as it is towed so the tubing is paid out. In the end, there is a petrol pipe-line stretching right across the Channel. (Doubtless, the scientific detail in the above is garbled, but it may make some sense to you.)

Another gadget is a thing called a Mulberry. Mulberries are huge floating piers, which it is intended to tow across the Channel to compensate for lack of landing facilities on the other side. Presumably, they will be rammed up against the shore to assist unloading. Yet another gadget is a kind of seaborne road, along which light traffic can cross the sea. This, presumably, is some kind of development, on a vast scale, of the pontoon bridge idea.

According to Section V officers now attached to 21st Army Group at Portsmouth, Brigadier Williams, who is Brigadier, General Staff (Intelligence) to Montgomery, takes an extremely gloomy view of the prospects facing the Allies. He is not thinking in terms of total failure. He thinks, however, that the establishment of a bridgehead will be an extremely slow and painful process, and he expects little progress to have been made before the end of the year. Williams, incidentally, is one of the outstanding intelligence officers of the British Army. He is aged only about 30, and was a Don at Merton College, Oxford, before the war. What is most remarkable about his rise to high position on Montgomery's staff is the fact that Montgomery does not like him!

Against this gloomy view, it should be said that, according to Dick White, who is principal Ib adviser to SHAEF, SHAEF's estimate is that, if the most optimistic expectations are realized, the Allies must be standing by November, the end of the campaigning season, on a line running through France from north to south, slightly east of Paris. This does not mean by a long way that SHAEF expects the Allies to reach this line by November. It's slightly encouraging, however, that SHAEF should ever dare to think of the possibility of Paris this year. Presumably, however, this estimate presupposes complete initial surprise, and a landing without effective opposition.

According to Wallace-Hadrill, now a member of Section V, formerly of MI14, the Germans have just moved an armoured division into Caen. This information was presumably obtained from his contacts in MI14, and may be based on military intercepts. It is conceivable that this indicated some foreknowledge of the place of the landing on the part of the Germans. But is just as likely that the move took place as part of routine German defence dispositions.

CONTROL COMMISSION MILITARY SECTION

The above organization, which is destined to function as the British Military Control Commission in Berlin, is just being formed. As its head, Major-General West has been appointed. He will perform the same role for CC (MS) as General Morgan performed for SHAEF, viz. he will prepare the nucleus of a staff.

According to present plans, the CC(MS) will be subordinated to SHAEF. SHAEF, however, will not be established in Berlin at any stage. The reason for this is that SHAEF is an integrated Anglo-American body, and it is not desired to confront the Russians with the appearance of an Anglo-American bloc in Berlin. The Control Commission in Berlin will therefore consist of three parts, British, American and Russian, all apparently independent of one another. The independence, however, as far as the British and Americans are concerned, will be more apparent than real, owing to the subordination of the British and American sections to SHAEF. (It is probable that SHAEF will not move beyond Paris.)

CHRISTO MILANOFF POPECHRISTOFF

Popechristoff (I am not quite sure of the spelling) has approached SIS in Istanbul. He claims to be Deputy Chief of the Bulgarian Counter-espionage Service in Istanbul. He says that his principal activity has been directed hitherto against the Russians, but he now offers to collaborate with the British on anti-German work. This proposal is being studied.

POLES

Lord Reay, of the Central Department of the Foreign Office, informed me on 17.5.44 as follows: Churchill recently had a meeting with three Poles who have recently arrived from Poland. Their names, which have been published in the papers, are: Pomian, Berezowski and Stanis-lawski. These Poles claimed that their organizations had established contact with the Russian command in Eastern Poland and were collaborating with the Russians, Churchill said that the Russians denied this. As it was impossible to verify either claim the subject was not pursued. Churchill was extremely bored throughout the meeting, and excused himself in the middle of it, saying (untruthfully) that he had an important meeting to attend. Others present were: Selborne, MEW, Harry Sporborg, SOE and O'Malley.

According to Reay, Churchill has begun to take an extremely anti-Polish line recently, and was bullying Mikolajczyk [the Polish prime minister in exile] on account of his failure to come to terms with the Russians. Reay added that it was taken for granted in the Foreign Office that the USSR would get all Poland east of the Curzon line, and that Poland would be compensated for its loss with chunks of German territory.

Reay also told me that O'Malley had recently made an extremely careful study of the Katyn evidence, and that, as a result of his researches, he had reached the conclusion that 'the less said about Katyn, the better' meaning of course that in his opinion the Russians had been responsible for the massacre. Churchill, however, had said that he was unable to accept O'Malley's conclusions.[2]

INTERNATIONAL BRIGADE

Sixty-two members of the International Brigade have recently been sent from Algiers to the USSR. Most of them were Germans or nationals of Central European or Balkan states. They had been interned in French North Africa ever since the end of the Spanish Civil War. Curry is making strenuous attempts to collect information about these individuals, since he argues on the analogy of the Green case,[3] that these men are all potential Soviet agents.

SIS ORGANIZATION

P.1 is Major Gentry. He is responsible for the work of the section as a whole, viz. for the collection of intelligence (overwhelmingly operational intelligence) from France, with the exception of a few decaying lines run by Commander Dunderdale (SLC). Some of Gentry's work represents independent British intelligence work; but by far the greater proportion is based on co-operation with the BCRA. P.1/FFF is Captain J.A.S. Golding. He is specifically responsible, under Golding, for liaison with the BCRA. P.1/I.O. is Mr Whitelaw, who is responsible for keeping the records of all P.1 work. P.1/Ops is Flight-Lieutenant Luce, who is responsible for the despatch of agents by air. He is assisted by a Mr Butler. P.1's communications with France consist of a widespread wireless network, and airborne courier bags. The bag service is maintained by the use of Lysanders on clandestine night flights. I believe that there are certain courier lines operating across Spain and Portugal.

P.2 is Mark Oliver. He is responsible for offensive espionage based on Spain, Portugal and Spanish Morocco. Portugal and Spanish Morocco are now of severely restricted value, since little operational intelligence is obtainable from those centres now. Madrid maintains a few lines of some importance into France. P.2 is also in charge of certain dying stations in Africa, eg Lagos, Pretoria and Lourenco Marques. Oliver contemplates resignation, in view of the small volume of work attaching to his post. His assistant is Mr Harris (P.2a). He concentrates chiefly on minor problems of administration.

P.3, 4, 6, 7, 8, 9, 10 are without assistants. P.5 (formerly Commander Dunderdale) has lapsed; he is now called SLC. P.11, which was formerly in charge of Africa, has also lapsed, its stations having been assimilated by P.2. P.10 has also lapsed, since the former P.10a (Major Hamilton-Gordon) has now become P.10.

P.12 is still Captain George Taylor RN, but he has almost passed out of the picture, owing to sustained illness. The effective head of the section is P.12a, Hoare, who is in charge of all SIS stations in the Western hemisphere. There is no espionage proper being carried out in the USA. All the work there consists in liaison with the various American intelligence agencies, OSS, FBI, etc. There is a certain amount of desultory espionage in central and South America, the stations in the Argentine and Brazil being the most active. P.12b is Mr Walter Bell. He is responsible for liaison with OSS (SI). He is extremely dissatisfied with his job, as it offers little scope for originality. It has some compensations, however, in that it involves a certain amount of entertaining, and Bell is a bit of a playboy. His political attitude, however, is Marxist.

The third group of documents found in the Philby archives are photographs of original SIS documents. This annual review of P.10, the SIS sub-section headed by Major Hamilton-Gordon which covered the Mediterranean, is the first of its kind to be published. Naturally the Russians were tremendously interested in SIS's activities in the region, and were in direct contact with Communist guerrillas in Yugoslavia, Albania, Greece and Italy. Although many of the individual personalities were disguised by SIS's convention of code numbers, Philby had already supplied sufficient information for them to be able to put names to virtually all the SIS personnel referred to, and probably a large number of their agents.

Very few authentic contemporaneous SIS documents have ever been released for public scrutiny, so this example, though a trifle mundane in some respects, has a special significance.

The Year 1943

The final monthly summary of this Section for the year 1943 is attached.

A brief review of the activity of the Stations is given below.

Mideast, the main controlling station, had in addition to their activities in the Balkans and 9th and 10th Army Areas, the responsibility for the Desert Campaign, both direct and through Malta, until the final fall of Tunisia. Operational secret information obtained by SIS on the Tunisian Campaign was undoubtedly a feature of the early part of the year. From January 1st until the end of the campaign 450 reports of immediate operational value to the SERVICES were produced. Seven of the agents were lost in the course of their duty, but eight received awards for outstanding services.

The Yugoslav Office began the year with one group in Yugoslavia sending accurate train watching information. By June five missions had been established, one of which was operating in the Trieste area of northern Italy, producing most valuable naval intelligence. The Yugoslav Office was strengthened towards the end of the year by the despatch of the whole of the Yugoslav Section in London, and was transferred to Bari in October.

At the end of 1943 fourteen stations were in operation in Yugoslavia, four of which were in charge of British Officers.

The change in the military situation which made the whole area one of immediate operational importance, proved the value of the missions which have produced a great volume of Military, Naval and Air target intelligence which has received most favourable comments from the Services. Five more missions, two of which will be in charge of British Officers, are in preparation for immediate entry. These are expected to cover the remainder of all Yugoslav military areas.

The Cairo Office, since the appointment of the new 17000, has produced increasingly valuable political information throughout the year.

Greece and Crete are partially covered by the Greek Office with 39000 and the two Offices at Istanbul and Smyrna. At the beginning of the year there were thirty groups in operation, while at the end of December thirty-nine groups were effectively producing secret intelligence.

The activities of 18904/3.33, 18904/3.45, 18904/63, 41280, 13904/S.41, 14135, 14561, 35300/P, 14135/N, 14671, 41217, 11905, 18875, 18863, 18904/S.49, 15904/S.46, have been of particular note and on no less than four occasions have personal congratulations been received from the Commander-in-Chief, Middle East, for prompt reporting of ship movements which have enabled the Royal Navy to disperse convoys and sink enemy shipping. During 1943 the Greek Office in Cairo entered nine successful missions to Greece and the Dodecanese and four to Crete. The Smyrna and Istanbul Office entered or recruited in Occupied Territory fifty successful agents.

The Istanbul Office under 22500 has shown steady improvement throughout the year. The number of agents directed from Turkey working in each Balkan country in December is as follows:

Rumania	20
Bulgaria	10
Yugoslavia	5
Hungary	10
Greece	10
Main agents	
Sub-agents	200

Close and satisfactory contact has been maintained with the Turkish SIS. Courier contacts with Germany and occupied territories have also proved of some value.

Contre-espionage work in the Istanbul Station has been much on the increase.

Mention must be made of the splendid work carried out by Smyrna Station during the evacuation of the Greek Islands by British Forces towards the end of the year. On the information side it gave accurate and advance reports of the enemy's impending attack, including vital information concerning the movement of airborne troops. Shipping reports were also accurate. The actual plan of evacuation was very greatly facilitated by Smyrna's intervention with the Turks in making arrangements for coastal reception areas and the expeditious movement of the parties through Turkish territory. Preliminary work in assembling and running a flotilla of 90 motor boats to aid the evacuation was carried out by our Smyrna Office.

Palestine, Syria, Iraq and Persia lost operational and post-operational interest during the year and have accordingly been whittled down both as regards staff and agents. Their activities have been reduced largely to political reporting and contre-espionage.

Number of agents, including aub-agents in Occupied enemy Territory: –

January 1943	353
December 1943	6,650

Number of operational reports of value from enemy occupied territory in 1943 6,650

Finally, 95500 special mission to Moscow, which took place during the year, has shown progress well beyond expectation and closer co-operation with the NKVD on a high level is expected.

P.10
1st January 1944

P.10 Monthly Report
December 1943

I. ACTIVITIES IN THE FIELD

A. Territory in Allied hands.

1. Iraq

82160, whose supply of commercial and military information has fallen off considerably during the past few months, is to be paid by results in future.

2. *Syria*

87425, who has been our Head Agent in Damascus, since September 1942 under AIO cover, has been taken onto the Mid-East Military ceiling u.o.f. 21.9.43

B. *Enemy Territory*

Albania

3. 4.135 is at Prumeti, Albania, awaiting the arrival of 41125 by parachute.

4. 41451, who is working on his own in the vicinity of Tirana, was unfortunate in getting himself mixed up in a skirmish and lost everything, including his XP outfit. Now equipment and supplies will be despatched to him with the next SOE sortie into that district.

5. Some good information has been received from 35612, 35612/A and 35612/B, the SOE/Naval party who landed south of Valone recently and are engaged on coast watching and naval intelligence.

6. An SOE proposal to establish a route for supplies by sea to the British mission in Albania was received by 35600 with enthusiasm. We will co-operate by providing a W/T operator and set for a coastal base between Durazzo and Lrin. The W/T operator will be able to undertake coast watching and send reports in our own code to Bari.

Yugoslavia
a.) *Adriatic Coast*

7. New Operation: 35644, a Canadian Serb recruited from the Canadian Army as an NCO, trained in W/T in England, arrived in Cairo in June. He left for Bari at the end of November and was entered from there to the island of Is in the Adriatic on December 18th. His first report was dated December 20th.

8. 35906/C has requested 3 W/T sets for operation by Yugoslav merchant Navy operators on the islands of Krk, Mijet and in Montenegro. The operators will be trained by 35654 to establish a coast-watching chain on the Dalmatian coast. All plans will work to Adriatic in codes supplied by 35600. The first report from the island of Mijet was dated December 20th.

b.) *Mainland*

'Judge' 35604 is sending much reliable information from Partisan HQ in Croatia, chiefly connected with shipping in the Adriatic and situation reports on the fighting between Partisans and Axis forces on the mainland. He has recently recruited a Partisan train-watcher who reports on traffic on the Belgrade/Zagreb line.

'Moth' In addition to information on Order of Battle and Lines of communication from Partisan HQ in Slovenia 35681 has been sending air intelligence obtained from Italian civilians specially sent by him for this purpose to North Italy. He has also sent a brief survey of railway lines in Slovenia and Venezis Oiulia. The Partisans have recently re-established contact with a source in Ljubljana who supplies detailed traffic reports passed to us by 35681. He is further arranging for a Partisan reception committee for the 'Spam' party.

'Century' and 'Moth' are sending morning meteorological reports which are passed immediately to YA. It is hoped that it will soon be possible to supply meteorological reports from Dalmatia, Croatia and East Bosnia.

'Cigar' Messages have reached Geneva by courier from 35610/B that 35621 has been captured by the Partisans. Another source thinks it possible that he is now interned with Novak's staff in a Slovene castle.

'Esquire' Geneva has forwarded a further report from 35610/B stating that 35610 has been murdered. No further details are given.

c.) Forward Plans

> 'Volt'   35906/B   (leader)
> 22640/B   (W/T Operator)
> 35642

A British party for entry to Partisan HQ, Primorsko, via Partisan HQ Slovenia, to take place shortly. Their mission will be to report on German troop movements through Slovenia and north-east Italy. Such information is regarded by Y as of the highest priority.

> 'Pipe'   35601   (Leader)
> 35916   (Assistant)
> 22640/A   (W/T Operator)

A British party for parachute entry in January to Partisan reception committee at their Headquarters in Macedonia, to cover rail traffic on the north/south line through Yugoslavia. Contact with Partisan GHQ during 35601's absence will be maintained as at present through 35621. The information is that 35601 should return to Partisan GHQ after establishing a train-watching service in Macedonia.

d.) New SOE sources

The following are particulars of new SOE sources: –

DUST-THROWER: British liaison officer with the Partisans in Macedonia. Information should be reliable.

DUENNA: British liaison officer with Mihailovic Forces in Vranjo area (Serbia). Information should be reliable.

Greece

Two agents, 41470 and 41454, who were captured by the Italians in Athens in December 1942, succeeded in escaping from prison and 41470 is back in Cairo.

41517, 41516 and 41546 were dropped successfully to the Yannina district on the night of December 19th.

41501 and 41502 at Larissa are doing good work, but are meeting with interference from the EAM.[4]

41495 (Patras) is now being quite expert at XII reporting.

41472 (Athens) has not come up to expectations and has been told to return to Mideast.

41280, operating from Athens, reported on December 18th that the Germans had captured a clandestine W/T station in Athens using the call sign LIK, and also an encoded message which it is believed the Germans have been able to decode. This set belonged to 41479/D, who escaped.

A message has been received from SOE to the effect that 41533 and 41528, who were being seriously hampered by the EAM in Nubcoa, have got away to Athens. They have, however, lost their W/T set and 41001 is endeavouring to contact them through SOE. If they can recover a W/T set they should be able to do useful work in Athens now that 41473/D has been captured and 41472 is to return to Mideast.

41538 and 41533 are working under difficulties, as they were betrayed by villagers who were captured by the Germans in the Cephalonia district. Although they were informed that we might be able to mount a rescue operation, they decided to take to the hills and carry on.

18904/63 in Athens has sent several reports of military activity in Eastern Thrace. (Hitherto our Athens agents have not succeeded in touching this area.)

18904/63 in Athens reports that the EAM political organization have captured – and, it is feared, executed – some members of his organization who were carrying a mail-bag addressed to 18904 at Smyrna.

18904/3.37 at Chios was arrested by the Germans on a charge of assisting persons trying to escape from the Island. He was soon released for lack of evidence, and resumed his duties. A point of interest is that he is sending some of his reports by pigeon.

41280 at Athens reports that three of his agents at Athens are being sought by the Gestapo and must leave Greece.

18904/S.41 is well into his work again, after his return to Salonika, and sends timely reports on the sailings of ships.

41128, at Kavalla, has had W/T difficulty, but has sent some reports on coast defences.

18904/S.43 has gone out on the Northern Caique Patrol (Tenodos–Dardanelles area).

18904/S.33, at Athens, has maintained his regular flow of naval, military, economic and political information.

41230, at Athens, is second only to 18904/S.33 in the quantity and quality of his information, particularly regarding the sailing of ships from the Piraeus.

41205, 41208, 41215/A and 41220 have also contributed their share of useful information from Athens.

19904/63 is a new agent sent by 18904/S.33 to Mykonos in the North-eastern Cyclades.

18904/61 is recently installed on Mitylene and 18904/S.37 on Chios has sent good reports on the defences of the Island.

The following are particulars of new SOE sources:

DEFAMER   In a ship manned by British officers operating in the Aegean near Naxos. Very reliable.

DEFAULTER   Group of Greek Officers, mostly engineers, operating in Athens. They are said to have an intelligence net covering Attica Right Wingers. Believed reliable.

DEFACER   Greek Army Lieutenant operating in Naxos. Reported to be reliable.

DEERHORS   Native fisherman at present on Scarpanto. Considered reliable.

DEFECTIVE   British Officer operating in North Central Macedonia near the Serbian frontier. Very reliable.

DEFENDER   British Officer. Liaison set with Zervas guerrillas in North Central Epirus at Kolanje. Considered reliable.

DEFIANT   W/T set allotted to GHQ of ELAS forces to be used for passing messages directly to Cairo – not through British controlled W/T set. Reliability of messages must be considered according to circumstances and signature of sender.

Crete

The 41451/A Group at Ierapetra is reported to be doing excellent work. Their movements have, however, been somewhat restricted on account of the presence of Italians round their camp.

41478 and 41491 (Sited) are also being hampered by the presence of two or three Italians. Everything possible is being done to get rid of the Italians.

41445 was successfully changed over with 41476 and 41477 on the night of December 19th. 41545 was despatched to Crete to relieve 41476 and 41477, who have completed one year's work on the Island and are due for a rest. Approval has been given to Mideast's suggestion to approach YN for a commission RNVR for 41477.

41450, 41498 and 41450/P. This party have had a tough time. After tramping across the Island and narrowly escaping capture on more than one occasion, they have returned to the vicinity of their original HQ south-west of Heraklion. A supply operation was laid on at the end of November, but owing to unfavourable conditions a good deal of the stuff was lost. A second attempt will be made as soon as possible.

W/T contact has been established with a new group in the Kastelli area, led by 41490.

The following are particulars of new SOE sources:

DETENT & DETROUSER Regular sub-sources of DETRIMENT in Crete. Believed reliable.

Dodecanese

18904/72 and 18904/75 on Leros – 18904/71 on Kalymnos – 41139, 18904/67 and 18904/70 on Kos – 18904/60 and 18904/S.49 on Rhodes – and 18904/S.44 Symi:- are agents (most of them recently entered) covering the Dodecanese. Of those, 41139 and 18904/S.44 have sent several good reports on the movements of small craft and the strengths of the German garrisons.

41500 and party arrived at Rhodes on December 20th.

Bulgaria

18060/1.A and 18874, in Sofia, have reported an increase in the number of German troops in Bulgaria, including some movement towards the south-east.

35300/G at Sofia has sent good reports on Bulgarian order of battle.

11005/C is carrying on at Skopl the work of the train-watching group, after 11005 had to take refuge in the mountains.

18921, at Istanbul, remains our most reliable source for Bulgarian order of battle

Hungary

14561/L is, after the arrest of 11561/D and 14561/E, continuing the work of the group at Budapest.

35300/F at Budapest continues to send reports on aircraft construction.

Roumania

14571 at Timisoara and 14135/H at Crclova, continued to send reports on Roumanian order of battle.

14135, at Bucharest, has added a new source, 14135/R, to his group, and continues to send regular military information.

14135/Z's reports from Constanza on shipping are as regular and full as ever.

14252/A at Istanbul, has been commended for his Roumanian oil reports.

II General

INTELLIGENCE CENTRE AT BARI

An Intelligence Distribution Centre is to be established at Bari. It will be controlled by SCI Levant and have representatives from MI14, Mideast, MI topographical Mideast, PRU plus four SOE Intelligence Officers and one from OSS. It is proposed that an SIS officer should also be attached to the Centre. The function of the Centre will be to co-ordinate intelligence from all sources, both secret and open and to distribute it to the local British Armed Forces. Secret Intelligence will be passed by the departments collecting it direct to the Centre. 'Y' material however will continue to be handled and distributed solely by SIS.

It has been agreed that if and when AFHQ or collating branches are established in Italy, normal procedures will be reverted to and secret intelligence will be passed through SIS.

CETNIKS

The work of all the allied intelligence and contre-espionage services in Italy continues to be considerably hampered by the establishment at Bari of the Cetnik Office. As a result of strong representations by the Services concerned, the Cetnik Committee was dissolved and the members were to be removed from Bari. The difficulties, however, continue, as not only are the Cetniks not under arrest, but are allowed to leave the camp and return to the town where their anti-Partisan activities are becoming a nuisance.

OSS ACTIVITIES

48000 reports in confidence that the OSS Italian Section are running their own W/T in Brindisi for communication with agents in Albania and North Italy.

In addition to one mission already in Albania, the OSS has established Albanian contacts through the Albanian representative in Istanbul.

The OSS hope shortly to establish communications between Brindisi and Albania by small aircraft. 48000 has requested that the above information should not be disclosed to the Americans in London.

SIM ACTIVITIES

Provided all communications are under our control, the Italians will be permitted to establish W/T communication with Albania. Their aims are to obtain military intelligence and contact the remnants of the Firenze Division, which they believe to be still fighting in Montenegro. The SIM have a suitable officer and an Albanian W/T operator. Communications will be to Bari and all reports will be at the immediate disposal of 35500.

SOE

The control and direction of SOE activities in Greece, Yugoslavia and Albania is now exercised by the Commander-in-Chief, Middle East, and their organization in Mideast and Italy, formerly known as MO4, has been renamed 'Force 133'.

OPERATIONS

69602 reports that arrangements are now complete for the American Squadrons at Brindisi to make way for the RAF and that the 624 and 148 Squadrons will be stationed there.

III Administration

A 35600 STATION

35600 Staff is now located as follows: –

Mideast	Adriatic	Special Missions
2 Officers (1 en route for Bari)	4 Officers	3 Officers
2 Secretaries	5 Other ranks (Instructors)	1 Other rank
1 Codist	1 Cipher clerk	
	1 Codist	
	1 Secretary (en route from UK)	
	1 WAAF Officer (Leaving shortly from UK)	

Promotions. The following promotions have been authorized: –

35601 to Acting unpaid Squadron Leader
35906/C to Local Captain

Both these officers need these ranks for their work in Yugoslavia.

XB Officer. Captain Crofts, to whom the symbol 35700 has been allotted (and not to Captain Anderson as shown on the Staff List) has arrived at Bari to take up his duties as special XB officer for Yugoslavia on 35600 Staff. His work as OC No. 2 SIS Unit will in no way conflict with these special duties. He has been joined by Sub/Lt. H.H. Finnis RNVR a qualified XB Officer, for special interrogation.

Transfers. 22667 and 22667/A arrived in England early this month and have been taken over by P.6

Djermanovac, a naturalised Cuban of Serbian origin recruited in Havana through 48000 and sent to Mideast, proved on arrival to be unsuitable for this organisation and is being returned to Cuba via this country. He left Mideast by sea on December 17th.

B MIDEAST STATION

New Staff

Officers	2 male
	1 female
Secretaries	5
Codists	2
Indexing clerk	1

Transfers

(i) Internal Officers	3
Clerical Staff	9
(ii) To Eastern Mediterranean	4
Clerical Staff	
(iii) To UK. Officers	2

Resignations

| Clerical Staff | 3 |

Travel

92000's movements, as given in para. 60 of our November Summary, have been cancelled. He arrived in Cairo on Dec. 22nd, and is expected to be in London about Jan. 8th.

90000 flew to Algiers on 15.12.43 for consultations with 92000. He returned to Cairo with him on Dec. 22nd.

17000 left Cairo on Nov. 25th on a visit to Jedda. He returned on Dec. 3rd.

Misses Edmonds, Shore, Taylor, Gambier-Parry, Fraser and Cameron arrived in Cairo from the UK on Dec. 5th.

89209 left Algiers for Bari on 29.11.43

22300 left Mideast for Jerusalem on 5.12.43

Ex-63000 left Teheran for Cairo on 7.12.43 and has now reached Gibraltar en route for the UK.

Ex-99702/3 and ex-65610/C arrived in this country from Mideast on 10.12.43.

16508 has arrived in the UK on duty from Istanbul

Ex-87000 and ex-37913 arrived in the UK on 10.12.43

Miscellaneous

89311 has been awarded the MBE

69709 has been promoted to Flight Officer

41001's promotion to the rank of Captain has been approved.

83000 (ex-93700) assumed control of Teheran Station w.o.f. 7.12.43. He left to visit Cairo on 14.12.43 for briefing in his new duties.

Apollonia W/T station has now closed. All plans have been taken over by Adriatic. The staff and equipment reached Cairo on Dec. 12th.

C. RUSSIA

Moscow

Travel

95500 has returned to this country for a short visit.

Philby's productivity as a spy is extraordinary and demonstrates his determination to go quite beyond what most commentators had believed to be the damage he caused to the Secret Intelligence Service. These documents are testament to his willingness to betray every scrap of information that passed through his office, and his desire to compromise every confidential source and every one of his colleagues. The consequence, of course, was that to the Russians there was nothing remotely secret about MI6 or its operations, which evidently remained handicapped for many years after these breaches of security.

Glossary of Soviet Intelligence codenames

The rules of *conspiratsia* (security) require the real names of people, places and organizations to be kept out of operational documents, even if they appear in the cipher text for the most innocent reasons. Winston Churchill, for example, was assigned the codename PEER and President Truman was referred to as SAILOR. To enhance security, individual codenames were occasionally changed, so the same source may appear in the traffic, over a period of years, under different cryptonyms: thus Goronwy Rees was both FLIT and GROSS, John Cairncross was MOLIERE, LIST, EDWARD and KAREL.

Immediately after the war a system of sporting terms was introduced: agents becames ATHLETES, Englishmen SKIERS, Frenchmen BOXERS, Germans WEIGHTLIFTERS and so on.

The British SIS gave its agents codenames based on numbers, while during the war the German system identified a Spanish Ambassador as DOLORES PAPA, Franco as URSULA and President Salazar of Portugal as her friend OLGA.

A–201	Willy Lehman	BEN	Konon Molody/
ABO	Harry Smollett/		Gordon
	Henri Smolka		Lonsdale
ADA	Donald Maclean's	BEYER	Bertold Ilk
	courier	BOB	Boris Kreshin
ADAM	Mikhail Shishkin	BOSS	Lord Hankey
ALEXANDR	Simon Kremer	BOY	British delegate to
ANATOLY	Yevgeny		the League of
	Mitskewich		Nations
ANDREI	Dmitri	BREITENBACH	Willy Lehman
	Bystrolyotov	BRON	Aleksandr V.
APOTHEKER	Soviet		Baranov
	intermediary in	BUNNY	Unidentified
	Paris		member of
ARKADY	Yuri Modin		the Oxford
ARNO	Ernest Oldham		Group
ARTYOM	Boris Berman	CASINO	British Military
ASYA	Ethel Gee		Intelligence
ATHLETES	MVD agents	CHAPSKY	Shuster
ATTILA	Unidentified spy	CHARLES	Klaus Fuchs
B–I	William Euer	CHARLIE	Ernest Oldham
B–13	Pavel Dyakonov	CHEMIST	Soviet Intelligence
BEER	Bertold Ilk		officer in Paris

CHIEF	Captain John Harvey	JOHN	Vasili Dozhdalev
COMPATRIOTS	CPGB members	JOHN	Unidentified Soviet spy in London
COOPER	Henri Pieck	JOHNSON	Anthony Blunt
D3	Francesco Constantini	JOSEPH	Soviet spy in French Intelligence
DARK ALLEY	British Foreign Office	JULIUS	Mauritz J Wanshtein
DELIUS	Otto Wagner		
DUCHE	Sergei Spiegelglas	KAP	Anatoli Gorsky
DUDLEY	Secondo Constantini	KAREL	John Cairncross
		KARO	Jurgen Kuczinsky
DUNCAN	Francesco Constantini	KELLY*	Unidentified Soviet atomic spy
EDITH	Edith Tudor Hart	KIN	Boris Bazarov
ENORMOZ	Joint NKVD-GRU atom project	KLATT	Richard Kauder
		KLIM	Adolf Chapsky
ERIKA	Bystrolyotov's assistant	KONRAD	Secretary of the Austrian Communict Youth
FIVE, THE	Cambridge group		
FLIT	Goronwy Rees		
FRED	Anthony Blunt	KORONA	Unidentified Soviet spy in London
FRIENDS	Soviet Bloc services	KURORT	Bletchley Park
FRITZ	Mally's assistant	LANG	Ilya Longin
GERTA	Unidentified spy in Vienna	LANGLE	Francesco Constantini
GOT	Percy Glading	LAROSH	Unidentified Soviet recruitment target in Prague
GRENADIER	Laurence Grand		
GROLL	Walter Krivitsky		
GROSS	Goronwy Rees	LESLIE	Lona Cohen
HANS	Dmitri Bystrolyotov	LIN	Guy Liddell
		LISZT	John Cairncross
HARDT	Theodor Mally	LORAN	Graham Greene
HEIR	ATTILA's son	LOUIS	Morris Cohen ('Peter Kroger')
HENRY	Anatoli Gorsky		
HERMAN	William Euer	LUDWIG	Ignace Reiss
HICKS	Guy Burgess	LUKSY	unidentified covername
HIRT	Bertold Ilk		
HOFMAN	Julius Hutschnecker	MADAM	Lucy Oldham
		MADCHEN	Guy Burgess
HOTEL	British Secret Intelligence Service	MADELEINE	Soviet intermediary in Paris
HUT	British Security Service MI5	MAG	Captain John King
IGOR	Konstantin Kukin	MAKAR	Zhuravlyov
INSTANCE	Central Committee	MANN	Theodor Mally
ISLAND, THE	Great Britain	MANOLI	Kavetsky
IVAN	Vasili Dozhdalev	MARR	Soviet illegal
JACK	Fyodor A. Karin	MATVEI	Belopolsky
JASHIN	Sumarokov	MAX	Boris Kreshin
JIM	Guy Burgess	MAYOR	James Klugmann

* Denotes change in original cryptonym

MISHA	Unidentified Soviet officer	RANCY	Soviet intermediary in Paris
MOLIERE	John Cairncross		
MOND	Ivan Kaminsky	RESORT	GC & CS, Bletchley Park
MOOR*	Unidentified Soviet atomic spy		
		ROLAND	KEMP
MORRIS	Unidentified source	ROSS	Nicolai Rodin/ Korovin
NATIONAL PARK	Los Alamos	ROSSI	Unidentified Soviet spy
NEIGHBOURS	Soviet Military Intelligence	SAM	Grigori B. Grafpen
		SCHWED	Alexandr Orlov
NICK	Nikita S. Deryabkin	SCOTT	Unidentified leader of the Oxford Group
NIGEL	Michael Straight		
NOOK	Foreign Office	SEMYON	Golst
NORA	Captain John Harvey's daughter	SHAH	Harry Houghton
		SHELLEY	British consular official in Geneva
OS29	German journalist		
OS42	English journalist	SHTURMAN	Soviet intermediary in Paris
OS43	Ramsay MacDonald's aide		
		SOHNCHEN	Kim Philby
OS44	Arthur Henderson's aide	STANLEY*	Kim Philby
		STEPHAN	Arnold Deutsch
OSKAR	N.N. Alekseyev	STRELA	Unidentified spy in Vienna
OSKAR	Markov	STUART	Donald Maclean
OST	Akselrod	TED	Unidentified cover name
PAUL	Unidentified spy at Bletchley Park	TEMNY	SIS source in Moscow
PAUL	Guy Burgess	TIRE	New York
PEEP	Bystrolyotov's assistant	TONY	Anthony Blunt
		VADIM*	Anatoli Gorsky
PFEIL	Unidentified Sovet spy in London	VALDEMAR	N.V. Rakov
		VALET	Unidentified Soviet spy in London
PLATON	Member of the Rome rezidentura	VIKTOR	Arkady Petrovich Kerr
		VITYAZ	Unidentified Soviet spy in London
PROBATIONERS	NKVD agents	WEISE	Donald Maclean
PYOTR	Stanislav Glinsky	YAN	Anthony Blunt
RAIMOND	Ignace Reiss	ZAKOULOK	Foreign Office
RALPH	Leo Long		

* Denotes change in original cryptonym

Source Notes

Chapter I: The Reds are Coming

1. Chart 1: 1 July to 1 September 1926.

Symbol	Total	Valuable	Average	No Value	Remarks
B-1	77	11	7	19	40 are being processed.
B-2	8	1	2	5	
B-3	8	–	4	4	
B-12	40	5	11	13	11 are being processed.

Chart 2: 1 September to 15 December 1926

Symbol	Total	Valuable	Average	No Value	Remarks
B-1	191	14	31	7	9 are not evaluated as they are of an operational nature and are being processed.
B-2	14	3	3	3	
B-3	45	8	17	5	
B-9	12	-	3	6	
B-12	57	10	17	7	

2. Telegram No. 925, Hodgson to Chamberlain, 7 December 1926.
3. Foreign Office Memorandum on British foreign policy, 5 April 1926.
4. File 521, Vol. 1, pp. 180–90.
5. Ibid., Vol. 2, pp. 191–3.
6. Ibid., pp. 193–9.
7. Ibid., pp. 200–4.
8. Ibid., pp. 221–6.
9. Ibid., pp. 228–90.
10. Ibid. Vol. 3, pp. 122–6. Other examples include: Despatches of the British Ambassador in Moscow, No. 919 of 16 December 1926 and No. 18 of 6 January 1927 on the 7th Plenary Session of the IKKI (Ibid., Vol. 3, pp. 127–38); Telegram No. 67 of 22 January 1927, from Sir Robert Hodgson, in reply to Foreign Office telegram No. 6 of 19 January 1927 on the alarm in the USSR about military intervention (Ibid., pp. 170–3); a selection of documents on the situation in China, as seen by the British Consuls-General in Shanghai, Mukden and Hankow, sent by Ambassador Sir Miles Lampson under No. 935 of 31 December 1926 to Chamberlain (Ibid., pp. 207–41); a selection of documents on relations

between France and Belgium with Germany: telegrams from the Ambassador to France, the Marquess of Crewe, No. 1497 of 8 July 1927 and No. 1639 of 27 July 1927; telegrams of the Ambassador in Rome, Sir Ronald Graham, No. 552 of 9 July 1927 and No. 735 of 22 September 1927; telegrams from (Sir) Hughe Knatchbull-Hugheson in Brussels, No. 559 of 12 July 1927 and No. 569 of 14 July 1927, to Chamberlain (Ibid., Vol. 7, pp. 62–89).

11. *Information on British Foreign Policy*, File No. 801, Vol. 1, p. 341.
12. Ibid., pp. 347–8.
13. Ibid., Vol. 3, p. 97.
14. Ibid., Vol. 1, p. 213.
15. File 521, Vol. 3, pp. 122–6.
16. Ibid.
17. File No. 801, Vol. 1, p. 367.
18. File 119/2, document a.o.
19. File No. 521, Vol. 7, pp. 302–9.
20. Ibid., Vol. 1, p. 155.
21. Ibid., p. 164.
22. Ibid., Vol. 3, p. 190.
23. File 521, Vol. 3, p. 188.
24. Ibid., Vol. 1, p. 212.

Chapter II: The Zinoviev Letter

1. *Provocation*, File No. 329, p. 208.
2. *The Orlov Archives*, File No. 30633, Vol. 1, p. 1.
3. Ibid., p. 3.
4. Ibid., pp. 25–6.
5. *Provocation*, File No. 329, Vol. 4, p. 209.
6. Ibid., p. 215.
7. *Pravdist*, File No. 11886, Vol. 1, pp. 6, 9.
8. Ibid., p. 17.
9. Ibid., Vol. 3, pp. 1132–3.
10. Ibid., p. 1133.
11. Ibid., p. 809.
12. *Provocation*, File No. 329, Vol. 4, p. 214.
13. Ibid., p. 218.
14. See *Trotsky* by Dmitri

Volgokonov (HarperCollins, 1996), Vol. 2, p. 446 for the text of Trilisser's letter.
15. *Provocation*, File No. 329, Vol. 3, pp. 216–17.
16. Ibid., p. 218.
17. Ibid., pp. 216–18.
18. Ibid., p. 214.
19. Ibid., p. 323.
20. Ibid., p. 362.
21. Ibid., p. 361.
22. *Pravdist*, File No. 11886, Vol. 1, p. 191.
23. *Provocation*, File No. 329, Vol. 5, p. 183.
24. Ibid., Vol. 3, p. 344.
25. *Correspondents*, File No. 9235, Vols. 1–2.
26. Ibid., Vol. 1, pp. 16–17.
27. Ibid., Vol. 2, p. 239.
28. *The Orlov Archives*, File No. 30633, Vol. 3, p. 273.

Chapter III: *Rezident* in London

1. *Miscellaneous Information on British Foreign Policy*, No. 521, Vol. 1, pp. 37–40.
2. *Germany*, No. 3588, Vol. 2, pp. 47–51.
3. *BEER*, No. 2454, Vol. 1, pp. 2–4.
4. *Correspondence with Group No. 1*, No. 17698, p. 89.
5. Ibid., pp. 5–7.
6. *Materials on British Intelligence and Counter-Intelligence*, No. 800, pp. 135–9.
7. No. 17698, Vol. 1, pp. 3–4.
8. Ibid., pp. 5–7.
9. HOFMAN, No. 10024, Vol. 1, p. 2.
10. Ibid., pp. 3, 4, 7.
11. No. 17698, Vol. pp. 5–7.
12. Ibid., pp. 3–4.
13. *Correspondence with Group No. 1*, No. 17706, Vol. 1, p. 196.
14. No. 17698, Vol. 1, pp. 68, 80.
15. Ibid., p. 68.
16. No. 10024, Vol. 1, p. 19.
17. No. 17698, Vol. 1, p. 73.
18. Ibid., p. 68.

19. Ibid., pp. 61–6.
20. No. 1002, Vol. 1, p. 94.
21. Ibid., pp. 47–53.
22. No. 17706, Vol. 1, p. 60.
23. Ibid., pp. 99.
24. No. 10024, Vol. 1, pp. 79–80.
25. Ibid., p. 69.
26. Ibid., p. 42.

Chapter IV: The Secrets of Room 22

1. HANS-ANDREI, No. 9529,
   Vol. 2, pp. 195–6.
2. Ibid.
3. Ibid.
4. Ibid., pp. 26–8, 128–30, 136–7.
5. Ibid., pp. 139–41.
6. Ibid., p. 142.
7. Ibid., p. 270.
8. Ibid., p. 197.
9. Ibid., p. 196.
10. Ibid., p. 119.
11. Ibid., Vol. 1, p. 190.
12. Ibid., Vol. 2, pp. 177–8.
13. Ibid., Vol. 1, p. 186.
14. Ibid., p. 173.
15. Ibid., p. 17.
16. Ibid., p. 186.
17. Ibid., p. 175.
18. Ibid., p. 176.
19. Ibid., p. 172.
20. Ibid., pp. 145–6; Vol. 2, 204–5.
21. Ibid., Vol. 1, p. 140.
22. Ibid., p. 143.
23. Ibid., pp. 131–2.
24. Ibid., pp. 121–5.
25. Ibid., p. 128.
26. COOPER, No. 27135, Vol. 1,
    pp. 2–4.
27. Ibid., pp. 29, 36, 49–51.
28. SHELLEY, No. 6432, Vol. 1,
    pp. 1–18, 38.
29. Ibid., pp. 67, 70, 80.
30. Ibid., p. 86.
31. Ibid., pp. 90–91, 97.
32. Ibid., pp. 105–6.
33. Ibid., p. 107.
34. MAG, No. 21870, Vol. 1, p. 3.
35. Ibid., p. 2.
36. Ibid., pp. 4, 8.
37. Ibid., pp. 9–10.
38. Ibid., pp. 11–14.
39. Ibid., pp. 24–6.

40. Ibid., pp. 27–8, 32.
41. Ibid., pp. 33–4.
42. Ibid., p. 35.
43. Ibid., pp. 46–8.
44. Ibid., pp. 56, 58.
45. Ibid., pp. 61.
46. Ibid., pp. 92.
47. Ibid., pp. 89–90, 243, 105, 111.
48. Ibid., pp. 108, 121–24, 164,
    109.
49. Ibid., pp. 159, 164, 167.
50. Ibid., p. 175.
51. Ibid., p. 181.
52. Ibid., p. 183.
53. Ibid., p. 185–186.
54. Ibid., pp. 265–8.
55. Ibid. pp. 280–5.
56. File COOPER No. 27135, Vol. 1,
    pp. 354–5, 321, 388.
57. MAG, No. 21870, Vol. 1,
    pp. 233, 235, 255, 236.
58. Ibid. p. 265.

Chapter V: Codename DUNCAN

1. File DUNCAN, No. 8862, Vol. 1,
   p. 67.
2. Ibid., p. 78.
3. Ibid., p. 17.
4. Ibid., p. 246.
5. Ibid., pp. 348, 365.
6. Ibid., p. 508.
7. Ibid., p. 572.
8. Ibid., p. 630.
9. Security of Documents in HM
   Embassy Rome, PRO FO 850/2
   Y775.
10. DUNCAN's contacts between
    1924 and 1927 were Umansky
    and Shuster (CHAPSKY), later the
    rezident in London.
11. Austrian Requiem by Kurt von
    Schuschnigg (Gollancz, 1947)
    p. 112.
12. Ciano's Diary (Heinemann,
    1947) pp. 96, 245. Although
    Ciano pretended to von
    Schuschnigg that the Italians
    possessed a source in the British
    Foreign Office, he was more
    candid in his diary entry for 11
    September 1940: 'It seems
    incredible, but we do not have a

single informant in Great Britain. On the other hand, the Germans have many. In London itself there is a German agent who makes radio transmissions up to twenty-nine times a day. At least, so it is stated by Admiral Canaris' (pp. 289–90). Ciano evidently believed that the Italian source in the British Embassy in Rome had been compromised on 20 April 1940 by the anti-Fascist journalist Luigi Barzini: 'From one of the usual documents lifted for us from the British Embassy it appears that he had informed the British that we have a secret service operating effectively inside the Embassy itself.'

13. *Hansard*, House of Commons, 8 December 1947, Col. 758.

Chapter VI: The Great Illegals

1. File STEPHAN, No. 32626, Vol. 1, pp. 2–3.
2. Biography, 15 December 1938, ibid., pp. 24–7.
3. Ibid., p. 232.
4. Ibid., p. 11.
5. Ibid., p. 87.
6. Ibid., p. 97.
7. Ibid., p. 190.
8. Ibid., p. 200.
9. Ibid., p. 207.
10. Ibid., pp. 239–40.
11. Ibid., pp. 214, 260, 322.
12. Ibid., p. 311.
13. Ibid., p. 437.
14. File MANN, No. 9705, Vol. 1, pp. 239–40.
15. Ibid., pp. 64–5.
16. Ibid., pp. 106–21.
17. Ibid., Vol. 2, pp. 5, 7, 9, 10.
18. Ibid., p. 26.
19. Ibid., pp. 41, 48.
20. Ibid., p. 90.
21. Ibid., p. 95.
22. Ibid., p. 115.
23. Ibid., pp. 172–8.
24. Ibid., Vol. 1, p. 1.
25. Ibid., p. 12.
26. Ibid., p. 239

27. Ibid., pp. 230–40.
28. History of the London *Rezidentura*, No. 89113, Vol. 1, p. 123.
29. File STEPHAN, No. 32826, Vol. 1, pp. 15–16.
30. File No. 89113, vol. 1, p. 123.
31. File KHATA, No. 75284, Vol. 6, pp. 278–82, 312–14.

Chapter VII: Burgess and Blunt

1. *History of the London Rezidentura*, File No. 89113, Vol. 1, pp. 125–32.
2. TONY, File No. 83895, Vol. 1, p. 240.
3. *History*, Vol. 1, p. 350.
4. TONY, Vol. 1, p.viii.
5. *History*, Vol. 1, p. 350.
6. TONY, Vol. 1, p. 21.
7. Ibid., pp. 15–16.
8. Ibid., pp. 27–8.
9. Ibid., p. 75.
10. Ibid., p. 26.
11. Ibid., p. 31.
12. Ibid., p. 88.
13. Ibid., pp. 31, 88.
14. In 1941 Oliver C. Green was convicted of petrol coupon misuse, and discovered to be the head of a GRU network of Spanish Civil War veterans.
15. Major Gilbert H. Lennox, then head of MI5's Operations Section.
16. Major T.A. Robertson, then head of B1(a), MI5's German double agent section.
17. Hugh Shillito, then head of F2(b) and F2(c), respectively Comintern and Soviet intelligence sections in MI5's subversive activities division.
18. TONY, Vol. 1, p. 60.
19. Ibid., p. 98.
20. Blunt's summary of the British Intelligence structure identified the following War Office branches:
MI-1 Intelligence in the field
MI-2 Intelligence in all foreign countries except Western Europe

MI-3 Intelligence in Western
Europe
MI-4 Maps
MI-5 Counter-espionage in
Britain
MI-6 Counter-espionage abroad
MI-7 Propaganda for the troops
MI-8 Wireless Intelligence
MI-9 Propaganda of an
unspecified kind
MI-10 Artillery and Gas
Intelligence

21. Ibid., pp. 111, 112, 126, 129.
22. Ibid., p. 144a.
23. ALBION, File No. 100605,
    p. 232.
24. *History*, Vol. 1, p. 434.
25. TONY, Vol. 1, p. 154.
26. Ibid., p. 155.
27. Ibid., p. 239.
28. Ibid., p. 190.
29. Ibid., p. 173.
30. Ibid., pp. 175-8.
31. Ibid., pp. 179-80.
32. Ibid., p. 192.
33. Ibid., p. 182.
34. In November 1927, Wilfred
    Macartney was arrested while
    passing classified data to Georg
    Hansen. Both men were
    sentenced to long terms of
    imprisonment, MI5 having been
    supplied with the evidence
    against them by a City
    businessman, George
    Monckland.
35. Information based on Blunt's
    conversation with Miss Ogilvy:
    TONY, Vol. 1, p. 273.
36. Ibid., Vol. 2, pp. 1-2.
37. Ibid., Vol. 1, pp. 206-10.
38. Ibid., p. 291.
39. Ibid., p. 211.
40. Ibid. Vol. 2, p. 16.
41. Ibid. Vol. 1, p. 168.
42. MADCHEN, File No. 83792,
    Vol. 1, pp. 476-7.
43. Ibid., p. 217.
44. Ibid., p. 216.
45. ALBION, Vol. 5, p. 233.
46. TONY, Vol. 1, p. 298.
47. MADCHEN, Vol. 1, p. 481.
48. Ibid., p. 252.
49. Ibid., p. 472.
50. Ibid., Vol. 1, pp. 6-8.
51. Ibid., Vol. 1, p. 473.
52. Gukasov's memorandum, dated
    27 June 1939, ibid., p. 203;
    Kreshin's memorandum dated 14
    March 1940, ibid., p. 307.
53. Ibid., p. 322.
54. Ibid., p. 404.
55. Ibid., pp. 475-6.
56. Ibid., Vol. 2, pp. 9-15.
57. Ibid.
58. Ibid., Vol. 4, p. 301.
59. Ibid., p. 302.
60. TONY, Vol. 2, p. 40.
61. Ibid., pp. 101-103.
62. Ibid.
63. Ibid., p. 65.
64. Ibid. p. 27.
65. Ibid., p. 137.
66. Ibid., p. 71a.
67. Ibid., p. 113.
68. History, Vol. 1, p. 506.
69. TONY, Vol. 2, p. 144.
70. Ibid., p. 169.
71. Ibid., p. 189.
72. Ibid., p. 161.
73. Ibid., p. 186.
74. Ibid., p. 170.
75. MADCHEN, Vol. 2, p. 185.
76. Ibid., p. 118.
77. *History*, Vol. 1, p. 506.
78. MADCHEN, Vol. 2, p. 134.
79. Ibid., p. 113.
80. Ibid., pp. 120-1.
81. Ibid., p. 177.
82. Ibid., pp. 161, 182.
83. Ibid., p. 100.
84. Ibid., p. 206.
85. Ibid., p. 211.
86. Ibid., p. 216.
87. TONY, Vol. 3, pp. 49-50.
88. Ibid., pp. 53-8, 64-6.
89. MADCHEN, VOL. 2, p. 230.
90. Ibid., pp. 247, 257.
91. Ibid., p. 261.
92. Ibid., pp. 265-6; Vol. 3,
    pp. 29-30.
93. TONY, Vol. 3, p. 219.
94. Ibid., pp. 134-5.
95. Ibid., pp. 149-50.
96. Ibid., p. 151.
97. Ibid., pp. 94-98.
98. After his retirement from the
    Security Service in 1971, George

Leggett wrote *The Cheka:
Lenin's Political Police* (Oxford
University Press, 1981).
99. TONY, Vol. 3, p. 277.
100. Ibid., pp. 238–240.
101. Ibid., p. 253.
102. MADCHEN, Vol. 3, p. 94.
103. Ibid., pp. 54–7, 59, 65, 77, 94,
     100.
104. Ibid., pp. 169, 170, 211.
105. Ibid., p. 69.
106. Ibid., p. 218.
107. Ibid., Vol. 2, pp. 316–18.
108. Ibid., pp. 254–55.
109. Ibid., p. 258.
110. Ibid., pp. 273, 275.
111. TONY, Vol. 4, p. 70. Professor
     E. Franklin Frazier (1894–
     1962) acquired his notoriety
     with the publication of *The
     Pathology of Race Prejudice*
     (1927) and *The Negro Family
     in Chicago* (1932).
112. Ibid., p. 107. In fact Halpern's
     role as the wartime head of the
     Minorities Section of British
     Security Co-ordination in New
     York was known to the Centre,
     as disclosed by a VENONA text,
     22 June 1943.
113. MADCHEN, Vol. 4, pp. 76–7.
114. Ibid., p. 99.
115. Ibid., pp. 80–2.
116. Ibid., pp. 117, 122, 125.
117. Ibid., pp. 132–3.
118. Ibid., p. 253.
119. Ibid., pp. 162–83.
120. Ibid., pp. 202, 231.
121. TONY, Vol. 4, pp. 212–21.

Chapter VIII: The KLATT Affair

1. KLATT, File No. 67044, Vol. 1,
   pp. 24–31.
2. Ibid., pp. 139–42.
3. MAX, File No. 25634, Vol. 2,
   pp. 131–87.
4. Ibid., p. 150.
5. Ibid., p. 29.
6. KLATT, File No. 67044, Vol. 1,
   pp. 127–36.
7. Ibid., pp. 145–9.
8. Ibid., p. 436.

9. Ibid., pp. 292–302.
10. Ibid., pp. 464–5.
11. Ibid., Vol. 5, p. 224.
12. Ibid., Vol. 1, p. 95.
13. *British Intelligence in the Second
    World War* by F.H. Hinsley and
    C.A. Simkins, Vol. 4, p. 199.
14. *Special Tasks* by Pavel
    Sudoplatov (Little, Brown,
    1994), p. 158. William Fisher
    was later to achieve some
    notoriety in America as the KGB
    illegal 'Rudolf Abel'. Whether
    Sudoplatov's MAX is the same
    spy, or simply another agent
    with the same codename, is a
    matter of conjecture: see *Novoye
    Vremya* No. 41, 1993, pp. 40–2.
    Sudoplatov masterminded a
    double-agent operation
    codenamed MONASTYR which
    was based on Aleksandr
    Demyanov (codenamed HEINE)
    who crossed into Nazi-occupied
    territory in December 1941 to be
    recruited by the Abwehr.
    Designated MAX, he was inserted
    back into Russia in 1942 and
    remained active until the end of
    the war, dying a decorated hero
    in Moscow in 1975. Considering
    that KLATT was already
    well-established by the time
    Demyanov slipped across the
    lines for the first time in
    December 1941, it is likely that
    there is no connection between
    the two cases, save for the
    coincidence of cryptonym.
15. *The Schellenberg Memoirs*
    (Andre Deutsch, 1956), pp. 307–
    8.
16. Reinhard Gehlen, *The Service*
    (World Publishing Co, 1962),
    p. 58. A detailed analysis of the
    Soviet advantages accomplished
    by MAX was undertaken by
    David L. Thomas in *The Legend
    of Agent 'Max'* in *Foreign
    Intelligence Literary Scene*
    (Vol. 5, No. 1, January 1986).
17. For further discussion of MAX,
    see *Burn After Reading* by
    Ladislas Farago (Walker & Co,

1961), pp. 116–18; *Hitler's Spies* by David Kahn (Hodder & Stoughton, 1978), pp. 312–17; *Their Trade is Treachery* by Chapman Pincher (Sidgwick & Jackson, 1981), pp. 103–6.

18. See *Questions, Questions, Questions: Memories of Oberursel* by Arnold M. Silver (*Intelligence & National Security*, Vol. 8, No. 2, April 1993, p. 203). For a personal account of Kauder's abduction, see Harris Greene's memoir *The Rescue of 'Max'* in *Foreign Intelligence Literary Scene* (Vol. 5, No. 3, May/June 1986).

19. 'Klop' Ustinov was a veteran MI5 agent and the father of the actor Sir Peter Ustinov. See *Klop and the Ustinov Family* by Nadia Benois (Sidgwick & Jackson, 1973). Klop's principal agent had been Wolfgang zu Putlitz, as recounted in *The Putlitz Dossier* (Allan Wingate, 1957), in which the author refers to Klop as 'Paul X'.

Chapter IX: The Vegetarian

1. LIST, File No, 83896, Vol. 1, pp. 1a–4.
2. Ibid., Vol. 1, p. 7.
3. Deutsch, depending entirely on his memory, evidently mixed up the time. Contact was established in February: see above, Mally's letter of 9 March 1937, and the dates of subsequent events in the text below.
4. *The History of the London Rezidentura*, Vol. 1, p. 351.
5. LIST, Vol. 1, pp. 8–9.
6. Ibid., p. 10.
7. Ibid., p. 15.
8. Ibid., p. 11.
9. Ibid., p. 16.
10. Ibid., p. 17.
11. Ibid., pp. 17, 21.
12. Ibid., p. 29.
13. Ibid., p. 42.
14. Ibid.

15. Ibid., p. 48.
16. Ibid., p. 61.
17. *History*, Vol. 1, pp. 351–1a.
18. 83895, Vol. 1, p. 66. Information about a British Intelligence agent in the NKVD was also received from Maclean, who saw a report on a Politburo meeting. See *Deadly Illusions*, p. 228.
19. 83896, Vol. 1, pp. 72–8.
20. Ibid., p. 856.
21. Ibid., pp. 94, 98, 126.
22. Ibid., pp. 99, 103, 110.
23. Ibid., p. 162.
24. Ibid., p. 163.
25. Ibid., pp. 167–77.
26. Ibid., p. 181.
27. Ibid., p. 209. Herbert Baggallay was the chargé d'affaires at the British Embassy in Moscow and then Kuibyshev.
28. Ibid., pp. 195–6.
29. Ibid., pp. 41–2.
30. Ibid., p. 22.
31. Ibid., pp. 23, 30.
32. Ibid., pp. 36–8.
33. Ibid., Vol. 2, p. 62.
34. Ibid., pp. 70, 72–9.
35. Ibid., pp. 80, 86–7.
36. Ibid., Vol. 1, p. 504, Vol. 2, p. 85–7.
37. Ibid., Vol. 1, p. 584, Vol. 2, pp. 129, 146–7, 152.
38. Ibid., Vol. 2, pp. 126, 156.
39. Ibid., pp. 170–6.
40. Ibid., p. 184.
41. Ibid., pp. 184, 189.
42. Ibid., pp. 212, 214.
43. Ibid., Vol. 3, pp. 37, 38, 45, 46, 88, 96.
44. Ibid., pp. 101, 183–5.
45. Ibid., pp. 299, 305–6.
46. Ibid., pp. 309, 311.
47. Ibid., pp. 374.
48. Ibid., p. 390.
49. Ibid., pp. 408, 412.
50. Ibid., Vol. 4, p. 30.
51. Ibid., p. 157.
52. Ibid., Vol. 4, pp. 169–70.
53. Ibid., p. 180–9.
54. Ibid., p. 338.
55. Ibid., p. 214.
56. Ibid., p. 311.

57. Ibid., pp. 370–5.
58. Ibid., Vol. 5, p. 64.

Chapter X: Atom Secrets

1 Interview with Barkovsky.
2. Ibid.
3. A VENONA intercept dated 14 August 1941 indicates that the GRU's Colonel I.A. Sklyorov held a meeting with Fuchs on 8 August in Birmingham.
4. *Beyond the Ocean and on the Island* by Aleksandr Feklisov, pp. 112–15.
5. *The Traitors* by Alan Moorehead (Harper & Row, 1953). Unusually, Fuchs's MI5 interrogator, William Skardon, was given official instructions to co-operate with the author.

Chapter XI: Codename shah

1. SHAH, File No. 83793, Vol, 1, p. 26a.
2. Ibid., pp. 181–2.
3. Ibid., p. 277; Vol. 2, p. 179.
4. Ibid., Vol. 2, p. 164.
5. Ibid., Vol. 3, pp. 6–8.
6. Ibid.
7. Ibid., Vol. 3, pp. 26–7.
8. Ibid., p. 62. *The Times* had reported the defection of S. Kryza, a Polish diplomat in his twenties, from the Polish Embassy on 17 August 1957.

9. Ibid., p. 87.
10. Ibid., p. 93.
11. Ibid., p. 104.
12. Ibid., pp. 199–200.
13. Ibid., p. 209.
14. Ibid., p. 264.
15. Ibid., p. 273.
16. Ibid., pp. 285–6.
17. Ibid., p. 301–2.

Postscript

1. See *The Eye of Conscience* by Edith Tudor Hart, edited by Wolf Suschitzky (Dirk Nishen Publishing, 1987).

Appendix II: The Philby Reports

1. *My Silent War* by Kim Philby (McGibbon & Kee, 1968).
2. German claims that the mass graves of Polish officers found at Katyn were evidence of a Soviet atrocity were repudiated in Moscow where it was asserted that the murders had been carried out by Nazi execution squads.
3. See Ch. VII, n. 14.
4. The National Resistance Front known by its initials EAM was actually a Greek Communist Party organisation, and the political wing of the guerrilla army known as ELAS.

Index

357